TABLE OF CONTENTS

PREFACE

O n an April day in 1789, on the balcony of Federal Hall in New York, George Washington was inaugurated President of the new republic. Among those present on Broadway was a Dominican friar from Ireland, John O'Connell, who was assigned to ministry in Manhattan. He was the first of an unbroken line of Dominican men and women on mission in the United States: friars, sisters, lay members and contemplative nuns who have shaped the history of the Order of Preachers in the new nation and affected the lives of ten generations of Americans. Theirs is an interwoven story which has never been told as a whole. Existing accounts have focused on single branches with little reference to others. In reality, however, there is one Order whose American members have been closely related throughout the years.

For the sake of present and future service to the Church, there is need to know the history of the Dominican family on mission together, beginning in the earliest years of the nation.

For to be Dominican means to say WE. To be Dominican means to be a FAMILY. In so doing we not only offer the Church another model; we find out for ourselves what it means to be Church, what it means to be Christ, what it means to be ourselves.[1]

An integrated study of American Dominican history was first proposed at a conference for Dominican novices and formation directors in 1975. The need for such a study has increased with the movement toward collaboration and closer union among member groups throughout the Order. In response to that movement, and as one of its early manifestations, in 1990 a team of Dominican historians and researchers initiated the study entitled **Project OPUS: A History of the Order of Preachers in the United States.**

This project is sponsored by the Dominican Leadership Conference of the United States, the first example of organized collaboration among American Dominicans. Its history goes back to 1935 when the congregations of Dominican Sisters formed the Conference of Major Superiors, joined later by the provinces of friars. OPUS members have owed a continuing debt of gratitude to the DLC officials and member groups of the Dominican Leadership Conference for their encouragement and support.

Project OPUS has been made possible by the generous, skillful participation of Dominicans of all branches of the Order in the research, writing and other required services. Many individuals and groups, in addition to members of the Dominican Leadership Conference, have supported them with generous financial assistance.

PROJECT OPUS

---

1. Donald Goergen, O.P., to an assembly of the Province of St. Albert the Great, 1989.

Initial Participants in Project OPUS

Dominicans	Affiliation
Albrecht, Mary Louise	St. Mary's, New Orleans
Beyenka, Barbara	Sinsinawa Congregation
Braun, Magdalen	Newark Monastery
Coleman, Mary Frances	Adrian Congregation
Dickey, Susan Karina	Springfield Congregation
Donnelly, Anna	Dominican Laity
Dougherty, Patricia	San Rafael Congregation
Flood, Marie Walter	Sinsinawa Congregation
Gerlach, John	St. Albert Province
Hammerschmith, Victorine	Tacoma Congregation
Hettich, Mary Elizabeth	Summit Monastery
Johnston, Thomas	St. Albert Province
Kress, Justinia	Sinsinawa Congregation
Langlois, John	St. Joseph Province
Liekweg, Lois	Sparkill Congregation
Lopez, Alfred	St. Albert Province
Masserano, Rose Marie	Nashville Congregation
Matthews, Mary Assumption	W. Springfield Monastery
Mc Caffrey, Mary	Columbus Congregation
Mc Donald, Mary Francis	Congregation of Hope
Mc Greal, Mary Nona	Sinsinawa Congregation
Mc Guire, Joan Monica	Kentucky Congregation
Mc Mahon, Mary Agnes	Columbus Congregation
Mihm, Margaret	Sinsinawa Congregation
Murray, Cecilia	Congregation of Hope
Noffke, Suzanne	Racine Congregation
Noonan, Paschala	Kentucky Congregation
Petit, Loretta	Akron Congregation
Quinlan, Louise	Kentucky Congregation
Ruthenberg, Michael	St. Albert Province
Ryan, Marie Joseph	Grand Rapids Congregation
Tancrell, Luke	St. Joseph Province
Trutter, Carl	St. Martin de Porres Province
Welsh, Janet	Sinsinawa Congregation
Wright, David	St. Albert Province

PRINCIPLES UNDERLYING PROJECT OPUS

From the beginning the participants have agreed upon three principles as the basis for their research and writing:

1 The history should include all branches of the Order in a single integrated narrative

Branches of the Dominican family have been founded in the United States in the following order: friars in 1805, sisters in 1822, laity before 1865 (date uncertain) and contemplative nuns in 1880. Each foundation has written its own history, recording, along with its growth and difficulties, its contribution to the mission of the Order and the life of the Church. OPUS researchers cannot replace those valuable histories, but only provide a broad, documented record of the Order on mission for two centuries in the United States. Our hope is that this history will strengthen the ties that have bound us from the beginning and contribute to the growing spirit of collaboration among us.

Before 1863, references to Lay Dominicans are very few, although Edward Fenwick sought information about how to establish chapters at the founding of the American province. Individual men and women were received as tertiaries in the 1850's, but no chapters were founded until 1863 at St. Dominic parish in San Francisco. The second chapter was formed in 1865 in the parish of St. Louis Bertrand in Louisville, Kentucky.

Cloistered nuns came to the United States near the end of this period, as shown in Chapters 13, 14 and 15. Their mission required adaptations that led to their becoming active congregations. In 1880 the first foundation of a monastery was made, to be followed soon by others. Their story will be told in Volume II.

2 The American Dominican story should be studied within the context of the nation and the Church.

Dominicans arrived in the United States ten years after the Declaration of Independence. Only in the context of the nation's history, studied by regions, cultures and periods of time, can the story of the Order in the United States be presented as a whole.

The Church, however, is more than context. It is the fabric into which the life of the Order has been woven. When the first diocese was formed in 1790, Dominicans were already present, assisting the nation's one bishop, John Carroll. When the single Diocese of Baltimore was divided into four, an Irish friar was called to be bishop of New York. From that time until 1865 Dominicans were present as bishops or theologians at every provincial council. In 1865, members of the Order were active in eleven dioceses, including those along the Atlantic and Pacific coasts, the Canadian border and the Gulf of Mexico. They were forming American "households of the faith" as bishops, pastors, founders of parishes, teachers and preachers.

3 Research and writing should be based on assiduous study of original documents

The primary sources studied by OPUS researchers have included letters, annals and every other kind of record kept by, or relating to, Dominicans in the United States during the period being studied. Copies are kept in the central office of Project OPUS in Chicago, and sources are available for inquirers' further research. They include significant documents found in archives of the Order of Preachers and its American branches; in the Congregation of Propaganda Fide (now Evangelization of Peoples) and Catholic dioceses; and in the following archives.

ARCHIVES AND COLLECTIONS

Symbols	Archives
AAB	Archives, Archdiocese of Baltimore
ACHSR	American Catholic Historical Society Records
AGOP	Archives General, Order of Preachers, Rome
APF	Archives, Congregation of Propaganda Fide, Rome
ASF	Archives, Archdiocese of San Francisco
BBC	Bishop Baraga Collection
CAA	Cincinnati Archdiocesan Archives
CDS	Archives, Columbus Dominican Sisters, OH
CP I,II,III	John Carroll Papers
CRS	Catholic Record Society, Columbus, OH
CUA	Catholic University of America Archives, D.C.
DEA	Detroit Archdiocesan Archives
DNA	Diocese of Nashville Archives
DUA	Dubuque Archdiocesan Archives
EDP	Archives, English Dominican Province, Glasgow
FCA	Filson Club Archives, Louisville, KY
GUA	Georgetown Univ. Archives, Jesuit Province, MD
HNP	Archives, Holy Name Province, Oakland, CA
IDP	Irish Dominican Province Archives, Tallaght
KDS	Kentucky Dominican Sisters Archives
LS	Leopoldine Society Archives, Vienna
LVA	Louisville Archdiocesan Archives, KY
MAA	Milwaukee Archdiocesan Archives
MSJ	Mount St. Joseph Archives, Cincinnati, OH
NDS	Archives, Nashville Dominican Sisters
NYA	New York Archdiocesan Archives
PAA	Philadelphia Archdiocesan Archives
QA	Quebec Archdiocesan Archives
RDA	Racine Dominican Archives
SAA	St. Albert Province Archives
SCA	San Clemente Archives, Rome
SDA	Sinsinawa Dominican Archives
SHSW	State Historical Society of Wisconsin
SJP	St. Joseph Province Archives
SLA	St. Louis Archdiocesan Archives
SMNO	St. Mary's, New Orleans Archives
SPF-L, SPF-P	Society for the Propagation of the Faith, Lyon and Paris
SRA	San Rafael CA Dominican Archives
UFL	University of Florida, Gainesville
UNDA	University of Notre Dame Archives
USC	United States Catholic Historical Society
USNA	United States National Archives

ACKNOWLEDGEMENTS

OPUS researchers thank the archivists and curators of the above collections for their generous service. We wish to acknowledge especially the following persons:

Signorina Giovanna Piscini,
> whose study and translation of American documents in the Propaganda Fide Archives, following the work of Anton Debevec, have made them available to OPUS members and other researchers through the Franciscan Calendar.

The late Cornelius P. Forster, O.P.
> and his successors in the Archives of St. Joseph Province, who welcomed us to that bountiful source of American Dominican documents gathered originally by Victor O'Daniel, O.P.

Paul Thomas,
> Archivist of the Archdiocese of Baltimore, for his early interest and prompt response to OPUS needs for historic documents in his care.

Inez Ringland,
> Associate Dean for Information Services at Dominican University and her reference staff who have generously provided answers to our frequent inquiries.

Sharon Sumpter
> of the Archives of the University of Notre Dame for her patient searching and continuing service to members of Project OPUS.

We owe sincere gratitude to editors Dolores Liptak of the Sisters of Mercy of Hartford, Connecticut, and Clyde Crews of Bellarmine University of the Diocese of Louisville for their careful review and ideas for improvement of Volume I. We thank all others who have read the manuscript critically and offered helpful suggestions.

We thank these members of our Dominican family for their generosity, judgement, and unique gifts in the making of Volume I: Barbara Beyenka, John Gerlach, Lois Hoh, Justinia Kress, Margaret Mihm, Judy Miller, Luke Tancrell, Carl Trutter, and Mary Woods.

Mary Nona McGreal, O.P.
General Editor

Loretta Petit, O.P.
Associate Editor

CONTRIBUTORS TO VOLUME I, DOMINICANS AT HOME IN A YOUNG NATION

Members of Project OPUS who have contributed to this volume of American Dominican history are listed here with the titles of chapters for which they have done major historical research, or writing, or both.

FOREWORD

Four Dominican friars from Spain arrived in the Americas in 1510 to preach a Gospel of justice and love to the conquistadors, and one of hope to the natives. One of them was the eloquent Spaniard, Antonio de Montesinos, who with his community at Santo Domingo passionately defended the human rights of the natives and converted to their cause the priest Bartolomé de las Casas. Their mission was prelude to that of the Order in the United States; and in fact, Montesinos was the first known friar to arrive on our Atlantic shore, as told in Chapter 1, "Friars from Spain Preaching Justice."

Montesinos and his confreres belonged to a religious order called the Order of Preachers, or Dominicans, whose members had been in existence for nearly three centuries.

Who were the Dominicans?

What brought them to the Americas?

What led members of the Order to establish a mission in the United States at the time the nation was founded?

The Order of Preachers was founded in France in April of 1215 when two men of Toulouse asked to join the preacher Dominic de Guzman of Castile on his mission from the Church. He welcomed them as brothers and gave himself the same title. They and all who followed them by profession had one purpose: to proclaim the Word of God by preaching and teaching, and by the example of their lives. They would sustain that mission by study and contemplation of the Word and by their life in common, as modeled by the early Christians in the Acts of the Apostles.[1] The first friars were sent to towns throughout Europe to teach and preach, beginning in the university cities of Paris and Bologna, Madrid and Oxford.[2]

Before the close of the 13th century, lay persons joined the Dominicans as members of the "Third Order," known today as "Dominican Laity."

Women were members of the Order from its origin. Dominic invited them first to join "The Preaching of Jesus Christ," a group he gathered at Prouille in the south of France in 1206. In the new Order, women formed communities of contemplatives who supported the preaching friars by their monastic life of prayer. Women continue that life today as Nuns of the Order of Preachers.

Dominican friars first came to the Americas from Spain, England, Ireland and France. Their story is told in the chapters of Section 1, "*Preachers from Abroad, 1786 - 1815.*" In 1805, Edward Fenwick of Maryland founded the American Dominican province of friars on the Kentucky frontier. Then American women, at the call of the friars, were drawn to an active life in the Order as Dominican Sisters, beginning in Kentucky in 1822, Ohio in 1830, Wisconsin in 1847 and California in 1850.

By the mid-nineteenth century, American friars, sisters and lay Dominicans were established in far-flung posts in the United States. They moved with the itinerant pioneers and "settled in" to serve them by preaching and teaching. They helped the Catholics to build the Church parish by parish in Ohio and Michigan, Wisconsin and Tennessee, and the Mississippi Valley. With equal vigor they followed the hardiest pioneers to California and the Pacific coast. Others went east to offer service in Washington, D.C., New York, Connecticut and Rhode Island.

Wherever the first friars went, the sisters went also, to carry out their common mission. A brief review of their foundations and ministry from 1806 to 1865 is found in Section 2, *Americans on Mission Together, 1806 - 1865.*

As the first Dominican friars came from Europe to the United States, so did sisters come from Europe in the mid-nineteenth century. They were assigned from Germany and Ireland to serve the rapidly multiplying immigrants from those countries. Along with others from their homelands, they were pioneers in adapting to the unknown cultures and languages of the new nation. Their contributions to Church and society are described in Section 3, *Immigrants Called by Immigrants, 1853 - 1865.*

Following the Civil War, the formative years of the republic were coming to an end. While Americans would continue to be one nation, they would now be changed for better and for worse by its rapid development. Some citizens were moving from farm to city, some from manual labor to the assembly line. A few would "rise" from poverty to security, and even amass incredible wealth. All were affected by the multitude of inventions which they beheld in wonder and began to use.

During the years 1865 – 1910, as will be seen in Volume II, Dominican men and women would participate in many changes in society and respond to them in new ways. Members of the Province of St. Joseph moved their center of action and government eastward to New York and Washington, D.C. Communities of Dominican sisters who had been attached to the Province adjusted reluctantly to their independence from the jurisdiction of the friars. Lay Dominicans formed their first chapters in the rising cities of New York and Louisville and San Francisco. Women formed new communities of sisters to meet new needs. In this period cloistered nuns established their first monasteries in the United States. While these experiences had an element of newness, they continued to call American members of the Order of Preachers to the original purpose of St. Dominic de Guzman: to praise, to preach, to bless; and to share with others the fruits of their contemplation.

1. See M.H. Vicaire, O.P., **St. Dominic and His Times** (Green Bay, Wisconsin, Alt Publishing Co., 1964). See also Vicaire, **The Apostolic Life** (Chicago, IL, The Priory Press, 1966).

2. On the day of Dominic's death in August of 1221, the friars arrived in England and founded a community of students, preachers and teachers at Oxford. Their black cloaks prompted the people to call them "Blackfriars."

DOMINICAN FOUNDATIONS IN THE UNITED STATES 1805-1862

1805-06 Friars of St. Joseph Province, St. Rose Kentucky

1822 Sisters of St. Magdalen, Kentucky
(later St. Catharine, Kentucky)

1830 Sisters of St. Mary, Somerset, Ohio
(later Columbus, Ohio)

1844 Friars of St. Charles Borromeo Province, Sinsinawa, Wisconsin
(affiliated with St. Joseph Province, 1849)

1847 Sisters of Sinsinawa, Wisconsin

1850 Friars of Holy Name Congregation, Monterey, California
(Holy Name Province, Oakland, California, 1912)

1850 Sisters of Monterey, California
(later San Rafael, California)

1851 Sisters of St. Agnes, Memphis, Tennessee
(affiliated with St. Catharine, Kentucky, 1888)

1853 Sisters of Williamsburg, New York
(later Amityville, New York)

1860 Sisters of St. Cecilia, Nashville, Tennessee

1860 Sisters of St. Mary, New Orleans, Louisiana

1862 Sisters of Racine, Wisconsin

PREACHERS FROM ABROAD, 1786-1815

A PRELUDE: FRIARS FROM SPAIN PREACHING JUSTICE

With the Spanish invaders of the Americas in the 1500's came Dominican friars from Spain, sent to teach, heal and preach. Their mission reached from the islands of the Caribbean to Florida and Mexico, through Central and South America, and across the Pacific to the Philippines. In those places members of the Order of Preachers dedicated their lives to fighting oppression by teaching the truth of salvation; of human nature saved by Jesus Christ. Among those early friars only a few arrived in the land that is now the United States, but one of them was Antonio de Montesinos who raised the first cry for liberty in the western hemisphere.

Only two years after the death of Columbus did the saga of the Spanish Dominicans on mission in the Americas begin. On October 3, 1508, the Master of the Order

Map of the Americas (16th century) : route of the Dominicans from Salamanca to Sto. Domingo, 1510

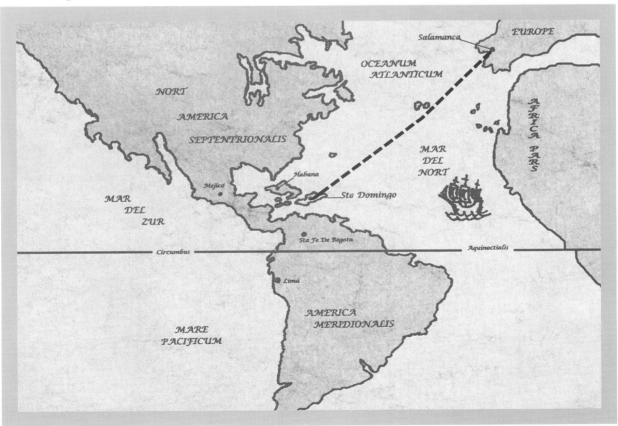

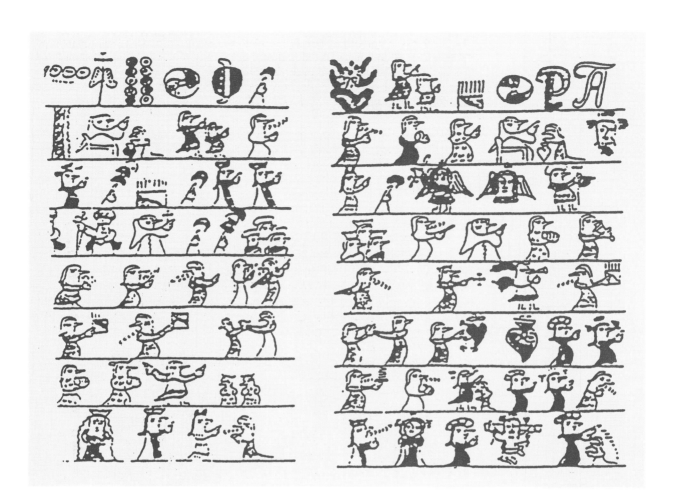

**Pictograph catechism
created by Pedro de Cordoba:
a page on General Confession**

of Preachers, Thomas de Vio, or Cajetan, had requested that fifteen friars be sent from the University of Salamanca to La Espanola, the island in the Caribbean which today includes Haiti and the Dominican Republic. [1] The first four men arrived in September, 1510 at the Spanish stronghold of Santo Domingo, and made it their mission base. They were Pedro de Cordoba, the prior; Antonio de Montesinos; Bernardo de Santo Domingo; and Pedro de Estrada. [2] These friars would leave an indelible mark on the early struggle for human rights for indigenous peoples. Without delay they denounced the abuses committed against the natives and studied their languages and cultures. Pedro de Cordoba led the way in writing books in native languages, beginning with the clear, attractive lessons of his pictorial catechism. [3]

The four friars found strength for their preaching and teaching in the life of their Dominican community: their common prayer, the study which their Constitutions required to be "assiduous," and the sharing of gifts in planning for ministry. Their first bold action was to refuse the comfortable quarters provided them by the invaders. They moved into one of the native huts and soon became a "communidad profetica" in Santo Domingo, openly supporting each others' preaching in the face of daunting power and wealth. The Word of God came to life in the western hemisphere when the friars denounced the injustices of the Conquistadores against the natives. They addressed with courage the evils of inhuman treatment of the conquered people: the long hours of killing work in the mines; the suffering of children and women forced to labor under the oppressive **encomendero** system on the vast **encomiendas** of the conquerors. These evils were widespread, despite the fact that by June 1500 the Catholic Kings formally approved a policy of liberty, not slavery, for the natives.[4]

In their mission across the Atlantic, the four friars, and many who followed them, took as their model the founder of their Order in the thirteenth century, Domingo de Guzman. He renewed the life of the Church by proclaiming the Gospel to the people. His followers in the sixteenth century sought to free the native peoples by proclaiming that same Gospel in the struggle between their mentality and culture and that of the invaders. The struggle would end with the cultural and religious annihilation of native civilizations.[5]

On the second Sunday of Advent in 1511, Antonio de Montesinos preached a rousing sermon to which all four friars had contributed ideas and added their signatures. The listeners included soldiers, colonists and officials who represented King Ferdinand and the Court of Spain. For the first time they heard a deliberate public protest against atrocities for which they themselves were responsible. Imagine their reactions to these words:

> . . . Tell me, with what right, with what justice, do you hold these Indians in such cruel and horrible servitude? On what authority have you waged such detestable wars on these people, in their mild, peaceful lands, where you have consumed such infinitudes of them, wreaking upon them this death and unheard-of havoc?
>
> How is it that you hold them so crushed and exhausted, giving them nothing to eat, nor any treatment for their diseases, which you have infected them with through the surfeit of their toils, so that they "die on you" [as you say]— you mean, you kill them— mining gold for you day after day?
>
> And what care do you take that anyone catechize them, so that they may come to know their God and Creator, be baptized, hear Mass, observe Sundays and Holy Days?
>
> Are they not human beings? Have they no rational souls? Are you not obligated to love them as you love yourselves? Do you not understand this? . . . How is it that you sleep so soundly, so lethargically?

Even before this crushing indictment the friar opened his sermon with these words: "You are all in mortal sin! You live in it and you die in it! Why? Because of the cruelty and tyranny you use with these innocent people![6]

The listeners were astounded and shocked. Never before, to their knowledge, had Christians been called to truth and justice among people whom many thought to be less than human. Thus developed in this hemisphere the first significant clash between human rights and human greed. Perhaps Montesinos awakened the moral conscience of some Spanish listeners, but it was too late to undo twenty years of destructive exploitation. However, by their intense, persistent protests, the four Dominican men became the first European spokesmen to defend the rights of natives in the Americas. They also determined the quality of the early foundations of the Order of Preachers in those lands.[7] Montesinos had challenged the system. The reaction of the colonists was far from positive. They brought their complaints to the prior, Pedro de Cordoba, who assured them that Montesinos had spoken for the Dominican community and would continue to preach the same message. On the following Sunday the sermon was still stronger. When the king heard all this, he was alarmed. He sent a **cedula** or royal letter to the governor of the island, Diego de Colon, voicing his extreme displeasure at the preaching; he ordered Colon to stop the condemnation of the **encomienda** system.[8]

To raise a voice in defense of the natives was only natural for Montesinos and his brothers, educated at the studium of San Esteban and the University of Salamanca, where theologians taught the fully human nature of all peoples. The natives possessed the natural rights of human persons, rights which could not be taken away despite their "primitive state." They were free by nature. Their lack of Christian faith gave no grounds to enslave them, make war against them or take away their lands.[9] However, this thesis was questioned not only by the invaders, but by some learned theologians in Spain. Even their Dominican provincial reprimanded the community. He threatened to send no more men if the friars did not refrain from such criticism.[10]

Montesinos and Pedro de Cordoba traveled to the Spanish Court to present their case to King Ferdinand. He called a **junta** of theologians and jurists whose deliberations resulted in the *Laws of Burgos*, promulgated December 27, 1512. The Dominicans were far from satisfied with them. A second **junta** framed another set of laws, which was issued in the following July. Although these fell short of the desired outcome, they did demand an end to child labor, to compulsory work for women and to the exploitation of laborers: principles which remain today the cornerstone of social justice and fair labor practices.[11]

Meanwhile, back at Santo Domingo, the firm stand of the friars and their example had influenced the dramatic conversion of a Spanish priest who had supported the **conquistadors** and was given a large portion of plundered land in Cuba; an **encomienda** worked by Indians under the harsh system imposed by the conquerors.[12] The priest was Bartolomé de Las Casas who had come to Espanola with the conquerors in 1502, ten years after Columbus. As an **encomendero,** Las Casas enjoyed the fruits of the people's labor, but gave scant attention to their human needs and neglected their religious education. For these reasons the priest had been denied absolution by a confessor in Santo Domingo, probably Pedro de Cordoba. The friars had decided together to withhold pardon from **encomenderos** who oppressed their workers and neglected to instruct them in their faith.

Las Casas himself tells of his conversion to a new way of life. As he was preparing to celebrate Mass and preach to the Spaniards on Pentecost, he began to consider some of the declarations from Scripture which denounced human oppression. First and foremost were words from Sirach (Ecclesiasticus) 34: 18, 21:

Tainted his gifts who offers in sacrifice ill-begotten goods! . . . Like the man who slays a son in his father's presence is he who offers sacrifice from the possessions of the poor.	The bread of charity is life itself for the needy, he who withholds it is a person of blood. He slays his neighbor who deprives him of his living; he sheds blood who denies the laborer his wages. [13]

When Las Casas realized how those words fit his life, he was deeply moved. Experiencing real conversion, he liquidated his property in Cuba and sailed to Santo Domingo. There he was stirred by the preaching of Montesinos and the counsel of Pedro de Cordoba and his community. On their advice he returned to Spain to work for justice. At the court of King Ferdinand he began in full force his crusade as "Defender of the Indians," both at the court and back in the Indies.

A second conversion of Las Casas occurred when, influenced by Pedro de Cordoba, he asked to become a Dominican friar. In April 1524, he made his religious profession, followed by four years of prayer and study at the convent in Espanola. There in 1527 he began his *Historia de las Indias*.[14] For the remainder of his life he defended the rights of the natives by preaching, writing, pastoral ministry and confrontation. However, as a man of his time, he still supported some forms of slavery, but later vehemently reversed his stand.

In 1517 an unnamed friar petitioned the king to inform the Pope of the inhuman treatment of the natives and the flaunting of the laws made five years earlier.[15] Continuing the struggle, the Dominican Bishop of Tlaxcala in New Spain, Julian Garces, sent the Pope an enthusiastic argument on behalf of the natives, defending them against charges of barbarity and cruelty. His letter, coupled with the persistent

21

pleas from Las Casas and others, resulted finally in the Bull of Pope Paul III, **Sublimis Deus**, of June 2,1537. In that document the pope declared:

> The Indians are truly men, and are not only capable of understanding the Catholic Faith but, according to our information, they desire exceedingly to receive it. . . . The said Indians and all the other people who may later be discovered by Christians are by no means to be deprived of their liberty or the possession of their property, even though they be outside the faith of Jesus Christ; . . . they may and should freely and legitimately enjoy their liberty and possession of their property, nor should they in any way be enslaved. . . .[16]

The ministry of Las Casas expanded and became even more critical when in 1544, at the age of seventy years, he was named Bishop of Chiapas, a vast and rugged area in southern Mexico. There he suffered intense antagonism from government and Church leaders, a confrontation which led soon to his resignation and return to Spain. There he continued his protests in his prophetic writings, and died in 1566. In retrospect, his influence has reached to the present day, but is still too little known. Although he never set foot in the present United States, his crusade for human rights has become in this country a rallying cry for justice to the Indians.[17] The principles for which Las Casas fought in Chiapas in the 16th century were upheld in that same diocese at the close of the 20th century by another Las Casas, the Dominican Bishop Samuel Ruiz.[18]

One source of the principles for which Las Casas and the other missionaries struggled was the Spanish theologian Francisco de Vitoria, who in 1526 had been appointed professor of theology at the University of Salamanca, at the request of students![19] Soon missionaries in the Americas were sending him their questions related to the human rights of the natives. By his assiduous study, Vitoria found many answers in the theology of Thomas Aquinas. Armed with these he joined the American crusade from a distance, sending his brothers clear and powerful responses to the protests of the colonists. Were not the Indians sub-human creatures? Were they not destined for slavery in order to benefit civilized peoples? How could the natives have any rights in relation to their conquerors?

Vitoria's response was based on the Thomistic principles of the God-given dignity and freedom of all human beings. First he condemned the conquest of Peru by Pizzaro; then he began to refute the arguments used by the invaders to justify the repressive policies of the conquest. Vitoria proclaimed in strongest terms the rights of the Indian peoples. He provoked a crisis of conscience in Spain as conflicting arguments were brought to King and Pope.

But Vitoria was not alone. His University colleagues joined him in defending a vigorous pastoral policy drawn from theological sources. Evangelization, they insisted, should promote human progress and liberation.

Centuries later, on the 500th anniversary of the arrival of Columbus in the Americas, a professor at the University of Salamanca, Luciano Pereña Vicente, republished a summary of Vitoria's basic teachings taken from his writings. Pereña published them in Spanish and English together in 1992. The English section is entitled, *The Rights and Obligations of Indians and Spaniards in the New World.*[20] Among the principles of Vitoria which Pereña lists under their broad categories are the following:

I. The Indians are human beings

• Inasmuch as he is a person, every Indian has free will and, consequently, is the master of his actions.

• By natural law, all are born equal. Legal slavery is a product of the law of nations and thus can be abolished, when nations so will, in favor of peace and human progress.

• The Indians may not be deprived of their goods or powers on account of their social backwardness, nor on account of their cultural inferiority or political disorganization.

• The [goods of] the Indians may not be expropriated, nor may their lands be occupied, if these actions are not based on the law that is common to Christians and non-Christians alike.

• Everyone has the right to truth, to education, and to all that forms part of his cultural and spiritual development and advancement.

• The Indians have the right not to be baptized and not to be forced to convert to Christianity against their will.

II. The Indian peoples are sovereign

• The Indian peoples are sovereign republics and, thus, are not properly subordinate to Spain, nor do they form part of Spain.

• The Indian rulers, whether natural or elected, enjoy the same fundamental rights as any Christian or European prince.

• By natural law and the law of nations, all the goods of the earth exist principally for the common good of humanity, to which end the natural resources of every nation should also serve.

III. The Indian peoples form part of the international community

• On account of natural human solidarity and by the law of nations, all men, . . . have equal right to the communication or exchange of persons, goods, and services, with the sole provision that justice and the natives' rights be respected.

• By reason of natural sociability, the Spaniards have the right to travel through Indian territory and to establish residence there on the condition that by so doing they neither prejudice nor injure the natives.

• The Spaniards have the right to trade with the Indians just as the Indians have with the Spaniards.

• A properly defensive war does not justify conquest when the Indians innocently believe, on account of ignorance, that they are justly defending their property.

• If war is waged against the Indians in order to free them from their inhuman and barbaric customs, when this aim has been reached, the "protector-state" cannot prolong its intervention; nor may it, on the pretext of defending innocent people, be permitted to occupy the Indian territories indefinitely.

• The "protector-state" has the right to remain in the conquered territory only so long as its presence is necessary for ending the unjust situation and for ensuring future peace.

IV. The responsibilities of government

• Wars are not waged to exterminate people, even though they might have been the aggressors in the war, but rather for the defense of law and the establishment of peace. It will be possible to guarantee the peace and security of the Indians only through relations marked by moderation, understanding, and tolerance. . .

• It is not sufficient for the king of Spain to promulgate good laws, appropriate to the capacity and development of the Indians; he is also obligated to install competent governors who are willing to enforce such laws against those who exploit the Indians or attempt to plunder them and seize their goods.

• Religious tolerance is a principle of political prudence that occasionally requires one to countenance certain pagan customs and laws, the abolition of which, even though they might be illicit in principle, would nonetheless be a crime against the social peace and the conscience of the majority of Indians.

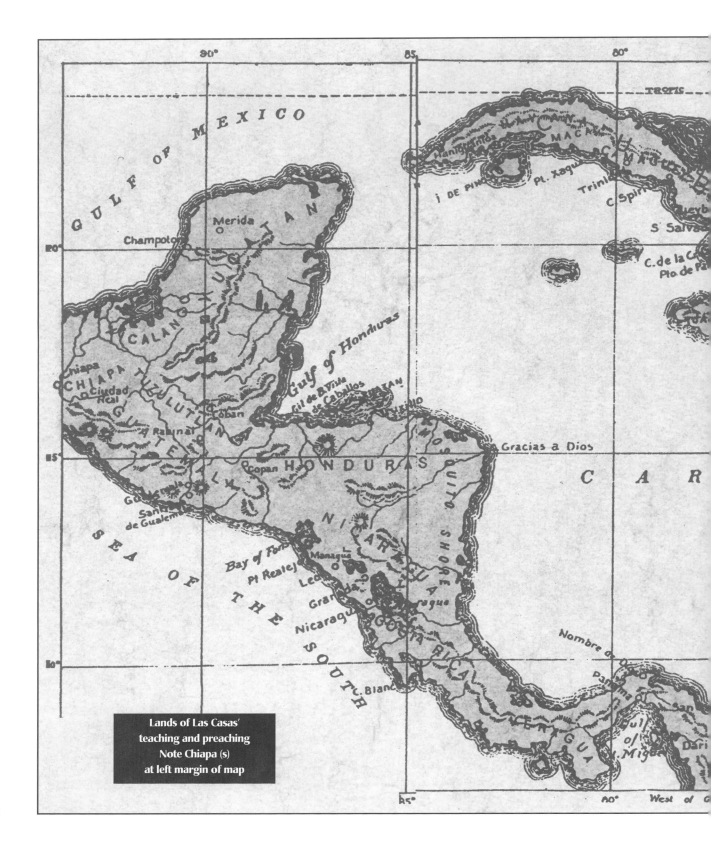

Lands of Las Casas'
teaching and preaching
Note Chiapa (s)
at left margin of map

24

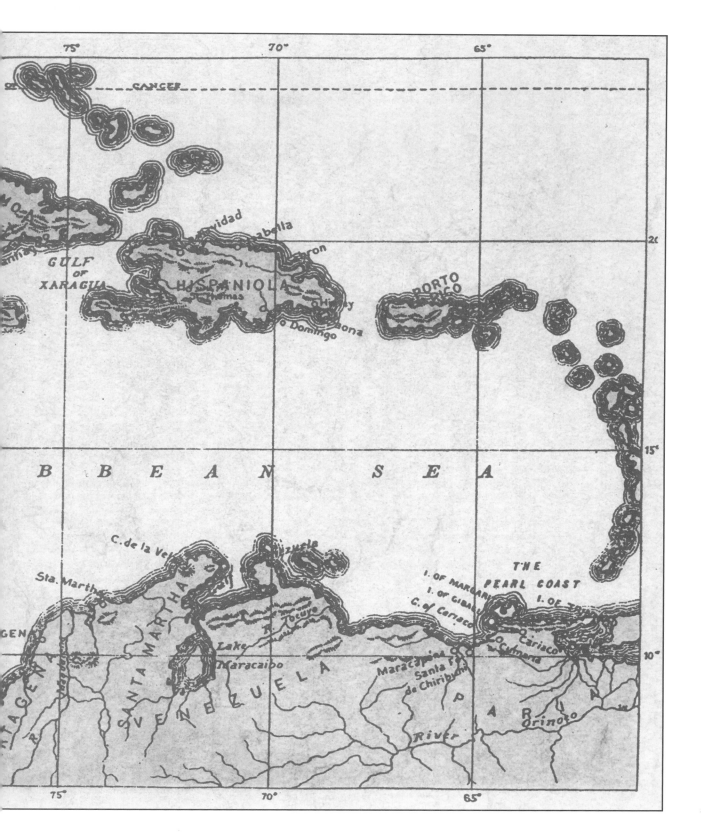

25

**Antonio de Montesinos:
Monument at Sto. Domingo
harbour**

While teaching about human rights, Vitoria studied the laws of various nations. He compiled from them the principles underlying relations among contemporary sovereign peoples. Those principles earned him lasting acclaim as the "Father of International Law."[21] Under that title his writings were cited by the United States Government in its formative years; especially in the 19th century, when making treaties with the Indians. However, despite the citation of Vitoria's teachings the government treaties with the Indians were in practice only shameful misapplications of Vitoria's underlying principles.

Although Vitoria never came to the Americas, his Dominican brothers brought to the natives his lasting principles, along with the Gospel on which they were based. Only with these could they confront the invaders who were seeking gold, land and power at the expense of other human beings.

The first Dominican known to have reached the land which is now the United States was the preacher Antonio de Montesinos. In July, 1526 he and two other friars left Puerto Rico with an expedition of six ships led by Lucas Ayllon Vasquez.[22]

His purpose was to establish a colony by peaceful means. Therefore it was not surprising that the friar Bartolomé de Las Casas stood on the shore at Espanola to bid farewell to the adventurers, and particularly to his Dominican confreres.[23]

The Ayllon party landed in the vicinity of the present Georgetown, South Carolina. Here the would-be colonists expected to encounter a "new Andalucia," a land rich in crops known in that part of Spain. It was also said to abound in pearls and gems![24] But the explorers found neither pearls nor abundant crops; only a sparse native population, a few villages, and no suitable place for a settlement. Three years earlier a Spanish ship had sailed to this coast and captured natives by persuading them to come aboard their ship. The crew took them off to Espanola, where they sold the Indians into slavery. This may have accounted for the Ayllon expedition finding few natives.

The Spanish expedition remained about three months and built near the coast a little church dedicated to San Miguel de Gualdape. The friars celebrated Mass, perhaps the first on the mainland, but left no record of baptisms. While still in their temporary settlement, Ayllon Vazquez died October 18, 1526, and was probably buried in the church of San Miguel. His death, coupled with the severe winter and the prevalence of hunger, disease and dissension, soon caused the party to return to Espanola. One baptism was administered to an elderly woman in present-day Georgia, but the friars were reluctant to baptize without certainty that the natives would be properly instructed beforehand and ministered to afterward.

On his return to the Caribbean, Antonio de Montesinos was appointed by the Crown to be protector of the natives of Venezuela. After nearly fifteen years in that delicate assignment, trying to prevent the wholesale exploitation of the natives, he was murdered by an officer of the Crown on June 27, 1540.[25] Montesinos' powerful cry for justice was finally silenced by the force which he had challenged so vehemently for thirty years. At Santo Domingo today he is honored by a monument showing him shouting his message of justice and love across the waters, out to the world.

Another forceful preacher of justice who came briefly to the shores of the present United States was Luis Cancer, who joined the Dominican community at Espanola in his youth. In 1521 he was assigned with Montesinos to the mission at San Juan, Puerto Rico. In 1542 he left Puerto Rico to join Bartolomé de Las Casas among the Mayans in Guatemala. That land was called La Tierra de la Guerra, the Land of War, because the natives had never ceased their rebellion against the invaders. The two friars brought to the natives the Gospel message of freedom and peace and named the region **La Tierra de la Vera Paz**. While studying the native languages, they discovered the riches of the Mayan culture, including a love for music. Cancer and Las Casas translated the Gospel message into rhymed couplets and songs and sent them to the natives with some merchants. The recipients were delighted. Fray Luis then went alone into their rugged land and was welcomed by the people, despite warnings of the danger awaiting any Spaniard.

Following the rugged Guatemala mission, Fray Cancer desired to go to Florida, where christianization had been unsuccessful because of cruelties inflicted by the conquerors. He obtained support in Spain for a peaceful journey into Florida, but could find no one willing to risk his life in that strange and hostile land. In the Espanola community, however, he discovered missionaries ready to accompany him. A native Christian woman, Magdalena, was also willing to go along as their translator. The party sailed up the west coast of Florida in the spring of 1548, but their mission ended abruptly. First to go ashore were the friar Diego de Tolosa and an oblate brother named Fuentes, accompanied by the interpreter Magdalena. They immediately disappeared. A captive of the natives informed the survivors that the friars had been murdered. Magdalena could not be found. On June 20, 1549, the feast of Corpus Christi, Fray Cancer and his companions celebrated the Eucharist on the shore and returned to their ship.[26] They sailed up the coast to Tampa Bay where Luis Cancer insisted on going ashore alone. He was immediately killed by the natives.[27] Fray Cancer and his fellow martyrs were the first Dominicans to be martyred in North America. Luis Cancer, valiant leader of many peaceful missions, has been named Proto-Martyr of Florida. He is now proposed for recognition by the Church as a saint, a man of love, faith, peace, courage and love.[28]

Before the Florida catastrophe, Dominican chaplains accompanied several other expeditions into the land that is now the United States. Hernandez De Soto in May 1539 sailed from Havana into the Gulf of Mexico to seek for gold, silver and gems. His mammoth party included more than six hundred soldiers. They battled with natives near the site of the present Mobile and destroyed their town, then moved along the Louisiana coast into the present areas of Mississippi, Arkansas and Texas until the summer of 1543. They found no treasures, and most of the members perished. Of the three friars in the party, the only survivor was Juan de Gallegos.[29]

Autograph of Luis Cancer, Florida martyr

27

Five friars were among the thousand passengers on a Spanish galleon bound for their homeland in 1554. Their ships encountered a fierce storm in the Gulf of Mexico and were destroyed. One friar, Marcos de Mena, was washed ashore on the coast of Texas near the present Padre Island. Cared for by natives, he returned to health and ultimately reached New Spain.[30] Carlos Castaneda calls Marcos de Mena and his companions the Dominican martyrs of Texas.[31]

Undaunted by previous tragedies of their brothers, several groups followed Luis Cancer to Florida. A mammoth expedition organized in June 1559 by Tristan de Luna y Arellano included Domingo de Salazar from Mexico, a friar eloquent in the preaching and practice of social justice. He would later bring those gifts to the Philippine Islands, where he became the first bishop. The De Luna expedition was doomed by poor leadership, scarce food, difficult weather and dissension.[32] Another expedition to Florida was led by Gregorio de Beteta, who had been there with Luis Cancer and was determined to return. He was named bishop of Cartagena, Colombia, but refused the office in hope of returning to Florida, which he did.[33]

In the summer of 1566, near the present St. Augustine, Florida, Pedro Menendez d'Aviles initiated an exploratory trip to Bahia de Santa Maria near Chesapeake Bay. On August 14 the group reached the entrance of Chincoteague Bay, off the Maryland-Virginia coast. Winds blew their ship out to sea, but on its return, the party laid claim to the area for Spain. Threatened by the seasonal hurricanes, they then set out for their homeland.[34]

Forty years after the last ill-fated voyage up the east coast of Florida, inhabitants of the successful Spanish settlements welcomed the first visit of a bishop to the present territory of the United States. He was the Dominican missionary Juan de las Cabezas de Altamirano, who arrived at St. Augustine from Havana in mid-March 1606 and visited all the Spanish settlements.

Two more centuries followed before the Order of Preachers would establish the Province of St. Joseph in the United States. The founder was an American who knew almost nothing about the early presence of Dominicans in Latin America. Yet his mission would be the same as theirs: to preach a Gospel of justice, peace and love.

1. Monumenta Ordinis Fratrum Praedicatorum Historica vol.17, Oct. 3, 1508, 7. By 1508, Ferdinand V had learned of heresies in Espanola. Ferdinand called upon the Dominican provincial of the convent of San Pablo at Burgos to send out virtuous, conscientious friars who could defend the purity of the Faith by their theological knowledge and preaching ability.

2. Victor F. O'Daniel, O.P., **Dominicans in Early Florida** (New York:The U.S.Catholic Historical Society, 1930) 2. O'Daniel was the first scholar in the United States to publish in English a complete historical work concerning the first friars in Florida. He used Justin Cuervo, **Historiadores del Convento de San Esteban de Salamanca.** 3 vols. (Salamanca:Imprenta Catolica Salmanticense, 1915).This was a publication of three manuscript histories of St. Stephen's Convent, Salamanca.

3. Pedro de Cordoba was an innovative provider of written materials for evangelization, ranging from his "Catecismo Pictografico" for the use of the natives, to his published guide for missionaries entitled **Doctrina Cristiana**, the first doctrinal text ever written in Espanola.

4. Lewis Hanke, **All Mankind is One** (DeKalb: Northern Illinois University, 1967) 7. A study of the disputation between Bartolomé de Las Casas and Juan Gines de Sepulveda in 1550, on the intellectual and religious capacity of the American Indians.

5. Gonzalo Balderas Vega O.P., "Una Comunidad Profetica: Los Dominicos en La Espanola," **Esquila Misional** (1989):12.

6. Bartolomé de las Casas, O.P., **Historia de las Indias**, Vol.2 (Mexico:Fondo de Cultura, 1951) 441-442. See Gustavo Gutiérrez, **Las Casas In Search of the Poor of Jesus Christ**, trans. Robert R. Barr (Maryknoll, N.Y.: Orbis Books,1993) 29.

7. Gutiérrez 29,30.

8. Coleccion de documentos ineditosrelativos al descubririmento, conquista, y organizacion de las antiguas posesiones espanolas de Americas y Oceania sacados de los Archivos; del Reino y muy especialmente de Indias, vol.1 (Madrid: 1864-1884) 32, 375-379.

9. Thomas Aquinas, **Summa Theologiae II-II**, Q.66, a. 2. (Madrid: Biblioteca Autores Cristianos, 1951) 450.

10. Lewis Hanke, **The Spanish Struggle for Justice in the Conquest of America** (Philadelphia: University of Pennsylvania Press, 1949) 19. See also Gutiérrez 36.

11. Mirtha Hernandez, "Fray Antonio de Montesino and the Laws of Burgos," M.A. Thesis, Louisiana State University, 1977, 104.

12. Lesley Byrd Simpson, **The Encomienda in New Spain: Forced Labor in the Spanish Colonies, 1492-1550** (Berkeley: University of California Press, 1929) 49.

13. Cited in Gutiérrez 47.

14. Gutiérrez xix.

15. Lewis Hanke, "Pope Paul III and the American Indian," **Harvard Theological Review** 30 (1937) : 69-70.

16. John Tracy Ellis, **Documents of American History**, vol.1 (Wilmington, Del.: Michael Glazier, 1987) 7-8. On June 9, 1537, the Pope issued another Bull, **Veritas Ipsa**, in which he strongly condemned the enslaving of the natives.

17. Among other groups who look to the Spanish friar as a model in their crusade for justice is the Las Casas Ministry of the Dominican Leadership Conference.

18. See **Bartolomé de Las Casas: Liberation for the Oppressed**; an adaptation by Dominican Sisters and Friars of "Bartolomé de Las Casas": A Saga for Today" by Helen Rand Parish. Mission San Jose Foundation, Mission San Jose, CA, 1984.

19. Vitoria had been teaching theology in Paris at the historic Dominican studium of St.Jacques. Because of its influence, Dominicans of France were widely known as "Jacobins." Centuries later the French revolutionaries usurped the friars' popular title as well as their property.

20. Pereña's work of 49 pages is printed in English and in Spanish. The Spanish title is **Derechos Y Deberes Entre Indios Y Españoles En El Nuevo Mundo**. (Washington D.C.:Catholic University of America and Salamanca: University of Salamanca, 1992) 17ff.

21. See **F.Cohen, Handbook of Federal Indian Law** (Charlottesville, VA: Michie, Bobbs-Merrill, 1982) 52.

22. Paul E. Hoffman, **A New Andalucia and A Way to the Orient** (Baton Rouge: Louisiana State University Press, 1990) 61.

23. Hoffman 34-59.

24. Hoffman, 320. John Gilmary Shea in his **History of the Catholic Church in Colonial Days**, vol.1 (New York: John G. Shea, 1886) 101-108, cited this landing at the Chesapeake Bay. Shea's theory was followed until recent studies indicate that the landing was near present-day Georgetown, South Carolina.

25. Hoffman 81.

26. O'Daniel 64.

27. O'Daniel 67.

28. See the pamphlet by Alberto Rodriguez, O.P., "Proto-Martyr of Florida. . . . Fray Luis de Cancer, O.P., Dominican Pioneer, Pacifist Preacher & Martyred Missionary," Southern Dominican Province of St.Martin de Porres, Metairie, Louisiana, 1999.

29. Ignacio Avelllaneda, **Los sobrevivientos de la Florida: The Survivors of The De Soto Expedition** (Gainesville: P.K. Yonge Library of Florida History,1990) 29.

30. Marcos de Mena, O.P., was left near death on the shore, where his brothers buried him in sand up to his neck to protect him from animals. Waking and finding his companions slain, he extricated himself and was cared for by natives. He found his way back to New Spain, where he told the harrowing experiences of the group.See Agustin Davila y Padilla, O.P., **Historia de la Fundacion y Discurso de la Provincia de Santiago de Mexico de la Orden de Predicatores**, 3rd edition (Mexico: Editorial Academia Literaria, 1955) 287-290.

31. Carlos Castaneda. **The Mission Era: the Finding of Texas 1519-1693**. vol.1 (Austin: Von Boeckmann-Jones Company, 1936) 141-156.

32. O'Daniel 115-120.

33. O'Daniel 195-196.

34. The Dominicans were blamed by some for the mutiny, but this accusation was later refuted. See Clifford M.Lewis S.J. and Albert J. Loomie, S.J., **The Spanish Jesuit Mission In Virginia 1570-1572** (Chapel Hill: published for the Virginia Historical Society by the University of North Carolina Press, 1953) 24.

CHAPTER 2

PREACHERS
IN THE SERVICE
OF BISHOP JOHN CARROLL

After Antonio de Montesinos returned to Santo Domingo from the Carolina coast in 1526, no other Spanish Dominicans established missions along the Atlantic coast for more than two hundred years. Then in 1786, one friar led the way for many men and women of the Order of Preachers to follow him to the United States in unbroken continuity. That forerunner was John O'Connell of the Province of Ireland, who came from his post in Spain in 1786 to serve as chaplain for the Spanish legation in New York. His was a prestigious and unique assignment: to serve with Don Diego de Gardoqui, a man of talent and influence in Church and State.[1] Don Diego introduced him to Catholic life in early New York as well as to the nascent American government. Gardoqui, a diplomat and treaty maker, was also a faithful Catholic. He helped the Catholics on Manhattan Island to build their first church of St. Peter on Barclay Street and encouraged O'Connell to give substantial assistance in ministry to their parish.

New York at this time was a city of about 30,000 people centered in Manhattan. Over the next decade, the population continued to increase as immigrants from Ireland, England, France and Germany streamed into its ports. Urban problems of housing, public health and education challenged its new leaders. Stop-gap measures provided for elementary schools, an office of public health, and a supply of fresh water for the principal streets. In 1789 citizens founded a social and political club called Tammany Hall, which in time became one of the largest political machines in United States history.

Following the Revolutionary War, Catholics, largely from Ireland and England, numbered about two hundred. Many were poor people who worked long hours to make a living. Many were lost to the faith because of the shortage of priests. Besides the small St. Peter's Church, Catholics had available the chapels of the French and Spanish legation,[2] the latter in care of John O'Connell. After three years of ministry in New York, O'Connell returned to Europe. Of him John Gilmary Shea wrote, "He was the first of the Irish Dominicans to serve in this country, and we may infer that he paved the way for the brilliant, able and good priests of the Irish province who subsequently labored in New York and Philadelphia.[3]

In 1790 Catholics of the young nation welcomed their first bishop. He was John Carroll, a native of Maryland and a member of the Society of Jesus until its suppression by Pope Clement XIV in 1773. He was called by Pope Pius VI to be Bishop of Baltimore, and therefore of the whole United States. His diocese then reached to the nation's western boundary at the Mississippi River.

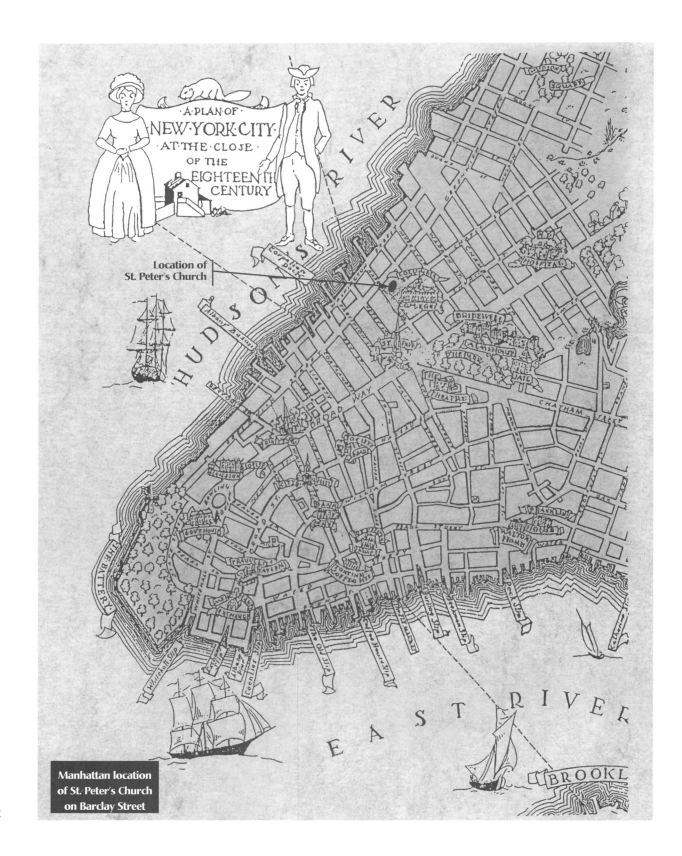

A PLAN OF
NEW·YORK·CITY·
·AT·THE·CLOSE·
·OF·THE·
EIGHTEENTH
CENTURY

Location of
St. Peter's Church

HUDSON'S RIVER

EAST RIVER

BROOKL

**Manhattan location
of St. Peter's Church
on Barclay Street**

John Carroll knew the challenges that lay before him. He had been facing them for six years as superior of the Catholic mission in the United States, a realistic internship for assuming episcopal authority. He took comfort in the fact that he was named bishop on the recommendation of his fellow priests.[4] Nevertheless, the clergy as a body were his greatest challenge, owing to their inadequate number, their coming from varied lands and cultures, and the uneven quality of their ministry. Of this challenge Carroll wrote candidly to a friend in England,

> You cannot conceive the trouble I suffer already & still greater which I foresee from the medley of clerical characters coming from different quarters & various educations & seeking employment here. I cannot avoid employing some of them, & they begin soon to create disturbances.[5]

Most of the bishop's clerical "medley" were men of religious orders.[6] The first to come from Maryland and eastern Pennsylvania were men of the English province of the Society of Jesus. When the Society was suppressed by the Pope in 1773, the members in the United States remained faithfully at their posts.[7] The Jesuits were soon joined by other religious men from Europe. Augustinian friars came from Ireland; Capuchins, Friars Minor and Recollect Franciscans came from Ireland and Germany. At the time of the French Revolution, men of the Society of St. Sulpice came from France.[8]

Many priests of religious orders from Europe came on individual missions without intending to make an American foundation. Some moved from place to place, perhaps deserving the label "strolling clerical fraternity" by the historian Guilday, who gave them only "a passing mention."[9] Some caused trouble for the bishop in their parishes. However, most of the missionaries gave to the Church in the new nation their talent and good will, and some even their lives. They deserve more than a passing mention.

Many of the clergy were Irish. John Carroll was warned by an English Jesuit, Charles Plowden, against receiving any Irish priests, and especially friars. Plowden's letter is not extant, but its tenor is clear from Carroll's reply:

> Your friends are alarmed at the introduction, or rather, at the arrival of Irish priests and fryars [sic] into our Country; but, my Dr. Sir, can I reject them if well recommended, and exclude numerous Xtians from every opportunity of receiving the Sacraments? I know from my own little experience that they are a poor resource, not for want of knowledge (for they have proved, in general, men of much information) but for want of virtue, temper, & disinterestedness.[10]

Whatever his experience, in 1787 the bishop was pleased to appoint an Irish pastor for the troubled Manhattan parish of St. Peter's on Barclay Street. He was William Vincent O'Brien, the Dominican who with John O'Connell was among the first of twelve friars to serve with Carroll. In the fall of 1787, O'Brien presented himself to the bishop for an assignment and easily passed the test of clerical ability. He brought gifts of zeal, intelligence and rich experience. He had entered the Order in the ancient Irish convent of San Clemente in Rome, then studied at Naples and the University of Bologna.[11]

**Portrait of Bishop
John Carroll,
(1736–1815)**

The bishop appointed O'Brien pastor of New York's only Catholic parish, St. Peter's, which was gravely divided.[12] So serious was the situation that Carroll made an arduous eight-day journey from Baltimore to install the new pastor. Facing the crisis caused by certain trustees and a former parish priest,[13] he presented O'Brien to the troubled parishioners with these words:

> My duty demanding of me. . .to provide a pastor for the care of your souls, I have invested with all necessary and requisite powers for that purpose the Rev William O'Brien, of whose zeal, virtues and talents for the work of the ministry I have received the most ample testimony and assurance.[14]

The majority responded with good will to his plea for unity and to O'Brien's leadership. The bishop remained at St. Peter's into November. On returning to Baltimore he wrote to O'Brien,

> I beseech you not to lose courage; for if you should, I candidly own that I do not know where to find the Clergyman in the U. States to replace you. I really consider your arrival in America, at so critical a period, as a providential designation of you to repair so dreadful scandals, & heal such dangerous wounds given to Religion at its first introduction into New York.[15]

He thanked "the good Providence of God that at this juncture brought to America a priest of the Order of St. Dominic."[16]

In the entire State of New York there were no more than 2,000 Catholics, mostly of Irish origin.[17] Some lived in Albany, but the majority in Manhattan. At this period the "papists"(not always a pejorative term) aroused little interest among other New Yorkers except when they were in trouble. Then the public was too ready to believe accounts of their misbehavior.

After leaving the city Bishop Carroll wrote that O'Brien's predecessor Nugent and his supporters were threatening dire recriminations against St.Peter's, fearing that the Catholics would not be spared open violence and bloodshed. He added,

> I leave it to you to consider how harmful to our religion this regrettable affair must turn out, especially in a city in which [the Catholic Church] was established barely three years ago and in which Congress, and consequently many persons from each of the States, reside.[18]

In that year of 1787 the Constitutional Convention met in New York, with George Washington presiding.

Despite the difficulties among the Catholics, William O'Brien was able to open at St. Peter's the first free school in New York City, which was also the first parish school in the State.[19]

During the yellow fever epidemics that struck New York in the closing decade of the century, the pastor encountered death daily in his compassionate rounds of the city. His life was spared, but failing health and increasing blindness curtailed his activity. The trustees complained to Bishop Carroll about the lack of ceremonies, especially High Mass and Vespers on Sunday.[20] In 1806 violence erupted again at St.Peter's, this time incited by a bigoted mob.[21] Afterward O'Brien's ill health and advancing age diminished his activity, but he had already served the Church of New York well. The historian Guilday wrote, "Father O'Brien kept order and harmony in the Catholic body of the city and State."[22]

On May 14, 1816, William O'Brien died at the age of seventy-six. He was buried in St. Peter's Church where the people placed on his tombstone an epitaph which said in part,

> WHO IS THERE THAT HAS NOT HEARD OF HIS PIETY,
> HIS BENEVOLENCE, HIS CHARITY, HIS ZEAL DURING
> THE RAVAGES OF THE YELLOW FEVER
> IN THE MEMORABLE YEARS OF '95 AND '98 ?
> YES; "I WAS SICK AND YOU VISITED ME."(Matt. XXV, 36)[23]

St Peter's in 1790

Long before the death of William O'Brien, Francis Antoninus Fleming, a professor in the studium at Lisbon, came to serve in the United States. Two Philadelphia Catholics had asked the bishop to bring Fleming to their parish, St. Mary's, and his cautious reply was,

> If he be really desirous of coming to America, and will bring with him sufficient vouchers for his good conduct and ability, I will be exceedingly glad of his service, receive him with cordiality and give him employment suitable to his profession.[24]

The vouchers came without delay and were impressive.[25] Fleming was permitted by his Irish provincial to volunteer for the American missions and was recommended by the Nuncio at Lisbon.[26] In December 1789 John Carroll welcomed Fleming to Philadelphia. Initially he described Fleming as "a Gentleman of amiable manners & temper, & a very excellent scholar." [27] Later he wrote, "We have a great acquisition in an Irish Dominican from Lisbon of the name of Fleming;. . . a well-informed, decent, & sweet-tempered man." [28]

The Irish Dominican found himself in a city far different from those cities he knew in Europe, although Philadelphia was the largest city of the new republic. In 1790 the first national census recorded a population of 42,000 counting natives, immigrants and free blacks.[29] The focus of American political life now moved from New York to Philadelphia, where George Washington began his term as president, and Thomas Jefferson returned belatedly from France to become Secretary of State.

Along with St. Mary's, Francis Fleming's pastoral responsibilities included the Chapel of St. Joseph in Willing's Alley and the distant rural outstations of Pennsylvania, New Jersey and Delaware. The people welcomed their new pastor as a good preacher. Philadelphia Catholics and Protestants alike, noted John Carroll, seemed to have "scarce any other test to judge of a clergyman than his talents for preaching."[30] They preferred their pastor's "live" sermons to the mere reading of a prepared text, which was then a common practice. They so valued Fleming's sermon for St. Patrick's Day in 1790 that they had it published.[31]

Bishop Carroll named Francis Fleming one of his two vicars general and gave him care of the northern district of the Baltimore diocese, which embraced Pennsylvania, Delaware, the two Jerseys, New York and New England! As vicar, Fleming participated in the first synod of the diocese, which Bishop Carroll convened in November 1791.[32] He defended Carroll vigorously when he was accused of favoring former Jesuits and discriminating against German Catholics.[33]

After only three years Fleming's ministry was cut short by death in 1793 while caring for victims of yellow fever. The epidemic caused 4000 deaths in Philadelphia alone between August and October. Fleming's assistant, the faithful former Jesuit Lawrence Graessel, suffered the same fate. Concerning their loss Bishop Carroll wrote to Archbishop Troy of Dublin,

> Your kind condolence on the loss suffered by the death of two of our most respectable and valuable ecclesiastical members. . . revived that remembrance of them which always affects me with the most lively grief, as well as deep concern for the well-being of my diocese. I can truly say that their loss is irreparable to me, for I have not, amongst the clergy here, any men capable of filling that void which their deaths have made. Your Lordship was acquainted with Mr. Fleming's merits, and they could not have been exercised anywhere more to the credit of religion than at Philadelphia, where he was universally loved and esteemed.[34]

Two friars who were students with Francis Fleming at Lisbon, Michael Burke and Christopher Keating, had followed him to the American mission in 1789. Burke was assigned to St. Peter's, New York, where, except for two years in Norfolk, Virginia, he remained until 1800. After courageous care of yellow fever victims, he drowned while crossing a river to attend the sick.[35]

As John Carroll was leaving for England in 1790, he wrote to Archbishop Troy, "Another of your brethren in religion, Mr. Keating from Lisbon, was just arrived when I left Baltimore. He is much commended by Mr. Fleming and will be fixed near Philadelphia."[36] Christopher Keating ministered to scattered Catholics in Pennsylvania, Delaware and New Jersey.[37] He was praised for his zeal and care of the sick and dying. During one epidemic Bishop Carroll wrote, "Mr. Keating exposed himself night and day with most exemplary charity, and gained the love and esteem of all."[38]

Keating loved Francis Fleming as a brother, who in turn treated the young man, as Carroll wrote, "with the tenderness of a father."[39] The yellow fever which took Fleming's life in 1793 also struck Keating. He finally recovered, but in his mourning for Fleming, he became an alcoholic. On learning this, the bishop wrote to him with firm kindness, suggesting a priest counselor.[40] To the regret of his Philadelphia parishioners, Keating returned to Ireland in 1795. There he died seven years later at the age of 39.[41]

Not all the Dominicans who served in the early Diocese of Baltimore were from Ireland. When John Carroll became bishop in 1790, two French Dominicans, Jean Antoine Le Dru and Gabriel Isabey, were at work in the Mississippi Valley. Each was unknown to the other, but both were in the service of Bishop John Carroll.

The first was French-born Jean Le Dru, whose ministerial adventures were bizarre and tragic.[42] He entered the Order of Preachers in 1772 in Paris, where he studied and was ordained at the historic convent of St. Jacques. The friars there were known in France as Jacobins; but when the French revolutionaries confiscated that priory in 1790, they also assumed for themselves the name given the Dominicans by the people.[43]

Following a grave illness, Le Dru was assigned in 1785 to the Island of Martinique to recover his health. When returning to France in the following year, he was shipwrecked on the Atlantic and brought by rescuers into Nova Scotia. There the Vicar General appointed him pastor of the Acadians at St. Mary's Bay.[44] Then began his many troubles in North America, ranging from the questioning of his priestly status to accusations that he was an American spy.[45] Late in 1788 he left Canada for Baltimore to request an assignment from John Carroll. He was asked for a recommendation from his provincial superior, but his request in early 1789 did not reach Paris before the French Revolution erupted there in May. No reply ever came.[46] John Carroll sent Le Dru to the French settlements in the Illinois country around Kaskaskia, which was now American, but the Bishop of Quebec claimed that it was still within his jurisdiction.[47]

Late in 1789 Jean Le Dru left the Illinois country for the Spanish territory across the Mississippi to accept a pastorate in St. Louis.[48] This dismayed John Carroll and seemed to confirm negative judgments he had heard from Canada. He thought Le Dru was an "apostate Dominican."[49]

After four years in St. Louis, Le Dru set out for Canada in 1794 to clear his name with Bishop Hubert of Quebec and then go on to Baltimore to see Bishop Carroll. He ministered to scattered French settlers along the way. On arriving at Mackinac Island in 1794, he was apprehended by the British commandant as an American spy and sent in custody through the Great Lakes from one British fort to another. His ship was wrecked on Lake Ontario and Le Dru was drowned, his life ending with the same kind of catastrophe that brought him to North America in 1786.[50] But there exists now in St. Louis a marker to commemorate his ministry in the Mississippi Valley, placed there by Dominicans who are there today.

The second French Dominican who served with Bishop Carroll was Gabriel Isabey whose birthplace in France is unknown. Following the American purchase of Louisiana, John Carroll was named head of the vast Diocese of Louisiana and the

Floridas from 1805 to 1812. In the bayou country of southwest Louisiana, the tribal home of the Attakapas Indians, the exiled Acadians from Canada began to settle in 1755.[51] Their first chapel, which Longfellow memorialized in the poem "Evangeline," was replaced in 1765 by the church of St. Martin of Tours in St. Martinville. To that parish a French friar, Gabriel Isabey, was assigned as pastor in 1804.[52] How or when he arrived from France is not known. Possibly he came from Bordeaux with a fellow refugee of the French Revolution, Miguel Barriere, who preceded him at St. Martinville.[53] Isabey traveled throughout the bayou region in compassionate ministry to the Cajuns, descendants of the Acadians from Canada. He remained with them until his death in 1823.[54] Of Isabey's pastorate a Louisiana historian wrote, "This priest was greatly beloved. . . . His gentleness and amiability gained all hearts, and when he died there was general mourning."[55]

Soon after John Carroll became bishop, he expressed the hope that the Irish Dominicans would establish an American province of friars to give stability to their mission.[56] Conditions in Europe made this impossible at the time. Priests were sent on individual assignments while they remained members of the Irish province. Among these were the last four men from Ireland to serve in the Baltimore Diocese entirely within the time of Bishop Carroll. They were Anthony Caffry, Dominic May, Francis Bodkin and Bartholomew McMahon.

Anthony Caffry entered the Order of Preachers at Esker in Galway, making his profession in 1777.[57] On coming to America in 1794, he was asked to form the first Catholic parish in the City of Washington, then under construction as the new "Federal City" to which the national government would move from Philadelphia in 1800. The Irish architect, James Hoban, it was said, persuaded Caffry to come there for the sake of the Irish laborers who were working on the government buildings.[58] While those buildings were under construction, Anthony Caffry and his parishioners worked nearby on their modest frame church of St. Patrick.[59] The laborers' parish was poor and funds were needed to continue construction. The pastor asked Bishop Carroll for help, reminding him that he had saved Carroll's life in a recent epidemic.[60]

The bishop and his parishioners soon learned that Caffry could be difficult, as when he insisted to the Coadjutor Bishop of Baltimore, Leonard Neale, that the area of St. Patrick's Parish must include the entire expanse of Washington City![61] After ministering more than ten years in Washington, Caffry was assigned to New York, and returned three years later to Ireland. In 1811 he died unexpectedly in Dublin. On hearing this, Bishop Carroll lamented the decease of "my good-hearted friend Dr. Caffrey."[62]

During the summer of 1794, Dominic May, O.P., set out from Dublin for Philadelphia in the company of the Augustinian John Rosseter and a diocesan priest, Michael Ennis.[63] Archbishop John Troy had recommended the trio to Bishop Carroll, based on the judgment of the Irish Dominican provincial. Father May, he wrote, was "well-informed, exemplary and laborious."[64] But his new ministry was hardly begun when, not three months after arriving, he was stricken with yellow fever. He died in Baltimore on October 2, 1794. The cathedral record described "a priest of the Order of Preachers, . . . lately from Ireland, deceased this day of a malignant fever, aged about 33 years."[65] Bishop Carroll wrote to Archbishop Troy,

> I had no opportunity of experiencing the good qualities which all accounts concurred in attributing to Mr. May.... He arrived very sick at Baltimore where [the fever] then raged.

> I lodged him at my house, though I did not much apprehend the nature of his disease. But it soon manifested itself in so visible a manner that he died three days after.[66]

One more sorrowful loss for the young Church in America!

If any Irish priest deserved the epithet "wandering friar," it was Francis Bodkin, who came to the Baltimore Diocese in 1794. By his own testimony he had studied in Rome and Naples, ministered to a parish in Spain, and brought very ample credentials from England and Ireland. The only remaining evidence of his studies are his Spanish Bible and moral theology text.[67] Bishop Carroll announced his coming when he informed Archbishop Troy of the death of Dominic May. "Since his death," he wrote, "another Irish gentleman, and of the Order of St. Dominic, Mr. Bodkin, arrived from London, destined to live with a private family, but the arrangements were not made agreeably to the promises given in London, and he went to seek a brother in the West Indies."[68]

Carroll's words revealed that Bodkin was ready to begin his restless journeying, first to Kentucky and Louisiana, en route to the West Indies! In 1804 he wrote to Carroll from New Orleans about the historic transfer of that city and the vast region west of the Mississippi to the United States. He said, "I witnessed the Spanish, French, and now the American flag flying."[69] It was good history, but his ministry was not revealed. His travels led him finally back to Galway, where he died on September 27, 1822.[70]

A fourth Irish Dominican, Bartholomew Augustine McMahon, arrived in Philadelphia in 1799. Bishop Carroll sent him to St. Peter's in New York, but within months he became a victim of the rampant yellow fever and died there in July of 1800.[71]

FRIARS WHO SERVED WITH BISHOP JOHN CARROLL
1786 - 1815

Name	Ministry	Location
John O'Connell	1786 - 1789	New York
William V. O'Brien	1787 - 1816 (d.)	New York
Francis Fleming	1789 - 1793 (d.)	Philadelphia
Michael Burke	1789 - 1800 (d.)	Philadelphia; New York
Christopher Keating	1789 - 1795	Philadelphia
Jean-Antoine Le Dru	1789 - 1794 (d.)	Mississippi Valley
Gabriel Isabey	1793 - 1823 (d.)	St. Martinville, LA
Anthony Caffry	1794 - 1808 (d.)	Washington, D.C.
Dominic May	1794 (d.)	Baltimore
Francis Bodkin	1795 - 1796	Maryland
Bartholomew A. McMahon	1799 - 1800 (d.)	Philadelphia; New York
John Ceslas Fenwick	1800 - 1815 (d.)	Maryland

Note: The entry (d.) designates those who died while on mission to the United States.

The last Dominican welcomed by Archbishop Carroll was not an Irishman but an American, born in Maryland not far from the estate of the Carrolls. He was John Ceslas Fenwick whose nephew Edward Fenwick founded in 1805 the first province of the Order of Preachers in the United States. The two Fenwicks belonged to that eminent Maryland family whose progenitor Cuthbert came in 1634 with Lord Calvert's colonists from England.[72]

John Fenwick was born around the year 1759 at the family manor on the Patuxent River in St. Mary's County, Maryland. In 1773 he went to Belgium to study at Holy Cross College in Bornhem, conducted by the English Dominican friars in exile.[73] While John was there, the Revolutionary War took place and the colonies declared their nation's independence. At seventeen John became an American citizen, to the joy of all his family.

On October 14, 1777, John became a Dominican novice in Belgium, the first American to enter the Order of Preachers; but he could not make his religious profession until 1783. It was forbidden to youths under 25 years of age, not by the Order or the Church, but by the imperial intruder in Church affairs, Joseph II of Austria.[74] John continued his studies at Louvain, was ordained there in 1785 and then received the degree, Lector of Theology. He was assigned to teach at Holy Cross College where one of the students was his nephew from Maryland. After graduation in 1794, Edward followed his uncle into the English province of the Order of Preachers.

When the French Revolutionaries swept into Belgium in the summer of 1794, the Dominicans fled from Bornhem, forced to leave their property in the hands of the invaders.[75] They returned to England and soon reopened Holy Cross College in the Surrey village of Carshalton near London. John Fenwick taught theology there until about 1800, when he returned home to begin years of pastoral ministry with Bishop Carroll in his native Maryland.[76]

Early in 1804 John's nephew Edward began to establish an American province of the Dominican friars in Maryland. Knowing his uncle John to be "a worthy confrere of the Order and missioner,"[77] Edward wrote to Rome that "Father John Fenwick, my uncle. . . is in Maryland, and will, I suppose, joyfully join me."[78] When Edward and his co-founders were sent by Bishop Carroll to Kentucky, John did not go with them. He remained in the service of Carroll in southern Maryland, probably at Carroll's request.[79] In 1804 Bishop Carroll assigned John Fenwick to a cluster of Maryland missions where the Jesuits had been the only missionaries for many decades. The professor from Belgium and southern England now began eleven years of exhausting ministry on horseback or on foot. His base was Port Tobacco, Maryland, where he lived at St. Thomas Manor with erstwhile members of the Society of Jesus.[80]

John's nephew Edward knew the hardships of the Maryland mission. He had experienced them briefly before going on to Kentucky. In 1805 he wrote to Rome from Maryland,

The distress of the Catholics in this country. . . is beyond description. The scarcity of priests, the numerous and dispersed congregations, their desolation and pressing solicitations for spiritual succor should move stones, if possible, to compassion. Scarcely a missioner in Maryland who has not two, three and four congregations to serve, which are 10, 15, and 20 miles distant from one another.[81]

In 1808 the vast Baltimore Diocese was divided, and the Dioceses of Boston, New York, Philadelphia and Bardstown were carved from its vast expanse. John Carroll was named Archbishop and his diocese was reduced from nation-wide to more manageable size. Yet within its limits Catholic settlers and parishes were multiplying, while the number of clergy increased slowly and veteran priests grew older.

Among those veterans was John Fenwick, who continued his arduous ministry in Maryland. Conscious of his dual allegiance to the Order and the diocese, but also of his decreasing strength, he wrote in 1813 to Archbishop Carroll,

> I have been long thinking of writing to you about retiring, which I mentioned to you before hearing of the intended journey [from Kentucky to Maryland] of the Rev. Mr. E.Fenwick. I waited his arrival. I have conversed with him, and think best to consult my superior [Samuel T. Wilson, of the new province] whether he would wish me to come to Kentucky or not. I now write to him, and shall leave myself in his hands. In the meantime I put my hopes in you, that you will grant me the place of retirement you mentioned to me, or any other more eligible. I wish now to give up immediately, or as soon as possible, as I find myself overpowered with hardships and difficulties, and wish to prepare myself for death.[82]

How the archbishop replied is not known, but Carroll was aware of Fenwick's overwork. He had written on November 11, 1812, to John Grassi that John Fenwick was "overpowered" at his post at St. Thomas, Port Tobacco.[83] But in the following year John Fenwick was assigned temporarily to one more Maryland mission, St. Joseph's at Deer Creek. There he must have expended all his remaining energy. His death occurred on August 20, 1815, not four months before that of John Carroll.

On hearing of "good Fr. John Fenwick's unexpected death," Archbishop Carroll wrote to Grassi, "The extent of his missions has been contracted since the Rev. Mr. Brooke has resumed the ministry; but yet it will be very difficult to replace his loss."[84] Grassi replied with details of John's death:

> From the letter that I wrote to Father E. Fenwick. . . Your Excellency will have understood how true and too much is the sad news of the bitter loss of the Rev. John Fenwick. Father Francis Neale wrote me from St. Thomas that that praiseworthy man died Sunday, August 20, and was buried the Monday following. Good Father John became overheated going on foot from one place to another, bringing on the sickness that soon reduced him to extremity. Behold us at a new impasse, searching for a missionary to make up for such a loss.[85]

The final word to Archbishop Carroll came from John Carey, S.J., with whom John Fenwick lived at Port Tobacco. He wrote,

> The unexpected & almost sudden death of our honoured & esteemed dwelling companion, the Rev. J. Fenwick, has undoubtedly much surprised your Lordship as it did all those who were acquainted with that amiable Missionary & knew the strength & habitual state of his constitution & his health. The nature of his first & last sickness is not perfectly known. However, [it] caused a dissolution of the whole system & from that moment rendered every medicinal art & remedy inefficacious.[86]

John Ceslas Fenwick was buried at St. Thomas Manor, Port Tobacco, among his deceased friends and co-workers of the Society of Jesus. It was ironic that while John remained faithful to his ministry in Maryland, his bishop had refused permission for his nephew Edward to establish a province in their home State, sending them instead to the Kentucky frontier.

Even a cursory review of the Irish Dominicans on mission in the American Church before 1815 reveals the significant role of two men who sponsored their coming and their ministry. They were John Troy and John Carroll, the heads of the Church in the country that sent the men and the county that received them. Before becoming bishops, both prelates had been members of religious orders, the first a

Grave marker of John Fenwick, O.P., in Jesuit cemetery, Port Tobacco, Maryland

Dominican, and the second, a Jesuit. Both kept before them, with vision and fairness, the good of the whole Church, and both were realists. No account of that period would be complete without a brief glance at the contributions of John Troy and John Carroll as collaborators. They formed a liaison of trust that bridged the Atlantic and lasted for more than a quarter of a century, from 1788 until Carroll's death in 1815.

John Troy (1739-1823) was an Irish Dominican who studied at San Clemente, the Dominican studium in Rome. Later, as prior, he prepared the young students for the far-flung missions of the Irish Dominican province. During his ten years as Bishop of Ossory, beginning in 1773, Troy became known for his wisdom and impartiality concerning the clergy, both of the diocese and of religious orders. In 1786 the bishops of Ireland chose him to be the Archbishop of Dublin.[87] In that office he transformed the Church in Ireland[88] without losing sight of the Church elsewhere, especially in North America. His constant concern was to provide fully qualified priests, first for Ireland, where he helped to found the renowned Maynooth seminary, and then for the missions of Canada and the United States.

The concerns of John Troy were those of John Carroll as well, when he was named successively the superior of the American missions, then first Bishop, then Archbishop of Baltimore. In collaboration the two Church leaders, each formed in the spirituality of his religious order, developed a friendship based on common ideals.

When John Carroll was made bishop, the two men had already begun their lasting correspondence. In 1788 Carroll had welcomed the first letter from Troy with these words:

> I am happy in taking this occasion to open a correspondence with a prelate of your distinguished character, and hope your Grace will allow me to apply to you with confidence and liberty in all matters which may intervene between this country and Ireland relative to the welfare of religion.[89]

Their letters were marked by mutual confidence as both bishops wrote frankly about the qualifications or limitations of men from Ireland.[90] Characteristic of Carroll was his request to Troy to send priests "of unblemished morality, sobriety & of good knowledge."[91]

Troy showed no favoritism in recommending men of religious orders. They were sent in fact, not by him, but by their own superiors. Nevertheless, the Dominican archbishop gave Carroll full information and counsel, sometimes expressing regret that certain men he had recommended did not meet their standards.[92] The record shows that the majority of those placed through their collaboration were exemplary priests.

The relationship between Carroll and Troy was strained when John Connolly, O.P., was made Bishop of New York without the consultation owed to Bishop Carroll by Church officials; but Carroll's recommendations had never reached Rome.[93] Worse in Carroll's eyes was the nomination by Irish bishops of the controversial William V. Harold, O.P., for the Philadelphia bishopric. (See Chapter 3). Believing that Troy had promoted his nomination, Carroll told him with his usual candor, "Would it not be resented as a very improper interference, if we the Bps in the US should presume to fill the Vacant Sees of Ireland?"[94] Troy hastened to respond,

> If I interfered in the appointment of a Bishop for Philadelphia by a direct recommendation of Revd. Mr. Harold, I must confess my having acted irregularly and improperly. But, if I recollect aright, I only stated the interference of others, for your Grace's information. However this be, I regret exceedingly that any irregular act of mine should afford a moment's uneasiness or anxiety to Your Grace."[95]

Troy's recollection was correct. His letter had mentioned Harold only in these words:

> Revd. Mr. Harold Senr. has procured recommendations from the Archbishop of Bordeaux & other Prelates in favour of his nephew Revd Mr. Wm. Harold to be appointed to the See of Philadelphia, which have been forwarded to Rome. Your Grace's knowledge of him dispenses me from saying anything more of him.[96]

The basis for the lasting relationship of Archbishops Carroll and Troy was each man's respect for the wisdom and gifts of the other, supporting their common love and labors for the Church. Their relationship continued to the end of John Carroll's life, and benefited the Church as much as the labors of the missionaries who came to the new nation.

Few documents can be found to tell the story of the Preachers in the United States at the time of Bishop John Carroll. Those few reveal features of their mission which, though not unique, substantially benefited the American Church. First, the Dominican friars followed the example of St. Dominic in putting the mission of the Church before the founding of a new province for the Order. They worked zealously with priests and people of the diocese to realize that common purpose.

Another element of Dominican ministry expected and appreciated by the people was their devoted preaching. The preacher's weaknesses, in the tradition of the Order, were absolved through his preaching; and if his sins were public, he sought forgiveness for them through public proclamation of the Word.[97] Another gift of the early missionaries to the faithful was their thorough study. They received excellent education in colleges and universities on the continent, from Rome and Bologna to Paris, Lisbon, Bilbao and Louvain. Some used this learning for writing, as did William O'Brien in writing the life of St. Paul, which provided substance for his sermons in the church of St. Peter's on Barclay Street.

The friars' preaching took another form as they gave days and nights to the care of the sick and dying. This was the ministry of William O'Brien which the people singled out in remembering his years of service among them. And in the same ministry the friars Francis Fleming, Michael Burke, Bartholomew McMahon and Dominic May gave their lives.

Although Bishop Carroll's mission was sometimes hampered by unstable clerics, most Dominican missionaries came to the diocese with the intent to remain. Of the twelve friars who came to the United States in Carroll's time, eight never went home. For most of them that time was very short, since death claimed them unexpectedly in the midst of their ministry.

To summarize the contributions of these friars is not to disregard their limitations and weaknesses. Rather, it should emphasize the good they did in working with John Carroll to lay firm foundations for the Church in the United States.

1. Gardoqui negotiated treaties with John Jay and won the respect of leaders of the new nation and the Church. John Carroll especially appreciated his gifts. He wrote to Rome, "I have repeatedly consulted the very excellent Spanish Representative about the state of religion and its spread throughout the States." To Cardinal Leonardo Antonelli, Maryland, March 18, 1788, Archives of Propaganda Fide,Rome(APF) Am.Centr.vol.2, 524r-527r.

2. The reader will find greater detail on the city of New York and its Catholics in the Profile of Bishop John Connolly.

3. John G. Shea, **The Life and Times of the Most Rev. John Carroll** vol.2 (New York: 1888) 268.

4. The election was described in the papal brief by which John Carroll was made Bishop of Baltimore. See John Tracy Ellis, ed., **Documents of American Catholic History,** vol.1(Wilmington, Delaware: Michael Glazier, 1987) 163.

5. Baltimore, Oct.23, 1789, Thomas Hanley, S.J.,ed., **The John Carroll Papers,** vol.1 (Notre Dame: Notre Dame University Press, 1976) 349. The **Carroll Papers** will be cited hereafter as CP 1, 2, or 3 designating the three volumes. Plowden, Carroll's confrere in the suppressed Society of Jesus, was a trusted friend to whom he could write of diocesan affairs in confidence, thus recording unintentionally the pulse of his episcopal ministry.

6. Among the 22 priests at the Baltimore Synod of 1791, there were three diocesan priests, three Sulpicians, and sixteen members of religious orders, of whom most were from the suppressed Society of Jesus. See the Synod Report in Peter Guilday, **The Life and Times of John Carroll** (Westminster, Maryland: The Newman Press, 1954) 428-429.

7. See Gerald Fogarty, Joseph Durkin, R.Emmett Curran, **The Maryland Jesuits, 1634-1833** (Baltimore: Maryland Province, Society of Jesus, 1976). The Society was partially restored in 1805, and fully in 1815.

8. These were the primary senders of religious men to the eighteenth-century United States. The Sulpicians, while not a religious order, served the Church admirably as missionaries and bishops as well as founders of seminaries, their chief work. See Christopher Kauffman, **Tradition and Transformation in Catholic Culture: the Priests of Saint Sulpice in the United States from 1791 to the Present** (New York: Macmillan, 1987).

9. Guilday 504.

10. To Plowden, Rock Creek, Maryland, May 26, 1788. CP, 1, 389.

11. Hugh Fenning, O.P., **The Irish Dominican Province, 1678-1790** (Dublin: Dominican Publications, 1990) 502. This is a richly documented source of information concerning the friars of the Irish province who came on mission to the United States.

12. Andrew Nugent, an Irish Capuchin, was temporary pastor in New York. He encouraged parishioners to join him in resisting Carroll's authority. He also caused civil disorders for which he was tried in the civil court. Cf. Carroll to John Thorpe, New York, Nov.7, 1787. APF Am.Centr. v.2, 510rv; also Carroll to Plowden, Maryland, Mar.1,1788. CP 1, 272-73 et passim.

13. Many trustees asserted the right of lay control over temporal affairs in the parish. See "Trusteeism" by Patrick Carey in Glazier, Michael and Thomas Shelley, eds., **The Encyclopedia of American Catholic History** (Collegeville, MN: The Liturgical Press, 1997) See also Carey.

14. Sermon given in the chapel of the Spanish legation, Oct. 1787. CP 1, 264. Nugent and some parishioners had blocked Carroll from celebrating Mass in St. Peter's Church.

15. Baltimore, Dec.8,1787. CP 1, 271-72.

16. To Cardinal Leonardo Antonelli, Maryland, Mar. 18,1788. APF Am. Centr. v. 2, 524r. Carroll showed his confidence in O'Brien by sending him to Boston to deal with a schism there, and also consulted O'Brien concerning the need for an American bishop.

17. Two years earlier the estimate was 1500.

18. To John Thorpe, New York, Nov.7,1787, CP 1, 265-67.

19. James Roosevelt Bayley, **A Brief Sketch of the Early History of the Catholic Church on the Island of New York,** 2nd ed.(New York: Catholic Publication Society, 1870) 65-66. Bayley noted that the school enrollment averaged 500. He was a nephew of Elizabeth Seton, who became a Catholic of St. Peter's parish in 1805.

20. Hearing this, Bishop Carroll sent O'Brien a letter of reproof. Washington, July 5,1796, CP 2, 184-85.

21. Bayley 68-69.

22. Guilday 427.

23. Reproduced in Bayley 66.

24. Carroll to parishioners of St. Mary's, Philadelphia, from Baltimore, July 21, 1788, CP 1, 321. Catholics often took the initiative in obtaining priests from their homeland. They sent inquiries, named possible recruits for Bishop Carroll's consideration, and requested his authorization for them.

25. See Fenning, 541-546, concerning the qualifications of Fleming and related facts about his vocation.

26. Charles Bellisoni to Carroll, Sept.4,1789. Archives of the Archdiocese of Baltimore (AAB) 8 A 35.

27. To Plowden, Philadelphia, Dec. 24, 1789, CP 1 398.

28. Carroll to Plowden, Rock Creek, Md., Feb.24,1790, CP 1, 431.

29. The census takers often listed free blacks in nameless groups, as they did the slaves. The latter were counted as three-fourths of their true number. The 1790 census revealed that more than 95 percent of the nation's citizens lived in rural areas. But most of the immigrants, especially those from Ireland, chose to live then in the city. Populations of the chief urban centers besides Philadelphia were recorded in 1790 as follows: New York 33,000 Boston 18,000 Charleston 16,000 Baltimore 13,000. The national population was 3,930,000, of whom Catholics numbered about 35,000, or fewer than 1%. See Gerald Shaugnessy,S.M., **Has the Immigrant Kept the Faith?** (New York: Macmillan, 1925) 52.

30. Carroll to Plowden, Rock Creek, MD Dec.15, 1785, CP 1, 196.

31. Fenning, 543. Very likely the publisher was their fellow parishioner, Mathew Carey, who was writer, patriot, bookseller and defender of the Church until his death in 1839. **New Catholic Encyclopedia,** 1967 ed.

32. CP 1, 526 ff.

33. Reported by the Apostolic Nuncio to Propaganda Fide, Lisbon, Jan. 20 and Feb. 3, 1791, APF Am. Centr. v.3 11-15.

34. Baltimore, July 12, 1794, CP 2, 120. Just previous to his death Graessl had been designated coadjutor for the diocese.

35. Michael Burke was often called by his second name, Nicholas. See Fenning 569.

36. Posted from London, July 23, 1790, CP 1,452.

37. From baptismal records, St.Joseph's chapel, 1791-1795, kept by Keating for the outlying stations. Philadelphia Archdiocesan Archives(PAA).

38. To Troy, Baltimore, Sept. 28, 1795. DDA 116/6, no.93, as quoted in Fenning 563, n.194.

39. Carroll to Troy.

40. Baltimore, July 16, 1795, CP 2, 144.

41. Fenning 564.

42. See the unpublished study by Michael Ruthenberg,"By Way of Oswego; Jean Antoine Le Dru, O.P.," Aquinas Institute, St. Louis, 1988. This work, carefully documented, provides the facts concerning Le Dru.

43. The term "Jacobin" was also given to Dominicans beyond Paris. Their church in Toulouse where the tomb of Thomas Aquinas is venerated has been known for centuries as the Church of the Jacobins.

44. Le Dru to Bishop Jean Hubert, Mar. 29, 1790, Archives, Archdiocese of Quebec.

45. Although Bishop Hubert gave him full faculties as a "missionary curé" among the Acadians, Le Dru was accused by two Irish priests of pretending to be a priest. In Nova Scotia the British residents did not welcome anyone from France. Ruthenberg 7.

46. Just before religious orders were suppressed Carroll wrote that "the Jacobin priest" had not yet obtained a letter from his provincial. To Pierre Gibault, Baltimore, Jan.20, 1790, CP 1, 421. A footnote on p. 422 of CP 1 states that James McHenry, writing to Carroll June 12,1796, accused Le Dru of "undermining American interests against the English." But McHenry's letter includes no such accusation. AAB 5 D 4.

47. See Carroll to Bishop Jean Hubert, Baltimore, May 5,1788, and Hubert's reply from Quebec, Oct. 6, 1788. Both are quoted in Guilday 296-298.

48. Ruthenberg, 15. Several missionaries among the French settlers left them because of lack of support, especially after widespread failure of their crops. In the Spanish colony they were assured at least of meeting the cost of living.

49. Carroll to Bishop Jean Hubert, Mar. 2, 1796. CP 2, 162. There is no evidence in Dominican records that Le Dru was an apostate. The inventory made by French revolutionaries in September 1790 lists him as an ordained Dominican of the Arras convent, which was closed in the following summer. Neither is there documentation concerning his alleged misdemeanors. Ruthenberg concludes that accusations were colored by anti-French prejudice among the clergy and people of Nova Scotia. Ruthenberg 6, 33 ff.

50. Ruthenberg, 36 ; 44-46. Victor O'Daniel, in his **Dominican Province of St.Joseph** (New York: Holy Name Society, 1942)129 states that Le Dru left the Order in France before coming to America, but the 1790 census of the Arras convent refutes this supposition.

51. Roger Baudier, **The Catholic Church in Louisiana** (New Orleans: Baudier, 1939) 171.

52. Roger Baudier 252, 266, 283.

53. O'Daniel 129-30.

54. M.A.C., "The Church of the Attakapas, 1750-1889," **American Catholic Quarterly Review** 14 (1889): 477-78.

55. Baudier 252.

56. Carroll to John Troy, Baltimore, Sept. 28, 1795. DDA 116/6, no.93, quoted in Fenning 563-64.

57. Fenning 561. There is some evidence that he studied at the Sorbonne. Bishop Carroll always identified him as "Dr. Caffrey."

58. Hoban's role is mentioned on the memorial tablet to Caffry erected on the grounds of St.Patrick Parish, but this is not documented. See "James Hoban, the Architect and Builder of the White House and the Superintendent of the Capitol at Washington," **American Catholic Historical Researches** 24 (1907): 35-52.

59. See the well documented study by William W. Warner, **At Peace with All Their Neighbors: Catholics and Catholicism in the National Capital, 1787-1860** (Washington D.C: Georgetown University Press, Oct. 1994) Ch.6.

60. Caffry to Carroll, Washington, Aug. 1800, AAB 8 A C 3.

61. Neale to Carroll, Georgetown, Jan. 27, 1804, AAB 5 P 5.

62. Baltimore, Jan.16, 1812. Spic. Ossor. 3, 533-34. Quoted in Fenning, 562, n.193. Caffry's name is spelled with an *ay* or *ey* in various documents. In his letters to Carroll he uses neither vowel in his signature.

63. Rosseter became a founder, with Matthew Carr, of the American province of the Augustinians in Philadelphia. The diocesan priest Michael Ennis has been mistakenly identified as an Augustinian, as in Hanley, CP 2, 143.

64. Dublin, Oct.18, 1794, AAB 8 M 1. In this letter Troy clearly identified Michael Ennis as a diocesan priest.

65. St. Peter Pro-Cathedral Internments 1794.

66. Georgetown, June 22, 1795, CP 2, 143.

67. According to Fenning, 565, "No evidence of his work, nor even of his presence in Ireland lies to hand."

68. June 22, 1795. CP 2, 143.

69. To Archbishop Carroll, New Orleans, Jan.3, 1804, AAB 1 T 8.

70. Fenning 569.

71. Guilday 626.

72. Cf. Victor O'Daniel, O.P., **The Right Rev. Edward Dominic Fenwick, O.P.,** (Washington, D.C.: **The Dominicana,** 1920) Ch.1. The Fenwicks, like the Carrolls, were families of faith who lived in St. Mary's County and were blessed from the beginning by the ministry of Jesuit missionaries from England. See Fogarty, Durkin and Curran.

73. Like the friars of Ireland, the English Dominicans conducted colleges and houses of formation in Belgium.

74. Victor O'Daniel, O.P.,"The Rev. John Ceslas Fenwick, O.P.," **Catholic Historical Review 1** (1915): 20-22.

75. The English chronicler indicated the friars fled in disguise and barely escaped detection while crossing the English Channel.

76. O'Daniel, **Fenwick.**

77. Edward Fenwick to Luke Concanen, O.P.,Carshalton, April 14,1804, Archives General of the Orders of Preachers, Rome(AGOP) XIII, 03150, 65.

78. Fenwick to Concanen, London, Sept 1,1804, AGOP XIII, 03150, 66.

79. So great were the needs in Maryland that Carroll persuaded Edward Fenwick and Robert Angier, one of the founding members of the American province, to minister there for a while before going on to Kentucky. Later Angier returned to the Maryland missions from 1816 to 1825. Cf. E. I. Devitt, S.J., "The Clergy List of 1819, Diocese of Baltimore", **Records** of the American Catholic Historical Society of Philadelphia, 22 (1911): 238-4l.

80. O'Daniel, "John Ceslas Fenwick," **Catholic Historical Review,** 1 (1915): 23.

81. To Luke Concanen, O.P., Piscataway, Md., Aug.1,1805, AGOP XIII, 03150, 73.

82. St. Thomas, Port Tobacco, Md., Dec.8,1813. AAB 3 R 14. Thomas Wilson came from English Dominicans in 1805 to assist Edward Fenwick in establishing a Dominican province in the United States. See Chapter 4.

83. Jesuit Archives, 203, B 2, Maryland Province, Georgetown University Archives (GUA).

84. Baltimore, Aug. 25, 1815, CP 3, 356-57.

85. Aug. 28, 1815, place unknown. The extract given here is translated from the original Italian. AAB 4 B 2.

86. St.Thomas, Port Tobacco, Md., Sept.11,1815, AAB 2 J 4.

87. H.E.Peel, "John Thomas Troy," **New Catholic Encyclopedia,** 1967 ed.

88. Emmet Larkin, "The Dynamics of Leadership in the Irish Church in the Nineteenth Century, 1786-1921," **Humanities** 9 (1988): 17-19.

89. Baltimore, Aug. 11, 1788, CP 1, 327.

90. More than once the two men voiced their concern in such words as these by Troy:" I notice what Your Lordship remarks respecting Missionaries, whether Secular or Regular, going from hence to America, & shall endeavor, so far as depends on me, that they correspond to Your Lordship's expectations." To Carroll, Dublin, Aug. 13, 1796, AAB 8 M 4.

91. Notes, Aug. 24, 1791, AAB 9 A 11.

92. One example is found in Troy to Carroll, Dublin, Oct.18, 1794. Troy regretted that he had erred in recommending a certain man, out of a desire to be fair to him. AAB 8 M 1.

93. Transatlantic ships carried the mails. Many were the delays and losses of messages going in both directions.

94. Carroll to Troy, July 22, 1815, AAB 9 T 3. Date given in Troy's letter of Sept. 8, 1815. AAB 8 B K 2. This was the last known letter from Troy to Carroll, who died on the following December 3.

95. Troy to Carroll, Sept.8, 1815.

96. Dublin, Mar. 22, 1815, AAB 8 N 8.

97. Cf. Simon Tugwell, O.P., **The Way of the Preacher** (London, 1979) 51-53.

THREE CONTROVERSIAL FRIARS

Many years after the fact, the provincial of the Irish Dominicans, William Vincent Harold, wrote to a friend in Dublin about his experiences in the United States. "If only those days could be changed. Even now, remembering them brings a blush to my cheek."[1] The passage was a rare indication that Harold had doubts about at least one (and perhaps several) courses of action he had so vehemently upheld during his American mission.

In the early years of the nineteenth century a number of Irish missionary priests came to the United States and died there. Others gave years of faithful service, but then chose to return to Ireland. Among the latter were three Dominican friars who left the States under a cloud of controversy. Each of these "controversials" had come as a mature priest with an excellent record. Each, upon returning to Ireland, continued where he had left off and served out his days as a highly respected member of the Order. Yet each man, while laboring in the American Church, ran afoul of the phenomenon known as "trusteeism." Depending on one's point of view of that system, William Vincent Harold, John Albert Ryan, and Thomas Carbry can be viewed either as martyrs or troublemakers. The trustee system was not unique to American Catholicism. Early Catholic settlers were merely adapting certain European practices to realities in the United States. For centuries in Europe a wealthy person or family who gave land and money towards the building of a church had a strong say in the temporal affairs of that church, and often exercised what was called the *jus patronatus,* or right to present to the Bishop the name of the man they wished to have for a pastor. In the United States the practice was much influenced by the Protestant tradition of allowing elected trustees to conduct temporal affairs. These men were chosen from among the "pewholders" – those who paid a regular fee which entitled them to the exclusive use of a particular pew in the church.[2]

Ethnic parishes tried to secure priests from their own background, but because of the acute shortage of ministers for the American mission, they often had to settle for whoever was available. The appointment of bishops also posed problems. The Vatican Congregation of Propaganda Fide, which was charged with the final selection of bishops in mission territory, was handicapped in its ecclesiastical appointments by the shortage of priests, great distances, and lack of specific knowledge of local circumstances. At least some of the tensions surrounding the American ministry of Harold, Ryan and Carbry can be traced to these causes.

William Harold and John Ryan became close friends during their early years as Dominicans. This relationship endured until Ryan's death in 1852. Even though they did not minister near one another during their American experience, their friendship, based on an almost uncanny similarity in thinking, caused them to be linked in the history of the Order.

William Harold was the first of the pair to arrive on the American scene. He came from Dublin, apparently drawn by the appointment of Luke Concanen, OP, to the See of New York in 1808. Not finding Concanen there when he arrived in that year, Harold heard that the recently named Bishop of Philadelphia, Michael Egan, OFM, was in need of a priest at St. Mary's, the cathedral parish. As Bishop Egan later told Archbishop Carroll, Harold had come with "strong recommendations from Doctor Troy and the provincial of his order," followed by letters from Ireland calling him "a gentleman of good sense and excellent conduct."[3] When Egan tested his worth by having him preach at St. Mary's, he announced, "He gave general satisfaction." In fact, a group of trustees afterwards congratulated the new bishop on obtaining "so able an appointment."[4]

William Harold's talent for preaching, joined with a natural ability for dealing with people, helped him to settle in at St. Mary's where he soon became Bishop Egan's trusted assistant. Six months after his initiation as preacher in 1809, Harold joined the bishop, the Augustinian friar John Rosseter and eight trustees in launching a major enlargement of the church to a size more fitting a diocesan cathedral. No one seems to have disputed the need for the reconstruction; what was questioned was the method of securing funds and their availability. Pastors and trustees addressed a circular, "To the Pewholders of St. Mary's Church," in which they admitted that "our funds are unequal to such an undertaking," and appealed to parishioners' generosity. They also cited a "well founded hope of liberal assistance from our brethren and fellow citizens in Philadelphia."[5]

The project went ahead, with the final cost nearing $30,000 and subscriptions amounting only to $17,000.[6] While renovations were being completed, formal installation of bishops for the four new dioceses of Philadelphia, New York, Boston and Bardstown were taking place. William Harold had the honor of giving the sermon at the consecration of Boston's Bishop Cheverus, which took place in Baltimore on the feast of All Saints, 1810. He spoke on the sanctity of ecclesiastical authority and so pleased the assembled prelates that they had the address printed.

Bishop Egan's consecration had been celebrated a few days earlier at St. Mary's. When Harold returned in triumph over his performance in Baltimore, there were new financial concerns to be settled. Besides the cost of church construction, the question of salaries now emerged. It was decided among the trustees that the bishop and two clergymen would be paid $2,400 a year.[7]

In 1811 John Rosseter left St. Mary's, owing to poor health. His place was taken by another member of the Harold family, a diocesan priest named James Harold, who was William's uncle. James had been exiled to Australia because of his alleged support of the rebels who had been his parishioners in the 1798 Dublin uprising. Broken in health by this exile, he was released from the penal colonies in 1810 but still barred from Ireland. Instead, he managed to reach Rio de Janeiro and enlisted the help of the papal nuncio to Brazil. News had reached him that his nephew William, who had been ordained a Dominican, was now pastor of "the largest and richest congregation in the United States."[8] He asked the nuncio for an introduction to Bishop Egan and help in reaching Philadelphia. The nuncio sent him on to the United States with a recommendation which called him "an excellent Irish ecclesiastic" who by his "piety and good conduct would render himself very worthy." [9] Egan received him graciously and wrote to Carroll that his coming "had made his nephew completely happy and should he remain with us, he will be a great acquisition." [10] Unknown to the participants, this combination of events and personalities would precipitate the disaster to follow.

Before the storm could break, one more actor arrived to foment the crisis. John Ryan, O.P., had been asked to accompany a priest friend, one Bernard Lonergan, on a sea voyage deemed necessary for his health. Both Lonergan and Ryan had relatives and friends in the United States. In New York the priests enjoyed the hospitality of the Jesuit Anthony Kohlmann stationed at St. Peter's. Kohlmann sent word to Baltimore of their arrival, mentioning that "Mr. Ryan is recommended to us as a most meritorious clergyman and excellent preacher." Though both men intended to return to Ireland after a short visit, Kohlmann clearly hoped that they both might stay in the United States. [11]

World events intervened. The embargo which accompanied the War of 1812 complicated plans for a quick return voyage. The two priests decided to visit Philadelphia, where, as Ryan put it, they would "spend some time with Doctor Egan . . . and with Mr. Harold my old fellow student and friend." [12] Lonergan then determined to return to Ireland despite the dangers of war. Because travel proved expensive, Ryan could not afford the trip. Before he sailed from New York, Lonergan tried to persuade Father Kohlmann to make a place for his friend John Ryan at St. Peter's. At first the pastor agreed and Lonergan wrote to Ryan telling him to come at once to New York. Harold traveled with Ryan. By the time they reached St. Peter's, Lonergan had left and Kohlmann had changed his mind. Lonergan had convinced him that both Ryan and his friends had expensive tastes, especially for fine wines. Regretting his invitation to Ryan, Kohlmann used the excuse that the parish trustees had said there was not enough money available to pay an additional salary.

Finding himself rejected, Ryan confronted Kohlmann and complained to Carroll, accusing the New York pastor of lying, insincerity and prejudice against Irish clergy. [13] Whether or not the accusation was correct, this representation to Kohlmann and the Archbishop weakened the good reputation once held by the two Fathers. What Dominican brethren were later to say of Harold probably applied to both men: they were, indeed, zealous priests, gifted preachers, but "ready for a fight." [14]

Ryan then left to visit his sister in Baltimore, and while there he was asked by John Carroll to fill a pastoral position in that city. This he did to the complete satisfaction of the archbishop, until his friend Harold became the beleaguered party in a Philadelphia dispute. Ryan went up to help him and the two friends eventually decided they had enough of American clergy. Both returned to Ireland in 1813, but not before a major conflict.

The same embargo that interfered with Ryan and Lonergan's plans to sail for Europe in 1812 wreaked financial havoc in American port cities, among them Philadelphia. Money needed to pay for the extensive renovations to St. Mary's evaporated, and the stress of financial shortfall began to erode the harmony of the bishop's household. There were also personality differences that had already surfaced between

Egan and the two Harolds. The bishop blamed the quarrels that erupted within the rectory on the presence of James Harold and cited him for unduly influencing his nephew to rebellion.[15]

As Egan described it, with Michael Hurley as a witness, open domestic warfare broke out when the bishop informed his two associates that his physician had advised him to preach as seldom as possible. Accordingly, he preached only occasionally and expected the Harolds to alternate at St. Mary's. This they refused to do. Nor would they help with the distribution of Holy Communion at Mass. Egan described a conflict concerning a baptism and an emergency sick call during which he asked James Harold to take the sick call. The elder Harold refused, saying that he was only bound to take calls that happened on his rotation.[16]

By this time, the bishop was asking Archbishop Carroll's advice about transferring James Harold to Pittsburgh, so that there might be some hope of his "living peaceably again with the nephew." James, however, was refusing to go unless his salary at St. Mary's would continue to be paid. Egan remarked that the elder Harold was very concerned "to make money, which he cannot do there."[17]

To complicate matters, in 1812 the trustees of St. Mary's reported that the parish was nearly seven thousand dollars in debt. They "saw no way of being freed from [that debt] unless the services of one of the pastors be dispensed with and the salary of the clergy be reduced."[18] When the July quarterly salary of six hundred dollars came due, there was nothing in the treasury. Efforts to secure a loan failed and by the beginning of August, the treasurer had managed to collect only two hundred dollars. This he offered to the clerics and it was refused.

The bishop and his two priests then issued a circular accusing the trustees of deliberately withholding the salary payment, asking if the parishioners truly wished "to submit your clergy to such humiliation from men such as these."[19] Without having a chance to explain their problems, the trustees were censured, and a subscription for the support of the clergy raised a thousand dollars in one week. The clerics had their salary and St. Mary's had more than its share of dissension. Protests and counterprotests were published and Archbishop Carroll received complaints from both sides.

Yet, by the end of October, the bishop had made his peace with the trustees, at the expense of the Harolds. He told Archbishop Carroll that he had never approved the circular against the trustees but had signed it "from a pliability of disposition." The ensuing controversy would be for him "an instructive lesson" for future occasions.[20] He was adamant about having James Harold resign. However, when it came to a final decision, it was Harold who outmaneuvered Bishop Egan by announcing from the pulpit on Sunday, February 21, that he and Father William Vincent would no longer officiate at St. Mary's. The outcry against Egan and the trustees which followed proved that both Harolds had a solid following among the ordinary people of the parish.

Once again there was a round of letters to Baltimore, calling "Mr. Harold, Jr. . . . a man of distinguished merit and talents: whose retention would "result to the advantage of Religion."[21] A Memorial signed by some three hundred members of the congregation begged the archbishop to restore the Harolds to St. Mary's, since the two priests possessed their "unbounded confidence" and were "supereminently adequate to all that can create respect and add dignity to our Holy Religion."[22] John Ryan came up from Baltimore to try to make a peace of sorts and Egan thanked him profusely for his efforts.

In the end, the Harolds held to their decision, and both left for Europe in April of 1813. Upon his return to Baltimore, John Ryan also announced that he was leaving the United States in April, evidently without consulting Carroll, who was chagrined at losing both Ryan and the younger Harold. Writing to William shortly after the February announcement, Carroll referred to his leaving as "a great loss to the diocese and the American Church in general." [23] The archbishop had tried to convince Egan to retain William Harold, but that prelate wrote that his mind was "unalterably set never to readmit" either of the Harolds to his diocese.[24]

Archbishop Carroll's good opinion of both Harold and Ryan was soon to change. When the two friars reached Europe, they painted critical pictures of conditions in the American Church. John Ryan indicted both Carroll and the Jesuits for trafficking in slaves and accused the archbishop of being "a great slaveholder." Carroll denied those charges and mentioned Philadelphia reports that Harold had insulted Bishop Egan.

The Philadelphia prelate continued to be plagued by salary disputes with his trustees as well as the ill health he had described to the Harolds during the winter of 1812. Worn down by the pressures of his position, Michael Egan died in July of 1814. Within days, one priest wrote that the only man St. Mary's would "peaceably" accept as pastor would be "the Rev. William V. Harold." [25]

Old St. Mary's church in Philadelphia

It was the first salvo in a campaign extending over several years that aimed at making William Harold the next bishop of Philadelphia. But those who were promoting

William Harold met with the considerable indolence of John Carroll. The Archbishop testified that while Harold was "of good morals and excellent in preaching," he was also "rather bold and arrogant to a degree that he was charged with harming his bishop." [26] Then Carroll sent in his own set of names for consideration: Fathers John Baptist David, Louis William DuBourg and Demetrius Gallitzin. Propaganda, under Cardinal Lorenzo Litta, recorded the conflicting recommendations and in the end, disregarded them all, selecting Doctor Henry Conwell, Superior and Vicar of the District of Lingannon in the Diocese of Armagh, Ireland.

Shortly after the appointment was announced, twenty-two of Conwell's fellow clerics sent a recommendation to Propaganda Fide. All agreed that, based on their knowledge of their "highly respected friend's constitution and period of life," he was not suited to be a bishop in the New World. They suggested that Conwell should not accept this honor but "spend the remainder of his days in his native land." [27] It was an opinion that numerous American clergy would have endorsed, but it came too late. In ignoring the advice of both Archbishop Carroll and the clerics of Armagh, Propaganda unwittingly set the stage for another disaster at St. Mary's.

During the years that Propaganda hesitated over naming a successor to the See of Philadelphia, the Congregation was receiving disturbing reports about conditions in the southern portion of the Baltimore Archdiocese. There was widespread discontent among the Irish Catholics in southern Virginia and the Carolinas, a good deal of it having to do with the rule of French pastors who served them. Into this volatile situation came another Irish Dominican missionary, one Thomas Carbry of Dublin.

Before coming to New York in 1815 at the age of sixty-five, Carbry had spent the better part of his priestly life in the service of the Dominican archbishop of Dublin, John Troy. He had been a student of Troy at the Irish Dominican college of San Clemente in Rome. Ordained in 1775, Carbry returned to Ireland and became known as a gifted preacher. In 1789, the Order honored him with the title Preacher General. By the time he arrived in New York City he had distinguished himself as a model cleric.

Carbry's decision to leave his homeland and undertake mission work at an advanced age was prompted by the appointment earlier that year of John Connolly as bishop of New York. The two had known each other at San Clemente in Rome. Now, Connolly was seeking the assistance of his old friend as he set out to shepherd a sizeable flock in the new world. [28] During the next few years in New York, Carbry proved to be a valuable assistant to the bishop and was well liked by the congregation. [29]

In a letter of April 9, 1818, Bishop Connolly informed Archbishop Ambrose Maréchal of Baltimore that Carbry had received a letter from the trustees of St. Mary's parish in Norfolk, Virginia, expressing their desire to have him as pastor. The Norfolk men had been involved for the previous two years in a dispute with their French pastor, Rev. James Lucas. Like many complaints raised against French pastors by English-speaking congregations, this one included dissatisfaction with Lucas' inability to preach effectively in English or to understand American customs and values.

Underlying the ethnic tensions was a far greater disagreement between Lucas and the trustees over ultimate authority in the Norfolk congregation. The disputes had come to a head on December 18, 1816, when Lucas appointed a new board of trustees to replace those who refused to cooperate with him. The former trustees retaliated by bolting the doors of the church and obtaining a court injunction against Lucas' use of the building. A month later, Archbishop Leonard Neale, who had appointed Lucas, placed under interdict the church controlled by the rebel group. Lucas then opened a chapel in his house which would serve as the parish church for the next four years. Believing themselves the victims of an overbearing pastor and an insensitive bishop, the disaffected trustees decided to bring their grievances to the highest authority by formulating a petition to the Holy See.

It was in that petition of 1816 that the name of Thomas Carbry first appeared in connection with the Norfolk crisis. After explaining the grounds for why they should be allowed to exercise the *jus patronatus*, the trustees continued:

> After the most minute and dispassionate enquiry into the characters and qualifications of the Clergy of these United States . . . , we have fixed our wishes and beg leave to present Reverend Thomas Carbry of the Order of St. Dominic, now residing in the City of New York; and we do not cease to offer to the Almighty Bestower of all gifts, our most ardent prayers that he may vouchsafe to inspire our Holy Father to confirm him our bishop and Spiritual Head to the States of Virginia and North Carolina (or the State of Virginia alone) with the title and dignity of Bishop of Norfolk.[30]

The petition ended with a threat "to have recourse to lay and unorthodox tribunals for redress" if the pope failed to heed their wish to have Carbry as bishop. From beginning to end, the document made surprising claims of lay rights in regard to spiritual authority. Even more astonishing was that the petitioners found a sympathetic ear in Rome when their case was presented to the Propaganda Fide in person by John Donaghey, one of the signers.

While being careful not to acknowledge the right of patronage, the officials of Propaganda nevertheless thought it prudent to address the request for a pastor whose native tongue was English. Otherwise the dissatisfaction might lead to schism. With an eye to preserving the unity of the Faith in Norfolk, Cardinal Litta wrote to Ambrose Maréchal, the new archbishop-designate of Baltimore, informing him of the Norfolk congregation's request for a separate bishopric in Virginia and asking his opinion. Litta suggested that, until a final decision was reached concerning the ecclesiastical status of Virginia, Maréchal should send an English-speaking priest as pastor to Norfolk as soon as possible. He went on to propose Carbry's name for the position, based on three highly favorable testimonials he had recently received.[31]

When Bishop Connolly wrote to Maréchal about the matter he described Carbry's response to the letter from Norfolk:

> He informed them that he considered their supplication of so serious and afflicting a nature that his charity could not refuse assistance. . . . It only remained for them to entreat their Bishop to request him to go there, and he would fly to their relief. . . . He asked my consent, which I thought myself in conscience bound to give him in such circumstances.[32]

Although Connolly was willing to sacrifice Carbry's assistance for the greater good of the Church in Virginia, Maréchal was not so willing to receive the missionary in his diocese. Despite highly favorable testimonials, the archbishop refused to appoint him pastor in Norfolk, based on information gathered from his own sources. After visiting Norfolk in June 1818, Maréchal wrote to Cardinal Litta that most of the people were devoted to the French pastor, and that the dissatisfied persons consisted of a very small group led by three trustees: Dr. Oliveira Fernandez, Mr. Thomas Reilly, and Mr. John Donaghey. He did not see any need to replace Lucas or erect a separate diocese in Virginia, as it was but a day's travel from Baltimore. As for Carbry, "he is a priest who would hardly be of help there, but would more probably prove a very great source of evils. He has been represented to me by men of weight as a priest of an ambitious and turbulent disposition."[33] This description stood in marked contrast to the earlier testimonials and to his reputation in both Ireland and New York. Maréchal's investigation seems to have been based on a single biased source of information, Peter Malou.

Malou was one of the Jesuit missionaries already working in New York when Bishop Connolly arrived in 1815. He had a penchant for stirring up trouble and maligning anyone who might oppose him in his schemes. While refraining from attacks on Connolly himself, he did not hesitate to calumniate Connolly's principal supporter, Thomas Carbry. In April of 1818 he made several more accusations, including the statement that Carbry had been suspended from his priestly duties in Ireland. This had no basis in fact. Yet, it was likely that Malou's accusations influenced Maréchal in his refusal to appoint Carbry as pastor in Norfolk.

Maréchal's depiction of the situation in Norfolk as one of relative harmony and satisfaction was as inaccurate as his portrayal of Carbry. In a letter to his friend Joseph Faraldi, Dominican prior of the Minerva in Rome, Carbry painted a far different picture of the situation, and one which proved more true to life. In June of 1818, he spoke of how dangerously close many Catholics in the southern states were to forming a schismatical church. They were seeking a priest who would travel to Utrecht, Flanders, to receive episcopal consecration from the schismatical Jansenist bishop there. As for the morality of their plan,

It serves no purpose to talk to them about the discipline of the Church and canon law. They will tell you that they know no law but that of the country . . . that popular elections are universal here in both civil and ecclesiastical affairs; and that the policy of the Catholic Church is old and should therefore be adapted to the laws and customs that are universal in these parts.[34]

Carbry thought that the only way to avert such a schism was to provide the people with pastors of their own tongue. Far from advocating a schism, Carbry was hoping to avoid it by warning Rome of the gravity of the situation.

Before long Carbry's predictions proved true. An Irish Franciscan, Richard Hayes, received an anonymous letter from South Carolina in March 1819 asking him to go to Utrecht for consecration as bishop of South Carolina. He in turn could consecrate other bishops for the disaffected Catholics of the American South. Although unsigned, the letter was followed by a postscript signed by Carbry who explained that he was only acting as intermediary for the anonymous writer. He also offered to transmit

Hayes' response to the writer. The document clearly implicated Carbry in a plot to form a schismatical church in the United States.

When Hayes exposed the whole affair to authorities in Rome, there was genuine shock over Carbry's role in transmitting the letter. Officials at the Propaganda compared it with Carbry's letters to Faraldi and Litta and sadly determined that they were written in the same hand. Despite his outright denial a few years later of any involvement in the affair, Carbry's good name was lost. The truth of the matter was to remain a mystery. If Carbry was not an accomplice in this scheme, then someone was trying to destroy his reputation. This was certainly a possibility. Only a few months before, Carbry had expressed deep concern over the possibility of a schismatical American Church. Would he have then taken an active role in promoting the very evil he had sought to avoid? [35]

A few months after transmitting the anonymous letter from South Carolina to Richard Hayes, Carbry left New York for Norfolk. He arrived on May 23, 1819, claiming to have been commissioned pastor of the congregation by Pope Pius VII. The following Sunday Carbry celebrated Mass in the church while the pastor Lucas celebrated in his own chapel. In June, Maréchal wrote to Carbry demanding that "before the first day of the coming month of July, you yourself bring Us the title (or send Us an authentic copy of it), on the authority of which you presume to exercise pastoral jurisdiction in our diocese." [36] The archbishop warned that should Carbry fail to comply, he would be appropriately censured.

Unfortunately, Maréchal's request went unheeded. One month later he sent a second warning, threatening Carbry with solemn excommunication if he continued to function in the diocese. Again, there was no response. Carbry's intransigence and his association with those who were schismatically inclined finally led Maréchal to promulgate the Norfolk Pastoral letter on September 28, 1819. He warned Norfolk Catholics "to avoid with religious fear any communication in spiritual things with that unfortunate priest . . .You cannot adhere to him as your Pastor without leaving the Church, from which he has separated himself." [37] Although Maréchal had now formally condemned the Irish missionary, he stopped short of excommunicating him.

What happened next, however, seemed to suggest that Carbry's claim of a papal commission might have had substance after all. On November 11, 1820, Cardinal Fontana of Propaganda informed Maréchal of Rome's decision to erect a diocese in Virginia with Richmond as the episcopal seat. Despite Maréchal's objections, Propaganda saw the appointment of a bishop in Virginia as imperative if schismatical tendencies were to be kept in check. The bishop-elect of the new diocese was Patrick Kelly, priest of the diocese of Ossory in Ireland. He was instructed to reside in Norfolk until there were enough Catholics in Richmond to support him financially.

Kelly came to Norfolk in mid-January of 1821, after receiving a cold reception in Baltimore from the archbishop. Within a week the Norfolk pastor Lucas reported to Maréchal that the new bishop had met with Carbry who told him that he had come to Norfolk only until a bishop should be appointed for Virginia. Such a statement from Carbry seemed to imply that these were instructions given to him as part of his commission. Lucas' next communication was even more enlightening. Said the frustrated French pastor, "It is a scandal to see Mr. Carbry continue to officiate without any interruption, submission, or punishment. . . . The Bishop lifted the interdict

**Henry Conwell,
second bishop of
Philadelphia**

Saturday, and gave Mr. Carbry permission to say Mass at eight o'clock." [38]

The fact that Bishop Kelly appeared to inflict no censure or any other punishment on Carbry would seem to indicate that Carbry had done nothing to incur a penalty. If indeed he had been ministering in Norfolk with neither the permission of the ordinary nor some higher authorization, he would not have been allowed to function so freely by the new bishop. Therefore, the assumption was that Kelly must have been given some proof of Carbry's papal commission.

If such evidence existed in a document, it was never found. [39] Of course, it is possible that the commission was a fiction. This would help to explain why Carbry never responded to Maréchal's requests for proof. However, if the missionary was in fact acting without authorization, it becomes difficult to comprehend Kelly's generous treatment of him. And why did Maréchal never excommunicate the Irish missionary, as he had threatened to do? Was it because he feared Carbry's account might be true? Whatever the answers, Thomas Carbry faded into the background with the coming of Bishop Kelly to Norfolk. The Dominican friar left that city in 1822 to return to Dublin. His departure coincided with the appointment of a new bishop and the return to Philadelphia of the two Irish missionaries who had left under a cloud. William Harold and John Ryan now reentered the country as rescuers.

During years of waiting for a bishop, the Philadelphians welcomed to St. Mary's parish a handsome young Irish priest named Thomas Hogan. He could preach a rousing sermon and attract the loyalty of parishioners, especially the ladies. However, he tangled with the Vicar Louis De Barth early in his career; there matters stood when the new Bishop of Philadelphia, Henry Conwell, arrived on December 2, 1820. The next day was Sunday and Hogan was the scheduled preacher. As one listener put it, "Father Hogan pitched into Vicar General DeBarth . . . on Tuesday he was deprived of his faculties by the Bishop for his language. Then the war was on." [40] Hogan did not intend to give up his berth at St. Mary's, but the new bishop withdrew Hogan's faculties. While the action was legitimate, the bishop did not endear himself to his new flock by suspending a favorite pastor within three days of his arrival. The congregation was divided over the issue. Hogan's supporters seized control of the church building and harassed the bishop and other clergy, and whoever backed them. Launching a pamphlet war, they forced the bishop's party to retreat to the Chapel of St. Joseph in Willing's Alley for parish services. The bishop's supporters among the parishioners, although they upheld episcopal authority and worshipped in St. Joseph's Chapel, had little love for Conwell.

At this time the Dominican William Harold was a professor at the studium of Corpo Santo conducted by the Irish Dominicans at Lisbon in Portugal. He received detailed accounts of the Philadelphia troubles from a parishioner, Thomas Maitland, who described Bishop Conwell as "an honest and sincere divine, [but] perhaps the most injudicious appointment made by the Sacred College for the course of a century." [41]

Maitland and several other parishioners asked Harold to return to Philadelphia to support Bishop Conwell in the battle against the Hoganites. The idea appealed to the Irish friar. He had already written an impassioned defense of his character and former actions in the States, seeking to clear his name with the Propaganda. Now he obtained from that office a patent as "missionary of honor" to Philadelphia and sailed to the rescue in the late spring of 1821.

Finding the situation incredibly complicated, Harold convinced Bishop Conwell to send for John Ryan to add another able cleric in Conwell's ranks. Ryan received permission from the Vicar-General of the Order, Pius Maurice Viviani, to transfer to the American Dominican province in May of 1822. He arrived two months after a violent riot attended an election of parish trustees, when only Hoganites were elected. But Hogan fell into disgrace through his relations with a woman parishioner and was removed from St. Mary's. The trustees then engaged a priest named Angelo Inglesi to replace him. However, thanks to clever detective work by William Harold, Inglesi was proven to be no priest at all. He was a former French soldier, adventurer, actor and missing husband of a Canadian woman.

Determined not to recognize Bishop Conwell, the trustees procured a young Irish priest named Thaddeus O'Meally for their church, which was now under interdict. The main point of the dispute now was the exercise of the *jus patronatus* and the trustees' claim that the right to govern the church rested not with the hierarchy but with the laity. [42]

Faced with these claims Archbishop Maréchal of Baltimore was goaded into action. By the end of 1824, O'Meally was excommunicated and another round of negotiations began that lasted throughout the following year.

Just as the bishop's party began to see the possibility of eventual victory, Conwell capitulated to the trustees. He made a separate peace with them and signed a concordat which gave them just about everything they wished, including a version of the *jus patronatus*. Two key provisions agreed to the "right of presentation" of pastors and a demand that Rome decree that no future bishops be appointed without "the approbation and at the recommendation of the Catholic Clergy of this diocese." [43]

Thoroughly disgusted at Conwell's capitulation, Harold, Ryan and others of the bishop's party promptly sent a copy of the document to Rome. Propaganda officials informed the bishop that his agreement with the trustees was unacceptable. Faced as well with the disapproval of Harold and Ryan, Conwell turned against them. On December 1, 1826, he gave Harold a note which read in part, "in consequence of your insulting language and behavior to me on many occasions, I cannot recognize you any longer as my Vicar General." [44] Harold protested his innocence and loyalty. He asked Conwell for a specific charge, since "that which you are pleased to allege is too vague and general to be susceptible of examination at the tribunal to which, I fear, I shall have to appeal." [45]

This threat goaded Conwell into more drastic action. On April 1, eight clergymen met at St. Augustine's Church and signed a resolution to the effect that "in consequence of the very reprehensible conduct of the Rev. Wm. Vincent Harold in regard to his Bishop for some time," the bishop would be justified in suspending his faculties. [46] Two days later the bishop withdrew the faculties of both Harold and Ryan. Harold reacted with a civil lawsuit against the eight priests, charging them with libel and demanding a public apology.

According to later commentators, Harold thus made the first of two major mistakes. To bring a civil suit against a fellow priest merited excommunication. Harold never intended to go through with the suit, his friends believed. He intended only to frighten the clergymen into a retraction and apology. This was what happened. Some of the men stated that they had never seen the charges before April 1; they were pressured into signing to support the bishop's authority. Harold achieved his purpose, but his method created doubts in high places concerning the soundness of his judgment.

When Harold protested his suspension to Archbishop Maréchal, the Baltimore prelate declined to interfere. The Holy See, he said, was the only tribunal to which Harold could appeal. Maréchal was bombarded with letters for and against the participants. On May 1 he received from an impressive list of trustees and pewholders a letter disapproving of the suspension of Harold. The writers were ready "to open a correspondence with proper authorities of the Catholic Church [to] obtain a speedy and permanent redress of the grievance of arbitrary suspension." [47]

Archbishop Maréchal soon abandoned his policy of non-interference. He sent a full account of the matter to the Vatican and explained to a friend in Rome that there would be "no peace as long as he [Harold] remains in Philadelphia. The same may be said of the Bishop." [48] Meanwhile Conwell took another turn, officially appointing Harold and Ryan pastors of St. Mary's! He gave them all the "necessary faculties for that purpose." [49] Finally at the close of 1827, everyone at St. Mary's seemed content.

However, the Propaganda officials had been studying all the previous complaints and had consulted the Master General of the Order of Preachers. On March 6, 1828, Capellari directed Bishop Conwell to come to Rome with all due haste and appointed a pastor for St. Mary's in Philadelphia. He directed the friars Harold and Ryan to leave Philadelphia for Cincinnati, to serve with Bishop Edward Fenwick, their confrere, in the " functions of the sacred ministry." [50] The Dominican Master General sustained the assignment from Propaganda, reminding the two friars that "the will of the pope is the law and rule to be obeyed at all times. . . . The spirit of our institute demands this kind of obedience." He went on to describe the work of the Order in Ohio and added words which the two friars later made good use of: "Should you not embrace the wise alternative, you know the consequences." [51]

The explicit directives, including the call of Bishop Conwell to Rome, sparked many rumors. To make the facts known, Bishop Conwell had Cappellari's letter printed in a pamphlet, to the dismay of Harold and Ryan. They believed that the public would take the Pope's order to leave as a slur on their characters. They refused to go to Cincinnati and waged an intensive campaign to have their assignment rescinded. They claimed that the publication of the Pope's order put a whole new slant on the matter. Fellow citizens would think that "a foreign prince" could pass a sentence of removal on other Americans, putting the Holy See in a very bad light. Americans were free to choose their place of residence. For an outside power to remove someone to another state was to violate the laws of the Republic. Harold and Ryan had a duty to preserve American Catholics from "any suspicion of a divided allegiance." [52] This argument remained the essence of all their protests.

William Harold was an American citizen, but John Ryan's request for citizenship was pending. Harold asked Henry Clay, Secretary of State, to intervene with the Vatican on their behalf. He claimed protection by the President from foreign interference with his American civil liberties. Ryan wrote that his removal to another state would delay by at least another year his achievement of citizenship. The request traveled from Henry Clay to two diplomats in France: the American minister and the papal Nuncio. Clay and the minister, James Brown, consulted various authorities and concluded that the controversy was a matter of the spiritual authority of a religious superior over subjects who had willingly joined the organization and agreed to keep its laws. [53]

On learning that the United States government would not interfere to keep them in Philadelphia, Harold and Ryan sent Clay their thanks for his efforts, summing up once more their case against Bishop Conwell and Rome. Minister Brown summed up the whole affair "a delicate subject to be meddled with by a government like ours founded upon the principle of letting alone all religions." [54]

Harold and Ryan lingered in Philadelphia through the winter. In the spring of 1829 they went, not to Cincinnati, but back to Ireland. Ryan eventually settled in the Dominican priory at Cork and was in much demand as a preacher throughout the country. Harold became the first head of the Dublin priory, then of the entire Irish Province, serving successfully in both positions. Their confreres evidently considered the pair "more sinned against than sinning." They had been instrumental, after all, in putting a stop to Hoganism in Philadelphia. Perhaps their impetuous errors of those years helped to prune them for later growth.

1. William Vincent Harold, O.P., to an unnamed lady of Dublin, **American Catholic Historical Society Records** (ACHSR) 14 (1897) :14.

2. Material on trusteeism is excerpted from chapter 2, "European Catholic Environment," Patrick W. Carey **People, Priests, and Prelates** (Notre Dame: Notre Dame University Press, 1987) 25-28.

3. Michael Egan to John Carroll, Philadelphia, Dec. 19, 1808, Notre Dame University Archives (UNDA) CABA 1/15.

4. Egan to Carroll, Dec. 19, 1808.

5. Circular "To the Pewholders of St. Mary's Church," Philadelphia, May 18, 1809.

6. :Bishop Egan and the Trustees of St. Mary's," ACHSR 21 (1904): 103.

7. ACHSR 14 (1897): 26.

8. "Reverend James Harold, the Botany Bay Irish Convict Priest of Philadelphia, 'The Cause' of the Direful Dissension at St. Mary's Church, 1812-12,," ACHSR 14 (1897): 25.

9. Papal Nuncio to Brazil to Bishop Michael Egan, Rio de Janeiro, Ja. 10, 1811, Archives, Archdiocese of Baltimore (AAB) 5 S9. In addition to a letter of introduction, the Nuncio had Father Harold bring a portrait of the Holy Father for Archbishop Carroll.

10. Egan to Carroll, Philadelphia, Mar. 16, 1811, UNDA, CABA 1/18.

11. Anthony Kohlmann, SJ, to Archbishop Carroll, New York, Apr. 1812, AAB 4 L 13.

12. John Ryan, OP, to Carroll, Philadelphia, May 21, 1812, AAB 7 L 10.

13. Ryan to Carroll, May 21, 1812.

14. ACTA, Propaganda Fide, 1821, ff. 158-159.

15. Egan to Carroll, Philadelphia, Jan. 14, 1812, AAB 3 I 5.

16. Egan to Carroll, Philadelphia, Jan. 25, 1812, AAB 11 B M1.

17. Egan to Carroll, Jan . 25, 1812.

18. ACHSR 14 (1897): 26.

19. ACHSR 14 (1897): 27.

20. Egan to Carroll, Philadelphia, Oct. 29, 1812, ACHSR 19 (1902): 410.

21. Chevalier de Onis to Carroll, Philadelphia, Mar. 6, 1813, AAB 11 B M 1.

22. Memorial addressed to John, Archbishop of Baltimore by parishioners of St. Mary's Church, 1813. Archives of the Riggs Library, Georgetown College, collection of J. G. Shea, Case 4.

23. Carroll to William Harold, Baltimore, Feb. 20, 1813, AAB, Carroll Letter Book.

24. Egan to Carroll, Philadelphia, Mar. 5, 1813, AAB 11 B M 1.

25. Patrick Kenny to Carroll, Philadelphia, July 26, 1814, AAB 6 R 3.

26. ACTA, Propaganda Fide, 1815, fol. 284.

27. Archives Propaganda Fide, America Centrale (APF), vol. 146. The petition, which the signatories had formally notarized, was dated Feb. 22, 1820.

28. In a letter to Cardinal Lorenzo Litta of Propaganda, Connolly relates that upon his arrival in New York his flock numbered about thirteen thousand with four priests to care for their needs. Three of the priests were Jesuits and the fourth was Carbry. John Connolly to Litta, New York, Feb. 25, 1818, APF, America Centrale, vol.IV, 74r-77r.

29. Shortly after his departure from New York, the trustees of the congregation wrote a letter of gratitude to Carbry for his devoted service. The letter was published in **The Norfolk and Portsmouth Herald,** June 16, 1819. Cited by Victor O'Daniel, The Carbry Case, 203, ms., SJP.

30. Peter Guilday, **The Catholic Church in Virginia 1815-1822** (New York: The United States Catholic Historical Society, 1924) 49.

31. The testimonials were from Patrick Gibbons, former provincial of the Irish Dominicans; Pietro Antonio de Pretis, Vicar of the Master of the Order; and John Chiesa, Procurator of the Order at Rome. APF, Sept. 13-14, 1817.

32. Connolly to Maréchal, New York, Apr. 9, 1818, AAB 14 T 3.

33. Maréchal to Litta, Baltimore, June 16, 1818. Cited in O'Daniel, Carbry Case 106.

34. Carbry to Joseph Faraldi, OP,

Nov. 22, 1818. Translation from the Italian found in the SJP, Carbry file. This is one of only two extant letters indisputably written by Carbry. The other contained similar information and was sent to Cardinal Litta at Propaganda, July 30, 1817.

35. In his research on Carbry, Victor O'Daniel, OP, discovered three different copies of the Hayes letter in Propaganda archives. Presumably, one of them should have been the original in Carbry's hand. But after careful comparison of the three with Carbry's letters to Faraldi and Litta, O'Daniel came to the conclusion, later corroborated by a handwriting expert, that none of these actually matched Carbry's handwriting.

36. Maréchal to Carbry, Baltimore, June 9, 1819, AAB, Letterbook, "Norfolk."

37. Pastoral Letter to the Catholic Congregation of Norfolk, Virginia, Sept. 28, 1819. Photostat copy SJP, Carbry file.

38. Lucas to Maréchal, Norfolk, Feb. 5, 1821, AAB, 18 I 44. Translation taken from O'Daniel, Carbry Case 364-65.

39. Two possible answers to the mystery: Carbry received his commission in the form of a secret **vivae vocis oraculum** or an oral command given by the pope through the mediation of Cardinal Litta, SJP, Carbry manuscript, 256-57 or authorization from Pius VII had come through the Dominicans at the Minerva, whom the pope visited with some frequency. Clodoald Mercier, O.P., to Bernard Walker, Rome, Apr. 24, 1936, SJP, Carbry file.

40. "The Church in Philadelphia in Early Colonial Days—St. Mary's and the Hogan Schism," ACHSR 17 (1900): 168-9.

41. Thomas Maitland to William V. Harold, Philadelphia, Apr. 17, 1821, APF America Centrale, vol. 6.

42. William Harold to Archbishop Maréchal, Philadelphia, Sept. 24, 1823, AAB.

43. Concordat signed by Bishop Conwell and Messers. Meade, Ashley and Randall for the Trustees, Philadelphia, Oct. 9, 1826. Copy in the Archdiocese of Philadelphia Archives (PAA).

44. Conwell to Harold, Philadelphia, Dec. 1, 1826, AAB 22

D 3.

45. Harold to Conwell, Philadelphia, Dec. 1, 1826. AAB 22 D.

46. "Against Harold," Philadelphia, Apr. 1, 1827. The signers were the priests Bernard Keenan, John O'Reilly, Edward Mayne, Michael Hurley V.G., Thomas Hayden, T.J. Donoghan, John Hughes, and R. Baxter – the last – named cleric, the one who served as secretary and drew up the document. APF, America Centrale 6. Copy in SJP.

47. Carey, Meade and Borie to Wm. V. Harold, Philadelphia, May 1, 1827, PAA.

48. Maréchal to Dr. Gradwell, June 22, 1827, AAB.

49. Conwell to the Trustees of St. Mary's, Philadelphia, Oct. 17, 1827, ACHSR 28 (1911): 325.

50. Cardinal Maurus Cappellari to Bishop Conwell, Rome, Mar. 8, 1828, ACHSR 28 (1911): 327-28.

51. Giuseppe Velzi, OP, to Very Reverend Father [Harold], Rome, Feb. 29, 1828, ACHSR 28 (1911): 327-28.

52. Harold and Ryan to Cappellari, Philadelphia, June 30, 1828, ACHSR 28 (1911): 335.

53. James S. Hopkins, ed., **The Papers of Henry Clay,** vol. 7 (Lexington, Ky.: University of Kentucky Press, 1982) 372. [Velzi's term "consequences" referred only to spiritual sanctions and not to physical coercion.]

54. James Brown to Henry Clay, Paris, Dec. 30, 1828, **Henry Clay Papers.**

JOHN CONNOLLY, BISHOP OF NEW YORK,[1] 1814-1825

In 1815 the records of the Diocese of Liége in Belgium described the recently-consecrated Bishop of New York, John Connolly of the Order of Preachers as "A man who conducts himself like an angel in all things. . . ."[2] The new Irish bishop was fluent in several languages, and had spent thirty-seven years working at high levels for his Order in Rome and the Vatican. He was sixty-four years old, and on his way to the New World as first resident bishop of New York, a diocese which had only four priests to serve it and comprised the whole state of New York and northern New Jersey.

On the international scene, the War of 1812 had ended in February of 1815, and an "era of good feeling" was about to begin. It was an auspicious time for a long-awaited leader to arrive in New York. Connolly had shown strength of spirit and courage in Rome seventeen years earlier when he resisted the French takeover of Dominican properties. But the likelihood that the newlynamed bishop would ever return to Europe was slim. He was now a bishop in his declining years, in a distant place with a different culture, and pastor to a different people.

John Connolly was born in the parish of Monknewtown in County Meath, Ireland, in October 1751.[3] His parents had a tenant farm on the hill of Slane where St. Patrick is reputed to have lighted the paschal fire in honor of Ireland's conversion to Christianity. He studied at home and in Drogheda, north of Dublin.

In his youth Connolly entered the Dominican Order and pursued his ecclesiastical studies at the Irish Dominican College of Holy Cross, Louvain. He was a member of the Convent of the Holy Cross when he was ordained on September 24, 1774, in the Cathedral of Saint Romuold in Malines (Mechlin), Belgium, by Cardinal John Henry von Frankenberg. He remained in the country to complete his classical studies until 1777. Then he was called, not to his native Ireland where small numbers of courageous friars were ministering, but to Rome.

When a teaching vacancy occurred at San Sisto and San Clemente in Rome, Connolly was appointed to fill it. He assumed the position of professor and master of students. The Irish Dominican community that he joined in this last quarter of the eighteenth century "generally numbered about fifteen priests, three or four students, and a few brothers. It was fairly well off, and with men such as Luke Concanen and John Connolly on the staff, was reasonably scholarly."[4] Here Connolly spent thirty-seven years in a variety of teaching, administrative and diplomatic capacities, challenged the troops of Napoleon Bonaparte and saved from destruction a major Dominican foundation. Here he was consecrated bishop.

Another Dominican who had received the habit at the Irish Dominican College at Louvain, was Richard Luke Concanen, whom the younger John Connolly eventually followed even to the bishopric of New York. To take Concanen's place as master of students and philosophy professor Connolly was assigned to Rome from Louvain. Subsequently, as Concanen moved out of a post it was entrusted to Connolly. In 1778 Concanen resigned as subprior because of other demanding responsibilities, and Connolly was appointed in his stead. In 1782 Concanen, now prior, withdrew as Regent of Studies, and Connolly assumed the post. In 1787 Concanen became assistant to the Master General at the Minerva and theologian of the Dominican Casanate library, while Connolly succeeded him as prior of San Sisto and San Clemente.

Before becoming prior, Connolly had received the highest honor the order could bestow, namely, the title of Master of Theology. The friars of the Irish Province, assembled in Dublin wrote, "For the mastership . . . we ask, in virtue of his teaching, the appointment of Father John Connolly, who has passed his examination . . . and is Regent of our College of San Sisto and San Clemente, Rome. His merits and character are well known to your Most Rev. Paternity." [5] This honor was granted without objection as proof of the worth and esteem in which he was held by the head of the Order who knew him well.

Connolly was prior of San Sisto and San Clemente until 1796 when he became procurator of that community, an office he held for ten years. During this time, Connolly also assisted Concanen, who bore the burden of heavy work and correspondence as assistant to the Master of the Order and who had to deal with the Irish bishops. Such activities required a high degree of intelligence, sensitivity, diplomacy, and linguistic ability. Both Connolly and Concanen were therefore well known and respected at the offices of Propaganda Fide and the Roman curia. But the calm spirit and diplomatic talents of John Connolly were about to be severely tested.

Napoleon's troops occupied Rome on the evening of Feb. 9, 1798. Connolly described the situation in a letter to Patrick Plunkett, the Bishop of Meath:

> . . . By an edict of the 16th, General Bertier declares the pope's temporal authority abolished, and the Roman Republic [sic] to be under the protection of that of France. By edicts of this morning the French emigrants are ordered away in the space of 24 hours, and the property of the church is to be sold in the space of two months, to extinguish the debts of the State. . . . [6]

In March Connolly reported that the French had seized and sold everything belonging to the English and Scotch colleges in Rome. Four thousand ecclesiastics had been ordered away, four cardinals were confined in the Dominican convent at Civita Vecchia, and the Pope was forced to stay in Siena. Despite all the movement, Connolly took up residence at San Clemente where he had leave to say Mass only on festival days.

Traumatic experiences continued well after the departure of the French army on October 2, 1799. In January 1800, Connolly described his actions regarding San Clemente, an important site of antiquity and property of the Irish Dominicans:

By having obtained leave from the Republic to open that church after its suppression, and serve the public in it as chaplain and confessor, without any emolument, I have saved it from destruction, as also the convent and library . . . It was to render this service to my order that I determined to stay here, if permitted by the Republic. This city is in a deplorable state, owing to a great scarcity of provisions, particularly bread, and the number of robberies committed almost every night in the streets, houses, and even churches.[7]

Confusion continued under the new Roman Republic, with financial negotiations and settlements of church properties left in poor condition. Connolly became vicar and bursar at San Clemente in 1800 and tried to cope with paying the bills. In 1809 the Papal States were incorporated into the French Empire and Pius VII was arrested and placed under custody in Savona. Restoration of religious life in Rome and repossession of properties began only after Napoleon's fall and the pope returned to the city. These difficult years of testing foreshadowed Connolly's days to come.

John Connolly, second bishop of New York

John Carroll, Archbishop of Baltimore, petitioned the Propaganda for the erection of four new American dioceses. In April, 1808, Pius VII divided the huge see of Baltimore into the dioceses of Boston, New York, Philadelphia and Bardstown. Carroll had suggestions for all these sees except New York. In 1807, he wrote to the congregation of Propaganda Fide, "It seems necessary that in the beginning the bishop of Boston should exercise jurisdiction over the territory [of New York] . . . . For none of the priests residing in that territory appear to me suited for the episcopacy. I therefore refrain from recommending anyone for that responsible post."[8]

The Cardinals acted quickly in 1808 and unanimously chose Luke Concanen, who was an agent and friend of John Carroll, as well as the personal choice of the pope. When Pius VII approved the selection of Concanen for New York, he added that should the bishop-elect be unable to sail for America because of poor health, John Connolly should be his replacement. Concanen spent over two years attempting to gain passage to America during the period of embargoes on Italian ports. He spent much time at Leghorn, exhausting his finances. Sadly, he died there on June 18, 1810.

With Bonaparte's abdication Pius VII returned to Rome in January, 1814. Restoration of civil and religious order began. The Propaganda took up its concern for filling the see of New York and in its general meeting of September 19, 1814, unanimously voted for John Connolly. He was consecrated bishop on Sunday,

November 6, 1814, but maintained responsibility for the repossession and repairs of San Clemente until time for his departure from Rome.

At last Concanen's replacement, John Connolly, was on his way to the New World. From Rome, the new bishop traveled to Belgium, England and Ireland and obtained two young priests willing to serve in New York. They were Irish-born Michael O'Gorman and James McKenna. Connolly sailed on the *Sally* with its fifty-seven passengers in mid-September of 1815. The transatlantic journey was a long and dangerous one of sixty-seven days, so unduly prolonged that he was believed lost at sea. He arrived ill, without fanfare, in New York on November 24, only to be confined for several weeks until his health returned.

In Baltimore John Carroll eagerly awaited Connolly's arrival. He wrote in mid-1815 to John Troy, Archbishop of Dublin, "We cannot account for Bishop Connolly's not being yet arrived; his Diocese is suffering for him; and for its sake, it is to be wished, that he may come, accompanied by a number of zealous, capable and edifying clergymen."[9] Carroll, who favored American-born and educated clergy, was not at all happy with Rome's choice of bishop for New York, a choice made without consulting him. He expressed his feelings to Charles Plowden, his Jesuit friend in England:

By letters from Abp Troy it is given me to understand, that a Rev. Mr. John Connolly, Dominican, resident at Rome for 37 years, was nominated in Sepr. And consecrated in Novr., as Bishop of N. York; that he was in Flanders about March 20th. On his way to Ireland, where he was to embark for his Bishoprick [sic]. It was known here that before the death of Dr. Concanen his Holiness at the Drs. Intreaty [sic], intended to assign to him, as his Coadjutor, the Rev. Mr. Maréchal, a priest of St. Sulpice, now in the seminary here, & worthy of any promotion in the Church. We still expected that this measure would be pursued; and therefore made no presentation or recommendation of any other for that vacant See; however, Mr. Connolly is appointed, with whom none of us are acquainted; nor has anyone in this country been consulted. I wish this may not become a very dangerous precedent, fruitful of mischief by drawing censure upon our religion, & false opinion of the servility of our principles.[10]

Carroll died before Connolly could learn from him his duties in New York. But the new bishop quickly learned from his environment and his fellow priests about the people, the city, and the Catholic Church in New York.

Under James Madison, the nation's fourth president, the United States was at peace. The Treaty of Ghent, 1814, brought a sense of greater unity and national pride to the new nation. Outside the country, there was little knowledge of the United States, and not a great deal of interest in it.

Social life in the United States seemed to some as agreeable as on the continent. The census of 1810 had reported over seven million inhabitants, of whom more than a million were slaves. A sense of independence prevailed and the spirit of Americanism was obvious. Illiteracy was common, duels occurred occasionally and drunkenness and gambling were common vices. But the absence of an official religion in the United States must have puzzled Connolly the most.

St. Patrick's
Cathedral,
New York,
dedicated
May 4, 1850

New York, the country's most important port, carried the label of a "forest of masts." It equaled European cities for its cosmopolitan flavor. It incorporated the lower end of Manhattan, or "hilly island," and Broadway that had long been a thoroughfare for the Indians. Workmen busied themselves in many areas of the city during their ordinary twelve to fifteen-hour working day. The traffic of carts, carriages and hackneys for hire clogged the streets, impeding the flow of traffic. The city had been the political center of the nation and the state in the 1790s. Yet foxes inhabited churchyards, and scavenger pigs roamed the streets. The lack of a good water supply and clean streets brought periodic bouts of cholera, yellow fever and other diseases. Almost every block boasted of one tavern. The population of the city in 1816 was 93,634: about 85,000 Caucasian, 8,000 free black, and 600 reported as slaves.[11]

For his part, John Connolly faced formidable challenges in a shortage of personnel and funds. Three Jesuits, Maximilliam Rantzau, Benedict Fenwick and Peter Malou, and one Dominican, Thomas Carbry, served the Catholics of New York – a small number indeed for their population. The parishioners could afford but little for the collection box in their parishes. In his adopted city, the bishop found a Catholic minority population of between 13,000 and 15,000. They were mostly poor and largely Irish immigrants escaping political and economic conditions in their homeland. Catholic English, French and Germans composed the smaller numbers. Most of the Catholic laity respected church authorities and a few prosperous laymen played key roles in the American church, exercising church property rights which later became a source of trustee problems.

Three churches existed in the diocese in 1815. The first was St. Peter's, located on Barclay Street and dedicated on November 4, 1796. The second was founded and incorporated by laity who had gathered secretly during the Revolutionary War in private homes, and often in a carpenter's shop on the same street. St. Patrick's church, under construction since 1809, became the new cathedral, and was dedicated in May of 1815. It was located about two miles northeast of Mott Street. St. Mary's, far to the north in Albany, was established in 1813.

It was in St. Patrick's Cathedral that Jean Cheverus, Bishop of Boston, installed Connolly as the second Bishop of New York. James Roosevelt Bayley described Connolly as a "small-sized man, very neat in appearance. . . . He was very simple in his manners, and most zealous—singing High Mass every Sunday without mitre or crosier." The writer continued, "many still living remember the humility and the earnest zeal with which he discharged the laborious duties of the confessional, and traversed the city on foot to attend upon the poor and sick."[12] He was more the humble scholar than a dazzling orator. His pupils remembered him as a man of more than ordinary mildness and gentleness of character. His zeal and experience had prepared him for the bishopric in Europe, but not for the problems he met in this new diocese where

everything was to be created; and whilst his resources were very small, the obstacles in his way were great. The trustee system had not been behind [him] in its early promise, and trustees had been so accustomed to have everything their own way that they were not disposed to allow the interference of even a bishop. Bishop Connolly was not lacking in firmness but the great wants of his diocese made it necessary for him to fall in, to a certain extent, with the established order of things, and this exposed him afterwards to much difficulty and many humiliations.[14]

The bishop regularly visited various areas of his diocese and in 1816 made his way to Albany. He was surprised at the number of Catholics there. In June of that year, he wrote that he was enjoying good health, but heavy priestly duties barely left him time to say the Divine Office.[15]

Financial burdens were ever present. Connolly wrote on February 13, 1817, that he was unable to advance customs charges in New York for books held there. "At this moment," he wrote, "I am not in a condition to advance money for any person, as the Trustees of this congregation have assured me two days ago, that they have not at present in their hands money enough to pay me the salary due to me for those three months last passed."[16] Even church services were without elaborate decorations because of meager resources of the time. Losses from unforeseen circumstances could always be expected. Minutes of the Trustees of St. Patrick's of February 20, 1821, record that thieves broke into the cathedral, stealing $300 worth of gold and silver, sacred articles and lace torn from vestments, as well as $90 from the collection for the poor. After rewards were offered, the articles were found in the city canal.[17] The cathedral owed $53,000, and having borrowed to build it, paid annual interest at seven percent. That financial burden prevented the bishop from supporting a sufficient number of priests. As a consequence, Connolly had to perform both night and day the duties of a parish priest, more than those of a bishop.[18]

Within a few years of his arrival, Connolly received some relief from his missionary activity with the coming of Irish priests. In October of 1817, Arthur Langdill came to serve.

Upstate, Charles D. Ffrench, OP, arrived in early 1818 to minister throughout the diocese. William Taylor, who appeared the following June, was assigned to the Cathedral. To compensate for the withdrawal of Carbry, John Power arrived in 1819 and three years later assumed the duties of pastor of St. Peter's Church. Within a span of five years, 1820 to 1825, Connolly ordained five priests in New York. All were needed to serve the growing population.

With additional priestly help Connolly took the initiative to establish some schools for the young. He brought three of Mother Seton's Sisters of Charity to conduct an orphan asylum in a wooden building on Prince Street in June 1817. A famous woman singer of the day gave a concert in support of this project. Starting with five orphans, the asylum housed twenty-eight the following year, all boarded, clothed and educated by the sisters. In 1817 St. Patrick's Charity or Free School opened in the cathedral's basement, accommodating over 240 boys and girls. A similar school already existed at St. Peter's, educating 344 pupils that year. Both educational facilities were supported partly by the state and partly by the two congregations.

Shortages of personnel and funds were small problems compared to the serious and protracted difficulty Bishop Connolly faced with the trustee system. Modeled on European and Protestant practices, and used for legal expediencies in incorporating church properties, lay trustees had assumed wide responsibilities in local church governance in the absence of priestly personnel and church funds. Bishops and clergy, accustomed to traditional episcopal control, found serious threats to religious authority in the trustee system. Trustee difficulties began in New York with its first Catholic parish and continued despite ecclesiastical opposition. Connolly reacted promptly if not wisely, as judged by one student of the trustee situation:

> Bishop Connolly was not well received by the New York City trustees nor did he do anything to win them over. In fact, having been warned about the trustees' dominance over the church prior to his coming to the United States, he did whatever he could to break the old trustees' stranglehold upon the Catholic community. Both St. Peter's and St. Patrick's . . . were under one board of trustees. Many of these men had served as trustees for thirty years. In April of 1817 Connolly single-handedly dissolved the sole board of trustees, established two separate boards of trustees, one for St. Patrick's and the other for St. Peter's, and appointed illegally, trustees who were favorable to episcopal rule over the churches.[19]

The angry trustees who had been replaced looked for support among the clergy. They found it in Peter Malou, a Jesuit, and assistant pastor at St. Peter's. Malou engaged in a letter campaign, and a majority of anti-episcopal trustees were chosen in the regular annual board elections that followed in March 1818. Among the clergy supporting the bishop was Charles Ffrench, the pastor of St. Peter's. William Taylor, recently-arrived from Ireland and assistant at St. Patrick's, opposed Connolly for this handling of the situation—or apparent lack of it. So the battle lines of clerics as well as trustees were drawn. As the annual trustee elections approached, clerical campaigning intensified. Charles Ffrench and the poorer people supported the bishop while Anthony Malou and William Taylor and wealthier parishioners backed the incumbent trustees. Ffrench appealed in the pulpit, the pubs and the press for Connolly's candidates. The incumbent trustees were pictured as manipulators of power. The opposition lauded the incumbents as pillars of society who had financed parish activities over a long period of time.[20] With the trustee election of April 1819, the pro-episcopal camp received a plurality of 80 votes out of 300 cast. In addition Connolly gained three trustees at St. Peter's and five at St. Patrick's, although two of the latter were found ineligible. But that did not restore peace.

In Baltimore, Archbishop Maréchal declined the request of the New York trustees to intervene and instead asked the beleaguered Bishop Connolly to settle the matter. Connolly had protested formally at the meeting of October 22, 1819, against any other ecclesiastical interference in the concerns of New York without the express permission of the Pope. In consequence, he answered Maréchal:

> . . . I am exceedingly sorry that it is not in my power . . . to do or suggest anything likely to quiet the minds of the two contending parties here, whereas the major part of the trustees of our church of Saint Peter labour to deprive me of my spiritual rights, while the major part of the trustees of our cathedral, and the mass of our numerous congregation are intent on supporting me in the enjoyment of them . . . Seeing, therefore the dispositions of their minds, I am persuaded that our disagreements will continue until next Easter Monday [1820] on which three of the trustees of Saint Peter's Church are to go out of office. . . . as I hope that these three new trustees will be men of moderation.[21]

After further elections of trustees who favored Connolly, and Malou's transfer to the Diocese of Boston, the greatest trial of the bishop ended. There is little doubt that those painful years took a toll on the health of John Connolly.

Active to the end, Connolly fell ill after attending a funeral on Tuesday February 1, 1825. Anticipating his death, he appointed John Power administrator of the diocese, and called to the cathedral Father John Shanahan, whom he had ordained the previous year. New York lost its bishop on the following Sunday evening. He lay in state at St. Peter's Church which was more convenient to visitors than St. Patrick's. It was estimated that 30,000 persons paid their last respects. Burial was at St. Patrick's on Wednesday, February 9. The bishop was eulogized for his prudent and unostentatious zeal. Although he was not known as a highly prized orator, yet his activities preached volumes to those who knew him best—the uneducated and the poor.

Upon his arrival in 1815, Connolly found only four priests and three churches, but he left his successor 35,000 Catholics in New York City alone, with 150,000 in the entire diocese and eight churches and eighteen priests.

1. This chapter relies to a great extent upon the initial work of Dominican historian Victor O'Daniel (1868-1960) who left an eighty-page typescript in the archives of the Dominican Province of St. Joseph. He gathered primary sources in the United States and abroad to prepare the manuscript.

2. Peter Guilday, "Trusteeism in New York," **Historical Records and Studies** 28 (1928): 49.

3. Though sources differ on the date of his birth, O'Daniel ascertained from the Archbishop of Mechlin that 1751 was the correct year. O'Daniel Ms., hereafter referred to as ODMS, Saint Joseph Province Archives (SJP).

4. Leonard E. Boyle, **San Clemente Miscellany I: the Community of SS. Sisto e Clemente in Rome, 1677-1977.** Apud S. Clemente, 1977, 59.

5. Quoted in O'Daniel manuscript on Connolly, 239-240. Original is in Tallaght Archives. A province can have no more than twelve Masters of Sacred Theology at one time.

6. Anthony Cogan, **The Diocese of Meath, Ancient and Modern,** vol. 3 (Dublin: Joseph Dollard, 1870) 318-319.

7. Anthony Cogan, (1870) 234.

8. Carroll to Michele Di Pietro, Baltimore, June 17, 1807. Thomas O'Brien Hanley, ed., **The John Carroll Papers III** (CP) ((Notre Dame, In.: University of Notre Dame, 1976) 26.

9. John Carroll to John Troy, Baltimore, 1815, CP, vol. 3 312.

10. Carroll to Plowden, Baltimore, mid-1815, CP vol.3 338.

11. Ira Rosenwaike, **Population History of New York City** (Syracuse, N.Y.: Syracuse University Press, 1972) 18.

12. James R. Bayley, **A Brief Sketch of the Early History of the Catholic Church on the Island of New York,** 2nd edition, (New York: United States Catholic Historical Society, revised 1973) 84-86.

13. Henry De Courcy, **The Catholic Church in the United States** (New York: Edward Dunigan and Brother, 1856) 384.

14. Bayley 83-86.

15. Connolly to Joseph Plessis, New York, June 7, 1816, **United States Catholic Historical Magazine,** vol. 4 (1892): 60.

16. United States Catholic Historical Magazine, vol.4, No.2 (1891-93): 193.

17. Mary Peter Carthy, **Old St. Patrick's New York's First Cathedral** (New York: United States Catholic Historical Society, 1947) 31.

18. John F. Maguire, **The Irish in America** (London: Longman's Green and Co., 1868) 370.

19. Patrick Carey, **People, Priests, and Prelates: Ecclesiastical Democracy and the Tensions of Trusteeism** (Notre Dame, In: University of Notre Dame Press, 1987) 134.

20. See Carey, **People, Priests and Prelates,** 134-135.

21. Guilday, "Trusteeism in New York" 57-58.

AMERICANS ON MISSION TOGETHER, 1806-1865

CHAPTER 4

OVER THE MOUNTAINS TO KENTUCKY

In 1788 John Carroll, who would be consecrated Bishop of Baltimore two years later, expressed the earliest known desire that the Dominican friars should form an American foundation of the Order. In response to Philadelphia Catholics who sought the ministry of Francis Antoninus Fleming, O.P., Carroll drafted an affirmative but cautious reply, colored by his experience with vagabond priests. At its close he wrote, "If Mr. Fleming be inclined to attempt an establishment for his order in Philadelphia, or any of the United States, they shall have every encouragement I can give as long as I retain any authority."[1] But Fleming died of yellow fever in 1793, and during his short ministry no Dominican establishment was formed.

Bishop Carroll did not give up. In May, 1796, he informed John Troy, Dominican Archbishop of Dublin, his regular correspondent, that the Irish Augustinians were forming a province in Philadelphia.[2] But hearing no more on the subject, he left it in abeyance for more than five years. Then in 1802 a proposal came from a new source: the English province of the Friars Preachers; or more precisely, from a single member of that province. And Bishop Carroll, consistent in his desire for the good of the nascent American Church, turned with interest toward this new possibility.

The Fenwick family coat of arms

During the summer of 1788 when John Carroll expressed his idea of a Dominican establishment in the United States, an American youth in Belgium was preparing to enter the English Province of the Order of Preachers. He was Edward Fenwick, Carroll's fellow Marylander, whose family counted five generations of colonists; and in Edward, the first generation of U.S. citizens. Their progenitor was Cuthbert Fenwick, who had come from England in 1634 with the first Catholic colony. Edward was born August 19, 1768 on the extensive family plantation bordering the Pawtuxent River in St. Mary's County. His father, Colonel Ignatius Fenwick, and his mother, Sarah Taney, belonged to the Maryland families who staunchly defended their beliefs during several periods of anti-Catholic oppression. Their pastors, from the days of Lord Calvert, were zealous members of the Society of Jesus.

Edward Fenwick's childhood was affected by two events of worldwide significance: one within the Church and the other in the land of his birth. In 1773 Pope Clement XIV suppressed the Society of Jesus throughout the world, including those houses in Maryland where the members were the only parish priests. Their scholastic institutions, including those in Europe to which American Catholic youth went for higher studies, were confiscated by the respective governments.[3]

Edward Dominic Fenwick, O.P.

Three years after the baleful event of suppression, the Fenwicks rejoiced with other liberty-loving colonials at the signing of the Declaration of Independence. Edward was eight years old. When he was sixteen he entered the College of Holy Cross, conducted at Bornhem in Belgium by the English Dominican friars. Edward's uncle John, nine years his senior, had finished college there and then entered the English province of the Order of Preachers. Setting out for Europe, Edward sailed from Baltimore in November 1784, mourning the recent death of his father Ignatius. His mother, Sarah Taney Fenwick, had died four years earlier.

On completing his studies in the summer of 1788, Edward asked to enter the Order of Preachers. He was accepted as a novice of the English province on December 4, 1788, and given the religious name of Dominic. Although his response to a religious vocation was whole-hearted, with no particular expectations of the future, the youth did have a dream: to establish the Order of Preachers in his homeland. This he stated clearly more than a decade later, on the eve of setting out for the United States. In an open letter from London addressed to "English Catholic Nobility and Gentry" he declared,

> I entered the holy Order of St. Dominick at Bornhem with the view of endeavoring, as soon as I should be duly qualified for so arduous an undertaking, to establish in my native Country a Seminary of Religious Men of the same holy Institute, who, actuated by an Apostolic Spirit, might effectually labor to plant Religion and virtue in the widely extended Continent of America."[4]

By a coincidence that Edward Fenwick would call providential, his request for help in founding an American province was published in England the same year that John Carroll wrote to the Irish provincial about sending friars to the United States. Two Maryland men, each without knowledge of the hopes of the other, looked to the day when there would be an American province of the Order of Preachers: the one an American novice, the other a leader of the Church in the United States who would soon be its first bishop. Neither Carroll nor Fenwick could have guessed that their hopes would be realized nearly two decades later by their collaboration.

While Edward Dominic spent his novitiate year at Bornhem, the French Revolution erupted in Paris, portending the dire events that would soon affect his community in Belgium. The Belgians themselves rose up against Austria and won a short-lived liberty. But at home in Maryland in that eventful year of 1789, the novice's relatives and fellow citizens were rejoicing in the stability of their new nation. The first President was elected, the first Congress convened, and the first States, including Maryland, ratified the Constitution. The novice Fenwick made his profession of solemn vows for life at Holy Cross on March 26, 1790. He pronounced the first words with an added identity, saying clearly, "I, Edward Dominic Fenwick, an American, make my profession. . . ."[5]

The new American friar continued his studies in a country on the verge of conquest, and on February 23, 1793, was ordained a priest at the Cathedral of Saint-Baron in the city of Ghent. During the following spring, the French revolutionaries entered Belgium, confiscating and destroying property as they went. The English Dominicans fled to their homeland, risking oppression and persecution there. They left behind Edward Fenwick, presuming that his American citizenship would keep him from harm. Instead he was imprisoned briefly, then freed. He crossed the channel to rejoin his confreres in southern England, where they re-established the College of Holy Cross. There Fenwick taught for five years and then was assigned to study at Woburn Lodge in Surrey with theologian James V. Bowyer. The assignment was too brief. Later he deplored his lack of further studies owing to the upheavals in Europe.

During nine years of ministry in the English province Edward kept before him his original dream of founding a Dominican province in the United States. Meanwhile Bishop John Carroll had again proposed that idea independently. Of that proposal he wrote, four years later in 1806:

> I had long encouraged their emigration from England, which offered no flattering prospects for the extension of their order, and so long ago as 1802 I had urged Mr. Short, then the Provincial of it in England, to embrace a fine opportunity which offered of obtaining a most advantageous settlement in the United States.[6]

Carroll's second letter of support was sent to Fenwick himself, who stated in 1804 that Carroll's encouragement was "clearly expressed in a letter his Lordship honored me with two years ago in which he approved, advised & urged the execution of the plan."[7]

And with reason. The English province at that time was reduced in number to a handful of friars, most of them past middle age. To lose any of these to a new foundation would be disastrous. However, the objections of the English provincial were overruled by the head of the Order who was urged by his vicar, the mission-minded Concanen. Therefore Edward Fenwick proceeded with plans for the American province, thanking Concanen for encouraging his "vague proposal" for a foundation in his native country "where the cries of religion and repeated solicitations of my friends pressingly call for me and all who feel for their spiritual wants."[8]

In the autumn of 1803, Luke Concanen again pledged his support and that of the Dominican Vicar General, Giuseppe Gaddi.[9] He assured Fenwick that he had all required permissions to go ahead. If the plan succeeded, he wrote, the first convent of friars in the United States would be accountable directly to Gaddi until Fenwick could "form a little American province after the example of the Augustinians." Concanen was not only Gaddi's assistant, but also the agent in Rome for the diocesan business of Bishop John Carroll. At the end of the year, when writing to Carroll on Diocesan matters, he added this word:

> A Mr. Fenwick, an American of my Order, proposed some time back his plan & wish for establishing a Convent or College in some part of that Country. I remitted him to Yr Lordship's Will & determination on this plan which if favourable he will have every due encouragement from this quarter."[10]

Before Concanen's letter reached Baltimore, Fenwick sent definite word to the bishop about his plans. On January 12, 1804, he wrote,

> The long conceived project of endeavoring to form an establishment under your Lordship's patronage for the education of youth etc. I now regard as the order of Heaven, since it is approved and much recommended to me by our General at Rome. I . . . shall embark as soon as I have made the necessary arrangements which suppose will be in May or June.

He said that he hoped to execute "in miniature" the plan of Bornhem College and Convent. His ultimate goal was made very clear: "Yes, my Lord the education of youth, the propagation of St. Dominic's Order, in fine, the cause of Religion is the object of my ardent wishes and ambition and feeble prayers." [11]

Fenwick then moved to his final preparations, seeking Dominican friars to carry out the new mission and financial support for it. These were his immediate concerns until he sailed for the United States in September, 1804. For financial support he looked first to his family in Maryland, where he could claim land and property by inheritance; but where in reality disappointment awaited him. [12] Meanwhile he appealed for help to the English people in an address to "The English Catholic Nobility and Gentry," published with the approval of the Bishop of London, John Douglas.

> The Primitive Christians did not confine their Charity and Solicitude to their own Churches, and we find St. Paul receiving contributions from the Churches of Greece and Asia Minor for the relief of their Brethren in Jerusalem.

In the future, he added, American seminaries could be "of the greatest service in the cause of Religion in England." [13]

Fenwick's quest for personnel began with a petition to Concanen to bring to America their Regent of Studies from Bornhem, Belgium, Samuel Thomas Wilson, O.P. This would seem feasible since Wilson's ministry in that country was curtailed by a papal decree which placed religious under the bishop of their diocese rather than their superiors. But the choice of Wilson, and subsequently of Robert Angier and William Tuite, all members of Bornhem college community, was a blow to the beleaguered provincial Underhill. The province could not afford to lose these valuable members. Even before the selection of Angier and Tuite, the provincial had voiced his objection, although he said he would leave all to the General. [14]

Finally, on August 29, 1804, Fenwick informed Concanen that the English provincial had given his reluctant consent. The American friar and Angier would sail from England to the United States on September 10. Although Fenwick was designated superior of the colony, he petitioned that Wilson be made prior in the United States – an office which became in 1807, not prior, but provincial, by authority of the general Gaddi. [15]

Fenwick arrived at the Norfolk seaport in November, accompanied by his English confrere Robert Angier. It was thirty years since he had left home to study in Belgium. Along with the joy of his homecoming, he met with unexpected disappointment. Although his brother James welcomed him to Maryland, nothing had been done to fulfill Edward's requests to sell lands he inherited from his father. Fenwick wrote to Bishop Carroll that, after all his planning, nothing was ready; then he described the situation.

> I have not yet seen my Brothers etc., shall take them all in on our way through the country to Baltimore – where we hope to wait on your Lordship as soon as possible after Xmas – I shall hear the opinion of Relatives & friends on the way, concerning our pro- jected establishment, shall make my own observations & submit the whole to your Lordship's superior light & deci- sion – Am sorry indeed to learn here that nothing is prepared for me, no place fixed upon, as I had flattered myself & others, there would be.[16]

The first disappointment was having no place ready for Fenwick's establishment in Maryland, where he could claim an ample portion of the vast Fenwick planta- tion. Far more discouraging was the possibility that, despite all previous communi- cations, the bishop would not encourage the founding of the Dominican college anywhere in Maryland. After the friendly and candid correspondence he had car- ried on with the bishop, this possibility seemed incredible to Fenwick. On receiving a letter from Carroll to this effect [an undiscovered document], he replied in aston- ishment and characteristic self-deprecation:

> I must observe for the present that it is totally owing to my inaccuracy & inattention which I am sorry for, if your Lordship did not clearly under- stand from my letter the chief & pri- mary object of my coming over to be that of establishing the Order of St. Dominic by any possible means which might hereafter afford assistance to the mission in my native country at large, and that I conceived the only way of establishing it would be in a college or convent. For this purpose alone, my Lord, I applied & with great difficulty obtained permission of my superiors as also the engagement of three of my confreres.[17]

He added that he hoped to see Bishop Carroll in Baltimore after Epiphany.

Actually, Bishop Carroll's objections were not with regard to the founding of the college or to the province. He had himself long desired that the Dominicans establish a permanent foundation in the United States. But he was opposed to a college being in Maryland. Fenwick could not understand this and considered Carroll's reaction to his plan totally new. He had been very clear from the beginning about Maryland being the locale of his enterprise, even asking Carroll to solicit help from his brothers James and Thomas in choosing a site for the college.[18] The objection was a blow to this sixth- generation Marylander, returning from England to his birthplace.

John Carroll's opposition was clarified when Edward Fenwick arrived in Baltimore early in 1805. In his first meeting with Carroll, the bishop cited two reasons for pre- venting a Maryland foundation. The first was to protect other interests in the Church, the second involved the need to evangelize the western frontier of his diocese. He was, of course, being protective of Georgetown College, which he himself had found- ed in 1789. As one of the former Jesuits, John Carroll had continued to be their guide. But by 1804 when Fenwick arrived with Angier, the Jesuits were in the process of par- tial restoration. At that point Carroll gave the struggling college at Georgetown into

**Stephen
Theodore Badin**

the care of the Jesuits. No other new institution could be encouraged, although in a few years the Sulpicians opened the same kind of dual institution: a college and seminary at Emmitsburg.

A second reason for locating Fenwick's enterprise away from Maryland was the insistent plea of settlers in far off Kentucky for priests to minister to their needs: needs which Fenwick had indeed foreseen but planned to address in his beloved Maryland. Yet he also knew that there had been at least sixty families of Maryland Catholics who had already gone to Kentucky and that Bishop Carroll had been receiving their petitions by mail and messenger. They were in fact both relatives and friends.

In 1804 the only priest in Kentucky was the zealous, eccentric French missionary, Stephen Theodore Badin. He had been ordained by Bishop Carroll in 1793, the first priest ordained in the United States, and proudly signed his myriad letters as "Stephen Vincent Badin, Proto-Priest." Assigned to Kentucky after ordination, he had served there alone, occasionally helped by itinerant clergy. He joined the crescendo of pleas from his people to the Bishop of Baltimore, which by 1804 convinced Bishop Carroll to send Fenwick and his Dominican brothers. The bishop concurred and sent the good news to Badin, but no hint of it to Fenwick. In fact, the first two Dominicans had not yet seen the bishop after their arrival when Badin was writing gratefully to Baltimore saying "I am happy to hear [from Carroll's letter of October 15] of the Dominicans coming shortly to this state." [19]

Fenwick and Angier finally met with Bishop Carroll early in 1805 in Baltimore. Whatever explanations they were given, Fenwick was persuaded by Carroll to go to Kentucky and see the region and the people for himself. This he did in the spring. Badin welcomed him joyfully. In a long letter to the bishop the veteran missionary expressed satisfaction at the coming of the friars and reminded Carroll that he had promised before the arrival of the Dominicans from England that they would be assigned to Kentucky. In his enthusiasm Badin asked to give all his property to the Dominicans, even suggesting he intended to enter the Order! [20]

By August of 1805 Fenwick had returned to Maryland, persuaded to make the new foundation in Kentucky. He informed Carroll that the final decision would depend on the approval of the Vicar General Gaddi and also the consensus of the four friars, when the other two would have arrived from England. The Kentucky Catholics promised to obtain funds to build the hoped-for college. And Fenwick had returned to pastoral ministry among the Maryland Catholics for the time being. [21] By now every needed authorization for the new province had been procured by Concanen from the Order of Preachers and from the Sacred Congregation of Propaganda Fide. Concanen also sent the necessary faculties for Fenwick to Bishop Carroll for his approbation. [22]

From Kentucky, meanwhile, came several serious questions newly raised by Stephen Badin. Using a pattern of interaction he would subsequently follow, Badin set aside his previous enthusiasm for the Dominicans and proposed caution in dealing with them. Apparently he had become influenced by a Belgian priest, Charles Nerinckx, who had arrived in Kentucky shortly after Fenwick returned from there to Baltimore. In two letters, mailed in the same post, Badin expressed caution about giving the friars any property, and fear of possible future errors in their teaching.[23]

On September 10, 1805, the number of founding friars was completed by the arrival from England of Samuel Thomas Wilson and William Raymond Tuite. Fenwick informed them of Carroll's request and of his own journey of exploration to Kentucky. They concurred with Fenwick and Angier in the decision to found the province in that distant mission. Wilson wrote to Rome from Georgetown saying he was now on the way to Kentucky, about seven hundred miles away. He added, "Ever since the Notice I recd from our Archbishop Mons. Roquelaire, that all religious in France being now secularized by his Holiness, were entirely under his jurisdiction; I have turned my thoughts to America, where a new prospect opens of labouring with success."[24]

As Wilson posted his letter to Rome, John Carroll was writing to his friend Anthony Garnier about the coming of the friars, saying,

The English Dominicans, at my request, have sent hither four of their number, worthy and zealous Gentlemen, & they are directed by their vicar General, and authorized by the Pope to establish, with my approbation, an independent province. Of these good Gentlemen I intend principally to make use, for the consolidation and extension of religion in the Western States, Kentucky & the part adjacent to the Mississippi and lakes of Canada. They are now departing for Kentucky where they will form a college; to the great joy of the most active and zealous Mr. Badin.[25]

Bishop Carroll had never gone west of Maryland. His words reveal how his purpose differed from the original Fenwick plan for a college, and also how little he knew of the extent of the mission he proposed for the Dominicans. Actually, they would find challenge enough for the next thirteen years in the central counties of Kentucky, where most of the Catholics had settled.

In the year 1805, with formal approval by the Order Of Preachers, the first steps were taken to found the American province, the realization of Edward Fenwick's dream. His sponsor Luke Concanen thanked Bishop Carroll for his encouragement, saying "You are the father and protector of this infant colony."[26] The initial members of that colony, Wilson and Tuite, arrived on the Kentucky frontier, but not without some difficulties.

Accompanied by Fenwick's nephews, Robert and Nicholas Young, Wilson and Tuite began their journey westward. The bumpy ride in a farm wagon over primitive roads of the Wilderness Trail took them in a southwesterly direction from Maryland through Virginia to the border of Tennessee and Kentucky. There they had to cross the Cumberland Gap. On the western side of the pass, the horses suddenly bolted, and dumped their passengers from the wagon. The only ones to sustain injuries were the less agile Dominican friars. Wilson broke his arm and Tuite suffered a deep cut in his forehead. First aid was applied and the ride continued.

Back in England the future of the Dominicans seemed bleak. It took encouragement for their confreres even to stay in existence. That they had lost four of their brothers to the American mission, as the 1806 chapter minutes record, was almost a fatal blow. The remaining English friars felt the crisis in much the same way that the first Dominicans mourned the loss of the great St. Dominic.[27] For the next quarter century they came close to dissolution. But the British perspective was written into their province history: "While in the United States things were thus triumphantly marching to success, in England the Province seemed only to grow more enfeebled."[28]

The American friars did not see themselves as triumphant. They were merely eager for the enterprise of evangelization. Thus Samuel Wilson and William Tuite spent the first months of their mission getting acquainted with both the land and people: the knobs and creeks of Kentucky; the struggling Anglo-Americans who had settled there. Sixty families had begun the trek from Maryland two decades earlier and in 1793 had welcomed, first, Stephen Theodore Badin and then in 1805 the Belgian Charles Nerinckx. Now they welcomed Wilson and Tuite, the vanguard of the Dominicans.

With the help of Father Badin the two friars became acquainted with the needs of the area. Because Badin had no room for both priests and Fenwick's two nephews, other families boarded the group. Father Tuite lived with the family of Thomas Gwynn and Father Wilson with the family of Henry Boone on the Cartwright Creek settlement. Wilson opened a school in the Boone home and took charge of the mission of St. Ann. By July Edward Fenwick was freed from his temporary service in Maryland to set out for Kentucky. Robert Angier would not arrive in the Kentucky hills until the fall of 1807.

Fenwick's arrival in the Bardstown area inaugurated several activities essential to the foundation of the first Dominican priory and province.[29] Although he had spent nearly thirty years abroad, the Maryland native brought to his new responsibility essential "American" qualities. He was energetic, restless, inventive, adaptable and even self-effacing. It was the perfect combination for leadership on the American frontier. Fenwick and Wilson traveled on horseback, stopping at newly built log cabins in the forest, as well as at farm homes, greeting their fellow Catholics. Their welcome always depended upon the experience the Kentuckians had had with Badin and Nerinckx.

In 1806, Badin wrote about the differences he felt between himself and the new evangelizers, "They long to be united in a college or monastery." Despite this realization, Badin withdrew his offer of property. Using Fenwick's Maryland patrimony the Dominicans purchased in his name the John Waller farm near Cartwright Creek, in the midst of the Catholic population of Washington County. On the 500-acre property stood a two-story brick house, a grist mill, and a saw mill. The farmland was hilly, but its soil was fertile. And the sturdy house was adequate for present numbers. The Dominicans had realized their first dream.

By Christmas of 1806 the friars established their community and dedicated it to the first Dominican saint of the Americas, Rose of Lima. It became their priory where a new province of the Order of Preachers was established. The first exception was made, since priories were to have twelve professed members, while provinces could not be established without the existence of three priories. This first test of viability would be matched by many other challenges as the young Province of St. Joseph struggled to stay alive.

At St. Rose, the friars also established a school for young boys and for youths interested in joining the Order of Preachers. The plan was similar to the one begun by Father Wilson at the Boone farmhouse. Bishop Carroll gave approval for the school even before Fenwick left Maryland, stating publicly that he greatly rejoiced at the plan for it, which he said would produce beneficial effects for "improving the minds and morals of the rising generation, and fortifying their religious principles." [30] On this point Carroll and Fenwick were of one mind. Fenwick had been determined to build both school and seminary in his native Maryland. Now he would fulfill his dream in Kentucky.

The Dominicans named this pioneer educational institution after St. Thomas Aquinas. It was open to boys eight to sixteen with tuition $125 a year. Offerings included "Greek, Latin, French, English, Reading, Writing, Algebra and Geometry . . . ." Extra charges were assessed for "clothes, mending, books, postage, medical attendance and medicine." [31] The flyer made no mention of length of school year, but supervision was assured.

One of the best-known pupils to attend St. Thomas was the future President of the Confederate States, Jefferson Davis. At the age of eight in 1816, he traveled from Mississippi to attend the school. In his old age, he recalled:

> The Kentucky Catholic School, called St. Thomas College, when I was there was connected with a church. The priests were Dominicans. They held property; productive fields, slaves, flour-mills, flocks, and herds. As an association, they were rich but individually they were vowed to poverty and self-abnegation. . . . When I entered the school, a large majority of the boys belonged to the Roman Catholic Church. After a short time I was the only Protestant boy remaining, and also the smallest boy in the school. From whatever reason, the priests were particularly kind to me.
>
> As the charge has been frequently made that it is the practice in all their schools to endeavor to proselytize the boys confided to them I may mention an incident, which is, in my case at least, a refutation. At that period of my life, I . . . thought it would be well that I should become a catholic, and went to the venerable head of the establishment, Father Wilson, whom I found in his room partaking of his frugal meal, and stated to him my wish. He received me kindly, handed me a biscuit and a bit of cheese, and told me that for the present I had better take some Catholic food. [32]

Rev. Charles Nerinckx

Relations between Badin, who had originally rejoiced to hear of the Dominican venture, and the friars grew worse. Within months of their arrival Badin had a complete change of heart. For one thing, Nerinckx had warned him not to give his property to the friars, or any other religious order, who might use it to gain ecclesiastical power and "allow error or heresy or any substantial deviation from morals or discipline" to take place. As to the Dominicans, Nerinckx "does strongly suspect the purity of their faith." In Belgium they strolled around freely "among the lawless soldiery of the French revolution," [33] seeming to indicate collaboration with the invaders. If Fenwick had read these lines, his mind would turn wryly to his own imprisonment by the revolutionaries, as his brethren fled back to England in disguise. Carroll, now grown used to Badin's anxious concerns, must have been surprised at his rapid change of attitude toward the friars.

Upon Fenwick's arrival the friars experienced the crescendo of criticism on the part of Badin and Nerinckx, matched by the rising voices of people who objected to the rigid practices of both men. In frequent letters to Bishop Carroll, Fenwick and Wilson cited Badin's strictures on dancing, and his unreasonable penances. Badin had actually commanded some to hold one hand over a candle flame while reciting the Hail Mary. Both Badin and Nerinckx continued to make implacable decisions about people's behavior. One young woman seeking a dispensation for a mixed marriage was told to spend six months fasting and praying as a penance. Still the permission was not given.[34]

Wilson judged such cases pastorally. As a Master in Theology, he was always in a quandary about decisions made by the two diocesan priests. In August, 1805, Wilson made known his apprehension to Bishop Carroll:

> No place in the world, Dr Sir, is more in want of a prudent Bishop than Kentucky, where thousands are living in constant neglect of the Sacraments, through the too great zeal I fear of the former Missioners. Young people are not admitted without a solemn promise of not dancing on any occasion whatever, which few will promise & fewer still can keep. All priests that allow of any dancing are publicly condemned to Hell. People taught to believe that every kiss lip to lip between married persons is a mortal sin. . . People publicly warned on our arrival, that there are all sorts of Priests good & bad, etc. Women refused absolution for their husbands permitting a decent dance in their house, not to mention a thousand things far more ridiculously severe.[35]

Such reports were certainly not new to Bishop Carroll. Letters from Kentucky laity of this period abound in the diocesan archives at Baltimore. Yet Fathers Badin and Nerinckx were not easily convinced they were creating a problem. Their rigorous practices were merely expressions of their zeal for their people. Stephen Badin wrote:

> Missioners in these parts must descend into the huts of the poor, and be satisfied with any sort of treatment by day or night; they must be inquisitive and indefatigable in the search of stray sheep. They should have at hand catechism books, pictures, beads, etc. to procure admittance or secure to themselves easier success; they must be dexterous, disinterested, humble and patient . . .They must expose themselves to disagreeable weather, cross-rides, disappointments, and even insults. They are not to be backward in . . . making known their sacerdotal character. They should be always ready to give a sermon, an exhortation or a controversial speech, publicly or privately." [36]

Even as Badin wrote, the Dominicans continued their own missionary ventures and made great progress. In 1806 Edward Fenwick sent a full report to the Dominican headquarters in Rome.[37] In that letter he gave a description of the geography of Kentucky, the social life of the people and the various Protestant sects in the area and requested faculties for forming the Rosary Confraternity and a local unit of the lay Third Order.

Wilson and Tuite continued to conduct the school while Fenwick directed the building of a new convent at St. Rose to house their increasing numbers. The building was ready in March 1807 on the feast of St. Joseph, the provincial patron. The same house would be maintained for more that 150 years as the center of the province mission. Its construction was a matter of realistic hope, since the numbers of friars and students were gradually increasing.

The year closed with two helpful events. In October Robert Angier, the fourth founding member of the province, arrived after a prolonged ministry in Carroll's Maryland parishes. He would soon be sent to St. Francis' congregation in Scott County. Two days later came a letter from Rome to the community, enclosing the appointment, made on the previous February 27, of Samuel Thomas Wilson as provincial. This word had been long-awaited by Edward Fenwick who in the formation of the province had placed Wilson's name before his own as being more able for that responsibility.

Hardly was the Kentucky mission begun when a series of letters to Bishop Carroll from Ohio settlers led the way to a new frontier for the Dominicans, one which would be significant for the Order, the Church, and Edward Fenwick. One petition came from two laymen in the tiny capital of Chillicothe, near the western end of the National Road. On February 1, 1807, they wrote in part: "Dear Sir, if you would be so kind as to make a trial and send a priest, there is nothing would give us more pleasure on account of our children as well as ourselves." [38]

One year later, on February 1, 1808, Bishop Carroll received a second plea, this time from Jacob Dittoe of New Lancaster near Somerset, representing three Catholic families. He described some good land suitable for the Church and said,

> We will exert ourselves in making improvements on the said land, if you have any prospect of sending a priest. We will have a good house for him to go in with a tenant and maid. Perhaps a tenant and some decent women to wait upon the priest might be found in your part of the world to come with the priest.[39]

Rt Rev. Benedict Joseph Flaget

In the summer after Carroll received this letter which he labeled "Important," he received a visitor from Kentucky, Edward Fenwick, who undoubtedly shared his concern for the Ohio Catholics. Before the end of the year 1808, Fenwick rode into the Ohio forests seeking the Dittoe family. The sound of an axe led him to a clearing on the Dittoe property. This was the beginning of the Dominican mission and of the Church in Ohio. Meanwhile, the little colony of four Dominican friars at St. Rose gathered for their first provincial chapter on May 10, 1808. Two weeks later the cornerstone was laid for St. Rose Church. Their Kentucky parishioners rejoiced as changes began to take place.

Then from the single Diocese of Baltimore were carved four new Catholic dioceses to serve a population that was expanding and moving westward. Along with the expected choice of three urban centers, New York, Boston and Philadelphia, the people on the western frontier were honored with the designation of little Bardstown in Kentucky as an episcopal see covering the vast area that reached north to the Canadian boundary and west to the Mississippi. Baltimore had now become the archdiocese, with John Carroll as archbishop over all.

Two of the new episcopal appointments were of keen interest to the friars in Kentucky. The first was that of Benedict Joseph Flaget, who would be their bishop at Bardstown. The second was the naming of a Dominican confrere, Luke Concanen, to be the first bishop of New York. As Vicar General of the Order of Preachers and also as agent in Rome of Bishop Carroll, Luke Concanen had been the most effective sponsor of the American province since Fenwick first expressed the idea of its establishment. Even more significant was the new role given Concanen by the head of the Order: to be his vicar with authority over all the Dominicans in the United States.[40] What this would have meant to the life and growth of the American friars, including the possibility of their being called to ministry in New York, soon became a moot question. Concanen was prevented from leaving Italy by Napoleon's embargo, and before it was lifted he was taken by death. The Dominican named in his place, John Connolly, arrived in New York only at the end of 1815. He had no previous ties with the American friars.

In 1809 Stephen Badin conveyed to Bishop Carroll news of the Dominican friars. Seven American youth were received as novices in the spring, and Badin told Carroll that it gave him much pleasure that "the Dominican monastery of St. Rose begins at length to assume a regular appearance."[41] In 1810 Badin reported enjoying peace with the Dominicans concerning their theological-pastoral differences.[42] In May he would join the friars in rejoicing at the first religious profession of new members. These were: Richard Pius Miles, of a family that had come to Kentucky from Maryland in 1796 when he was five years old; Samuel Louis Montgomery and Stephen Hyacinth Montgomery (not related), two sons of Maryland families transplanted to Kentucky;

Journey by flatboat on the Ohio River

Robert Young, the nephew of Edward Fenwick; and William Thomas Willett, the only native Kentuckian. In 1811, Nicholas Young made his profession.

Some time after the profession at St. Rose, Edward Fenwick set out for New York to meet the newly elected bishop, Luke Concanen. It would be a meeting of brothers and friends in the Order: Concanen as sponsor, Fenwick as founder of the Province of St. Joseph. Only upon arriving in Manhattan did Fenwick learn to his profound sorrow that Luke Concanen had died in Italy, before Napoleon's embargo on American ships was lifted. Fenwick became ill and could not participate in the memorial Mass for Bishop Concanen at St. Peter's on Barclay Street. He was still there recuperating in mid-November before he could return to Kentucky.

The year 1811 was a banner one for Kentucky Catholics. One year after his consecration as Bishop, Benedict Joseph Flaget was conducted by flatboat down the Ohio River. Accompanying him on this journey into Kentucky, to his new diocese at Bardstown, were three future bishops: Jean Baptiste David and Guy Ignatius Chabrat, both Sulpicians, and the Dominican Edward Fenwick.

Father David's account of the flatboat journey is charming in its realism:

> The roof is high enough not to oblige anyone to stoop. Imagine on this comfortable Ark Monsignor Flaget, who is its life and delight, together with three priests; for you must know that Father Edward Fenwick joined us at Pittsburgh, and in giving us a pleasant, useful travelling companion, he has freed us of the discomfort (which they say is extreme) of having a horse on board, since he sent our horse overland by two of his nephews who are taking his own horses. . . . Imagine, then, this family living in the greatest harmony (with a good-natured pilot who speaks little, but who is always in a good humor and very obliging, etc.) performing our regular exercises; edifying one another, cheering one another, and not refusing to put our hands to work, all knowing how to man the oars; keeping watch in turn; with book in hand marking all the places we pass; counting faithfully the hundreds of miles passed and the hundreds still to go; making guesses as to the probable hour of our arrival in Louisville. . . . [43]

The arrival of Flaget was a blessing for every Kentuckian. Not only did they have a bishop to serve the vast region, but the people could breathe more easily with one who they hoped could modulate the practices of Badin and Nerinckx. Now the Dominicans could serve them with less restraint. Two months after Bishop Flaget arrived at Bardstown he wrote to a fellow Sulpician, Francis Nagot, "The Messrs. of St. Dominic appear very attached to me. I do everything in the world to support and augment . . . good understanding: we often visit one another reciprocally, and we do it always with pleasure." [44]

The early growth of the Province of St. Joseph was neither rapid nor steady. The members from 1806 to 1820 counted only nine, besides the four men from the English province and the six professed in 1810. Of the latter, Robert Young died in 1812, and none was ready for ordination until 1816. Moreover, the seminary was the responsibility of Samuel Wilson, a task he shared with his office of provincial and his regional ministry. So difficult was his threefold role that in 1815, the year before the first ordinations, Wilson was cautioned by Bishop Flaget to give more time to the students to insure their proper preparation in theology. He suggested this, not because the students were lacking in ability, or because their teachers were unqualified. No ecclesiastic in Kentucky, Bishop Flaget acknowledged, was more learned than Wilson. Exhorting the prior to form the young men in prayer and recollection as well as theology, the bishop added that he did not intend to interfere with their internal affairs. Rather, "Your family is very dear to me, and will one day be too important in the affairs of my diocese for me not to do what in me lies to make it more pleasing to God and more useful for my diocese." [45]

Because of the shortage of priests, Edward Fenwick pined over his inability to remain in ministry to the Ohio settlers. On receiving a letter from Jacob Dittoe in May, 1812, the Dominican declined a visit and explained the duties which kept him from returning to Ohio:

> Yours of the 9th inst. is before me. I am sorry you have been so much disappointed, and so long neglected, and am the more sorry it is not in my power to visit you at present, having my hands and head all full. But take courage and patience a little longer, and you shall be comforted.

Then he tried to make clear the flurry of activities that overwhelmed him at St. Rose: building a brick church and college, finishing a new saw-mill and grist-mill, having "three companies of workmen about me, carpenters, bricklayers, all lodged and boarded – besides a large plantation and six congregations to attend to. Thus you see I have no time to spare. I have mentioned you all to the good Bishop. He pities you, and will do his best to provide for you." [46]

Despite all this activity, Bishop Flaget asked Fenwick in May 1816 to replace the ailing Robert Angier in Scott County. Angier was suffering from depression and had asked to go back to Maryland. The Dominican provincial Wilson, writing to the Jesuit provincial in Maryland, asked whether the Jesuit superior might recommend Angier to someone for "a little occasional consolation in case of a relapse." [47] With the departure of Angier, only three of the original founding friars remained. In the following September, however, four men were ordained to the priesthood: Richard Miles, Stephen and Samuel Montgomery, and William Willett.

Now Edward Fenwick was free to attend to the Dittoe family and the other settlers in Ohio. As an itinerant preacher, he sought his fellow Catholics in the forest clearings and new settlements. In 1818 his recently ordained nephew, Nicholas Dominic Young, joined him in Ohio. Together they built a log church and house. Over the next three years they would work together to bring the message of the Gospel to Catholics through out the state. The blessing of their church of St. Joseph, the first in Ohio, took place on December 6, 1818. This parish and its missions began to match in scope and intensity those in Kentucky at St. Rose. The two sites would become dual mission centers of the Order. The detailed story of these parishes is reserved for Chapter 6.

Bishop Flaget did not forget the efforts of the Dominican missionaries in Ohio. He himself visited that state, listened to the requests of the settlers, and marveled at the work of Edward Fenwick and his nephew. So vast was the Bardstown diocese that Flaget became convinced of the need for two new dioceses to be separated from Bardstown; one for Ohio, the other for the Territory of Michigan, which extended across Lake Michigan to the Mississippi River and beyond.

1. First draft, Carroll to "Petitioners for Fleming," July 21, 1788, Archives, Archdiocese of Baltimore AAB 9 A G 2. Whether his proposal remained in the final draft or not, it expressed an idea that would be conveyed later to the English Dominican province, with fruitful results.

2. Baltimore, May 25, 1796. Spic.Oss.3, 520-522. Cited in Hugh Fenning, **The Irish Dominican Province, 1697-1797** (Dublin: Dominican Publications, 1990).

3. John Carroll had gone to St. Omer in France for studies with the Society of Jesus and was ordained a Jesuit in 1761.

4. The address, published in London on Aug. 21, 1804, was a plea for financial support for the new province; a plea authorized by the Vicar Apostolic of London, Bishop John Douglass, Saint Joseph Province Archives, O.P., (SJP).

5. Handwritten profession document, ms., English Dominican Province Archives (EDP), Edinborough, Scotland.

6. John Carroll to Luke Concanen, O.P., Baltimore, Nov. 21, 1806, Archives General, Order of Preachers, Rome (AGOP) XIII, 03150, 76. Short had completed his term as provincial in 1798 and died in 1800.

7. Fenwick to Concanen, Carshalton, Jan. 23, 1804, AGOP XIII, 03150, 63.

8. Fenwick to Concanen, Carshalton, Mar. 15, 1803, AGOP XIII, 03150, 63.

9. Concanen to Fenwick, Rome, Nov. 19, 1803, EDP. Gaddi, the major superior of the order of Preachers, held the title Vicar General because of papal action in response to Spanish political interference. See R.P,. Mortier, O.P., **Histoire des maîtres généraux de l'Ordre des Frères Prêcheurs**, vol. 6 (Paris: Picard, 1914) 427-455.

10. Concanen to Carroll, Rome, Dec. 20, 1803, Archives Archdiocese of Baltimore AAB 2 W 2.

11. Fenwick to Carroll, Carshalton, Jan. 12, 1804, AAB 2 W 2.

12. Fenwick to Concanen, London, Jan. 23, 1804, AGOP XIII, 03150, 64.

13. Fenwick to "The English Catholic Nobility and Gentry," AGOP XIII, 03150, 66.

14. Fenwick to Concanen, London, Jan. 23, 1804, AGOP XIII, 03150, 64.

15. Fenwick to Concanen, London, Aug. 29, 1804, AGOP XIII, 03150, 67. This appointment would hold until the friars could move to the customary election of their provincial.

16. Fenwick to Carroll, St. George's, Southern Maryland, Nov. 29, 1804, AAB 3 R 3.

17. Fenwick to Carroll, Washington, D.C., Dec. 15, 1804, AAB 3 R 1. He offered, while in the new "Federal City," to minister to the Catholics of the area. The coadjutor Bishop Leonard Neale gratefully accepted his offer.

18. Fenwick to Carroll, Carshalton, England, Jan. 12, 1804, AAB 3 R 1.

19. Badin to Carroll, St. Stephen, KY, Dec. 6, 1804, **American Catholic Historical Society Records**, ACHSR 23 (1906): 155.

20. Badin to Carroll from "near Bardstown," May 15, 1805, AAB 1 G 9.

21. Narrated in Fenwick to Concanen, Piscataway, MD, Aug 1, 1805, AGOP XIII, 03150, 73.

22. Sources of those authorizations were: Cardinal Dugnano of Propaganda Fide to John Carroll, Rome, Dec. 22, 1804, AGOP XIII, 03150, 70; Propaganda to Fenwick Rome, Mar. 11, 1805; Concanen to Fenwick, Rome, June 22, 1805, AAB 3 R; Giuseppe Gaddi, Rome, to Fenwick, June 22, 1805.

23. Badin to Carroll, Kentucky, Oct. 5 and 12, 1805, AAB 1 G 10. Nerinckx, like Badin, had leanings toward rigorism. Also, he had been in Bornhem when the French revolutionary soldiers seized the town. He believed, mistakenly, that the soldiers treated the Dominicans and property with leniency. If the soldiers were lenient to the friars, it was because the commander happened to be an American, Major Eustace, who showed respect to religious men and women.

24. Wilson to Concanen, Georgetown, Oct. 14, 1805, AGOP XIII, 03150, 74.

25. Carroll to Garnier, Baltimore, Oct. 15, 1805, Thomas Hanley, SJ, ed. **The John Carroll Papers** (Notre Dame: University of Notre Dame Press, 1976) Hereafter CP, vol 2, 492.

26. Concanen to Carroll, Rome, Jan. 30, 1806, SJP.

27. Bede Jarrett, **The English Dominicans** (New York: Benziger, 1921) 197.

28. Jarrett 198.

29. This was the first American province of any religious order. Although the Irish Augustinians came to the United States in 1796 to establish a province, the foundation did not become a formal province until 1874. See Arthur Ennis, O.S.A., **The Augustinians: A Brief Sketch of their American History from 1796 to the Present** (Philadelphia: Augustinian Press, 1985) 9-19.

30. John Carroll to the Public, Apr. 25, 1806, Baltimore, AAB 3 R 6.

31. Flyer, **St. Thomas College,** n.d., near Springfield, Washington County, Kentucky, SJP.

32. Varina H. Davis, **Jefferson Davis, Ex-President of the Confederate States of America: A Memoir** vol. 1 (New York: 1890) 13-14.

33. Badin to Carroll, "near Bardstown," Oct. 12, 1805, AAB 1 G 10.

34. This controversy between the rigorists Badin and Nerinckx, and the moderate Dominicans has received much attention in the past. See John B. Boles, **Religion in Antebellum Kentucky** (Lexington: University Press of Kentucky, 1976) 62-65, and Victor O'Daniel, **A Light of the Church in Kentucky** (Washington, D.C.: The Dominicana, 1932) 109ff.

35. Wilson to Carroll, Kentucky, Aug. 25, 1806, AAB 8 B 16. "The former missionaries" were Badin and Nerinckx, whose place Wilson took in St. Ann's parish and other missions.

36. Badin to Carroll, near Redstone, KY, "alias Brownsville," Oct. 17, 1807, AAB 1 I 15.

37. Fenwick to Luke Concanen, Springfield, KY, Sept. 25, 1806, AGOP XIII, 03150, 75.

38. Whaland Goodee and Major Philips to Carroll, Chillicothe, Feb. 1, 1807, AAB 10 I 6.

39. Jacob Dittoe to John Carroll, New Lancaster, OH, Feb. 1, 1808, AAB 3 D 8.

40. This appointment was reported by Concanen in a letter from Rome to John Carroll, July 23, 1808, AAB 2 W 5.

41. Badin to Carroll, Bardstown, Jan. 8, 1809, AAB 1 J 1.

42. Badin to Carroll, Kentucky, Feb. 5, 1810, AAB 1 J 7.

43. David to Simon Bruté, Bardstown, June 4, 1811, Notre Dame University Archives (UNDA) II 3 n. The two nephews of Fenwick were Robert and Nicholas Young, professed a year earlier as Dominicans of St. Joseph Province.

44. Flaget to Nagot, Bardstown, Sept. 6, 1811, Filson Club Archives, Louisville, KY. (FCA).

45. Flaget to S.T.Wilson, Bardstown, 1815, A rough draft found in SJP.

46. Fenwick to Dittoe, near Springfield, May 25, [1812], SJP.

47. Wilson to John A. Grassi, S.J., Jesuit Provincial, St. Rose, KY, May 5, 1816, Archives of the Maryland-New York Jesuit Province (GUA) 205, 17.

CHAPTER 5

FRIARS AND SISTERS ON THE FRONTIER

The 1820s were a time of change and stress on the road to maturity for the first American province. They were united in the difficult work of laying foundations for their life and mission, including pastoral ministry unlike that of the former rigid pastors. Would they remain united when more men joined them and traveled far abroad, often alone, on mission?

During the summer of 1821, the provincial Wilson described the frontier life of the Kentucky friars in these words:

We carry out community life to perfection. No one has a farthing of his own, nor does anyone wish to, for in this region there is nothing you can buy – neither books nor other desirable items to buy. The tonsure is worn here just as at the Minerva and I am sending you enclosed a sample of the cloth used in making our habits. Our main objective is to be self-supporting and independent of the need for money; and this we have satisfactorily achieved. The principal art is to live without need to purchase things . . . except clothing for the missions. We have a blacksmith, a shoemaker, and a tailor; we still lack a joiner and a mason, so it costs us about two hundred dollars per annum to keep our mills in repair.

We are 12 in number in this community. Lately we have suffered severe financial loss for like most people in this part of the country we have been obliged to sell on credit losing about 600 dollars. But don't let this discourage you, nor prevent you from bringing along the religious you mentioned and some laybrothers as well; for we have well over 500 acres here which can easily support any additions to the community. We can assure the recruits of an abundance of pork, bacon, cabbage, turnips and even some inferior potatoes. . . . Indeed, if Americans could only cook decently, we would be as well off as you in Europe, but we don't have much luck in raising vegetables.

You Europeans will find the days of abstinence especially trying. Although we have a creek at our doorstep we never have fresh fish . . . so we substitute apple pie and other pastries for fish. We must, since a salt mackerel costs a dollar and a quarter . . . . When you get here I hope I am able to treat you to a couple of glasses of beer, at least.

Here is the schedule we follow: Rise at four A.M. every day. First off, a half-hour of meditation, then solemn silence until the community Mass at seven, during which we say Prime, Tierce and Sext. Then come collation or breakfast consisting of milk warm from the cow or a little tea for those who prefer that . . . .[1]

Tilbury carriage used by Fenwick's party on their journey from Bardstown to Cincinnati

The year 1821 opened with growing excitement and some apprehension. Would the expected announcement of a diocese for Ohio affect the friars favorably? Who would be the bishop? They had not long to wait. On June 19, 1821, the Holy See formed the new Diocese of Cincinnati, naming as its first bishop the pioneer Dominican apostle to Ohio, Edward Fenwick. He received the appointment late in 1821 with grave reservations and absolute certainty of his own inadequacies. The Dominicans, however, were pleased that one of their own was chosen. As provincial Samuel Wilson used his strongest exhortation to convince Fenwick to accept the office. Fenwick repeatedly refused, but no one was listening. He wrote to a confrere, "I was reluctantly compelled by the counsel, admonitions, & even threats of superiors."[2] He would never be convinced that he belonged in that exalted position.

During the period of suspense the friars welcomed some long-awaited assistance from Europe. In September 1821, John Augustine Hill, a native of England who had been corresponding with the American provincial, arrived from Rome with three other Dominican volunteers. They were John Hynes of the Irish province and Jean Baptiste de Raymaecker from Belgium, both ready for ordination; also an Irish novice, Daniel O'Leary. On arrival, Hill joined the St. Rose community, but expected to work in Ohio.

On hearing news of Fenwick's appointment, Bishop Flaget of Bardstown and the friars planned together for the consecration of the new Bishop of Cincinnati. The event took place at St. Rose church on January 13, 1822, attended by the parishioners for whom he had built the church fifteen years earlier. The ceremony was presided over by Bishop Flaget, assisted by his diocesan vicar, Samuel Wilson; also by John Hill and the newly ordained Hynes and De Raymaecker. All four men would now go to Ohio with the new bishop. The Kentucky friars would be affected for years to come by the departure of their zealous missionary founder, their provincial, and three priests only recently ordained.

The bishop's party set out for Cincinnati, experiencing many difficulties. Raymaecker recounted the hardships experienced by the party on their trip north in the raw March weather. The five men traveled in a two-wheeled carriage called a "Tilbury" that broke down often as it jolted over log roads and became mired in muddy traces cut through the forests. Worse yet was their need to swim the half-frozen Kentucky River in order to arrive at last in the "Queen City of the West," now the see city of the Diocese of Cincinnati. Their arrival was a boon for the Church of Ohio, but proved to be a grave setback for the Dominican community and mission in Kentucky.

Early in 1822, before the new bishop and his companions left St. Rose for Ohio, an event took place that delighted Fenwick and would affect the history of the Church, not only in Kentucky but also in the entire country. This was the realization of Fenwick's long-held dream to see American Dominican women religious share the mission of the friars in America. That dream had been delayed by Fenwick's itinerant mission in Ohio, but never abandoned. Its fulfillment remained for Samuel Wilson. One Sunday in February 1822 at St. Rose, he publicly invited young women to consider forming a community of Dominican Sisters, not cloistered as in Europe, but leading an active life and pronouncing simple vows.[3]

The response to Wilson's pulpit call was gratifying. Nine young women presented themselves as candidates. On April 7, four of the group persevered and were received formally into the Order of Preachers. All were members of the parish, accustomed to pioneer life: Angela Sansbury, Margaret Carrico, Magdalen McMahon, and Columba Tarleton. Wilson returned from Ohio for this historic ceremony. In August of the same year, six more candidates received the habit of the Order.

Wilson gave these courageous women a daily schedule which was quite monastic. They rose at midnight to recite the Office, were up again for meditation and morning prayer at five, then attended Mass and returned to chant the office. This routine, combined with teaching, was so strenuous that it had to be modified. Richard Pius Miles, a man of understanding and zeal, succeeded Wilson as the mentor, teacher, and director of the nascent community.

Even before the sisters were established the friars had visualized an active religious life for women. They believed it would fit the needs of the people as well as the purpose of the Order: proclaiming the Word of God through preaching and teaching. In fact, three years before Wilson's invitation, the friars had requested permission from the Pope to establish such a community. That authorization was given in 1820 in response to this petition:

> The Dominican Fathers of Kentucky in the United States of America, realizing the great benefit which, for the successful propagation of our Holy Religion, is reported by their missionary confreres of the Philippines, Tonkin [Viet Nam] and China,[4] with the establishment of colleges of tertiaries who are responsible for the education of girls, humbly beg Your Holiness to permit the aforesaid Fathers to establish comparable foundations in the Provinces [i.e. States] of Kentucky and of Ohio, under the direction of the same Order for the same pious purpose.[5]

There was considerable ambiguity connected with the forming of this community which would become the first active congregation of women in the Order of Preachers. Coming from Europe, the founding friars knew only cloistered nuns, but they soon came to realize that the life of enclosed women religious would be impossible in the frontier region of America.

In January 1823, Angela Sansbury became the first pioneer woman to pronounce vows. Later in the year, Magdalen Edelen, Benven Sansbury, Ann Hill, Margaret Carrico and Frances Sansbury made profession. Judith (Magdalen) McMahon, one of the first to be received, soon returned to her native Ireland.

In June, Angela was confirmed first prioress of St. Magdalen's convent with this official document addressed to her by the provincial Wilson:

> I, Brother Thomas Wilson, Prior Provincial. . . by the authority of my office, and empowered by His Holiness to that effect, do hereby declare, establish and confirm you, the said virtuous Sister Angela Sansbury, first prioress of our said college of Saint Mary Magdalen. . . . I hereby give you all spiritual and temporal authority over said college and religious nuns, as all prioresses of our holy Order possess and our holy Constitution authorizes . . . .[6]

Preceding the formal announcement Wilson stated that the sisters had petitioned to have Sister Angela at the head of their community.

The infant community was in competent hands. As the eldest daughter of Alexis and Elizabeth Sansbury, Sister Angela, the Prioress, had learned to take initiative. The life and customs embraced by the sisters fit the surroundings. Their first convent was a log cabin. They wore a religious habit in the convent but when traveling they used the dress of the day. On July 23, 1823, the Dominican sisters opened a school in a small "still house" building formerly used to make hard liquor, a building all too familiar in Kentucky. They enrolled fifteen pupils at St. Mary Magdalen, the name they gave to their new school.

Log Cabin Convent of St. Magdalen, 1822

Problems of sharing personnel and finances now arose, affecting the Order and the two needy dioceses. A few weeks before the transfer of the friars to Ohio in March 1822, John Hill had anticipated such difficulties. He requested Benedict Olivieri, vicar general, to create a special position in the Order that would allow Bishop Fenwick to engage Kentucky friars for the Cincinnati Diocese. Hill proposed that Fenwick be named Prefect of the Missions of the Order in the United States "with the faculty of placing subjects as he may think profitable to religion." Hill did not consult the new bishop on the matter but stated with naiveté and incredible self-confidence that if the bishop could not be given this faculty "it could be given to me, which would be the same thing, as long as he wishes me to be in his diocese. . . ."[7] The letter revealed Hill's foresight but also his ambition.

This boldness would eventually complicate Fenwick's freedom to serve. As provincial, Samuel Wilson took another position. John Hill naming himself as Prefect of the Missions dismayed him. He complained about Hill's self-promotion. "If he succeeds in getting himself nominated, what a confusion will this not bring. The Bishop . . . now sees thro' several of his plans." [8] There is no evidence that Hill's letter was ever answered.

Bishop Flaget became involved in this internal matter when Wilson transferred to Ohio three friars: Stephen Hyacinth Montgomery, John McGrady and Thomas Martin. Fearing that the Kentucky Church would lose more Dominicans, the Bishop of Bardstown requested Propaganda to forbid the removal of priests from Kentucky without his consent. The petition was granted.[9] In an effort to keep peace,[10] Wilson resigned as Fenwick's vicar in the Cincinnati diocese and returned to St. Rose Priory.

Next, financial relations became complicated with the division of the Ohio province from that of Kentucky. The bishop and friars in Ohio had to depend upon Sunday collections, often amounting to a total of two or three dollars at most, to support them all. By this time Fenwick believed that some recompense should come from his patrimony, the Kentucky property, to serve the Ohio missionaries. As founder of the Order in the United States, he understood the poverty and sacrifices they were enduring. Then he had rendered an account to the provincial, Wilson, of all property that he had been allowed to use, even goods and furniture.[11] Now Wilson, whom he considered both friend and supporter, suggested that he could not in conscience share the goods of St. Joseph province without consulting their Roman superior. The distraught Bishop Fenwick wrote:

> The convent in Kentucky which we 4 priests coming from Europe with permission began, has now increased in number to 13 priests, one deacon, simply professed novices 6, lay members 3, the number of religious still increasing and the convent having an abundance of possessions. Now you . . . may judge whether it is suitable and fitting for me to receive . . . in proportion to my labors and dignity, a part of the resources . . . for my brethren who will assist me in the care of souls and in the spread of the Order . . . .[12]

Wilson was aware of the plight of the Ohio priests. As early as 1820 he had declared that the friars hoped one day to see a Dominican bishop in Ohio. They planned to help maintain that bishop by buying a plantation on the bank of the Ohio River opposite Cincinnati.[13] They would send the income from that property to the bishop for his support and for the school he planned to establish in Cincinnati. Caught in the dilemma of concern for his diocese and for the friars of the province, Bishop Fenwick determined in 1823 to journey to Rome to explain his plight.

After numerous conferences between the Bishop and the Provincial, it was decided that the friars would form two provinces corresponding to the two states and dioceses in which they served. As a tentative step toward this end, Fenwick and Wilson co-signed a request to Viviani, Master of the Order in Rome, to form separate provinces: the original province of St. Rose in Kentucky and a new province of St. Louis Bertrand in Ohio.[14] Fenwick carried this joint petition with him to Rome. Early in the following year, 1824, the division was approved, with this proviso: consent for the division must be given by the friars of the province as a whole. The friars of St.

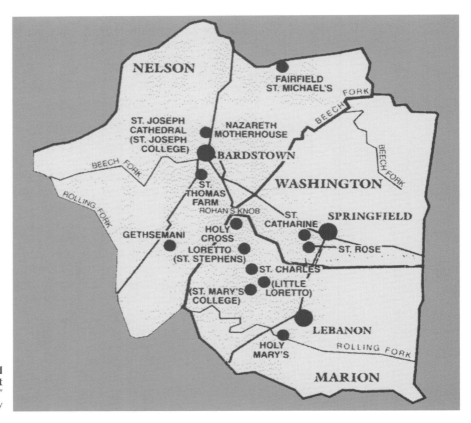

St. Rose priory and
St. Catharine convent
in the "Holy Land"
of Kentucky

Joseph Province would remain in Kentucky and those in Ohio would form St. Louis Bertrand Province. Neither Fenwick nor the authorities in Rome could foresee what complications would result from this condition.

In Rome the bishop received news that brought both joy and sorrow. Events at home dominated. For one thing the sisters at St. Magdalen were experiencing growth problems in their academy, which was filled to capacity with 29 pupils and 14 sisters. An extension was needed on the original building. Then came tragic word for Fenwick and the province. In May, two of the Kentucky friars died. William Thomas Willett, one of the first Dominicans ordained in the United States, became a victim of tuberculosis. Then came the devastating news of the sudden death of the provincial, Samuel Thomas Wilson. Fenwick could think of no one to replace this wise English friar. The loss was a tremendous blow to all concerned. Ironically, the Propaganda meanwhile sent the directive Fenwick had requested. The Dominican provincial was to send from Kentucky to Cincinnati "a sufficient number of subjects of his Order to provide in a stable manner for their temporal needs."[15] Wilson's death prevented its realization.

While the Kentucky friars were still shocked at their loss, the English confrere and co-founder William Tuite assumed the role of prior of St. Rose without authorization. Some of the friars resisted, making it clear that they found him an unacceptable candidate. So, too, did Bishop Flaget. Within the year Flaget wrote letters of complaint to Rome, citing Tuite's failure as teacher and preacher and the serious alcoholism which affected his life and ministry. In one letter he stated:

> Tuite is utterly unable to instruct the young men in Theology [which had been Wilson's forte] . . . He never preaches nor is he able to preach. . . . The four professed clerics are excellently disposed to acquire sacred learning and piety if they had but the opportunity . . . . The Sisters of St. Catharine who are under Miles' charge give an example, far and wide, of their Christian virtue, and they are doing a splendid job in the education of young ladies. But unless Tuite is removed, even this fine work will be doomed, for the Sisters ultimately depend upon the Fathers for their guidance. . . .[16]

The truth was that Tuite was deluded. He was convinced that no one else was capable of serving as superior. Among those he disdained were not only future priors and provincials but also the first Bishop of Nashville, Richard Pius Miles.

Certainly it would have been better if Tuite had returned to England after Wilson's death. He had little in common with the young men with whom he now lived at St. Rose. It is possible that William Tuite was never reconciled to life in Kentucky. Many years earlier Wilson had described the problems of European missionaries in the United States. He said,

> I will observe that daily experience teaches us that the European missionaries find such differences between our way of life and that of Europe that for many years we continue to recall the fleshpots of Europe. If they are secular priests they try to gather a little money to be able to return home; if they are Religious they have lost so much zest for life from excessive fatigue, [they] manifest their discontent.[17]

On his return from Rome to the United States early in 1825 Fenwick first learned about Tuite's self-appointment as prior. He also discovered that John Hill had been appointed vicar provincial for the incipient Ohio province.

In dismay, Fenwick wrote to the Dominican vicar general whom he had seen only recently in Rome:

> When that appointment was made I was in Rome but no one intimated to me anything about it. . . . Of Fr. Hill's talent and piety I have no doubts at all. He is an excellent missionary and a splendid Religious. But I do not think he has much capacity in the administration of temporalities. He is over-zealous and unpredictable in executing orders; and one must be very cautious in accepting any advice he may give. With him as its head, unless I am mistaken, this new Province will be in grave danger.[18]

Even more disconcerting was the news that both William Tuite and Samuel Louis Montgomery, two of the Kentucky friars, had withheld their consent to form the new province.

The question of provincial entities and jurisdiction was immediately reopened. Were there now two provinces or only one? The question remained unanswered until

1827, when both Fenwick and Hill addressed Roman officials. Fenwick proposed to Propaganda that the next bishop of Cincinnati be a Dominican, assisted by Fathers chosen by the Holy See.[19]

Hill sent to the Vicar General a dual proposal. First, since the division of St. Joseph Province was "vaguely obtained but never executed," he supported Bishop Fenwick in seeking the restoration of the single province, and a Dominican bishop for Ohio. But unknown to Fenwick, he proposed an added burden for him: to be the superior of the Order in the United States, with two Fathers to assist him.

Moreover, Hill said, the one reconstituted province should have its headquarters in Ohio, not Kentucky, with its patron changed from St. Rose to St. Louis Bertrand! [20]

Propaganda officials and the Dominican vicar general responded jointly to the two major questions. In a long and thoroughly developed memo, Propaganda issued a series of related decrees,[21] of which three were outstanding:

> **1.** The division of the original province, for lack of a fully affirmative vote among the friars, was now null and void. The Province of St. Joseph was to remain intact. Two friars were chided for over-ambition: John Hill for assuming the office of vicar provincial in the Ohio province before it "existed in reality," and William Tuite for assuming the office of prior and provincial in Kentucky based on seniority alone. The vacillations of Bishop Flaget concerning the province division were noted in the document.
>
> **2.** Concerning the current tensions arising from jurisdictional questions, Fenwick was directed by Propaganda to unite in himself, along with the dignity of bishop, the responsibility of Commissary General of his Order in the United States. The Master General conferred this responsibility for life.
>
> **3.** When the Bishop of Cincinnati ceased to be a Dominican, the Province of St. Joseph was to pay the new prelate an annual subsidy of $300. The significance of this puzzling requirement, and of others given in the Propaganda document, will be seen in Chapter 6.

The decree regarding the dual role to be held by Fenwick struck the friars like a thunderbolt. Fenwick detested the decree because it brought greater strain on the relations between himself and his fellow religious, and nothing was said in the document about sending additional Dominicans to assist the overburdened bishop. Some responsibility for the appointment of Fenwick to this unwanted position may be ascribed to Frederic Rese, who served as vicar general for the diocese of Cincinnati. He had been sent to Rome by Bishop Fenwick in 1827 to explain and promote the bishop's petitions. He wrote a few years later, that as a result of his representation in Rome, peace had been restored to the Dominicans by the appointment of Bishop Fenwick as Commissary General and thus the province "was saved from imminent ruin."[22] As a diocesan priest, Rese was defensive about his role in the appointment:

> True there are a few Fathers who consider this an infringement upon their constitutions and privileges, and in the last analysis they always have recourse to the trite subterfuge that the decision was made upon false representation, when they see me solicitous for the execution of the Apostolic Brief in all its provisions, and they insinuate that I am an enemy of the Order. But such is not the case.[23]

The unusual situation of a bishop being head of a province of men religious remained a problem for Fenwick and the friars. The 1828 decree pleased no one. The friars complained about questions of obedience. Fenwick pleaded that he had his hands full just being bishop.

To carry out his new responsibility Fenwick traveled to St. Rose, Kentucky, where he learned that under William Tuite as prior, regular observance had collapsed. The bishop hoped to remedy that situation by sending Raphael Munos from Cincinnati to serve as prior in August of 1828. But this move proved to be disastrous. Munos was a Spanish priest who came to Cincinnati in response to Fenwick's requests for priests from Europe. He held the degree of Master of Sacred Theology and was highly respected for his integrity and exemplary life. However, he did not understand American ways.

The three years Munos spent in Cincinnati had not convinced him that the friars should conduct a school where secular subjects were taught. When he reached St. Rose, where St. Thomas College was still educating young boys, he closed the school.

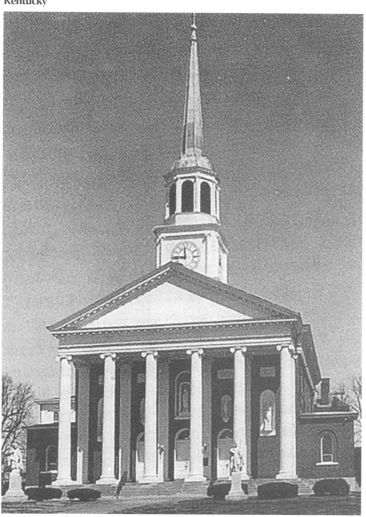

Cathedral of Bishop Flaget at Bardstown, Kentucky

Apparently Fenwick did not object, perhaps because of the possibility of opening a school in Ohio. Nor would Bishop Flaget oppose the move, since St. Thomas College was competing for students with his College of St. Joseph in Bardstown.

Munos' critical mentality about the school was also directed at the sisters at St. Magdalen. Dominican women in Spain were cloistered; sisters simply did not teach. Munos required the sisters to go to St. Rose if they wished daily Mass. He would not allow them to have the Blessed Sacrament in their convent. When he learned that they still owed $2000 on their enlarged facilities and had lost the help of Miles when he was transferred to Ohio, Munos urged them to disband. His reaction to Miles' concern for the sisters was almost ruthless. The St. Rose Council omitted Miles' name from the "Deeds of St. Rose" principally because he owed the priory "about $2000 on account of the Nuns. . . ."[24] Munos' authority for such a move was questionable, and the future of the sisters was a sensitive issue among the friars, especially with Bishop Fenwick.

Action was called for. Fenwick wrote immediately to the Vicar General in Rome, Tommaso Ancarani, to review the facts. Richard Miles, who was responsible for the welfare of the sisters had contracted a debt of $2000 for them to build an addition to their school. Then, just before Munos' arrival in Kentucky, the bishop was required to call Miles to Ohio and leave his responsibilities to Munos. But Fenwick wrote, "With chagrin I have learned that he considers the care of the Sisters foreign to his office"; consequently, "they very often cannot attend to their religious duties, and at the same time are suffering great need." The debt assumed by Miles had to be paid. Otherwise Miles could be brought to court and even imprisoned. The bishop's solution was to have the sisters leave Kentucky for Ohio. The sale of their convent and some of the friars' property at St. Rose would dissolve the debt. In Ohio they could do different works in the diocese until changed circumstances would permit them to be reunited in a community. The bishop reminded Ancarani that the matter was urgent and requested an early response.[25] Miles himself, before he left Kentucky and in letters from Ohio, urged the sisters to stand firm. Their respectful resistance to Munos' strictures was not disobedience.

Several months earlier Bishop Flaget, fearing that the Dominican friars would leave Kentucky, deplored that possibility in a strong letter to Propaganda. He was convinced of the necessity "that the convent at St. Rose, established already a good many years ago, will remain inviolate: and the care of souls which has been connected since its foundation with the Church of St. Rose will be diligently cared for by those Fathers who happen to live there." The sisters, as well, should not be encouraged to leave Kentucky:

> I am also confident that in the Monastery of St. Magdalen in which live pious women who follow the life of nuns and wear the habit of the Third Order of St. Dominic – which was built within a few years especially by the donations of the faithful – should be preserved for the educating of girls therein, as these religious women themselves promised to do when they sought the aid of the faithful to build it.[26]

He bemoaned the loss of Richard Miles, who on going to Cincinnati left many duties at St. Rose, including chaplaincy to the sisters. He worried that "the care of souls has suffered since the prior is not sufficiently skilled in English." Flaget explained that the care of St. Rose parish now fell entirely to Thomas Polin, "a man of feeble health," since two other priests in the convent "were kept under strict discipline as was fitting." These two were William Tuite and Samuel Montgomery, well known to the friars and the people as alcoholics.

Bishop Flaget went on to reveal another fear. Richard Miles had recently returned to St. Rose "endowed with the authority to sell the Monastery of St. Magdalen together with nearly a hundred acres of land annexed to it in order to repay the borrowed money and transfer the pious women to the Diocese of Cincinnati." The Kentucky bishop implored Propaganda to forbid the sale of the sisters' monastery, the friars' convent, and the Church of St. Rose without his consent. Such a sale would be a clear violation of the covenant the founders signed when they were seeking assistance from the faithful. He concluded, "Not without scandal to the faithful will that Monastery be sold which was built four years ago with their money in the assured hope of educating their daughters there and imbuing them with the holy principles of religion." [27] Along with their spiritual and physical deprivations, the sisters anguished over their possible disbanding.

In early December the response of Propaganda officials to Fenwick's request arrived. It was negative. Fenwick wrote in distress to the Dominican Vicar General:

> The reply received from the Sacred Congregation of the Propaganda about the sale of the convent of St. Rose did not satisfy me at all. I do not find in it any objection to the very strong reasons which I outlined, and I am led to believe that it was mere regard for the Bishop of Kentucky which dictated this reply. Bishop Flaget lacks neither money to buy the Church of St. Rose nor missionaries to send there. And since the favor that I requested is not being granted to me, I would prefer, if it were possible, that the Convent of St. Rose should be under the direct jurisdiction of the Bishop of Kentucky. I have too much to do in my own diocese to be able to take care of a community existing in another. . . . I have neither the time nor the money to spend for such a purpose.[28]

Matters in Kentucky had now come to a point where more than letter writing was imperative. Although Fenwick knew from several sources that Munos had restored the community of friars to regular observance, he had done so with extreme severity. He alienated the friars because of his rigor and his lack of proficiency in the English language. Munos, too, experienced much unhappiness at St. Rose. At the end of three months as prior, he had written to the Vicar General that religious observance at the convent had been relaxed for several years, and he had to initiate a reform of the place. He said that results were beginning to show as the men gathered for mental prayer every day, chanted the office in choir with regularity, and held the Salve procession daily after Compline. He noted that although Fenwick had congratulated him on the improvements in religious life, the bishop transferred to Ohio two priests who were the sole support of the Prior.[29] Of the two priests remaining at St. Rose, one was suspended by the Bishop of Bardstown, leaving the place with practically no assistance for the spiritual care of the sisters and a parish of 2000. Munos believed that he was not bound to obey Fenwick in releasing the two priests from St. Rose or disbanding the sisters. He felt that Fenwick was "acting as a bishop and for the good of his own diocese, not for the Order." Munos asked the Vicar to determine whether he was bound to obey a bishop

Notice of St. Magdalen Academy in the 1836 issue of The United States Catholic Almanac or Laity's Directory

who was acting in this way. He wrote a similar letter to Fenwick, indicating he could not believe that the bishop would do this to him without even consulting him. Roman officials assured Munos that Fenwick's authority over the Dominicans in Kentucky was legitimate. They were willing to send him a copy of the decree appointing Fenwick Commissary General of the reunited Province of St. Joseph.[30]

The Vicar General Ancarani could not have received the pejorative letter of Munos concerning Fenwick before the bishop himself wrote about the conditions in the province since he became Commissary General. Fenwick would have known, however, the nature of Munos' complaints. He gave Ancarani his version of the situation:

Last August [1828] I appointed as prior of St. Rose Father Munos who was staying with me in Cincinnati, I having some hope that he would be able to remedy the many spiritual and temporal disorders. In order to correct the extreme relaxation he passed very quickly to an extreme rigor. He knew neither prudence nor discretion, and our Order cannot hope for any help from him in America. . . . The 4 novices have been professed from 5 to 6 years, youths of irreproachable ways, but they study neither philosophy nor theology.. . . Father Munos, instead of giving them lessons in theology, has them memorize the Constitutions, not only the text but even the **declaramus.** As superior of this poor Province I find myself greatly embarrassed; I do not have religious of whom I can avail myself for the affairs of the Order. I cannot in good conscience receive novices at St. Rose, not having there teachers in the necessary subjects. The two convents, 300 miles distant one from the other, are weighted down with debts without hope of being able to pay them, and are in need of repair. After having asked God for divine assistance, and considered well all means of bringing the Province to a better state useful to the mission, I do not find other recourse than to sell the Convent of St. Rose in Kentucky, that is the building, the land . . . and with that money buy a piece of land in my poor diocese, and to build there a convent and a church dedicated to St. Rose.

Fenwick continued:

The reasons that have determined my course are the following:

1. The impossibility of governing and maintaining a Province composed of two convents 400 miles distant . . . in two different dioceses.

2. The very difficult communication and the heavy expense, as much for the superior as for the Religious, since the simple journey from one convent to the other costs 30 scudi [about $30.].

3. One cannot without great difficulty and expense send to St. Rose those young men in my diocese who present themselves to become Religious.

4. The visits which, alas, are necessary to that convent, are almost impossible for me, having to go outside of the diocese, lose very much time and precious money given for the missions of Ohio.

5. The convent is on the other hand of little use in Kentucky, a rich diocese with a well-filled seminary, with many missionaries, with a college and various religious establishments . . . . I hope through the goodness and mercy of the Lord . . . not only to obtain the requested faculties but to see even yet in the State of Ohio our convent as a mirror of religious life and a seminary of holy and scholarly missionaries.[31]

Although short of personnel in his diocese, Fenwick agreed to the requests of Munos and Flaget for an able-bodied priest. He sent Thomas Martin in September of 1829 to preach and minister to the congregation attached to the Church of St. Rose.

The welfare of the Dominican men and women in Kentucky and the failing health of Munos caused Fenwick in January 1830 to recall the Spanish priest to Cincinnati, where he died a few months later. Stephen Hyacinth Montgomery assumed the office of prior at St. Rose, where he remained until the summer of 1831. Exactly how the debt of the sisters was handled remains uncertain. One undocumented account presumed that Stephen Montgomery assumed the debt and the sisters repaid it by cooking, washing and ironing at St. Rose.[32] That the debt was discharged subsequently we know from a letter of Fenwick to Thomas Martin, Prior at St. Rose in early 1832. He wrote:

> As to the Sisters: I shall not fail to pray for them & to think of all the means I can devise to relieve & assist them – I have yet in my possession a letter authorizing me to dispose of property of St. Rose's Convent to pay their debts – but as it is a delicate point which I knew would be opposed by some and as I was informed at the time I recd that letter, that their debts were nearly paid, I did not communicate it to anyone. [33]

After all communications had ended, Miles stayed in Ohio, the sisters remained in Kentucky on their property and Martin was sent to St. Rose.

In 1830, the friars rejoiced at the ordination to the priesthood of four young men, the first in almost a decade: James Bullock, Joseph Jarboe, Charles Bowling, and Charles Pius Montgomery, younger brother of Samuel Louis Montgomery. All these men served the province for many years either in Ohio or in Kentucky. Charles Montgomery became Provincial and subsequently for reasons of health, refused the mitre for the Diocese of Monterey, California.

As the work of the friars continued to expand in areas where there were fewer Catholics, Fenwick sought and received the faculty of dispensing from the Dominican constitutions so that,

> Outside a Dominican Convent, even in sacred places. . . they can, in place of their habit, use the black clerical dress as secular clergy. In this there would be external uniformity, which is most suitable here; derision or criticism of Protestants would be avoided, and at the same time it would also be very helpful in their great poverty. For since the material which the Dominicans use in their habits is extraordinarily expensive and very easily soiled, it would cause him expenses which he could not meet without incurring loss in things more necessary. [34]

That measure solved some external difficulties, but many internal ones remained.

Early in 1831 Fenwick called a provincial chapter in Cincinnati. It was attended by Stephen H. Montgomery, Prior of St. Rose, Samuel L. Montgomery, Richard Pius Miles, Nicholas Young, Joseph Jarboe, subprior of St. Rose, and Charles P. Montgomery.

Fenwick indicated in his letter to Rome that some were not able to attend. At that meeting the troublesome question of the right of properties in Ohio was amicably settled, according to the directives sent from Rome in 1828. Fenwick agreed not to call men to Ohio from St. Rose Convent without the consent of the current prior and the majority of his council. Fenwick concluded the minutes, written in his own hand, with this personal intervention concerning his post as Commissary General:

> I resolved to request the Genl & Propaganda to accept of my resignation of Vicar General, Province of St. Joseph & transfer it to R. P. Miles or N. D. Young, either of whom is capable to discharge the duty and I believe it will give more general satisfaction to the Brethren as regularity, subordination & piety are reestablished in the province - & the cause of my appointment no longer exists.[35]

When Fenwick reported the chapter to Rome he added concerning his resignation, "Nor should it be overlooked that, if I should die, the occasion would doubtless give rise to quarrels and dissension with this authority position not being specifically arranged for." He then recommended that an election be held in the province, or that an appointment be made of one of three friars, Richard P. Miles, Nicholas Young, or Joseph Polin." [36]

In July of 1831, before Stephen H. Montgomery relinquished his office of prior at St. Rose, he reported that in the province there were thirteen Fathers, several of them on the Ohio missions, three professed novices, and two professed lay brothers. He indicated that Americans were little inclined to embrace the poor and mortified life of a Religious, but regular observance at St. Rose was continued in a spirit of peace and charity.

Historical marker at St. Rose, Kentucky

The sisters, he wrote, were doing well despite the problem of the debt. They totaled sixteen in two houses: the original in Kentucky, and the second in Ohio since 1830. With permission granted by the Master of the Order at Fenwick's request, the sisters were allowed to wear a black veil and say the little office of the Blessed Virgin.[37]

As for Fenwick's resignation as Commissary General, Montgomery wrote, "I have consulted the Fathers about it and they appear almost unanimously to wish that he be continued in it during his life as it is more than likely that the Fathers could not agree amongst themselves on a successor. . . ." [38]

Thomas Martin became prior of St. Rose in 1831. Fenwick who had worked closely with him in Ohio and often confided in him wrote often to the new prior, expressing his concern for the welfare of the friars. He continued to inquire about the recalcitrants, William Tuite and Samuel Montgomery. Above all, the bishop wanted to be reassured that Dominican life and practice were still being observed. He encouraged Martin to "have patience and courage and confidence in God under all troubles & cares." [39]

Cartwright Creek, Ky., locale of the initial Dominican foundations

A month later, despite illness, the Bishop was still inquiring about the two men who refused to follow either the prior's or his directives. He continued, "I hope to hear that all goes well with you, order and peace & mutual edification prevailing – all content & happy as far as this miserable world can render them." [40] In concluding the letter obviously written from a sick bed, Fenwick assured the prior, "If I can lighten any burden or afford any comfort whatever I will do it as far as in my power consistently with justice and other duties." A short time later he told Martin he wished only the good of the province and encouraged the friars to write to the head of the Order remonstrating against his selection as Commissary General. [41]

While St. Joseph Province was still struggling to attain its maturity, the idea of merging the new American group with the ancient Province of England was proposed. The English novice John Augustine Hill first suggested it in 1820. In polite but insistent language, Hill urged the English provincial Pius Potier to consider the union for the sake of both provinces, since both were struggling for existence. Potier resisted Hill adamantly (a feat not easily accomplished). He stated that the obstacles were too great; namely, the immense ocean that separated them, and the lack of sufficient personnel in the English province. Potier suspected that Hill wanted a share of the funds from the sale of the Bornhem property in Belgium. [42] Nothing came of this exchange.

Bishop Fenwick reopened the question of a merger after Hill's death in 1828. He was more cordial than Hill. He still had many friends in the English province to which he had belonged for ten years. Despite the possibility that time had radically altered the situation, he urged the merger in his correspondence with the English provincial Pius Potier. Thus in 1831 Fenwick inquired, "I should be glad to know what situation your province is in, if prosperous, & if you have a community at Hinckley. If you are not prosperous, I would again suggest & earnestly recommend to all able to labour to come over & apply to the general for leave to come . . . & cooperate with us in Ohio. [43] His courteous approach contrasted with the threatening tone of Hill's letters.

109

Several months later Fenwick proudly delineated to Potier the contributions of men and women of their Order to the Church in Ohio and Kentucky. The Dominicans had

> four excellent Brick churches besides four of wood, making eight in all – seven priests of the order on the mission in my diocese & six at the convent of St. Rose in Kentucky.
>
> You inquire about female convents. There is one at St. Rose's & another at Somerset in this state – both of third order – at the latter place there is a very flourishing school, & small as the number of ladies is, there is prospect of its assuming a very important station and an academy for young ladies. . . . Almost all the priests of the order who are employed in the missions in this diocese have been ordained by me.

He then expressed his regret that the English friars were suffering so much from government oppression and that their college and mission had declined. His suggestion to Potier followed:

> It is my candid opinion, that the best thing you could do would be to come to the assistance of our new province with what funds you might have, where I can assure you the prospect of promoting the good of our holy religion is boundless. . . . I beg of you to think seriously of this matter as it may result in a great deal of good to religion.[44]

There is no evidence that the English friars ever felt inclined to consider the move.

The repeated letters of Fenwick to Rome asking for release from his burden as Commissary General brought no relief. He wrote to Thomas Martin at St. Rose, "I have tried in vain to be divested of this galling & hateful authority. . . . I submit to my fate & advise all concerned to the like."[45] Six months later while on his last episcopal journey in the north, he wrote to his friend, an Irish Dominican in Rome,

Historical marker at St. Catharine, Kentucky

SAINT CATHARINE

Cradle and Mother House of the Dominican Sisters in U.S. First settlement at St. Rose Farm, 1822. Known as St. Magdalen Academy from 1823 to 1851. Renamed, 1851, St. Catharine of Sienna. Mother Angela Sansbury, O. P., and Rev. S. T. Wilson, O. P., co-founders. Former buried in Columbus, Ohio. Latter in St. Rose. The Academy chartered, 1839. College in 1931.

> I feel myself sinking under the weight of solicitude and infirmity. Arrived at my 64th year of age. . . I cannot add with confidence that a crown of glory awaits me because man knoweth not if he be worthy of love or hatred . . . I am sorry to say our little Province of St. Joseph does not flourish. It is poor in purse and spirit, is destitute of an able and active head to animate and promote its success. In fine it lingers for want of funds and efficient subjects.[46]

A few days later he confided to a benefactor in Europe that he was asking God to spare him until he could see his Order solidly established in the United States. This was not to be.

Fenwick died on September 26, 1832, during his last journey to the northern missions. At last he was freed of his double burden. Two months after his death, and more than eighteen months after his first request for relief, Roman officials, still ignorant of his death, sent the acceptance of his resignation as Commissary General.

1. Wilson to Hill, St. Rose, KY, July 23, 1820, APF IV, 609r-610r.

2. Fenwick to Maréchal, Kentucky, Feb. 9, 1823, Archives Archdiocese of Baltimore (AAB) 16 W 1.

3. An excellent source for the full story of these first American Dominican sisters can be found in Paschala Noonan, OP, **Signadou** (Manhasset, N.Y.: Brookville Books, 1997).

4. The Vietnamese Dominican communities of women named in the petition had been founded two centuries earlier for an active apostolate; but members did not take vows until the mid-20th century, a time of rapid growth for them. They suffered with their people through Communist oppression and the Viet Nam War. Some escaped to the United States. Providence blessed them with the welcome of the Kentucky Dominican Sisters.

5. Dominican Fathers to Propaganda Fide, Kentucky, Nov. 26, 1820, Archives, Propaganda Fide, Rome (APF) XXXVI, 849rv and 852v.

6. Wilson to Angela Sansbury, St. Rose, KY, June 6, 1823, Archives of Columbus Dominican Sisters (CDS).

7. Hill to Olivieri, Kentucky, Jan. 27, 1822, APF v.921, 446rv-449v. John Hill possessed a flamboyant personality with the talents of an outstanding preacher. Early in life Hill had married and joined the British Army, but resigned his commission when he became a Catholic. About 1818, when he decided to become a priest, he and his wife agreed to a separation. Hill had been friendly with the Dominicans in Belgium, so he chose to enter the Dominican Order. While studying in Rome he received every concession because of his experience and education. So rapid was his progress toward ordination that he celebrated his first Mass on Christmas Day, 1819, not

even a year from the time of entering the Order. Throughout his priestly career he never lost his penchant for the leadership which was evident from his early army days, and which caused annoyance to others.

8. Wilson to Francis O'Finan, Somerset, July 1, 1822, San Clemente Archives, Rome (SCA).

9. Consalvi to Flaget, Rome, July 27, 1822, SJP. Enclosed in the letter to Flaget was the directive to be delivered to Wilson.

10. See V.F.O'Daniel, **A Light of the Church in Kentucky** (Washington, D.C.: The Dominicana, 1932) 253.

11. Fenwick to S.T. Badin, **The Catholic Spectator of London**, I, 1823, 351. When Stephen Badin received in Paris a letter from Fenwick, he invariably sent it for publication to England . For that purpose, some letters were appropriate, others not.

12. Fenwick to Viviani, Rome, [Sept] 1823, APF, IX, 117rv-118r.

13. Wilson to Hill, St. Rose, Sept. 11, 1820, APF IV, 609r-610r. Wilson deplored the economic conditions in Kentucky, as elsewhere in the country crippled by the Panic of 1819. St. Rose was in debt for land the friars had purchased for expansion near the Wabash River. After the purchase, Flaget forbade them to use it. Surplus crops at St. Rose could not be sold, and tuition could not be collected. Everyone in the area of St. Rose felt the pinch.

14. Fenwick and Wilson to Viviani, Cincinnati, n.d. 1823, APF, VII, 123r-125r.

15. Caprano to Viviani, Rome, Aug. 9, 1823, Archives General of the Order of Preachers, Rome, (AGOP) XIII, 03150, 89.

16. Flaget to Velzi, Bardstown, Nov. 2, 1825, SJP.

17. Wilson to Hill, St. Rose, Sept. 11, 1820, APF IV, 609r-610r.

18. Fenwick to Velzi, Cincinnati, Apr. 5, 1825, SJP.

19. Fenwick to Propaganda Fide, Cincinnati, Jan. 12, 1827, APF IX, 191rv-192rv.

20. Hill to Velzi, Cincinnati, Jan. 12, 1827, SJP.

21. Bartolomeo Cappellari to St. Joseph Province, Rome, Apr. 20, 1828, APF IX, 626rv.

22. Rese to Propaganda Fide, Cincinnati, Feb. 16, 1832, APF X, 645rv-646rv.

23. Rese to Propaganda, Cincinnati, Feb. 16, 1832, APF X, 645rv-646rv. The writer added that the bishop had given the friars churches and property even beyond what was decreed by Propaganda, for two reasons: his intention was formed before the Brief was published, and he understood that subsidies from Europe should be given to missionaries of religious orders as well as those of the secular clergy.

24. Council Book of St. Rose, ms. Nov. 18, 1828, SJP.

25. Fenwick to T. Ancarani, Baltimore, Oct. 10, 1829. APF X. 223rv.

26. Flaget and Kendrick to P.F., Bardstown, May 12, 1829, APF X, 108rv-109r.

27. Benedict Joseph Flaget and Francis Patrick Kenrick to Propaganda Fide, Bardstown, May 12, 1829, APF X, 108rv-109r.

28. Fenwick to Ancarani, Cincinnati, Dec. 20, 1829, AGOP XIII, 03150, 139.

29. Munos to Ancarani, Kentucky, Nov. 10, 1828, AGOP XIII, 03150, 731.

30. Propaganda Fide to Munos, Rome, Feb. 14, 1829, APF X, 310, 94v-95r.

31. Fenwick to Ancarani, Cincinnati, Mar. 28, 1829, APF V, 230rv-231rv.

32. Anna Minogue, **A Hundred Years of Dominican History**. (Cincinnati: Pustet & Co., 1921) 70.

33. Fenwick to Martin, Washington, D.C., Jan. 23, 1832, SJP.

34. Castracane to Fenwick, Rome, Aug. 2, 1829, University of Notre Dame Archives (UNDA). This document enclosed in Cappellari to Fenwick, Aug. 8, 1829, III 2 g.

35. Fenwick, "Minutes of Provincial Chapter," Cincinnati, Apr. 23, 1831, SJP.

36. Fenwick to Ancarani, Cincinnati May 2, 1831, APF XI, fol., 102-103.

37. This request would indicate that heretofore the sisters wore a white veil and recited the Divine Office.

38. S.H. Montgomery to T. Ancarani, St. Rose, July 1, 1831, SCA.

39. Fenwick to Martin, Washington, D.C., Nov. 21, 1831, SJP.

40. Fenwick to Martin, Washington, D.C., Dec. 16, 1831, SJP.

41. Fenwick to Martin, Washington, D.C., Jan. 23, 1832, SJP.

42. Pius Potier to Hill, Weybridge, England, Nov. 25, 1820, English Dominican Archives (EDP).

43. Fenwick to Potier, Cincinnati, Dec. 1, 1831, EDP.

44. Fenwick to Potier, Cincinnati, June 12, 1832, EDP.

45. Fenwick to Martin, Washington, D.C., Jan. 23, 1832, SJP.

46. Fenwick to Francis O'Finan, Detroit, Aug. 13, 1832, SJP.

CHAPTER 6

FOUNDING THE CHURCH IN OHIO

Hardly was the Dominican mission well started in Kentucky when letters to Bishop John Carroll from Ohio settlers led to a new missionary venture. It would be significant for the Order and the Catholic Church in the United States, and particularly for the first bishop of Ohio. The first letter on record was that of Jacob Dittoe who arrived in Ohio two years after it achieved statehood. In 1805 he wrote on behalf of a colony of thirty German Catholics around Lancaster, promising land for a church if the nation's first Catholic bishop could provide a priest for them.[1]

A second letter was sent to Baltimore by two men of the small Ohio capital of Chillicothe near the western end of the National Road. On February 1, 1807, they wrote,

> We join our hands as one man in supplication to you desiring a priest, as there is no teacher of our Church in this part of the country; and if it is convenient for you to send us one we will do everything that is reasonable to support him. We have made no calculation of what might be collected yearly as we did not know whether we could be supplied or not; neither can we give a true account of the number of Catholics; but as nigh as we can come, is betwixt 30 and 40 which came from the Eastern Shore . . . .[2]

In the summer of 1808 Bishop Carroll, having read this letter and endorsed it "Important," received Edward Fenwick on a visit from Kentucky. He probably expressed his concern for the Ohio Catholics. Before the end of the year Fenwick rode into the Ohio forests seeking the letter-writers and was led by the sound of an axe to the Dittoe home in a clearing. For Fenwick this journey to Ohio was the impetus to become an itinerant preacher, a role he would never abandon. His response marked the beginning of the Dominican mission in Ohio and the founding of the Church among the Catholics in that State.

With the welcome addition of five ordained friars in 1816, the provincial Samuel Wilson was able to free Edward Fenwick to return to the Dittoes and their fellow settlers beyond the Ohio River. He became totally itinerant there, traveling constantly in forest areas, finding settlers and inquiring about Catholic families among them. To a friend in London he described his lonely journeys in these words:

I have become, as they call me here, an itinerant preacher. It often happens that I am obliged to traverse vast and inhospitable forests where not even a trace of a road is to be seen. . . . Many times, overtaken by night, I am obliged to hitch my horse to a tree and making my saddle a pillow I recommend myself to God and go to sleep with bears on all sides.[3]

In December 1817, a year after the ordination of Fenwick's nephew Nicholas Dominic Young, the youth was assigned by the provincial to join his uncle in the Ohio mission. Coming from a visit to his family home at "Nonesuch" near Washington, D.C., he began his new life in the hamlet of Somerset in Perry County, welcomed by the Dittoes and their fellow settlers. He wrote home about his mission beginnings:

I presume you begin to expect a letter from me by this time. . . . We commenced house-keeping yesterday in a comfortable log house, tho' no ways furnished as yet with large trees almost every sort so that we have a good collection to choose out of to leave for shade, ornament for the yard. The situation is very handsome, being on a gradual eminence. At present the view is much contracted, but will be extensive when the place and country about is opened. I think that in the course of a few years we shall make it a very pleasant place. All we shall want will be money sufficient to enable us to erect good buildings. As for ourselves we can do very well with the present house as long as the family remains small. But the church is what I allude to. That is what we shall want in the very beginning. The one that is now finished and adjoining the house, besides being of rough logs, is entirely too small to contain the present congregation which is almost double in number to what it was when I past [sic] this place in the Spring, and is daily increasing. The Greatest part of the new settlers are Germans from Connewago Congregation.[4] We shall perform divine services in the church for the first time next Sunday, and dedicate it to St. Joseph . . . I must make a request of you . . . . please send me the **National Intelligencer** one-year. I should be glad to have it . . . to see the debates of Congress etc.[5]

Fenwick among his people in the Ohio forests

St. Joseph church,
Somerset Ohio,
1818

Nicholas Dominic Young never lost his interest in the political life of the nation as he continued his zealous mission in Ohio.

The blessing of the little log church of St. Joseph, the first Catholic place of worship in Ohio, took place on December 6, 1818. A tiny log house adjoining the church served as a residence for the two friars. St. Joseph's was the center for the friars' visits to outlying missions and soon began to match in scope and influence the Kentucky establishment at St. Rose. The two sites became the dual mission centers of the American province.

In 1819 the settlers at Lancaster, Ohio rejoiced to complete still another log church, St. Mary's. The dedication of their new church occurred on Easter Sunday 1819. Spurred on by Michael Scott and other generous lay men and women, Christ Church, Cincinnati, had begun with a meeting held on Christmas Day in 1811, as announced in the town newspaper under the heading, CATHOLIC MEETING. It read:

As the Constitution of the United States allows liberty of conscience to all men, and the propagation of religious worship, it is earnestly requested by a number of the Roman Catholics of Cincinnati and its vicinity, that a meeting be held on the 25th of December, next, at the house of Jacob Fowble, at 12 o'clock. . . when it is hoped all those in favor of establishing a congregation and giving encouragement will attend and give in their names, and at the same time appoint a committee of arrangements.[6]

Heeding the announcement were nine men, seven women and four children.[7] These determined Catholics, like others throughout the State, pursued their objective for seemingly endless years. In 1817 they were still meeting, hoping, and praying, and even using the press to call for help from Catholics in the East. Their notice read in part, "Considering ourselves like the lost sheep of Israel, forlorn and forsaken. . . without Guide, Church, or Pastor; we are compelled. . . to call upon our brethren throughout the Union for their assistance towards the erection of a Catholic Church."[8] Their efforts finally bore fruit in 1819 with the blessing of the first Catholic church in the city of Cincinnati. Only three years later they would become members of the cathedral parish of the same city.

Still, Edward Fenwick and Nicholas Young were the only priests stationed in Ohio. From Somerset, the two Dominicans rode out to scattered, rapidly growing settlements. Even the cities were experiencing great growth in the early 1820s. Many families traveled by stage or Conestoga wagon from the East, along the National Road, beckoned to the area by rumors of plentiful and cheap land.

Generally before 1821, Catholics were served in mission stations, that is, private homes or public buildings, used only occasionally for the liturgy. Some of these earliest missions, like Somerset and Chillicothe, were set up by the initiative of local Catholics. In other areas Catholics were sought out by Fenwick who loved to say he was seeking "lost sheep" in the wilderness. There had been intermittent visits by missionaries before 1800 in the area that would later become Ohio. The Jesuits had accompanied explorers and as early as 1751 had built a chapel in the Sandusky area. Other missionaries attended Catholics as they traveled through the territory, but none remained long.[9]

Residence of Dominican friars, Somerset, Ohio

The lot of the missionaries was very difficult. Travelling mostly by horseback, they were constantly exposed to extremes of heat and cold through forested areas. Having no fixed salaries, they survived through the trifling collections they received or because of the farm produce the faithful donated. In a period of seven months in 1826 alone, two of the Dominican missionaries calculated that they had traveled 2500 miles.[10]

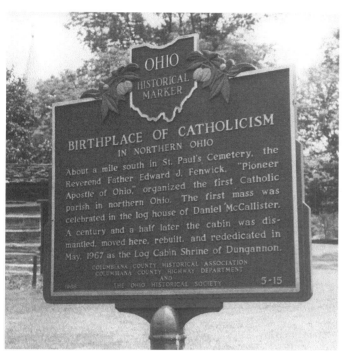

Historical marker at log house, Dungannon, Ohio

Before becoming bishop, Fenwick had served Catholics in northern Ohio in Canton, Wooster, Dalton, Chippewa and Marshallville. Some other early sites where he or Young brought the sacraments included Canal Fulton where Masses were celebrated in the Matthew Patton home. At Danville and Walnut Creek, Fenwick officiated before 1820, as well as in nearby Mt. Vernon. A Youngstown cabin, owned by Daniel and Jane Sheehy, situated almost on the Ohio state border, was the site where Fenwick celebrated the Eucharist for the first time in that area. The tiny village of Dungannon in Columbiana County maintains a shrine to Fenwick who celebrated the first Mass there in 1817. The original McAllister Cabin has been maintained over the years and the wooden dresser that served as the altar of sacrifice still demonstrates to visitors the importance of that occasion to the people of Ohio. The log cabin itself is on the list of state historic buildings.

The works of those early Dominican missionaries were greatly appreciated by Bishop Flaget of Bardstown, who had spiritual responsibility until 1821 for the entire Old Northwest, as well as for Kentucky. He himself visited Ohio, listened to the requests of the settlers, and marveled at the work of Edward Fenwick and his nephew. He it was who called for the creation of two new dioceses to be separated from Bardstown. One would serve Ohio, the other the Territory of Michigan, which extended north to the Canadian boundary and westward across Lake Michigan to the Mississippi River and beyond. The Dominican provincial Samuel Wilson agreed in principle with Bishop Flaget's ideas for Ohio. However, he feared that Flaget would suggest adding another French bishop to those who were already governing four of the six American dioceses. He wrote his fears to the head of the Order in Rome, urging some action which would lead to a Dominican being named bishop in Ohio.[11]

Flaget meanwhile was testing his ideas with the five other American bishops, all far removed from the frontier. He first proposed for Ohio either of two Fenwicks: the Jesuit, Benedict, well qualified by his theological knowledge and preaching, or the Dominican Edward, a cousin of Benedict, who had knowledge of the country and was "very popular" there. The latter, he knew, could get help from the men of his Order.

To serve Michigan Territory Bishop Flaget suggested Demetrius Gallitzin, the royal Russian missionary in Pennsylvania; his second suggestion was the French Sulpician Jean-Jacques Lartigue. In the same letter Flaget had a second thought about Gallitzin:

that he would be the right man for Ohio where German Catholics would receive him warmly. He even added a curious suggestion, namely that the Russian priest could make it easier for all involved by becoming a Dominican! The question of personal choice in response to an authentic vocation did not trouble the Sulpician bishop.[12] But lest that arrangement should entail insurmountable difficulties, Flaget wrote a second letter. This time he proposed again the Dominican Edward Fenwick for Ohio, since he was "a missionary full of zeal and humility." He mentioned the Dominican's lack of theological studies. Fenwick himself had always deplored the deficiency. In fact, Flaget admitted: "he has from all appearances . . . as much [learning] as I. If I have been made a bishop I do not see why the same dignity could not be conferred upon him."[13] Archbishop Maréchal concurred.

Unaware that the focus was on him, Edward Fenwick had in the meantime been busy describing the Ohio missions to his English confrere, John Hill, then in Rome. In a letter written in 1820 Fenwick estimated there were probably 3,000 Catholics scattered widely over 700 or 800 miles. The people were principally German and Irish, and the two Dominican missionaries had urgent need of a priest who knew German. The greatest need was for "apostolic men who can carry the burden of heat and cold, weariness, thirst; and who will not find it too difficult to travel across mountains and through valleys to seek out stray sheep." Pleased that Hill would soon be coming to join the friars in the United States, Fenwick expressed his hope that the English friar would bring from Rome the true spirit of the Order and that the newcomer would be "the Instrument in the hands of God to communicate it to others; truly a difficult thing in this wild country, and it costs something to form Religious according to the spirit of our holy Founder."[14]

In 1821 the official document arrived from Rome naming Edward Fenwick as the first Bishop of Cincinnati. With strong protests, citing his unworthiness for the task, Fenwick finally accepted the nomination as Bishop of Ohio. He assumed that responsibility in 1822. His charge included Catholics in the entire state of Ohio, and over the vast Michigan Territory that comprised the present states of Michigan and Wisconsin.

Jurisdiction of Bishop Fenwick, Cincinnati, Ohio, and missions of Michigan Territory

Territory of Michigan

Ohio

Cincinnati

Bishop Fenwick wrote officials in Rome expressing his formal gratitude for the favor bestowed on him. He realized that this position in the Church meant much to his Dominican brethren. Then he gave a panoramic view of his responsibilities as he saw them. Unlike some previously named bishops, he knew well the people and the territory now under his care. He described the length of Ohio as 240 miles and its width as 281 miles; an area in which he counted 6000 Catholics among its widespread population. He told of building the church at Somerset and "others in different parts of the province."[15] His people, mostly German, Irish and Swiss, were industrious and desirous of religious instruction. He recommended that a separate diocese be set up for Michigan Territory. To strengthen his suggestion, he described the extensive territory that embraced three Great Lakes, Huron, Superior and Michigan. He described the inhabitants as migrant fur traders, and thousands of Indians converted years before by the Jesuits. Both groups were without resident priests to serve them.

The new bishop did not wait long to begin the journey from Kentucky to Cincinnati, the Queen City of the West. Samuel Wilson, John Augustine Hill, and two young friars, John de Raymaecker and John Hynes, whom he had recently ordained, accompanied him. After a wet, cold journey, the bishop's party reached the Queen City on March 23 and there found temporary shelter. They were scarcely settled in the see city when they heard rumors of trouble in Kentucky. Bishop Flaget had expressed the fear that Wilson's presence in Ohio meant that all the Dominican friars would now be called to the Cincinnati diocese. Accordingly, he appealed to the office of Propaganda Fide to forbid such a move. The Roman officials obliged Flaget by sending Wilson a stern warning. He was told emphatically that he could not transfer his friars to another diocese without the consent of the local bishop.[16] After only four short months in Ohio, Wilson returned to Kentucky. His departure greatly concerned Fenwick, who had been fortunate to have the learned theologian whose wise counsel he valued. Now he did not have the support of a capable vicar. This would prove especially frustrating when he was required to be away from his diocese. But the bishop quickly immersed himself in the duties of his office and in learning about the affairs of his see city.

Established in 1788, Cincinnati had grown rapidly from a small frontier settlement to a prosperous river city. Now it surpassed in importance every other city in Ohio. Its position on the Ohio River attracted diverse economic interests, including trade, navigation and manufacturing. After the War of 1812, many New Englanders sought fortunes there; by 1830 Europeans, principally German and Irish, migrated in great numbers in search of employment. By 1830 the city had grown to 25,000. Rapid growth contributed to social crises. The first years of the nineteenth century were seriously charged with anti-Catholic bias. Cincinnati's immigrant population, already suspect to "nativists," could not expect to escape the prevailing bigotry.

Despite the apparent prosperity of Cincinnati, it was clear to the bishop that Catholics in the city and other areas in the state did not have sufficient income to support the pioneer church. They had little money to put into the collection basket on Sundays. At the frame cathedral, the donations on a Sunday amounted to two or three dollars. "With this modest sum," Fenwick wrote to the head of the Order, "I am forced to manage a household of 7 persons with 2 horses. Now I seek from your . . . Paternity how it is possible for me from such a small resource to provide not only for my own metropolis but for the entire region of Ohio."[17] He said he found joy in propagating the Order in America, but was not prepared for the difficulties entailed. In the same poignant letter he pleaded for priests and material aid. He told his superior he had hoped for greater support from the friars in Kentucky where he had given so much. He concluded by begging for attention to his needs.

To present his case to Roman officials, Fenwick borrowed money for the journey and left Cincinnati for Europe on May 30, 1823. He landed at Bordeaux on August 5 and continued on to Rome. Because of the death of the reigning pope, he had time to finalize his plans. On October 5, the new Pope Leo XII assumed office. When Fenwick met the pontiff the following day, he begged him to accept his resignation for reasons of incapacity and unworthiness. Leo would not grant this request but was touched upon hearing of Fenwick's poverty and his need for personnel. He gave Fenwick $1200 and many ecclesiastical articles needed in the new diocese.[18] The bishop referred to other offices in Rome his additional requests, such as the creation of two provinces in order to divide monetary resources, establishment of a diocese for Detroit, and assignment of a theologian for Ohio.

As Fenwick waited for a response to his requests, he lost no time in appealing for financial assistance from the Italian people. He described his diocese, the number of inhabitants, and its poverty. He told them of his welcome among Catholics who had not seen a priest for five or ten years, of his plans for building up a Church that included Indians and European immigrants as well as native-born Americans.[19] The bishop repeated this appeal in France, in Belgium, and in England. He varied the plea depending upon his audience, often telling about his parishioners' crude log cabin homes, their simplicity of lifestyle, and their eagerness to hear the word of God. He liked to explain that even those of other faiths came to hear the word of God when they learned that a missionary had come into their area.[20]

Financial assistance came Fenwick's way after these rousing talks. But he still needed personnel to carry out his dreams of spreading the Gospel. In Rome a German diocesan priest, Frederic Rese, offered his service for the German immigrants in Ohio. Encouraged by Rese's generosity, Fenwick left Rome for France hoping for more volunteers there. He was not disappointed. For ministry to the Indians and French-speaking fur traders in Michigan Territory the bishop obtained two French diocesan priests, Jean Bellamy and Pierre Déjean. For his continuing dream of having women religious to educate the young, Fenwick secured Sister Mary St. Paul, a French Sister of Mercy. All of the new volunteers departed for the United States, leaving Fenwick to continue his begging tour. Two experiences highlighted the bishop's travel in France. In Paris, Stephen Badin, the American missionary who had spent the previous five years in France, embraced Fenwick and introduced him to many Parisian Catholic authorities. The bishop quickly made his appeal to this sympathetic audience.

The second outstanding experience occurred when Fenwick reached Lyon. There he laid his financial problems before the Society for the Propagation of the Faith, a lay organization for raising and distributing monies to aid missionaries abroad. Fenwick's affability and modest demeanor favorably impressed the grand almoner, who awarded him eight thousand francs (equivalent to about 8000 dollars). In fact he promised to send Fenwick an annual donation.[21]

Fenwick ended his stay in Europe with a stop in England. There he made another appeal for funds. More important, he greeted many of his friends of the Order and assured the English friars that he sought no compensation for the years that Wilson and the other co-founders of the American Dominicans had labored for the English province. This compensation had been an earlier source of contention between John Hill and the provincial Pius Potier. With assurances of friendship Fenwick sailed from Liverpool toward the end of October 1824.

On the sea voyage home Fenwick had time to reflect. He counted as disappointments the fact that the Pope had refused to accept his resignation, that he had not obtained a theologian for Ohio, and that there was no new Detroit diocese to diminish his huge responsibility. He had mixed feelings about the feasibility of forming two separate provinces. He surely was happy about the amount of money safely deposited with Wright & Company of London and especially about the coming of Sister St. Paul and the three priests. It was well that Fenwick did not know of the changes that had occurred since his departure seventeen months earlier.

Fenwick reached the United States on December 1, 1824. While in the East he visited relatives, gave his fellow clergymen the latest news from abroad, and assisted wherever he could. When winter had passed he arranged transportation for his return to Cincinnati. Nicholas Dominic Young, Fenwick's nephew, asked John Dugan of Zanesville, a businessman and good friend of Fenwick, to drive his coach from Baltimore to Ohio. Gabriel Richard, missionary and Congressman from Michigan, joined the group for the journey westward. Near Cumberland, Maryland, on March 11, the horses bolted and ran away. Everyone was thrown from the coach and the baggage scattered. The only person seriously injured, however, was the driver, John Dugan. Only a few hours later, he died in Fenwick's arms.

Several weeks later, Fenwick finally reached Cincinnati. Many surprises awaited him. Without Samuel Wilson he had no one to supply a clear picture of the state of the diocese. Hill, head of the newly created province of St. Louis Bertrand in Ohio, was too busy at Somerset to be of service to him in Cincinnati. However, the bishop did enjoy visiting the little school recently organized by Sister Mary St. Paul. He expressed his pleasure with the good work of the other new recruit, Frederic Rese, who "learns English very fast and is working miracles with his Germans. He has already unearthed thirty-three Catholic families and has almost ruined the Lutheran Church, the pastor of which is spitting fire and flames against him. He preaches in German every Sunday and will soon begin in English." [22]

St. Peter's Cathedral, residence and Athenaeum, Cincinnati, 1830

Fenwick found one surprise distressing. In the bishop's absence, Hill had arranged for the building of a three-story brick house as an episcopal residence. This pretentious structure stood in great contrast to the humble little frame church that served as the

cathedral. Hill left the bishop with a debt of $4000 for the episcopal residence.[23] The contrast between his imposing house and the little frame church did not last long. Fenwick made plans to build a fitting cathedral immediately. He secured the land, hired an architect and by August of 1825, the walls of the building were nearly finished. Work progressed so rapidly that on June 29, the first Mass was celebrated in the yet unfinished structure. The new cathedral, named St. Peter's, measured 100 feet by 50 feet, a large church for this area of the country. Cincinnati residents delighted in this elegant yet simply appointed place of worship.[24]

With the completion of the cathedral, Fenwick devoted more time to securing priests to preach the Gospel and placing the ones already in his diocese. In Michigan Territory he could rely on Gabriel Richard, a Sulpician sent to the Detroit area by Bishop Carroll in 1798. Now the bishop sent two more missionaries, Anthony Ganilh and Vincent Badin, the younger brother of the veteran Kentucky missionary, Stephen Badin. Vincent was the first man ordained to the priesthood by Fenwick in Ohio, at the end of March 1822. Just two years later Pierre Déjean and Jean Bellamy arrived from France to lighten the clerical burdens in Michigan. These men served wherever Gabriel Richard sent them until Fenwick could become better acquainted with the needs of the area.

The number of priests in Ohio and Michigan Territory fluctuated from year to year. There were defections, requests to return to Europe or serve in other dioceses, and deaths of young and old. Through the 1820s, Fenwick and his fellow Dominicans established many parishes and helped parishioners build their churches. By mid-decade they were ably assisted by diocesan clergy. Two parishes still bear witness to the friars' attempt to give permanence to local congregations. They are St. Thomas in Zanesville and St. John in Canton.

The historic city of Zanesville took its name from Zane's Trace, the first road through Ohio. Ebenezer Zane, with the help of relatives, blazed the trail from Wheeling to Maysville, Kentucky, and started settlements along the trace. The city of Zanesville, named for him, was settled in 1799. There the friars ministered to Catholic settlers and encouraged the erection of a new stone and brick church in March 1823, on land donated by John Dugan. Stephen Hyacinth Montgomery, who served as first resident pastor, solicited funds far and wide, and even abroad, to pay for the new church. Dominican priests still serve St. Thomas Church in that city.

St. John Parish in Canton, where Edward Fenwick celebrated Mass in 1817, was an important mission station of the Dominican friars of Somerset. One of the earliest settlers in the city in 1806, John Shorb, offered his home for the celebration of the Eucharist until the new brick church was built in 1824. He donated five acres of land suitably located for the structure, but did not live to see the work completed. During construction, in July of 1824, Shorb suffered a fatal blow from a falling beam. Bishop Fenwick himself dedicated the new church and offered the first Mass in it. John Augustine Hill, much beloved as the first resident pastor of St. John's, used this parish as his missionary staging ground, riding many miles in order to preach the Word. Hill attended to the spiritual needs of the parishioners of St. John's until his death in 1828.

Somerset's close proximity to Zane's Trace and the National Road accounted for its rapid growth. By 1828, its first log church had reached its capacity. Nicholas Young, founding pastor, and his uncle Edward knew a larger structure was needed.

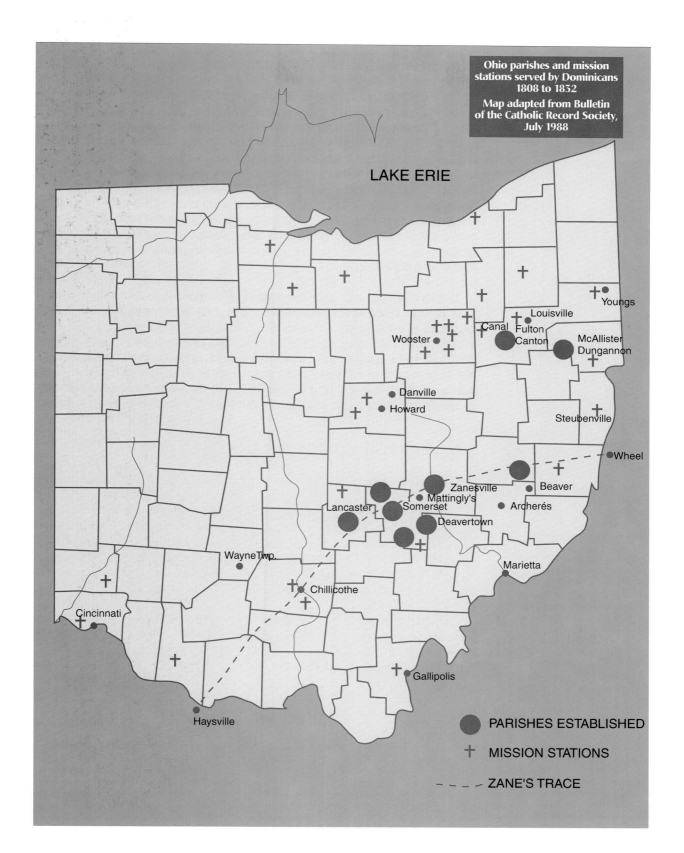

LAKE ERIE

Youngs

Louisville

Wooster   Canal   Fulton
Canton

McAllister
Dungannon

Danville

Howard

Steubenville

Wheel

Zanesville   Beaver

Lancaster   Mattingly's
Somerset   Archerés

Deavertown

WayneTwp.

Marietta

Chillicothe

Cincinnati

Gallipolis

Haysville

⬤   PARISHES ESTABLISHED

✝   MISSION STATIONS

- - - -   ZANE'S TRACE

123

This second church with a steeple visible for miles around opened in 1829, with N.D. Young officiating.

The friar Thomas Martin also devoted many hours on horseback to bring the Gospel to Catholics in northern Ohio. After the historic ground breaking for the Ohio Canal in Cleveland in 1826, Martin tended to the spiritual needs of the Irish laborers brought to the Cleveland-Akron area for that project. Daniel O'Leary, a young Dominican brought to America by Hill, served in Ohio after his ordination and profession. At Somerset he became an inspiration to his brothers. One wrote that in March of 1830, "at nine o'clock on a pitch-black night, while a torrential rain was falling, a man knocked at the door, asking for a priest to carry the viaticum to a gravely ill person ninety miles distant. Father O'Leary, . . . not in the least disconcerted by the storm and darkness, . . . mounted his horse, and set out cheerfully."[25] The witness, Samuel Mazzuchelli, the young Dominican missionary, stated that such happenings were common in Ohio.

Diocesan priests soon made significant contributions to building the Church in Ohio. Frederic Rese, the first of the diocesan priests whom Fenwick relied upon, came specifically to minister to German-speaking parishioners of the cathedral and nearby missions. But he did more than that; he cared deeply for Fenwick and in the bishop's declining years reminded him of duties and obligations he was prone to forget. James Mullon, ordained as a diocesan priest by Fenwick in 1825, proved to be one of the most successful preachers, especially in Ohio. It was he who accompanied Fenwick on his visit to the Indians in Michigan Territory in 1829 and left a written account.

Parishes in the Cincinnati diocese and the new diocese of Detroit (1833). Parishes then served by Dominicans are underlined.

John de Raymaecker ministered to the Germans in Canton, and later assisted Young and Martin. He made a considerable contribution to the preaching mission when Fenwick sent him to Europe in 1827, to secure more priests for the Ohio diocese. He returned bringing three diocesan seminarians who were a credit to the Church: John Martin Henni, Martin Kundig, and John Baptist Clicteur.

In 1829, Fenwick ordained the three seminarians brought by Raymaecker as diocesan clergy. Henni's first assignment was to be resident pastor at Canton. He carried on the Dominican practice of reaching out to many settlements in northern Ohio. Martin Kundig served first as teacher at the seminary in Cincinnati, then as travelling missionary to the German-speaking Catholics in southern Ohio.

John B. Clicteur became Fenwick's secretary after ordination. In that capacity he informed the Society for the Propagation of the Faith in France about the Ohio church. In one longer report, he wrote of many converts attracted by the kindness of Ohio priests; of the diocesan seminary that would open in a few months; and of the coming of socialist Robert Owen. Clicteur attended a lecture by this controversial figure, describing him as "somber and neglected" in appearance, whose face "carried visible marks of trouble and combat."[26] In commenting on Owen's failure at New Harmony, Indiana, Clicteur said, "the spirit of the people in this country is not disposed to a system of unbelief." This young priest's days of service were abruptly ended by death seven months after ordination. Hill's death in 1828, Clicteur's in 1829, and that of Munos in 1830 must have been a severe blow to Fenwick's hopes for a sufficient supply of laborers in his vineyard.

Two unusual priests who ministered under Bishop Fenwick in Michigan Territory deserve mention. They served the native tribes in the territory north of Ohio. Samuel Mazzuchelli, O.P., and Frederic Baraga arrived late in Fenwick's tenure as bishop, but after the bishop's death rendered valuable service for many years. Both became aware of Fenwick's needs during Rese's visit to Europe in 1827. The story of Mazzuchelli and his ministry is told in chapter 7. Even before Mazzuchelli left for his mission territory, Frederic Baraga was writing from Austria that he wished to transfer to the Cincinnati Diocese. He had become aware of Fenwick's need from a little booklet in German, edited by Fredric Rese "in which I read with tears how few workers there are in your diocese, while the harvest is most abundant."[27] He noted that he had the necessary permissions from his bishop and from Austrian Emperor Augustus. He needed only Fenwick's acceptance.[28] There was no hesitation on Fenwick's part. In his mind Baraga was already placed in Michigan, since the departure of Father Bellamy for China and the return of Pierre Déjean to France. Baraga arrived in Cincinnati in January 1831 where he joined the Bishop's household. There he studied both English and the Ottawa language while waiting for the journey north in the summer of that year. Fenwick was delighted to have Baraga as his travelling companion to the Ottawa Nation where he replaced Déjean at Arbre Croche.

To Fenwick, the last and perhaps the greatest surprise candidate who volunteered to serve in the rugged Michigan Territory was his old friend, Stephen Badin. Now almost seventy years old, Badin had returned from France in 1828, and offered his services for the Indian missions. Fenwick's wise suggestion that he serve at Mission St. Joseph with the Pottawatamies proved to be pleasing to Badin as well as to Pokagan, their chief. Badin gave himself tirelessly as he had always done, setting up a school for children, and writing frankly of all the needs of his mission.

Later several clergymen who had served under Fenwick distinguished themselves as bishops in various American dioceses: John Henni in Milwaukee, Richard Miles in Nashville and Frederick Baraga in Marquette.

Bishop Fenwick's plans for the American Dominican missions always included women religious working in collaboration with the friars. He rejoiced at the establishment of the Kentucky Sisters and wanted a similar group in Ohio. He was not alone in his wish to have Dominican sisters in the state. In 1825, John Hill wrote to Nicholas Young suggesting that he persuade Miles to bring the sisters to Ohio, adding that "Somerset would be better for them and for us" and listing the advantages for such a move.[29]

Fenwick's first effort to have the service of women religious was disappointing. He held great hope for the school that Sister Mary St. Paul established in Cincinnati. Shortly after her arrival in 1824, she had opened a school for girls with the help of Eliza Rose Powell, a convert in Kentucky. So pleased was Fenwick with the school when he returned from Europe in 1825, that he wrote the Mother Superior in France asking for more members of her congregation.[30] The disappointment that no more sisters arrived was compounded by the death of Mary St. Paul in September of 1827. Of necessity the school was closed.

The second venture was of even shorter duration. Both Fenwick and Stephen Badin had invited the Collettine Poor Clare nuns in Bruges to come to Cincinnati. Two of them, Francoise Vindevoghel and Victoire de Selles arrived in 1826. The third arrival was a Beguine from Ghent, Adelphine Malingie. They joined Sister St. Paul in her school in 1827 and taught seventy pupils. When Adelphine decided to leave the group the school was closed. The Poor Clares accepted an invitation to Pittsburgh, rejecting Fenwick's request that they go to Canton.[31] Thus they stayed in Ohio only fourteen months.

Fenwick was not satisfied with only one school. In 1825 he asked for women of Mother Seton's Sisters of Charity. John Dubois, the priest who acted as guide for the sisters, refused unless Fenwick could guarantee their financial security.[32] This the Bishop could not do. Undaunted, he waited for better times. In 1829 Fenwick wrote to the superior of the Charity Sisters, inviting them to open "a female orphan asylum under your zealous & charitable care. . . ."[33] He assured them of a "good & comfortable house" rent free, and $200 in cash annually for their support. They accepted this generous offer. Escorted by James Mullon, four sisters arrived in Cincinnati in October: Francis Xavier Jordan, Victoria Fitzgerald, Beatrice Tyler, and Albina Levy.[34] The Sisters of Charity continue to give generous service, not only in Cincinnati, but also in many parts of the country today.

Fenwick still had dreams of Dominican Sisters sharing his ministry in Ohio. His hopes finally became reality early in 1830. On January 11, four sisters from St. Magdalene, Kentucky, escorted by Stephen H. Montgomery, left for Ohio. The women who opened this first Dominican convent in Somerset were Benven Sansbury, Emily Elder, Agnes Harbin and Catherine Mudd. To break the long journey, the sisters rested a week in Cincinnati where they met and conferred with Fenwick. **The U.S. Catholic Miscellany** for February 20, 1830, noted that "Four sisters of the order of St. Dominic called from their monastery in Kentucky . . . passed through Cincinnati on their way to Somerset, Perry Co., Ohio." They planned to establish a female school there; they were "qualified, devoted to the cause of moral and religious instruction," and much good was anticipated from their presence.

The sisters arrived in Somerset on February 5 and named their establishment St. Mary's. Emily Elder became their first superior, and Benven Sansbury, the procurator. The story of their coming to Ohio is best told by Benven herself in her valuable journal written in pencil on brown paper, appropriately called the "brown paper annals." She wrote

The Sisters of St. Mary's Community at Somerset in 1830, having been invited by Bishop Fenwick . . . some times previous to their departure . . . had a rugged journey to Louisville. Staid [sic] there a few days in company with Father Montgomery [Stephen] who was their pilot to their destination. Staid [sic] a week with Bishop Fenwick under whose auspices the foundation of St. Mary's was made. When the Sisters arrived at Somerset the place where they were to stop, the house that had been purchased for them was not vacated. . .they had to find hospitality with H. & Peter Dittoe's for three weeks. . . .the Dominican Sisters created quite a sensational stir among the citizens.

The residents of Somerset had never seen a religious Sister. Benven recorded that their first house was a small brick structure on an acre of ground that also included a carpenter's shop. Shortly after settling in, the sisters opened their "female academy." When the bishop found there was demand for a boarding school, she reported that he "gave them the money to build a house & was doing his very best in every way. . . .

St. Mary's, Somerset, 1834

ST. MARY'S SEMINARY, Somerset, Ohio.

This Seminary was commenced about three years ago, and has been as liberally patronized as its friends could have expected.

The institution is under the immediate inspection of the Rev. N. D. Young, who occasionally examines the pupils and encourages their progress. To reward merit and excite emulation, medals are monthly distributed. On the last of July a general Examination is held, and the month of August annually observed as vacation.

The ladies who govern this Seminary have consecrated themselves to the service of God and the instruction of female youth. Among them is a French lady, well qualified to teach the French language. By a conscientious care of their pupils and strict attention to their advancement, by inculcating neatness, good manners, politeness, and moral principles, they hope to merit public patronage. The religion professed by these is the Catholic; parents, however, need not apprehend, that any solicitations will be used to induce children of a different persuasion to embrace the Catholic. Pupils of all denominations are received, from the age of 6 to 16. They will be required to submit only to the general regulations of the Seminary, viz. to attend morning and evening prayer and Divine service on Sundays and Holidays: this being a necessary regulation for the observance of discipline.

THE SYSTEM OF EDUCATION

Embraces the English and French Languages, Orthography, Reading, Writing, Arithmetic, Geography, (with the use of the Globes,) History, Rhetoric, Plain Sewing, Marking and Ornamental Needle Work, Music on the Piano Forte, Drawing, Painting, Fancy work and Embroidery.—Particular attention is paid in teaching Orthography, Reading, Writing, and the Grammar of both languages.

Terms for Day Scholars.

Orthography, Reading, Writing, and Arithmetic, $8 per annum—$2 per quarter.

to raise up the school, gave a piano, celestial and Terrestial globes, a valuable relic case with 30 & more relics . . . . some oil paintings and very many things."

The sisters' convent was in Holy Trinity parish, Somerset, a foundation still staffed by the Dominican friars. Father Nicholas Young and local parishioners assisted them in building a new convent in the fall of 1830. "The first building," Benven wrote, "was a two story-brick, 40 by 35 feet, with good basement and useful attic." Members of the parish made the brick, put up the building and did the carpenter work. She noted that "Brick could be got $3 per thousand – carpenters worked for a dollar per day – all kinds of provisions could be bought for a mere trifle. Chickens, eggs, butter in great or small quantities for 2 & 3 cts per [unit] – Beef & Pork 2 – Wheet [sic] 37 – Corn 25 cts. Oates [sic] 15c" [35]

The number of sisters at St. Mary's increased with the arrival of Sisters from Kentucky and prospective candidates. In 1831 Helen Whelan and Columba Walsh came from Kentucky. In the same year came Ursula Grignon, a parishioner of Samuel Mazzuchelli's mission in Green Bay, Wisconsin, who as a novice took the name of Sister Mary. She was the daughter of a French-Canadian father and a Chippewa mother. Fluent in French and the Chippewa language, Sister Mary planned to return to Green Bay later to teach her tribal people.

Bishop Fenwick himself escorted Ursula to Somerset in 1831 when he returned from one of his visits to various Indian tribes living near Lake Michigan. About a month after her arrival in Ohio, Ursula wrote to her parents about her new life. There were six sisters at her convent and a superior "whom we call Mother, who is very amiable." Ursula wanted them to know something of her daily routine:

> I am now going to tell you the state of affairs. In the morning at 3:30 the bell rings and we must get up without fail. It rings again for community prayer and a half hour of meditation; at six we go to work, at seven the rosary, after breakfast we recite our lessons, at 8 to work. There is not a minute lost. . . . I am going to tell you all I study: geography, grammar, etymology of words, correct the incorrect syntax, American history and arithmetic. Now for the [crafts]: sewing work on marquise lace, make flowers, knit, learn notes (music). That is what I am studying at present.

She concluded her letter, "May God keep you all, my dear and darling family." [36]

When her novitiate ended Ursula taught French in the Sisters' Academy which by 1832 numbered 60 young women. Another candidate, Jane Lynch from nearby Zanesville, joined St. Mary's community in 1832. She received the religious name Rose and later served the community as Mother Rose for many years. The record of receptions notes that she received the habit on April 30, 1832, and that "her noviceship began May 5, 1832." She was the first of six Lynches to enter the Dominican Order, including Monica, the mother of the family, and a brother who joined the friars.

A few months after the sisters arrived from Kentucky, Bishop Fenwick indicated to the Vicar General some reasons why he wished all the Dominican Sisters could be brought to Ohio:

OHIO.
RECEPTION OF A NUN.
From the U. S. Catholic Press.

Mr. Editor—On the 13th of Feb. being in Somerset, Ohio, I was much gratified in witnessing the edifying ceremony of the reception of a young lady to the religious habit of the order of St. Dominic, in the catholic church of that pretty little village. Being by casuality a spectator, and seeing the admonition of our divine Lord or rather his evangelical counsel to renounce " all things," even " father and mother," for his sake, practically observed by this female. I thought as one of your subscribers, who take great pleasure in reading such information in your and other catholic publications, that a short account of this ceremony, the first I have ever had the pleasure to witness, would not be uninteresting to the generality to your readers.

The establishment situated in the precincts of Somerset, was commenced two years ago. The ladies, six in number, were procured from a similar house in Kentucky by the Right Rev. Dr. Fenwick, who, I believe, is of the order of St. Dominic, and its superior general in this country. They commenced in a small house purchased for them with one acre of ground attached, by the same zealous prelate. The house soon proving too confined for the discharge of their religious duties, the end of their institute, and the instruction of youth, they were compelled to build one more suitable last year. This house which I had the pleasure of examining, (as all strangers have that liberty,) is very commodiously arranged, but is, I am persuaded even already too circumscribed to answer their purposes. The young female, the subject of this communication, as I am informed, is a French lady, who came here sometime last year for the object of dedicating herself in the life she has now so solemnly embraced ; at least, I understood from the preacher on the occasion, after one year's trial or noviceship as he called it, she will solemnly ratify by vow, what she has begun, should she persevere in her desire, and the other sisters who have already made their vows, elect her to be a future member of their community. Every thing of importance, I am told, is decided among these sisters by the ballot box, and one of the Rev. gentlemen of the Dominican order observed to me in my examination of the establishment, that this was a peculiar feature in their constitutions, and made the order like a little republic. " The principles," said he, " by which it is governed varying but little from our republican system." But to return to the ceremony--I was told that the young lady had a good French education; she will of course prove a great acquisition to the establishment, as a French teacher in the seminary. The ceremony of reception was indeed very impressive. Not long after I had taken my seat in the church, a procession of young ladies forming two rows came from the convent; these I presume were the pupils of the seminary; after them followed the candidate for the veil, dressed in the finest style, decorated with flowers and other ornaments used by the *beau monde*; on her side were two of the largest girls, she bearing a cross in her hand, emblematic I suppose of her intended change, from the worldly to the religious life. After them followed six nuns, dressed in the humble habiliments of their order, of white domestic flannel, a striking emblem of the purity, we may suppose, that adorns their hearts. The procession advanced into the church with slow pace as far as the railing of the sanctuary, when the girls turned to the right and left, leaving the candidate in the middle making her prostration. The sisters were directed by the officiating clergyman to take their seats on the gospel side of the sanctuary.

Professions in the Convent of St. Mary

I hereby make it fully appear to my satisfaction, that I made my profession in the above mentioned Convent according to the rule and Constitution of the Order of St. Dominick being legally constituted and authorized to receive my profession Sister Benvenuta Sansbury, Superior of the said Convent, Sister Helen Whelan, Mother of Novices. & Very Revd. F. Dominick Young. Pro. of the same Order, & Director of the Community.

I do, therefore, by virtue of these present, and in testimony thereof, I have here unto subscribed my name, This 19 Day of February A. D. 1833.

Sister Mary Grignon

Sister Agnes Harbin
✝ Sister Rose Lynch at Nesi

Witnesses

129

> We have called to the Diocese of Ohio four Sisters of St. Dominic from Kentucky giving them an establishment here: they already have a large number of scholars and are prospering. And we have sent other maidens, good young women, to the Kentucky Mother House to make their novitiate and then to be recalled here. . . . We can never spend our alms for the Dominican Sisters of another Diocese and therefore we will strive to have them all come into Ohio where they will then be able to participate in the alms which we beg from Europe because their reestablishment . . . will redound to the good of our diocese by their undertaking the education of youth. They play the office of missionary among us.[37]

The residents of Somerset and its environs patronized St. Mary's Seminary, as the academy was officially called. The *Catholic Telegraph*, the diocesan newspaper, praised the work of the sisters and the excellence of their school. The enrollment grew as the number on the staff increased. The *Prospectus* of the school listed details of terms, the system of education, and regulations for entrance. One of the offerings was French, no doubt taught by Sister Mary (Ursula) Grignon.

Correspondence indicates that both Fenwick and Nicholas Young continued to show concern for the sisters. Young wrote to Fenwick that "the sisters' house goes on slowly. All are well except Sister Catharine. . . . Ursula is sometimes a little melancholy."[38] The following March 1832, Fenwick wrote to Ursula's father, Louis Grignon, that she was in perfect health, contented, happy, and beautiful in her [Dominican] habit."[39] The sisters were incorporated by the Ohio State legislature under the title of St. Mary's Female Literary Society on December 17, 1832. The Act of Incorporation stated that "Elizabeth Sansbury, Elizabeth A. Harbin, Ann C. Walsh, and Julia Mudd and their associates . . . are hereby created a body politic and corporate with perpetual succession." The stabilizing effect of this act was emphasized by Nicholas Young, "I have received the Act of Incorporation for our sisters—this will save [them] much trouble and will make the institution more generally known."[40]

Although the Dominican friars in Kentucky maintained St. Thomas Aquinas College successfully, Fenwick felt that he could take little credit for it because he was so seldom there. However, letters indicate that his earliest plans to establish the Order in Maryland had included an institution of higher learning in Cincinnati. The bishop decided this would be a seminary to form a native clergy accustomed to the habits of the people, their language, and the primitive terrain. The seminary opened on May 11, 1829, with the best staff possible from his clergy.

The last building Fenwick planned was a college. This was surely an ambitious project, well beyond the responsibility of a bishop on the frontier. Known as the Athenaeum, it opened in October, 1831 with Fenwick as its president. Since that position was incompatible with his other duties, the bishop named James Mullon as the president. *The Catholic Telegraph* listed tuition for a year as $150, including boarding, washing, and mending. Students furnished their own beds and bedding. In addition to tuition for the regular curriculum of classical courses, there were fees for Music, Drawing and Painting, Italian and German languages. For Natural and Experimental Philosophy, each enrollee paid $10 "to supply the many instruments usually broken by the young experimenters." [41]

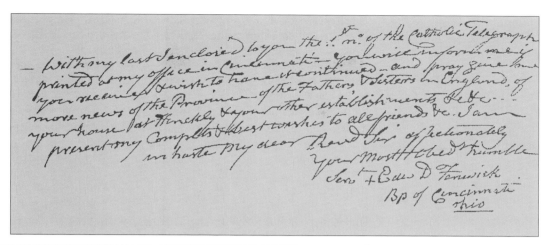

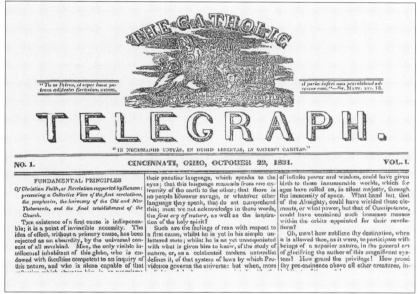

The Cincinnati *CATHOLIC TELEGRAPH*, first issue

In addition to formal structures of education, Bishop Fenwick considered the newspaper an instrument of instruction. Beyond communicating with his own people on matters of faith, he could use the paper to answer unjust accusations constantly leveled against Catholics by Protestant journals. The initial issue of the *Catholic Telegraph* appeared on October 22, 1831. Thus Cincinnati had the honor of sponsoring the first diocesan paper west of the Alleghenies. The newspaper continues to the present time.

Tensions between bishops and men of religious orders occurred from the earliest days in the United States. John Carroll had his differences with the Sulpicians in Maryland, and Benedict Flaget with the Dominicans in Kentucky. So the strained relations that developed in Ohio between Fenwick and his friars over the ownership of church properties were not new. It is to the credit of both parties that these tensions did not impede the spread of the Gospel.

As long as Fenwick and his friars constituted the sole missionaries in Ohio, there was no problem with deeds for church properties being in the name of the Dominicans. Once he became bishop, however, Fenwick's perspective changed. His first challenge arose early in 1825. While he was in Europe during the years 1823 and 1824, his Vicar, John Hill, directed diocesan affairs. He conveyed five different properties to the Dominican friars in his own name or in the name of other members.[42] Fenwick complained to Archbishop Maréchal of Baltimore, "All this was done in my absence & by a presumptive or tacit consent on which the clergymen, my Bro. Dominicans acted." Fenwick felt he had been betrayed. He wrote to Bishop Louis Dubourg of New Orleans that he was considering the removal of Hill from his confidence. Dubourg counseled Fenwick not to engage in a fatal rupture with Hill. "Though he may be impractical and rash he is very zealous," Dubourg wrote.[43]

Previously, Fenwick himself had signed over to the Dominican Province the properties in Ohio that had been deeded to him as he journeyed throughout the state as an itinerant missionary. Now worried about his right to do so, he again asked the opinion of Bishop Dubourg. The older bishop, then serving the Diocese of New Orleans, assured Fenwick that he saw no breach of the vow of poverty in disposing of the property in favor of the Dominicans. The property had become that of his Order because the vow of poverty made Fenwick merely the agent of the transfer.[44] Francis Patrick Kenrick, theologian for Bishop Flaget of Bardstown, aptly summed up Fenwick's dilemma:

> The Bishop is crucified in spirit, doubting what goods he ought to cede to his Order, what to retain for himself, what churches to be handed over to their control and with what accompanying conditions. Illustrious to be sure in purity of morals but by no means expertly informed about the Sacred canons. . . .[45]

Kenrick's private judgment was that Fenwick should have put all these properties into the hands of the bishop of the diocese. The friars, unable to solve the dilemma themselves, wisely submitted the matter to officials in Rome so that preaching the Word could continue.

Bishop Fenwick in 1829 was able to turn his attention, at last, to a mission dear to his heart: the Indians and fur traders in Michigan Territory. From his first days as bishop, he demonstrated concern for their plight. He wrote to Stephen Badin in 1823, "I intend . . . to have two missionaries travelling continually from place to place, especially devoting their labors and services to the Indians. For that purpose, it is necessary I should have a fund or fixed pension for such laborious and useful men. . . ."[46] In northern Ohio alone, as he told Badin, there were two thousand Indians. Some of these were Catholics who had to cross Lake Erie to Canada to have their marriages celebrated and their children baptized by a Catholic priest.

Because of the American removal policy, the Indians were pushed farther and farther west by the United States Government. As white settlers encroached upon Indian lands, no government action prevented their seizure of tribal territory. By Fenwick's time, various migrant tribes had become identified with certain locations. The Ottawas, centered in Arbre Croche, occupied lands on the eastern shores of Lake Michigan. The Chippewas or Objibwas settled at Mackinac Island near the junction of Lakes Huron and Michigan, while the Menominees remained around Green Bay, near the northwestern shores of Lake Michigan. Close to the foot of Lake Michigan, the Pottawatomies lived at River St. Joseph. Fenwick sent missionaries to all these tribes.

Besides sending available diocesan priests, the bishop encouraged his friars to seek out any Indians still remaining in Ohio. John Hill was the only Dominican of whom Fenwick wrote concerning his Ohio mission to the Indians: "His journeys took him to the shores of Lake Erie during the great heats of July and August. He made many conversions, baptized twenty-two adults, among them two Indians, reconciled four marriages and heard many confessions."[47] In the 1820s and 1830s, when Fenwick felt impelled to evangelize the Indians, some bishops of the Catholic Church seemed unmindful of these forgotten peoples. Fenwick himself visited the natives on three different occasions during the years 1829, 1831, and 1832. He praised the fervor of the native tribes for their eagerness to hear the Word from their beloved "blackrobes."

In 1829 the bishop returned to Ohio with two fifteen-year-old Ottawa youths from Arbre Croche: William Maccatebinessi and Augustine Hamelin. He wrote to a friend abroad that he would enroll these boys in English classes in Cincinnati, and if they still had aspirations toward the priesthood, he would send them to Rome to study. [48] These were the first known tribesmen to journey to Rome as candidates for the priesthood.[49]

On the night of June 13, 1832, Fenwick and August Jeanjean, a priest of the New Orleans diocese, began what proved to be the bishop's last trip north. They reached Michigan in early July, having visited mission stations in Ohio before boarding the boat in Cleveland for Detroit. At this point the dread cholera recurred. The bishop wrote to Rese that several sailors had died from it and were carried ashore and buried.[50] The travellers reached Mackinac on July 17. There the bishop became ill. He was able only to visit his beloved Ottawas and their pastor Frederic Baraga at Arbre Croche. He could not go to Green Bay because he was so ill.

Frederic Baraga (1797–1868), missioned to the Ottawa and Chippewa tribes of Michigan by Bishop Fenwick

On Mackinac Island at the cottage of Samuel Mazzuchelli, Fenwick spent time with the intrepid missionary. His illness gave rise to a deep sense of sadness, and the prospect of death haunted him. Mazzuchelli wrote in his *Memoirs* that it pained him to see the suffering and even the sense of guilt that Fenwick endured. The young Dominican reminded the bishop of all his labors during many years in Kentucky, Ohio and Michigan and that his "upright intentions would be seen by a just and merciful Judge." [51] When he was again able to travel, Fenwick returned by way of Detroit where he found Gabriel Richard also gravely ill with cholera. He then journeyed on, stopping to minister at several places in Ohio.

The cholera only heightened Fenwick's premonition of approaching death. Weakened from years of exhausting travel, he was a prime subject for contracting the disease. He reached Canton, Ohio, before he felt the full effect of his illness. There he visited the pastor of St. John's, John Henni, and his long-time friend and teacher in the parish, Eliza Rose Powell. When Miss Powell noticed the deterioration in the bishop's condition, she determined to travel with him to Cincinnati. This was September 25, 1832. When their coach stopped at Wooster, Fenwick went to an inn where he died the next day. Attended by doctors, he had only one person he knew, Eliza Powell, with him during his last hours. Because of fear of the spread of cholera, Fenwick was buried that day in Wooster. Later his body was laid to rest in a mausoleum at St. Joseph Cemetery in Cincinnati.

Although little has been written about Fenwick's role in preaching the Gospel in Ohio, the facts show that he led his Dominican brethren in bringing the Word to all parts of the state and revived the faith in many parts of Michigan Territory. He deserves the title "Apostle of Ohio," and remembrance of his ministry to the Indian tribes whose needs were ignored by society and even the Church. The Archdiocese of Cincinnati still benefits from institutions that Fenwick built when workers in the vineyard were few and resources were a precious commodity.

1. Jacob Dittoe to John Carroll, Lancaster, Jan. 5, 1805, Archives, Archdiocese of Baltimore (AAB) 3 D 7.

2. Whaland Goodee and Major Philips, Chillicothe, OH, Feb. 1, 1807, AAB 10 I 6.

3. Fenwick to A Friend in London, Washington, D.C., 1818, Saint Joseph Province Archives (SJP).

4. Conewago was an early Jesuit mission in Pennsylvania from which many settlers moved west to Somerset, Canton, Cincinnati and other towns in Ohio.

5. N.D. Young to his father Nicholas Young Esqr., Somerset, Dec. 4, 1818, SJP. In their generosity the Youngs had contributed two sums to young Nicholas for the Ohio mission: the one of $500, the other, $30. Elsewhere in this letter the young friar tells of losing the smaller sum kept out for traveling money; but not the $500, which he had prudently deposited in his saddle bags.

6. Liberty Hall, Cincinnati, Dec. 11, 1811, Cincinnati Public Library.

7. Copied in the Catholic Telegraph, 1858, XXVII, 4.

8. The plea published in the **Mirror** of Baltimore, signed by a committee of four men, was copied in the **Catholic Telegraph** 1867, XXXVI, 4.

9. See Thomas W. Tifft, "Ohio, Catholic Church in," **The Encyclopedia of American Catholic History,** 1997 ed., 1084-1086.

10. U.S. Catholic Miscellany, Feb. 24, 1827.

11. Wilson to John Hill (for transmission to Giuseppe Gaddi, Vicar General, O.P.), St. Rose, Mar. 6, 1820, Archives, Propaganda Fide, Rome (APF) IV, 608rv. At that date there were five dioceses besides the Archdiocese of Baltimore, whose bishop was Ambrose

Maréchal. The other bishops were Jean-Louis Cheverus, Boston; Benedict Joseph Flaget, Bardstown; John Connolly, New York; Michael Egan, Philadelphia; and Louis Dubourg, New Orleans.

12. Flaget to Ambrose Maréchal, Bardstown, March 7, 1820, University of Notre Dame Archives (UNDA), B.C.A., Box 3.

13. Flaget to Maréchal, Bardstown, Mar. 16, 1820, UNDA, B.C.A., Box 3.

14. Fenwick to John Augustine Hill, Georgetown, MD, June 1, 1820, APF Am.Cent., IV, 610r-611r.

15. Fenwick to Propaganda Fide, Kentucky, Jan. 25, 1822, APF VII, 143rv-144rv.

16. Propaganda Fide to S.T.Wlson, Rome, July 22, 1822, SJP.

17. Fenwick to Viviani, Rome, Sept., 1823, APF IX, 117rv-118r.

18. Propaganda Fide to Fenwick Rome, Jan. 12, 1824, UNDA II 4 d.

19. Fenwick to the Italian People, Rome, Oct. 12, 1823, SJP.

20. The Catholic Miscellany, III, 1824, 92.

21. "Mission de L'Ohio," **Annales** (1826): 94.

22. Fenwick to (unknown), Cincinnati, March 29, 1825, **Catholic Columbian,** Columbus, Ohio, Oct., 1882.

23. Samuel L. Montgomery to O'Finan, St. Rose, Aug. 16, 1832, San Clemente Archives, Rome (SCA).

24. U.S. Catholic Miscellany, May 3, 1828, 343.

25. Samuel Mazzuchelli, **The Memoirs of Father Samuel Mazzuchelli,** (Chicago, Il: Priory Press, 1967) 19.

26. Clicteur to Rigagnon, Cincinnati, June 28, 1829, **Annales** 514-521.

Several years earlier, a prominent citizen of Cincinnati asked Fenwick's opinion of Robert Owen. The bishop wrote that Owen's philosophy "is flattering to the senses & dazling [sic] to the mind. . . but confined only to temporal prosperity. . . ." Fenwick to George Guilford, Cincinnati Apr. 26, 1825, UNDA II 4 d. This letter is unusual because Fenwick seldom wrote about political and social events of his time.

27. Baraga to Fenwick, Illyria, Nov. 13, 1829, UNDA II 4 d.

28. Baraga to Fenwick. He wrote the same letter on Apr. 5, 1830, thinking that Fenwick never received his earlier letter. Because of the union of Church and State in his native country, Baraga needed the permission of the head of State, Augustus.

29. Hill to Young, Somerset, May 31, 1825, UNDA II 4 d.

30. Fenwick to Madame la Superiore, Cincinnati, July 8, 1825, SJP.

31. Charles Maguire, OFM to Fenwick, Pittsburgh, Apr. 28, 1828, Cincinnati Archdiocesan Archives (CAA).

32. M. Agnes McCann, **The History of Mother Seton's Daughters,** vol. 1 (New York: Longmans, Green & Co, 1917) 59.

33. Fenwick to Venerable & Dear Mother, Cincinnati, May 9, 1829, Archives, Emmitsburg Daughters of Charity.

34. John H. Lamott, **History of the Archdiocese of Cincinnati** (Cincinnati: Pustet, 1921) 246.

35. Benven Sansbury, Brown Paper Annals, ms., Somerset, n.d. but after 1832, Columbus Dominican Sisters, Archives (CDS).

36. Ursula Grignon to Louis Grignon, Somerset, Sept. 24, 1831, State

Historical Society of Wisconsin (SHSW) XXVIII: 26, 1831.

37. Fenwick to T. Ancarani, Cincinnati, Apr. 15, 1830, Archives General, Order of Preachers, Rome (AGOP), XIII, 03150, 140.

38. Young to Fenwick, Somerset, Oct. 4, 1831, UNDA II 4 d.

39. Fenwick to Louis Grignon, Cincinnati, Mar. 25, 1832, SHSW – Grignon, Lawe & Porlier Papers 29B: 17.

40. Young to Frederic Rese, Somerset, Dec. 19, 1832, Archives, Ohio State Legislature: 31 O. S.L.4.

41. Catholic Telegraph, I, 2, 14-15.

42. Fenwick to Ambrose Maréchal, Somerset, May 26, 1826, AAB 16 W 10.

43. Dubourg to Fenwick, New Orleans, Apr. 22, 1825, SJP.

44. Dubourg to Fenwick, New Orleans, January 10,1826, UNDA, II 4d.

45. F.P. Kenrick to Propaganda Fide, Bardstown, Jan. 30, 1826, APF VIII, 566rv-567rv.

46. Fenwick to Badin, Bordeaux, Aug. 8, 1823, SJP.

47. Fenwick to the Society for the Propagation of the Faith, **Annales** III, 298.

48. Fenwick to M.R., Cincinnati, **Annales** IV, 521.

49. See Robert Trisco, **The Holy See and the Nascent Church in the Middle Western United States 1826-1850** (Rome: Gregorian University Press, 1982) 212.

50. Fenwick to Rese, Mackinac, July 18, 1832, UNDA II 4 e.

51. Samuel Mazzuchelli **Memoirs,** 68.

The old oak tree
at Boone's chapel

ANGELA AND BENVEN SANSBURY

A giant oak tree, over two hundred and fifty years old, stands some twenty miles east of Washington, D.C., in the woodlands of Prince George's County, Maryland. The tree grew in the churchyard of Boone's chapel, the religious center of Maryland Catholics since colonial times. It is not difficult to imagine two small children, close enough in age to be taken as twins, playing ring games around this old oak tree. As Catholic colonists finally found religious freedom in the new republic, Elizabeth and Mariah Sansbury would find themselves at home in both Church and state.

Although records differ, it appears that Elizabeth and Mariah Sansbury were born in 1794 and 1795 respectively. Their parents, Alexis and Elizabeth Hamilton Sansbury, married on February 16, 1782,[1] and reared three daughters and four sons. The family probably lived on the land Thomas Sansbury, the grandfather of Elizabeth and Mariah, willed to their father Alexis in 1781. This land, east of the Patuxent River and southwest of Upper Marlborough, was near Boone's chapel.[2] There they worshipped either in a church or in private homes which Jesuit missionaries routinely visited.

The strength of character displayed by the amiable Mariah and the benevolent Elizabeth undoubtedly can be traced back through the centuries when persecutions and penalties affected their English Catholic ancestors. Both the Sansbury and Hamilton progenitors left England in the 1600s, probably for economic as well as for religious reasons. The Hamiltons could trace their Catholicism back to England. The Sansburys were early contributors to the building of Boone's chapel in 1710. Thus, both heredity and environment blessed Elizabeth and Mariah Sansbury.

The amount and quality of their education is unrecorded, although its effects seem almost as impressive as their religious inheritance. An aunt by marriage, Jane Coomes, was an educated woman; she migrated to Kentucky in 1775 and became the first teacher in that state.[3] Records indicate that Elizabeth and Mariah's mother signed numerous financial statements after the death of her husband. Books were listed as part of the contents of Alexis Sansbury's estate.[4] That the Sansbury children were educated while in Maryland seems a reasonable assumption. With their economic resources, the Sansburys could have their children attend either a small private school established by wealthy planters, a county free school, or classes in the home of family or relatives.

Relatives and friends of the Sansburys began to move to Kentucky as early as 1775. Some came with a colony in 1785. Economic hardship in Maryland and the prospect of more fertile land in Kentucky were the primary reasons for going west. Probably because of the father's poor health – Alexis died in 1816 – his family remained in Maryland until late 1819 or early 1820.[5] The years after his death must have been extremely difficult for the family. In 1816-1817, crops failed and food became scarce. In that "year without a summer," Elizabeth and Mariah's brother Alexis, Jr., became a member of an organization to provide relief for the poor.[6] Yet the 1818 family records indicate that the widow Elizabeth Sansbury was still paying the debts of her husband's estate, which was valued at over five thousand dollars. Most of that amount represented the current "value" of sixteen slaves.

Cartwright Creek became the destination of this branch of the Sansbury family. Its waters begin in the knobs of central Kentucky in what is currently Marion County, then cut through Washington and Nelson Counties where it joins the Salt River. As the horse-drawn coach or wagon carrying the Sansburys lumbered down Bardstown Road near what is now Springfield, the most imposing sight that met their eyes was the cluster of buildings belonging to the Dominican Friars of St. Joseph Province. These included St. Rose Church and priory, St. Thomas College and Seminary, a mill, and a farm. As told in Chapter 4, the Province had been established at St. Rose in 1806 by the American Edward Fenwick and the Englishmen Samuel Thomas Wilson, William Raymond Tuite, and Robert Antoninus Angier. This Dominican presence on the banks of Cartwright Creek changed the lives of Mariah and Elizabeth Sansbury dramatically.

There is some evidence that the Sansbury family did not live with relatives during their first days in Kentucky. Instead they may have spent time in a house on the McAfee property adjacent to the Dominican establishment. This 106-acre farm was purchased by the widow, Elizabeth and her daughter, Mariah, in March, 1820. When their mother died in 1822, the two daughters, Mariah and Elizabeth, received it as their inheritance and it became their dowry in 1823.[7] For several years Mariah and Elizabeth lived at the new property.

Life at Cartwright Creek took on special meaning for the two young women in 1822 when the parishioners of St. Rose Church witnessed a series of historical events occurring each month from January through April. No doubt, Elizabeth and Mariah Sansbury were present and took more than ordinary interest in these parish activities. In January, Edward Fenwick was consecrated Bishop of Cincinnati in St. Rose Church by Benedict Joseph Flaget, Bishop of Bardstown. Unless the Sansbury sisters had met Fenwick during his short time in Maryland, this was their first meeting with him.

In February, Samuel Wilson challenged the young women of the parish to establish a Third Order of Dominicans who would live as a religious community. He explained the advantages of religious life and reminded them of the great necessity of a Catholic school for young women. He shared with Fenwick a long-time dream of men and women of the Order working together to carry out the mission of the Church. Now as provincial, he made the first general appeal to St. Rose parishioners. Friars and parishioners awaited some response to the call of their pastor.

On March 2, Fenwick ordained four Dominicans to the priesthood at St. Rose before leaving for Cincinnati to take up his duties as bishop. Meanwhile Father Wilson's call reaped a parallel harvest. According to the Profession Book of the Kentucky sisters, on

February 28, nine young women of the pioneer families, including Mariah and Elizabeth Sansbury, told Wilson of their intention to become Dominicans. By March all nine were planning to form a Dominican community. Five of the nine were related to Mariah and Elizabeth. "Four were ready for reception but had not yet come together in community since they had no house, no means and no provisions, so St. Rose [the friars] fixed up a log cabin for their dwelling." [8] They named this small building Bethany. The candidates' slight knowledge of religious life would soon be broadened. "They had not as yet the habit to put on or even an idea how to make it, therefore, the Very Rev. Father Provincial instructed them and provided for them the habits." [9]

Six weeks after Father Wilson's pulpit invitation, on Easter Sunday morning, April 7, 1822, Mariah Sansbury entered the parish church of St. Rose and in the presence of the parishioners accepted the habit of the Order of Preachers from Wilson. She received the name of Sister Angela. In the afternoon young friar Richard Pius Miles gave the habit to three more women and Wilson examined the other five respondents. They received the Rule of St. Augustine and the constitution which Wilson had translated from the Latin. It was taken from the Second Order and Third Order constitutions with such adaptations as circumstances of the country would require. The introduction compared the sisters to the deaconesses of the early Church.[10]

Elizabeth Sansbury and Theresa Edelen sought admission into the Order in March. Elizabeth became known as Sister Benvenuta, shortened informally to Benven. Theresa received the name Magdalene. The two Sansburys, now known as Angela and Benven spent less than four months living in their newly organized religious community when they began to suffer personal losses. Their mother died in the summer of 1822. Shortly thereafter, their sister Sophie joined another congregation, the Sisters of Loretto, which had been established in Kentucky by Charles Nerinckx in 1812. The losses may explain why the Sansbury home was made available for the Dominican sisters. In view of the growing community, it seemed prudent to move from tiny Bethany to the larger house on the Sansbury property. By 1823, Angela and Benven found themselves back "home," but now the home was known as the St. Mary Magdalene Convent of Dominican Sisters. Eleven months after the first call, there were seven new novices living the Dominican life at St. Magdalene Convent. As yet, none had pronounced vows.

On January 6, 1823, Angela Sansbury made her profession into the hands of Samuel Thomas Wilson. He apparently had received or presumed a dispensation for Angela to make vows before she completed her year of novitiate. On June 6, the provincial confirmed Angela as the prioress of the new community. With joy, the sisters of St. Mary Magdalene Convent heard his historic words: ". . . being well acquainted with your exemplary conduct and zeal for regular discipline . . . influenced by that affection which your virtuous sisters testified toward you on a former occasion when they petitioned to have you placed at the head of their community, I . . . Brother Wilson . . . do hereby declare, establish and confirm you . . . first Prioress of our said College of Saint Magdalene. . . . " [11] On August 30, 1823, Benven and four companions made profession before Angela in the presence of Wilson. Thus they became the first women of the United States to pronounce vows as Dominican Sisters.

Six months after the move to the Cartwright Creek valley, the St. Mary Magdalene community made another historic move. On July 15, 1823, they opened the first school conducted by American Dominican women. Fifteen students studied in a building that once housed a still on the Sansbury property. They gave it the prestigious name of St.

Sister Angela Sansbury

Mary Magdalene Academy. The community and the school continued to grow. By February 1824, there were seven professed sisters, seven novices, and twenty-nine boarders.

Along with growth, however, there came new losses. Angela and Benven suffered the death of their sister Sophie who had joined the Sisters of Loretto. She had been received on April 3, 1824, and professed two days later on her deathbed.[12] The following year, the Mary Magdalene community suffered its first death; in fact they experienced the death of one sister every year for four consecutive years. Among them were two young cousins of Angela and Benven and a young Boone relative who took her vows on her death-bed.

The most devastating loss was the death of Samuel Wilson on May 23, 1824. Although the provincial had appointed Richard Miles to take responsibility for the sisters, still the loss of Wilson's wisdom and experience proved deeply traumatic. The few years that this highly respected churchman had provided them meant much to Angela and Benven and their small community, even if the horarium he crafted for them seemed strict. In view of the rigorism of some clerics in the area, however, the liberal, non-Jansenist teachings of Fenwick, Wilson and Miles were a beneficial influence on the life and spirituality of the Sansbury sisters and their companions.

The death of Wilson initiated another series of significant activities in the province. St. Mary Magdalene Academy had attracted so many students that an addition to the buildings was needed. This the workmen completed in the summer of 1825. The sisters had solicited money for the work, but lacked enough to cover all costs. Father Miles approved the addition, gave his personal pledge for the payment and signed a $2000 note. The note signed by Miles just before he was called to Ohio, as well as the appointment in 1826 of the Spaniard Raphael Munos as prior of St. Rose, caused the St. Magdalene community much sorrow. Munos objected to the unpaid debt, and in 1828 proposed that the sisters disband. As commissary general of St. Joseph province, Edward Fenwick sought a resolution to the problem. He wrote to the Master of the Order asking permission to sell the monastery and transfer the sisters to another place, or to establish them in Ohio.[13] This permission was refused. With encouragement from Miles in Ohio, the sisters discussed the proposed move, but decided against it. Little by little the community paid off the debt and remained in their beloved Kentucky.

Edward Fenwick's wish to have Dominican sisters share in the missionary work of his friars in the Cincinnati diocese soon became a reality. In 1830 he asked the Kentucky community for four sisters to serve in Ohio. On January 11, Benven, Emily Elder, Agnes Harbin and Catherine Mudd left for Somerset, Ohio. For Angela and Benven this separation, the first in their lives, was painful but was also a sign of growth for the community. Angela and the remaining twelve waved their good-byes as the chosen four went resolutely to their new adventure.

Piety Hill, the highest point in the village of Somerset, was the location of Dominican life in Perry County, Ohio. Adjacent to Holy Trinity Church on this hill, Fenwick purchased land and buildings that were to become St. Mary Convent and Academy. Here Benven encountered, not fifth generation English Catholics of Maryland or Kentucky, but recent German Catholic immigrants. The four pioneers derived much satisfaction from being the first Dominican women religious in Ohio and the second Dominican foundation in the United States. They recorded the event in these words:

Sister Benven, Sister Agnes, Sister Emily, and Sister Catherine of the Order of St. Dominic, being invited by the Right Reverend Bishop of Cincinnati to make an establishment in Ohio, having obtained leave, left St. Magdalene's Kentucky, on the 11 of January, 1830, and arrived at Somerset Ohio, their place of destination, on the 5th of the following month, where they found a gratified public ready to receive and support them. The said Sisters took possession of the house and lot purchased by the Reverend Bishop of Cincinnati and commenced housekeeping February 25th, 1830, and commenced their school April 5 in the same year with forty scholars the first quarter. [14]

The school building had served previously as a carpenter shop. Of this new St. Mary's Academy Sister Benven reported, "They commenced the building in the fall of 1830 and got it nearly finished before the winter of 1831 came on too cold." [15]

For the next three years, until 1833, Angela and Benven remained apart. Benven and her companions busied themselves organizing their school and getting acquainted with the people of Somerset who had never seen women religious before. During these years of separation, the two sisters were often at the heart of crisis. For one thing, cholera epidemics were rampant. The Kentucky sisters and friars distinguished themselves for their unselfish ministry to the sick and dying. Benedict Flaget, Bishop of Bardstown, had only praise for their dedication.[16] But the death of Bishop Fenwick, victim of the cholera, on September 16, 1832, in Wooster, Ohio, brought great sorrow. Especially affected were those who had recently come to Somerset at the bishop's request.

After a brief respite from her six-year duty as prioress in Kentucky, Angela decided to join Benven in Ohio. On April 15, 1833, she made her will,[17] leaving all real and personal property to the St. Mary Magdalene community. On that same day she and her cousin Ann Hill left for Somerset. With their departure, none of the Sansbury-Hamilton cousins, so integral to the foundation of the Dominican women was left in Kentucky.

A Note on the Sansbury Portraits

The likeness of Angela reveals an oval face, a heart shaped mouth, a somewhat distant look in her eyes and a relaxed pose: features that suggest a contemplative person. Her image reveals Mother Angela to be sensitive, intelligent, perceptive, anxious, artistic, beautiful, and distinguished in bearing. The portrait belies both the stereotypical rough frontier woman and the extraordinary achievements of this active contemplative.

The portrait of Benven shows a face square in shape. The mouth is firm with a small upper and full lower lip. The eyes are clear and resolute. With head erect and an open mantle over her shoulders, she appears to be ready to step forward to meet any need. The photograph presents a woman with a face that is kindly but strong; one can surmise that Benven could be either witty or determined. Those who knew Benven characterized her as stately, dignified and an observer of the Rule.

The portraits of the Sansbury sisters reveal stalwart Dominican women of the first two communities of vowed apostolic women in the United States. Through the choices and responses of Angela and Benven Sansbury, the Sisters of St. Catharine and St. Mary of the Springs congregations inaugurated what would become a procession of women who would join the friars as missionaries in the New World.

Sister Benven Sansbury

The two Sansbury sisters are remembered for the leadership they provided, especially for the St. Mary's community in Ohio. Over the years, Benven served either as prioress or sub-prioress, treasurer or novice mistress, in the three communities where she lived. After Angela's move to St. Mary's, she, too, was elected prioress and held that position until her death.

Under Benven's leadership as prioress, the academy flourished and the number of students increased rapidly. In 1832 Nicholas Dominic Young, O.P., the Dominican Provincial and mentor, arranged for the incorporation of the school as St. Mary's Female Literary Society. "I have obtained an Act of incorporation for our sisters, this will save them much trouble and make the Institution more generally known." [18] Following the Kentucky procedure, building a chapel took precedence over other structures. Angela and Benven sought financial assistance jointly from their friends abroad and at home. They avoided the dilemma of their earlier Kentucky experience.

Angela's death came in the midst of the flurry of building activities at St. Mary's. She had been ill for only eight days. She was forty-five years of age. One of the students at the Academy gave this account:

I have to tell you that which is most painful. Mother Angela died Saturday night, on the 30th of Nov., between 10 and 11 o'clock. The affection of the sisters, I should judge is very great at being deprived of a member so amiable. We were all present when she died. We attended her funeral on Monday at ten o'clock. There were three Rev. Fathers attended by a concourse of people; the church was crowded. . . . [19]

Benven succeeded Angela as prioress at Somerset. She continued to serve St. Mary's and its missions for more than thirty years. She also demonstrated her loyalty and concern for the welfare of the St. Mary Magdalene community. She ensured that the property in Kentucky remain in the hands of the Literary Society of St. Mary Magdalene. On March 11, 1847, for one dollar, she gave the Society her undivided interest in the 106 acres in Kentucky. She framed an agreement in strong legal terms. "The said Literary Society and the said Elizabeth Sansbury [sic] does further covenant and agree that she will warrant and forever defend the above sold land . . . from and against the claim or claims of all. . . ." [20]

If Benven's continuous calls to leadership were difficult, her ministry demands were no less taxing. She was called at age sixty to be involved in caring for infants in Tennessee. In 1855 she answered the call of the friars in Memphis to establish St. Peter's Orphanage there, and she remained for almost two years. Less than ten years later in 1864, at the age of seventy and in the midst of the Civil War, she and two companions arrived in Nashville, Tennessee, to staff an orphanage established by St. Mary's Orphanage Association. [21]

Benven endured two years in Nashville, years troubled because of the war. Shortly after they arrived, one of her companions, Gertrude O'Meara, became ill and died. Benven and her only other companion cared for the fourteen orphans until more sisters joined them from Kentucky. However, on December 1, 1864, a real crisis occurred when the sisters and orphans were notified they would have to leave immediately because of shelling by the Union armies. With the help of Father Joseph Kelly and friends, all were evacuated to the basement of the cathedral. The orphanage was leveled by the ensuing barrage, but rebuilt in 1865.

Benven was back in Ohio just three weeks when fire destroyed St. Mary's at Somerset on June 6, 1866. After the fire, Benven helped establish a temporary academy at St. Joseph Priory in Somerset. There she was prefect of the boarders and teacher. Although she often expressed her great love for Somerset and its people, yet as subprioress she voted on July 7, 1866, to move the sisters' convent and academy to Columbus, Ohio, a city with much more promise for growth.

During her long life, Benven had lived about twenty-five years in Maryland, ten in Kentucky, and, with the exception of a few years in Memphis and Nashville, over thirty-five years in Ohio. The mutual love between Benven and the citizens of Somerset in Perry County is expressed in her letter to the editor of the local paper when she was on her way to Nashville. She wrote,

My feelings urge me to tender . . . a most grateful farewell . . . . I say from my heart: I thank you for your many kindnesses . . . . Yes, most valued. . . yet much more so for the feelings of mutual esteem which they bespeak to exist between us. . . . When I shall be in a far-off land, my prayers, in unison with those of the little orphans, shall ascend in behalf of my esteemed friends in Perry. [22]

Now in her declining years, Benven "devoted her time principally to prayer, meditation, and a daily preparation for death." [23] She died just before she was to celebrate her golden anniversary as a Dominican sister. Death came quickly after only a week of illness, on May 31, 1873, at the age of seventy-nine. In her life she served her Order and Church generously. In four different communities, and in three states, she had made many friends who grieved for her.

The announcement will be received with feelings of intense grief at all the convents of the order. The telegraph, before this, will have conveyed the sad intelligence to her sorrowing sisters, not only throughout this State, but in Kentucky, Tennessee, Washington, D.C., Delaware, Florida and California. In all these convents, her name is a household word, and her sisters had hoped to have her live to see the 50th anniversary of her religious profession, the golden jubilee of which was to be celebrated on the 30th of August next, the Feast of St. Rose of Lima.[24]

Benven was the last to die of the original, founding members of St. Catharine's, Kentucky, and St. Mary of the Springs, Ohio. Her accomplishments and those of Angela were immeasurable. Angela, the angelic, and Benven the good, were rarely separated in life. Together they are finally at rest, buried near each other at St. Mary of the Springs, Columbus, Ohio.

1. C.M.Brumbaugh, Maryland Records: Colonial, Revolution, County and Church (Prince George County) 150.

2. Flaherty-Knox to Cameron, Branson, MD, Feb. 3, 1992, Kentucky Dominican Sisters Archives (KDS).

3. Clyde Crews, **An American Holy Land** (Louisville, Ky: Ikonographics, Inc., 1987) 36.

4. Prince George County Records, July 10, 1818.

5. Alexis, Sr., is listed in Prince George County census of 1810, but not 1820. Elizabeth his wife is listed in Washington County, Kentucky, census of 1820.

6. Lee R. Van Horn, **Out of the Past-Prince Georgians and Their Land** (np, 1976) 268.

7. Washington County, Ky, Deed Book F, 356, I, 280-281 and Will Book, C, 472.

8. SCA, First Profession Book, p.4.

9. SCA, First Profession Book, p.4.

10. SCA First Profession Book, pp 17-18.

11. Copy of letter of appointment – Original in Archives of St. Mary of the Springs, Columbus, Ohio.

12. Notes from Loretto Archives, KDS.

13. Fenwick to Thomas Ancarani, Baltimore, Oct. 10, 1829, Archives General of the Order of Preachers (AGOP) XIII, 03150, 136.

14. Council Book, ms., Archives of Columbus Dominican Sisters (CDS).

15. Benven Sansbury, "Brown Paper Annals," ms. Somerset, 1830, CDS.

16. Flaget to Louis DeLoul, Bardstown, July 5, 1833, The Filson Club, Louisville, Ky. (FCA).

17. Apostolic women religious with a simple vow of poverty retain possession of personal property, but not its use without permission. So making a will was appropriate.

18. N.D. Young to Fredric Rese, Somerset, Dec. 19, 1832, University of Notre Dame Archives (UNDA), II 4e.

19. Jane Lawe to R.L. Lawe, Somerset, Dec. 12, 1839, copy at CDS.

20. Washington County Records, Kentucky, Deed Book Q, 323.

21. Thomas Stritch, **The Catholic Church in Tennessee** (Nashville: The Catholic Center, 1987) 114.

22. **Democratic Union**, Somerset, Ohio, May 11, 1864.

23. Council Book, ms., CDS.

24. **Freeman's Journal**, New York, June 14, 1873, 3.

CHAPTER 7

To Michigan, Wisconsin and the Mississippi Valley

In 1830 Edward Fenwick extended the American Dominican mission beyond the frontier to the Mississippi River. Into the wilderness he sent alone, as he himself had gone into the Ohio forests, a newly ordained priest twenty-three years old. He was Samuel Mazzuchelli, a native of Milan and descendant of sturdy Celtic Lombards who had once moved down through the Alps to the welcoming Po Valley. In the years ahead Samuel Mazzuchelli would broaden dramatically the American mission of the Order of Preachers, evangelizing natives and newcomers of many cultures. He would preach and teach without ceasing, and establish communities of friars and sisters to do the same. He would found a multitude of parishes, build their first churches and open schools for their children and a college for youth.

When Samuel arrived at his first mission, such possibilities were unimaginable; but the spiritual hunger of the people was clearly evident and his vocation certain. In the spirit of his biblical patron Samuel and from his own experience he could later say,

> Let us wake up then,
> open our eyes,
> and if we are called, set out for any place where the work is
> great and difficult; but where, with the help of Him who sent
> us, we shall open the way for the Gospel.[1]

Why Samuel became a Dominican is not known. In his youth there were no friars left in Milan and no Dominican house in Lombardy. All religious orders in Italy were close to extinction.[2] He was sent to study in Rome when the reviving Province of Lombardy was reopening the ancient center of Dominican study at Sta. Sabina. With the new class of students Samuel, whose religious name was Brother Augustine, profited from the courses of excellent professors, along with wise directors of formation in religious life.[3] From his courses and readings Samuel compiled handbound notebooks which he kept with him all his life and used in his preaching and teaching.

In the summer of 1827 the Milanese youth was ordained a subdeacon. During the following final year of study he met a German-American priest, Frederic Rese, who was sent to Rome by Bishop Fenwick to seek missionaries for his needy diocese. On hearing him Samuel decided to volunteer for the American Dominican mission in the Diocese of Cincinnati.

The new head of the Order of Preachers was Giuseppe Velzi, who as provincial of Lombardy had brought Samuel to study in Rome. In spite of the critical needs of the Order in Europe, he consented to Samuel's desire and sealed his approval by "constituting as missionary for North America" one who was not yet a priest.[4] With Frederic Rese as guide, Samuel set out for America at the end of June, 1828. He stopped in Milan to bid farewell to his widowed father and try to help his family understand his mission.

The travelers then went on to France. On reaching the old Roman city of Lyon, Rese suddenly changed his travel plan. He went to Germany, and after two months directed the youth to go on alone to the United States. On October 5, 1828, Samuel Mazzuchelli boarded a small sailing ship, the *Edward Quesnel*, bound for the Port of New York. The passenger list of twenty-nine persons reflected the diversity of the early immigrants. A Scottish merchant, an English lace maker, a French watchmaker, and the American wife and daughter of the ship's captain accompanied the Italian novice as they journeyed together toward their future.[5]

After forty days on a sea of recurring storms, the ship docked in New York on November 15, 1828. Samuel set out alone by stage and riverboat for Cincinnati. Arriving at last at the "Queen City of the West" after eight days on the Ohio River, the youth whom Rese had written as "sent by the Master General" was welcomed warmly by Bishop Fenwick. In that kindly veteran of the missions, Samuel found a friend and lifelong exemplar, who in the spirit of St. Dominic had given himself wholly to the service of the Church.

For almost two years Mazzuchelli prepared for ordination to the priesthood, mentored by the bishop and the Dominican friars of Somerset, Ohio. From them he learned how to respond at any hour to the pastoral challenges of preaching, teaching, and consoling the sick and dying on the frontier. Early in February of 1830 he was present to welcome the first Dominican sisters who came from the convent of St. Magdalen in Kentucky to found the community of St. Mary in Somerset. Their zeal, and that of the Dominican women he met briefly in Kentucky, would inspire him later to found the third American community of Dominican women at Sinsinawa, Wisconsin.

On September 5, 1830, the Church of Cincinnati celebrated the priestly ordination of Samuel Mazzuchelli.[6] Several weeks later Bishop Fenwick sent the young priest to the place where the needs of the people seemed most urgent: the northernmost part of the old Northwest. Far beyond Ohio, and larger than that state, the region spread west from Lake Michigan to the Mississippi River and north to Canada.[7] The wilderness was interrupted only by scattered Indian villages, fur trading posts, and a line of American forts reaching diagonally from the Canadian border southwest to the Mississippi River. The mind-boggling assignment given the new priest was to be "missionary and parish priest of the North-West Territory, with particular care for Mackinac Island, Green Bay and Sault Ste. Marie."[8] He would be the first resident priest in the entire area since the Jesuit Fathers had been withdrawn fifty years earlier by the papal suppression of the Society of Jesus. All Bishop Fenwick could do for the bereft people was to send itinerant priests to them in succeeding summers and try to visit them himself each year.

After a journey of many days through Ohio forests to Detroit, then north by a fragile boat on the rough waters of Lake Huron, Samuel Mazzuchelli arrived at his mission base on Mackinac island as winter was literally closing in. There he met his first parishioners, a motley society of cultures and languages. There were French Canadians and Americans working for the fur-trade empire of John Jacob Astor. There were soldiers guarding the straits from the heights of Fort Mackinac. In the surrounding forests were scattered villages of Woodland Indians, chiefly of the Chippewa and Ottawa tribes. On the island were many **métis**[9] whom Presbyterian missionaries from New England were working zealously to educate, Christianize and Americanize.

Bishop Fenwick gave the priest two broad goals: to revive the faith of the neglected French Canadian Catholics and to bring the Gospel to the native peoples. The center of the young missionary's new life was the small church of St. Anne, a reminder of the days when the Jesuits, whom he called "the unforgotten padres," lived among the people and kept their faith alive. Now, he found, many Catholics were "indifferent and untroubled by devotion, owing to the lack of instruction, of priests, . . . and everything that could win them to virtue."[10]

Map of development of the "OLD NORTHWEST" in 1830

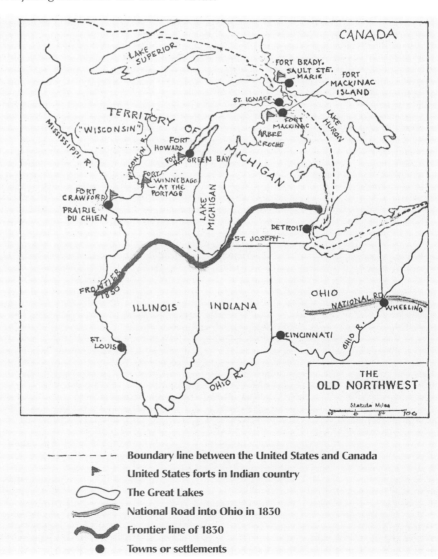

- - - - - - - **Boundary line between the United States and Canada**

⚑ **United States forts in Indian country**

〰 **The Great Lakes**

〰 **National Road into Ohio in 1830**

〰 **Frontier line of 1830**

● **Towns or settlements**

Father Mazzuchelli suddenly encountered the intense anti-Catholicism of the era.[11] The Mackinac Presbyterian minister, William Ferry, launched weekly lectures to discredit Catholic beliefs. The Dominican responded by inviting Protestants, Catholics, and Ferry himself, to a series of fourteen lectures on Catholic teachings to which listeners, could respond, and even interrupt the priest.[12]

The Dominican friar directed his energies not to polemical disputations but to the spiritual care of baptized and would-be Catholics. When possible he journeyed in all directions to minister to the people in scattered villages of Indians and trading posts. At Sault Ste. Marie on the Canadian border, he found no church building but preached to the people in the shade of a majestic oak tree beside the rushing waters of the rapids.[13]

Although a shade tree would do to begin with, settlers needed a regular place to gather for worship, a church to symbolize both their faith and the stability of their new settlement. Discovering this need very soon, Father Mazzuchelli helped the people in every place to build their own church. Only months after he arrived in the North, early in the spring of 1831, he initiated the construction of St. John the Evangelist church in Green Bay, the first Catholic Church in Wisconsin. The second was that of St. Gabriel the Archangel at Prairie du Chien on the Mississippi, which is still in use. Many have called the Dominican friar the "Builder of churches in the upper Midwest." In reality he was the builder of Christian communities, helping the people to form their first parishes in forty places in Michigan, Wisconsin, Illinois and Iowa.

Wigwams to which Menominee families welcomed the missionary to proclaim the Gospel

Their first building may have been made of mats, logs or stone, but each one sheltered a lasting parish, an *ecclesia* or church of living stones.

Members of the Indian tribes of the old Northwest were of great concern to Bishop Fenwick who visited them regularly and sent them missionaries when he could. Because of his zeal Father Samuel became the first Dominican friar to live and work among the Indians of the United States.[14] From 1830, when he first met the Menominee natives, to 1835, when other priests followed him in that ministry, Father Samuel ministered chiefly to the Menominee and Winnebago peoples, the latter now known by their original name, the "Ho-Chunk Nation." He also knew and served the Chippewas or Ojibway, and the Ottawa Nation.

The priest set out to learn the way of life of the natives by visiting their villages, accepting their hospitality, and eating their meager food. He went with families to harvest wild rice, make maple sugar, and fish through winter ice. Later he described each people's traits and customs, the work done by women and men, their love of children and respect for the elders. The priest experienced their severe hunger in winter and the suffering of families when the government plied them with liquor in place of needed goods and withheld unfairly their treaty annuities or funds for education. After studying the religion of the natives, the missionary stated with conviction that, contrary to the opinions of some Christian observers, their superstitious practices were not idolatrous.

In his catechetical effort, the missionary blended Indian ways and language with Catholic worship. At Sunday Vespers they chanted the Psalms of David, singing alternately one verse in Latin and the next in their own tongue. The missionary compiled a prayer book for the Winnebagos entitled *Ocangra Aramee Wawakakara,* the first printed work in a Sioux language. He had it printed in Detroit in 1833. In the fol-

The "DIGS" of lead miners along the Mississippi, showing the location of the Jones home at Sinsinawa Mound

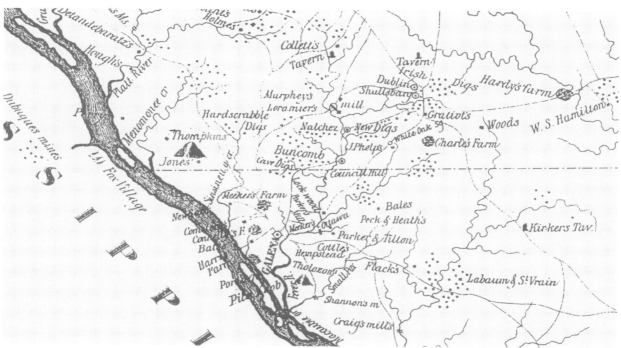

lowing year the first item ever printed in Wisconsin (then a part of Michigan) was his liturgical calendar, *Kikiwawadendanoiwewin*, or Almanac of the year's feasts in the Chippewa idiom. He preached the Gospel to the natives as to any other people. Father Mazzuchelli's appreciation of native languages and customs brought him into the arena of Indian education. In March of 1819, the United States Government approved a yearly appropriation of $10,000 for the "civilization and education of the Indian people." The Episcopalian mission received the entire fund. When the Menominee leader Chief Oshkosh protested, declaring that he would employ a lawyer and send the case to Washington, the agent threatened to have the chief "deposed." In 1835 Mazzuchelli wrote to President Andrew Jackson in protest, meticulously reviewing the injustice suffered by the Indian people, but in vain.[15] No school opened by the missionary received aid, despite the requests of tribal leaders, the allocation of funds for all Indian schools and the observance by the schools of all government requirements.

During the first five years of his labors among the native peoples, the young Dominican weathered the rigors of the frontier, experienced the anti-Catholic sentiments of government officials, and witnessed the tragic unfolding of the Jacksonian policy of Indian removal. He condemned the deleterious effects of the fur trade and alcohol upon tribal life, exacerbated by constant removal from their lands. Like many 19th century missionaries, he viewed the natives as "children of nature" who would become civilized once they embraced Christianity. Yet he affirmed many aspects of tribal life, marveling at the Indians' devotion to family and spirit of hospitality generously offered to strangers. He applauded the natives' sense of community and the common good. These traits, he noted, were not readily found in the nations of the world "among whom 'mine' and 'thine' are carried to such lengths as to necessitate so many laws. . . ."[16]

One day in the spring of 1835, Samuel Mazzuchelli left Prairie du Chien to ride south along the Mississippi to Galena, Illinois, to board a riverboat to St. Louis. On the way he discovered the flourishing lead region near the Illinois line where men were laying claims and digging ore from the richest deposit of lead in the world. The miners were coming from every direction, even from the British Isles. By 1835 families had begun to arrive to farm the rich soil near the two river cities of Galena on the east bank and Dubuque on the west. On arriving in the settlements, the traveler discovered nearly three hundred Catholics who had lost two priests in the recent cholera epidemic. They were pleading with Bishop Joseph Rosati of St. Louis to send a priest to this northern part of his diocese. When Father Mazzuchelli rode into their midst, they urged him to come to them.

The traveler soon boarded the riverboat to St. Louis, then went up the Ohio River to Somerset to see the Dominican provincial, Nicholas Young. The Catholic settlers upriver immediately petitioned the Dominican Master General, Tommaso Cipolletti, to send the missionary to their region. He gave his enthusiastic consent.[17] So began in 1835 the Mazzuchelli mission in the upper Mississippi Valley which lasted eight years. During the first four years, he was their only priest among the families settling rapidly on both sides of the Great River. His life now differed from that in the primitive conditions of the northern wilderness, but the mining frontier offered equally demanding pastoral challenges. For Italian readers he described the beginnings in Galena:

Samuel Mazzuchelli was loved by his parishioners, who called him affectionately Father "Matthew Kelly." He also gained the respect of Protestants. While Lyman Beecher announced from his Boston pulpit the immediate takeover of the West by the pope, life on the mining frontier necessitated a spirit of cooperation rather than fear of "Romish" conspiracy. As Mazzuchelli moved from place to place to form parishes and build churches, he soon made friends with Protestants. They contributed to the building funds and presided at the cornerstone layings of new Catholic churches.

The Italian friar who became an American citizen supported American ways of decision-making and collaboration and was held in high regard by all citizens. Less than a year after he arrived in the lead region, the Territory of Wisconsin was created from that of Michigan to extend from Lake Michigan west to the Mississippi. When the first territorial legislature met in 1836, its thirty-nine members, of whom only three were Catholic, chose Samuel Mazzuchelli to be their chaplain. After serving for one week, he declined the honor for the sake of his ministry and set out among the rising towns to form nascent parishes and build churches on both sides of the Mississippi River.

Samuel Mazzuchelli, O.P.

In July 1837, Pope Gregory XVI established the new Diocese of Dubuque, west of the Mississippi, a region soon to become Iowa Territory. There the Dominican friar was the only priest. The arrival of Bishop Mathias Loras in 1839 marked the beginning of a long friendship and partnership in ministry with the Dominican friar. The bishop depended upon Mazzuchelli's mature missionary experience and gifts, especially his zealous preaching. The two men often preached parish retreats together. After one retreat Loras reported to Bishop Rosati in St. Louis,

Mr. Mazzuchelli preached like an Apostle every night for 1 or 2 hours, and a half-hour in the morning, lasting to 12 days. As for me, I tried to accomplish something by my prayers and hearing confessions. [19]

In April 1843, Samuel Mazzuchelli accompanied Bishop Loras to Baltimore to be his theologian at the Fifth Provincial Council of the Church in the United States. Among the sixteen bishops present was the Dominican missionary Richard Miles, Bishop of Nashville. No council Act would be more welcome to

Mazzuchelli than the bishops' request for the formation of two new dioceses, Chicago and Milwaukee, which embraced his missions in Illinois and Wisconsin. Because his six-year assignment to the Diocese of Dubuque by the Master General was now ended, the priest's presence at the Baltimore Council was his last official service to Bishop Loras. However, he would return often to Iowa at the request of bishop, pastors and parishioners.

At the close of the Council Samuel sailed home to Europe. As he explained, the journey was made because of "several serious illnesses, the need of rest, the pressing needs of the missions, the very cordial consent of the bishop of Dubuque and many other reasons of less importance."[20] He went directly to Milan, where he soon regained his strength and began to pursue several projects for his stay in Europe. One was to write a full, reflective description of his fourteen years on mission in the United States. For this work he offered two reasons. The first, he wrote, was "to satisfy the eager wish of a number of devout persons, including the religious of the renowned Order of Preachers to which the missionary has the honor of belonging."[21] The second was to contribute from his experience to the Church history of the United States, especially with documents concerning dioceses recently erected in his mission region.

Soon the missionary learned that in response to the recent Baltimore Council, the Catholics in Wisconsin Territory would now belong to the new Diocese of Milwaukee, and those in northwest Illinois to the Diocese of Chicago. The missions up and down the eastern shore of the Mississippi were ready for the rapid development of the Church as growing numbers of families arrived hungry for the Word of God, the Eucharist and other sacraments.

Within a year the priest completed his Italian *Memorie*, or Memories of A Missionary Apostolic,[22] a work of 366 pages published in Milan. Then he turned to the project suggested seven years earlier by Tommaso Cipolletti, Master General, to establish in the midwest a second American province of Dominican friars.[23] He obtained without delay all needed authorizations from the Holy See and the Order. The Dominican Master General Angelo Ancarani appointed him Commissary Provincial of the new American province of St. Charles Borromeo, with authority to receive men and women into the Order, establish a novitiate, and staff missions in any place approved by the local bishop.[24]

In August 1844, Samuel Mazzuchelli returned from Italy. Before the end of October he purchased 800 acres of land in southwestern Wisconsin, a mile north of the Illinois boundary. On the height called Sinsinawa Mound, he established the center of the new province, calling it the "Missionary House of St. Dominic." It was to be a center of Dominican life and education, and of ministry to surrounding parishes. Only a few days after the purchase of "the Mound," as the place would always be known, a young German immigrant named Joseph Poelking came there "to live as a brother with the Rev. S. Mazzuchelli."[25] He was the first of twenty men who would enter the Order by way of Sinsinawa.

The new Bishop of Milwaukee, who had served in the Diocese of Cincinnati with Bishop Fenwick, was Swiss-born John Martin Henni. He offered Mazzuchelli a hearty welcome, stating that the greatest need of the region was for "missions, churches and common schools among those thousands of emigrants that are daily, & more than ever, pouring into Wisconsin & forming settlements."[26] Beyond the need for common schools, Father Samuel foresaw two additional needs for education: a college for men and an academy which would soon offer college studies to young women. In 1846 he opened Sinsinawa Mound College for men, which he dedicated to St. Thomas Aquinas.[27] The education of young women, he hoped, would be entrusted to Dominican sisters. He had already observed this model of ministerial partnership among the Dominicans in Kentucky and Ohio. He had asked for sisters from both those places, but none could yet be spared.

In 1847 Vincenzo Ajello sent three men from Italy to the new Wisconsin foundation. Unready for the hardships of community life and the frontier missions, they abandoned the enterprise one by one within three months, to the dismay of Father Mazzuchelli. His own Dominican nephew, Francis Mazzuchelli, who studied and was ordained in the United States, also returned to Italy.

However, new hope for the foundation came in the same summer when two young women of St. Dominic's parish at Sinsinawa asked Father Samuel to be received into the Order. By the end of 1847, four women had accepted the founder's invitation to form a Dominican community in Wisconsin.[28] Mary McNulty and Mary Routane were received as novices on August 4, 1847. They were members of St. Dominic parish, Sinsinawa, and teachers in nearby district schools. Both had been Sisters of Charity, founded by Elizabeth Seton, and were seasoned missionaries.[29]

Sister Josephine Cahill, one of the "Cornerstones" of the New Dominican Community

In December of that year two more women were received as novices. Margaret Conway, an Irish-born native of Canada, took the religious name of Sister Clara. Mary Fitzpatrick, an Irish immigrant, became Sister Ignatia. Early in April of 1848, Judith Cahill, whose family had come west by wagon from Pennsylvania, was received as Sister Josephine. The little community did not experience steady growth. Rather, its stability seemed quite tenuous and it appeared destined to fail. The hardships of frontier life and the founder's difficulties with the Italian friars seemed to anticipate failure.

By the close of 1848 the community numbered seven women. Several taught in the district schools while others attended to the household duties at the Mound. Sister Josephine recalled that in the village of Shullsburg they had no furniture; they slept on straw beds on the floor and lacked even a table for meals. Theirs was "always a cold dinner, often not enough. A piece of bread and a glass of water; a glass of milk was a luxury."[30]

Discouraged, the prioress Seraphina McNulty concluded that the group should disband. Early in 1849 she and Ermeline abruptly withdrew from the community. Father Samuel proposed that, after a day of communal reflection and prayer, the four remaining novices gather to determine their future. On February 5 they asked the youngest novice, Sister Rachel, to decide. She responded, "In the name of God let us remain together in our present community."[31] Four women made their religious profession in St. Dominic's church on August 15, 1849. They were Sisters Clara Conway, Ignatia Fitzpatrick, Josephine Cahill and Rachel Conway. Their founder called them, fittingly, the "four cornerstones" of the new Dominican community of Sinsinawa.

The year that followed was critical for the new community and its founder. They endured together a series of crises that affected the future of the sisters, the province and the Dominican mission in mid-America. Although officials of the Order and bishops of the region fully supported the mission, they could not help with money or personnel.

Father Mazzuchelli believed that the difficulties in the establishment of the Dominican province resulted from his own inability to govern. He asked several times to be relieved of the position of Commissary Provincial, a petition finally granted in 1849. By arrangement with Joseph Alemany, provincial of the friars' Province of St. Joseph, Samuel Mazzuchelli formally resigned, an action soon confirmed by the head of the Order. He moved to the village of Benton, Wisconsin, fourteen miles from Sinsinawa, and continued to minister to parishes at New Diggings, Shullsburg, Benton and neighboring stations. He assisted the Fathers who came to administer the Sinsinawa college by teaching, serving on their board of trustees and giving student retreats.[32]

The sisters remained at the Mound. When their founder learned that they were asked to do more housework than teaching, he objected to the provincial Joseph Alemany that "the four excellent Sisters will be kept mainly as servants, and the children of the country without Christian education."[33] Soon they moved to Benton to join the mission of their founder who helped them find places to teach in the district schools.[34] Their earnings enhanced the financial welfare of the young community and contributed to the operation of St. Clara Academy, which they opened in Benton in 1852 with Father Samuel as superintendent.

The move to Benton proved fortuitous for the growth of the young community. After five years with no new members, in 1853 an Academy student, Ellen Barry, was received as a Dominican novice, taking the name Sister Agnes.[35] During the following summer the annalist of St. Mary's, Somerset, recorded that on July 15, 1854, "The Sisters Joanna Clark, Magdalen McCurnan, Mary Louisa Cain & Mary Rose Callerher left St. Mary's to go to Benton, Wisconsin."[36] Their arrival in response to an earlier request by Father Mazzuchelli brought joy and hope to the fledgling Wisconsin community, which grew overnight from five members to nine! A year later three of the newcomers returned to their Ohio community, but Sister Joanna Clark remained in Wisconsin. She was elected prioress (a responsibility she had held in Somerset) and became the founder's valued associate, beloved by all.

The sisters opened St. Clara Academy in Benton to offer secondary education to daughters of the settlers. Samuel Mazzuchelli was superintendent, and instructed both students and teachers in scripture, literature, astronomy and physics.

The academy drew increasing numbers of young women to the little mining town. They came from such distant places as Kentucky, Tennessee and New England. Some of the "scholars" asked to enter the Dominican community. One of these was Cassie Stevens, a lively learner from a Presbyterian family of Boston who had become a Catholic while at the Academy. Two years after returning to her home on Beacon Hill, she became a novice among the Dominican women whom she had known in the Academy. Later she wrote of the spirit of generous poverty which she experienced among the sisters:

As the sisters lived, worked, studied and prayed together, they created common bonds based on the spirit and traditions of the Order. Their founder lived that spirit and taught them the Dominican way of life. After several years of experimentation Father Samuel presented to the Master General Jandel a translation of the Latin Rule of the Dominican Third Order, giving for each section a full commentary on its meaning for the life and active ministry of Dominican women religious in the United States. Together with the Rule, the volume included a brief history of the Order of Preachers, lives of more than twenty Dominican women of the Third Order, and the Rule of St. Augustine translated by Bishop John England. There were also notes on keeping community records. All were bound into a handsome volume printed by D.J.Sadlier Company of New York and known as the Rule of 1860. The compiler hoped it would be used by many Dominican communities in active ministry in the United States.

The Sinsinawa women kept no cloister or rigorous fasts; nor did they rise during the night to pray the Divine Office. Such practices, wrote their founder, were "of little or no use" where the sisters kept schools or the climate was extremely cold. Dominican life and mission on a frontier called for adjustability and common sense. However, many Dominican women in the United States lived an active life and tried to observe the rules of the cloistered nuns.[38] Several adaptations in the Rule of 1860 revealed the Italian priest's grasp of the political and economic realities of life in the United States. The Rule contained no reference to choir or lay sisters. All enjoyed the same rights and obligations, regardless of education or family background; all voted for community leaders.

Samuel Mazzuchelli envisioned all the Dominicans as one family in the Order of Preachers. He shared that vision in his prophetic dedication of the Rule of 1860 to the Master General Jandel. He wrote,

THE RULE

OF THE

Sisters of the Third Order of St. Dominic,

CONFIRMED AND APPROVED

BY POPE INNOCENT VII. IN THE YEAR 1405,

AND

BY POPE EUGENE IV. IN THE YEAR 1439.

WITH

USEFUL AND PRACTICAL EXPLANATIONS

ADAPTED TO COMMUNITIES OF SISTERS OF SAID ORDER
IN THE UNITED STATES.

NEW YORK:

D. & J. SADLIER & CO., 164 WILLIAM STREET.

BOSTON:—128 FEDERAL STREET.

MONTREAL:—COR. NOTRE DAME & FRANCIS XAVIER STS.

1860.

The Rule of the Third Order translated into English by Samuel Mazzuchelli, O.P., with commentaries useful for the Dominican Sisters of the United States

The profession shall be made either in the Church, served by the Father Preachers, or in the private chapel of the Convent. The relations and friends of her who is about to profess, as well as the friends of the Order, should not be refused admittance. When done in the church, the congregation of the faithful has a right to be present. The Bishop, or the Director, who is to receive the profession, shall be seated on the platform of the altar, which shall have at least two lighted candles. The Sisters shall stand on either side of the altar, and the Novice in the middle of the sanctuary. The Bishop or Director shall begin the *Veni Creator Spiritus*, in Latin or in English, as on pages 70 and 71.

After the *Oremus* he may give some words of admonition to the Novice, who at its conclusion, shall kneel below the steps of the altar, and the Prioress shall take a seat on the right side of the Novice, who, in the manner prescribed in the fourth chapter, shall recite the words of the Profession.

If the ceremony of giving a cross be adopted, the Bishop or Director, in presenting it to the newly professed, shall say :

Sister ———, receive this silver cross as the adorable sign of your being a spouse of Christ, and of the holiness of the Catholic faith, which, as a daughter of St. Dominic, you are called to preach and defend. Amen.

Then, all standing, the *Magnificat* shall be chanted by the choir, or recited by the Sisters, in Latin or in English.

**Selection from the Rule describing the ceremony of religious profession
for Sisters of the Third Order**

While he was establishing the community of Dominican women Father Samuel did not neglect his pastoral responsibilities or decline any call to preach and teach. On Sundays he gave the people of his parishes in Benton and New Diggings an instruction before Mass and a sermon on the Gospel of the day. The instruction was usually on the books of the Bible, studied throughout the year. One young listener described his preaching in these words:

> His long lectures before mass on the Old Testament & the usual sermon after the Gospel were always most inspiring & listened to by us, his poor ignorant congregation, with such rapt attention that you could hear a pin drop in the church. His language was always so simple & unctuous that any child could understand it.[40]

The priest did not write out his instructions or sermons, but recorded them throughout each year in sturdy account books. Preceding his topic of instruction [*In*] and subject of the Sunday sermon, he noted weather and road conditions which might affect his rural parishioners. A page for February 1851 includes the following entries:

Page from Father Samuel's record of sermons and instructions, February 1852

The priest's profound understanding of the meaning of *call* made him respond if possible to every summons, whether from a distant mission or a person close by who was in need. So it happened that the summons of a dying parishioner led to his own final call. Going into the country in the bitter cold of winter led to his death from pneumonia on February 23, 1864, at the age of 57. He answered that summons joyfully, recalling aloud the words of the psalm, "How lovely are thy tabernacles, O Lord God of Hosts!" The mourners knew that some of those tabernacles were the churches he had built, the parishes he had formed, and the hearts of people to whom he had brought the good news of the Gospel. One eulogy at the time of his death spoke for many persons in these words:

He who was once the only priest west of Lake Michigan has left the people of the extensive region in mourning. He was a good man, faithful to his vocation, prompt and zealous in the performance of every duty, inflexible in principle, but so mild, affable and obliging that in him seemed to have been centered for a time all the reverence and respect of a heterogeneous and frontier people.[41]

How lovely is your dwelling place,
        O Lord of hosts!
My soul is longing and sighing
        for the courts of the Lord:
My heart and my flesh cry for joy
        to the living God:
Even the sparrow finds a home,
        and the swallow a nest to shelter her young—
Your altars, O Lord of hosts,
        my King and my God!

Blessed are they who dwell in your house, O Lord,
        without ceasing they praise you:
Blessed is the man who finds his strength in you,
        when he sets his heart on the sacred journey:
Going through the dry valley, they make it a spring,
        the first rain clothes it with blessings:
They go from strength to strength,
        they shall see the God of gods in Sion.

The psalm recited by Father Mazzuchelli on his deathbed

1. The Memoirs of Father Samuel Mazzuchelli, O.P. Tr. Maria Michele Amato, O.P. and Mary Jeremy Finnegan, O.P. (Chicago: The Priory Press, 1967) 8-9; hereafter **Mem.**

2. In Europe the Dominicans, like other religious orders, suffered from the effects of the French Revolution and the succeeding political oppression. Property was confiscated, convents and houses of study were closed, libraries stolen and scattered. Common life was nearly obliterated, chapters and elections were suspended. No friars were found in France, where the Order was founded, until it was restored there by Henri Lacordaire. In 1850 when Alexander Vincent Jandel was appointed Master General, he stated "I am surrounded by ruins." Under his leadership, the Order in Europe returned to life. See Benedict M. Ashley, O.P., **The Dominicans** (Collegeville, Minnesota: Liturgical Press, 1990) Ch. 8.

3. Velzi was appointed Vicar General in the absence of Dominican elective chapters. His efforts to restore the Lombard Province and establish a flourishing study center were notable, beginning in 1825 when Mazzuchelli was professed.

4. The unique ceremony is recorded among Velzi's official acts in Archives General, Order of Preachers (AGOP) IV, 269, 31. As head of the Lombard province of the Order, Velzi, along with his assistant Tommaso Cipolletti, knew the youth well, and both were pleased at his request.

5. Manifest of the ship *Edward Quesnel*, arriving in New York from Le Havre November 15, 1828. SDA XI, 9.

6. Mem 20.

7. The mission area lay outside the Diocese of Cincinnati, but was assigned to Bishop Fenwick's jurisdiction. It would later include the Upper Peninsula of Michigan Territory, created in 1837, and the State of Wisconsin (created in 1848).

8. The missions in French Canada were abandoned after 1773, when the Society of Jesus was suppressed by the pope. Catholics were left without a resident curé for fifty years.

9. The **métis** at Mackinac and Green Bay were children of French-Canadian fathers and native Indian mothers.

10. Mem 23.

11. See Ray Allen Billington's classic history of American anti-Catholicism, **The Protestant Crusade 1800-1850: A Study of the Origins of Nativism** (New York: Macmillan, 1938.)

12. Mem 31. The conflict at Mackinac lasted through a second year, and is described with careful documentation in Keith R. Widder, **Battle for the Soul** (Michigan State University Press, 1999) Chapter IV, "Evangelical Ministry to the Multi-ethnic Community at Mackinac, 1822-1837," 69-101.

13. Mem 56.

14. One early Dominican missionary from Ireland, Charles Ffrench, O.P., ministered to Abenaki Indians in Maine in the 1830s.

15. Samuel Mazzuchelli to President Jackson, St. Louis, May 10, 1835. SDA II, 23.

16. Mem 50.

17. Cipolletti knew Samuel Mazzuchelli well from the years he was a student at Sta. Sabina. In responding with enthusiasm to the request from the lead region, he proposed that the priest consider establishing a house of the Order there, and possibly a province! Tommaso Cipolletti to Samuel Mazzuchelli, Rome, Jan. 30, 1836, SL. Copy SDA. XII, 133.

18. Mem 151.

19. Mathias Loras to Joseph Rosati, Dubuque, Oct. 24, 1839, SL. Copy SDA II, 55.

20. Mem 274.

21. "To the Reader" **Mem** XIV.

22. Memorie Istoriche ed Edificanti d'un Missionario Apostolico dell'Ordine dei Predicatori. (Milano: Ditta Boniardi-Pogliani, 1844).

23. Cipolletti to Mazzuchelli, Rome, (Oct. or Nov.) 1836, Draft, AGOP XIII, 04600:53. Copy SDA II.

24. Angelo Ancarani, **Patent to Samuel Mazzuchelli as Commissary of the Master General,** Jan. 12, 1844, AGOP XIII, 04600:18. Copy SDA PA 29.

25. Recorded by Mazzuchelli in his small handwritten "History of the Missionary Establishment of Sinsinawa Mound, Wisconsin, 1844-1847." Original SDA II, 167. Poelking was professed as a lay brother. Later,

at the request of Mazzuchelli, he was ordained a priest. He died in 1866 at St. Rose, Kentucky.

26. Bishop John Henni to the President of the Society of the Propagation of the Faith, Milwaukee, June 22, 1846, SDA XIII, 56.

27. The Sinsinawa Mound College was incorporated by the first legislature of the State of Wisconsin in 1848. It drew students from families in the Mississippi Valley. It was closed at the end of the Civil War, but its influence was spread to distant places by young men who entered the Dominicans from Sinsinawa.

28. "Book of Records of the Convent of St. Clara in the Diocese of Milwaukee, State of Wisconsin, . . ." Aug. 4, 1847; Dec. 26, 1847. Autograph record by Samuel Mazzuchelli. SDA.

29. No information has been found about the early life of Mary McNulty, but she had served in St. Louis, taught at St. Joseph's Boys School in Philadelphia, and directed a German orphanage in Cincinnati. Mary Routan was born in England in 1822 of a French Presbyterian family and became a Catholic through the Oxford Movement.

30. From the Personal Journal of Josephine Cahill, 6. SDA.

31. Book of Foundations, Appendix I, 1849, 4. SDA.

32. One student, Charles McKenna, was inspired by a Mazzuchelli retreat to enter the Order. He became the founder of the Holy Name Society in the United States. O'Daniel, **Very Rev. Charles Hyacinth McKenna, O.P.** (New York: Holy Name Bureau, 1917) 39.

33. Mazzuchelli to Joseph Alemany, Benton, Wisconsin, Mar.11, 1850. UNDA. Copy SDA II, 160.

34. Sister Clara Conway taught in the Benton district school for a salary of twenty-five dollars a month. The usual monthly salary for a female teacher in 1860 was $14.50.

35. "Book of Records," Aug. 15, 1853. SDA.

36. Annals of St. Mary's Convent, Somerset, Ohio. Columbus Dominican Archives. The four women traveled by riverboat on the Ohio and Mississippi Rivers and by stage from Galena to Benton.

37. Sister Charles Borromeo Stevens, **Golden Bells in Convent Towers** (Chicago: R.R.Donnelley, 1904) 69-70.

38. See Mary Cecilia Murray, O.P., "From Second to Third Order: Transition in the Regensburg Family of American Dominican Women from 1853-1929." (Ph.D.dissertation, Drew University, 1994) 36-41.

39. Samuel Mazzuchelli to Alexander Vincent Jandel, Benton, Wisconsin, Easter Sunday [Apr. 24] 1859. SDA, P.A. 43.

40. Vincentia Williams, "A School Girl's Impressions of Father Samuel When She was Fifteen Years Old." n.d. Original SDA XIV, 122.

41. Judge Charles Corkery, "Death of Very Rev. Samuel Mazzuchelli, Proto-Priest of the Northwest," **San Francisco Monitor**, May 28, 1864. Copied in the **New York Metropolitan,** but with author unnamed.

CHAPTER 8

WITH SETTLERS ON THE MOVE

E veryone was moving. Americans earned the title of "transients" as they hastened north and west along new roads and canals and rode "the cars" on the first short railroads.[1] They traveled with hope and anticipation. At the same time, the families of Indian tribes were also on the move. In sharp contrast to their seasonal migrations of the past, or those caused by intertribal conflict, most tribes were being forced out of their homelands into a tragic future. The Indian Removal Act of 1832 only whetted the appetite of Americans for new land.

Dominican men and women did not migrate to obtain land but to reach the people who did. Among the settlers they intended to proclaim the Word of God, teach their children, and help to build their Church. To do so they covered immense distances, as members of the Order had done from the time of Dominic. One circumstance differed, however. Women of the Order in the United States introduced a unique pattern of mobility, virtually unknown among women religious early in the 19th century.[2]

A roadside inn: a welcome site for travelers westward bound

For most Americans, including the Dominicans, movement led to settlement. After 1832 the regions through which the pioneers had gone from one clearing to another were dotted with settlements. People of those settlements called for help to build their communities of faith. Together, priests, sisters and laity founded parishes, churches, schools and convents.[3] These appeared one by one on the landscapes of Kentucky, Ohio, Michigan Territory, the upper Mississippi Valley and Tennessee.

Seeing the urgent educational needs of the pioneer families, the women of Dominican communities were eager to carry on the teaching mission of the Order, and their work was valued. At St. Mary's Academy in Somerset, for example, Bishop John Purcell of Cincinnati expressed his appreciation in these words:

> The system of education is judiciously concerted and far more extensive than even flattering report had taught us to expect. The Catholics and the Protestants of the neighborhood, as well as of Cincinnati, Wheeling, and other distant towns, appear to begin to appreciate it as it merits. We know of few institutions which more successfully aspire to public patronage.[4]

Students in Kentucky and Ohio, impressed with the life of the sisters, asked to join them in increasing numbers. Although beset by the prevailing poverty and illness, the three foundations of Dominican sisters made before 1850 remained sturdy and promising. They were St. Magdalen's, Kentucky; St. Mary's, Somerset; and the new community at Sinsinawa, Wisconsin.[5]

In 1833 the Province of St. Joseph counted fifteen friars. There were thirteen priests and two lay brothers listed in the Catholic Directory as serving in two dioceses:

CINCINNATI, OHIO	**BARDSTOWN, KENTUCKY**
(centered at St. Joseph, Somerset)	(centered at St. Rose)
Charles Bowling	Joseph T. Jarboe
James Bullock	Thomas Martin
John McGrady	Bro. Patrick McKenna
Richard Miles	Thomas J. Polin
Charles P. Montgomery	Bro. Patrick Shepherd
Joseph O'Leary	William R. Tuite [6]
John Baptist DeRaymaecker	
Nicholas Dominic Young	

The ministry of the friars was chiefly spiritual and pastoral: preaching the Gospel; witnessing to poverty and the evangelical counsels; forming parishes, gathering the settlers for worship, and building churches. Until 1850, the two centers of ministry of St. Joseph Province remained St. Rose, Kentucky, and St. Joseph, Somerset, Ohio. Friars were called from one or the other as the missions required. From St. Rose they served at St. Dominic's, Springfield, and Holy Rosary, Manton, as well as St. Magdalen's convent. From St. Joseph they were missioned at Lancaster and Zanesville as well as Holy Trinity, Somerset. In addition, they visited outlying stations.

Critical needs of the people sometimes called the Dominicans beyond their ordinary ministry, as when the 1833 cholera epidemic struck suddenly in Kentucky.

The care given stricken families by the friars at St. Rose and the sisters at St. Magdalen's was praised by Bishop Benedict Flaget of Bardstown in these words:

It is especially in the congregation confided to the Reverend Dominican Fathers [St. Rose] that this frightful scourge has made itself felt and has immolated more victims.

Although the religious of the Third Order of St. Dominic [Dominican Sisters] have always been among the dead and the dying, not one has succumbed to those painful and charitable labors.

The five Dominican Fathers employed in that parish, the most numerous in all Kentucky, have deployed a zeal worthy of the first ages of the church. For more than three weeks, night and day, they were constantly employed in fulfilling their ministry among the sick, taking rest only half-clothed, and I would say almost all their meals on horseback.

When I betook myself to their convent, they were so extenuated and deplorably worn out that it was almost impossible for me to keep back my tears. A holy joy all the same appeared on their visages because their ministry had been blessed by the happiest success both among Catholics and among Protestants.

Two lay brothers of this order have wrought unbelievable good; never would I have known the hundredth part of the merit of these venerable religious, if that frightful scourge had not appeared in the country. God in his mercy has preserved them all, without doubt to give them new occasions of deploying their zeal worthy of all admiration and almost above all praise. I hope that one day I will be able to give an exact account of their works which will certainly be most edifying.[7]

One of the victims of the epidemic was William Raymond Tuite, the third of the English friars who had accompanied Edward Fenwick to the United States to found St. Joseph Province.

The two lay brothers cited by Bishop Flaget were the first ones received in the American province. Brother Patrick McKenna was professed in 1830 and remained at St. Rose for the rest of his life. At his death his goodness was praised in these words: "Brother Patrick was a man of exemplary piety and obedience. . . . And being both kind and charitable to his brothers he was truly beloved by all."[8] Brother Patrick Shepherd was professed at St. Rose in 1831. When Shepherd died in 1860, he was praised in the press as a stonemason who had worked with the Fathers in the establishment of the Church in Ohio; in Kentucky as a gardener widely known and respected; and among his brethren of St. Rose, a man of ardent prayer.[9] Before 1850 the two men would be joined by six other Irish brothers.

In the fall of 1832 the Dominican mission in Ohio was changed dramatically after the death of Bishop Fenwick. His authority in Church and Order was now transferred to three men. John Baptist Purcell, an Irish-born priest and scholar from Mt. St. Mary's College in Emmitsburg, Maryland, succeeded him as Bishop of Cincinnati.[10] Some thought that the new bishop should have been chosen from the Order of Preachers.[11] With Purcell's appointment the argument ended, but the issue did not die. What relationship would now exist between the bishop and the Dominicans of St. Joseph Province? A second responsibility of Bishop Fenwick was given to Frederic Rese, his former vicar, who was appointed Bishop of Detroit in 1833. His new diocese covered the remainder of Fenwick's original jurisdiction, the vast Territory of Michigan, reaching to the Mississippi.

Fenwick's third responsibility, that of Dominican superior, was given to Nicholas Dominic Young, first as vicar provincial.[12] He represented the Order at the consecration of Bishop Purcell in Baltimore on October 13, 1833, and from there accompanied the new bishop back to Cincinnati. Purcell appointed him vicar general of the diocese; a move which led to the first dispute between the two men. Because Purcell did not announce the appointment of his vicar, Young published the news himself in the diocesan paper, the *Catholic Telegraph.* Purcell responded with an episcopal scolding.

**Bishop John Baptist
Purcell of Cincinnati**

> I can see no occasion for formally announcing your appointment. . . My object in making it in your favor was that in managing the affairs of the churches confided to priests of your order, you may be, *ad aedificatione,* under less restraint. . . . These are points of no great moment to men whose calling is to save immortal souls. Let this be our main occupation of mind & heart and life, to the exclusion of minor things such as St. Paul disdained to notice that he may gain Christ.[13]

Young replied that he had made the announcement in order to quiet rumors of a break between the bishop and the province.[14] But the announcement seemed only to encourage such a break. Within the year Young decided to resign as Purcell's vicar.

Strain continued between bishop and provincial as each upheld his own sphere of authority. One example of opposing perspectives was the manner of dealing with a Dominican priest, Stephen Hyacinth Montgomery, whose misdeeds led Young to restrict his activity.[15] The bishop brought Montgomery to live with him. This seemed a flagrant disregard of Young's jurisdiction over the internal affairs of the Order. The crusty correspondence between bishop and provincial revealed a relationship of reluctant admiration and indignant response between two stubborn men who found different ways to serve the Church.[16] Nicholas Young was certainly well meaning, and a strong leader in the struggling Province of St. Joseph. Yet he often aroused resistance and frustration among his Dominican confreres as well as others. He demanded from the friars a blind obedience that was incompatible with Dominican spirituality. He seemed not to know how to persuade and lead those of good will.

The ministry of Nicholas Dominic Young among the people was zealous and knew no limits. In Ohio alone no other Dominican was so well known and honored by the earliest settlers, as told in this tribute:

> Many were the early Catholic missionary priests whose work in Ohio earned for them appointments to bishoprics, the enduring recognition of historians, and even full-length biographies. No priest was more important, however, to the Catholic people of frontier Ohio than Father Nicholas D. Young O.P. This devoted son of St. Dominic must have been known to every Catholic family which lived in Ohio before 1830. There could hardly have been a Catholic family here who did not have at least one child baptized by his hand and voice or one marriage blessed by him for the Church.[17]

The portrait caption reads: MOST REV. JOHN B. PURCELL, D.D.

Bishop and provincial collaborated in 1833 to negotiate a major transfer of property from the Province of St. Joseph to the Diocese of Cincinnati. The early Catholic settlers, in recognition of the friars' ministry among them, had given Edward Fenwick and the friars the title to properties of the following churches in Ohio:

Trinity in Somerset, Perry County	St. Barnabas on Jonathan Creek, Morgan County
St. John, Zanesville	
St. John Baptist, Canton	St. Patrick, Perry County
St. Paul, Dungannon near New Lisbon	St. Mary, Lancaster
St. Dominic, Beaver, Guernsey County	Sapp's Settlement, Knox County

In his will, signed in 1830 and approved by the Holy See, Bishop Fenwick bequeathed these properties to the Province of St. Joseph. This was as the people intended.[18] But there were not enough Dominican priests of that province to care for all nine churches. Thus in 1833, after the execution of Fenwick's will, the province surrendered five church titles to the Diocese of Cincinnati. At the close of 1833 the friars remained only at Holy Trinity in Somerset, St. Mary's in Lancaster and St. John's in Zanesville, as well as at their proto-church of St. Joseph in Somerset.[19] This transfer of churches was not merely a matter of real estate, but related essentially to the parish ministry in each place. The need of the diocese, like that of the Dominican province, was for priests more than for property. Bishop Purcell now had to supply priests for the parishes originally served by the Dominicans, whom he often praised for their faithful mission.

Nicholas Dominic Young, O.P., Provincial

Until 1834 the original convent of St. Rose, Kentucky, was the only priory in the province. To the disappointment of the men there, Nicholas Dominic Young had chosen for his residence as provincial the community of friars at St. Joseph's, Somerset. Since the growing Catholic population in Ohio demanded the presence of more priests, an unproductive rivalry began to develop between the two houses and Young had difficulty establishing his authority among the St. Rose friars. He had to be assured by Olivieri, the master general, of his right to transfer men from Kentucky to Ohio.[20]

On January 18, 1839, the friars' Convent of St. Joseph was made a formal priory and novitiate. While this status was long desired, it would intensify the competition between St. Rose Priory and that of St. Joseph. Their rivalry did not cease until the focus of the province turned to the east, leaving both Ohio and Kentucky at the western extremity of the province.

Meanwhile, on April 22, 1837, the year of widespread financial panic, one event gratified all the friars. As a province, they elected Richard Pius Miles to be their American provincial. It was their first effective election in the province, an indication of its increasing maturity.[21] Following Young, Miles soon became widely respected. As provincial he was mild but firm, just and kind. However, the friars would benefit only briefly from his guidance.

Only six months after his election as provincial, Richard Miles received word that he had been appointed bishop of the newly created Diocese of Nashville, Tennessee. He refused the appointment, citing the needs of the province and his own shortcomings. His American confreres and Dominican officials in Rome joined him in protest, but to no avail. Richard Miles was consecrated Bishop of Nashville on September 16, 1838. The new bishop kept in close touch with the province, and turned to its members for assistance and encouragement. His real need was for priests, since there were none attached to the diocese when he was appointed. Eventually, several Dominican men and women came to his aid.[22]

Before Miles could undertake his episcopal duties, a serious difficulty for the province arose with Bishop Purcell. In an early letter to Miles, the Ohio bishop raised the matter of the annuity owed him by the Dominicans, which he now calculated to amount to $1500.[23] Province members, including Young, thought the matter was a dead issue. Why Purcell decided to initiate the demand at this time is difficult to understand. He knew that it could not be paid without depleting the limited funds needed for the sustenance of the friars. In addition, the Dominicans felt that they had already benefited the diocese by giving it properties of much greater value than the designated sum. Besides, they continued serving several parishes and missions without expense to the diocese.[24] Charles P. Montgomery, who succeeded Miles as provincial, summed up the feelings of the friars when he wrote Purcell, "Were a person to ask you your advice, whether the payment of a note which had been given under erroneous suppositions could be conscientiously demanded, you would certainly answer in the negative . . . . Where then is the justice of your claim?"[25] The annuity remained a tense issue, involving consultation with Rome until 1852. At that point Robert White, an Irish Dominican visitator of the province, joined Bishop Purcell in bringing about cancellation of the obligation.[26]

To replace Miles as provincial, the master general Angelo Ancarani appointed Charles Pius Montgomery on November 24, 1838.[27] While such a position would not have been Montgomery's ambition, he tried to carry out his duties diligently. By this time there were fifteen priests and three lay brothers in the Province of St. Joseph, of whom six priests and two brothers were at St. Rose, and nine priests and one brother at Somerset.

Before Richard Miles left his responsibilities as provincial, he assigned two young friars to study in Rome: Nicholas Raymond Young, nephew of Nicholas Dominic, and the subdeacon Thomas Langdon Grace of Charleston, South Carolina. The policy of sending students to Rome, rather than bringing European lectors to the United States, had been urged by major superiors to satisfy the need for lectors in the American province. Balancing study with ministry was a fundamental issue for the Americans, as it had been for the Order elsewhere. From the beginning, study was as essential to Dominican common life as liturgical and contemplative prayer. But study and ministry have always existed in tension. Among the early American friars, the tension was unending. Some of the older men cited Fenwick as their model, forgetting that he himself deplored his lack of scholarship, which was a by-product of the French

Revolution and its aftermath. They argued that the frontier Church did not require advanced theology, and demands of the missions made impossible any long period of preparatory study. Some friars, led by Eugenio Pozzo and supported by Nicholas Young, Charles P. Montgomery, and George Wilson, countered that contemplation, study, and strict observance of the Constitutions of the Order were essential. Others insisted that observing the letter of the Constitutions (which had not been officially revised since 1690) was almost impossible for missionaries at locations many miles apart.

In 1840 the arrival of three well-educated Dominicans from Europe stirred some self-examination on the part of province members. Joseph Sadoc Alemany and Francis Cubero came from Spain, via Italy, to serve the missions. Eugenio Pozzo left his chair of theology at the University of Turin to come to the United States, and effected the most immediate impact. He was made Regent of Studies and placed in charge of the provincial studium, or house of studies at Somerset. He also hoped to bring about stricter observance of the Constitutions and customs of the Order.

Eugenio Pozzo from Turin leads list of regents of studies of St. Joseph province

PP. Moderatores Studii Gen. Ohiens. Conv. S. Joseph.

Anno 1841.
Stud. Reg. Rv. P. Fr. Eug. Nyac. Pozzo litteris patent
datis die 17 Sept. ab A.R.P. Fr. Pio Montgomery Priore Prov.

Anno 1842.
Stud. Reg. Rev. P. Fr. Eug. Nyac. Pozzo.

Anno 1843.
Stud. Reg. Rev. P. Fr. Eug. Nyac. Pozzo.

Anno 1844.
Stud. Reg. Rev. P. Fr. Eug. Nyac. Pozzo.

Anno 1845.
Stud. Reg. Rev. P. Fr. Eug. Nyac. Pozzo.
Philos. Lector. Rev. P. Fr. Sadoc Vilarrasa Lit. pat. diei 17
Septembris a P. Fr. Th. Jarboe Vic. Prov.

Anno 1846.

The studium offered candidates courses necessary for their ministry of preaching and teaching in the United States. Some of the Somerset students were chosen to continue studies for graduate degrees. Later, Pozzo was assisted in his lectorship by the scholarly Spaniard Francis Sadoc Vilarrasa and some of the better students, including James Whelan. Coming from the University of Turin, Pozzo must have found the young men from farms or villages of Kentucky and Ohio raw material indeed. He wrote to the master general Vincent Ajello, "I have to work with people who are not capable of forming an idea of the order, the necessity of studies, who are blind to formal and colorful ideas."[28] Nor did he receive much support from some of the friars, who lent a sympathetic ear to students experiencing difficulties in classes. Pozzo returned to Europe after promoting the Dominican ideal of "assiduous study" among the Americans for nine years.

In the fall of 1842 George A. J. Wilson was appointed provincial on the recommendation of Nicholas Young.[29] He was a recent convert from Methodism and said to have a "fire and brimstone" style with its emphasis on total abstinence. Some considered him a harsh judge of men. He enjoyed the confidence of superiors of the Order to whom he sometimes conveyed a negative picture of the province. In May of 1844, Wilson left for Rome to attend a general chapter and beg for funds for the province. He developed such a liking for Europe that it proved difficult to keep him in the States thereafter. Nevertheless, his travels also benefited the people and the province. In Ohio he was known for his zealous preaching and long, difficult journeys to the sick and others in need. In 1852 he built the church of St. Dominic in the nation's capital, and in 1867 he opened the parish of St. Vincent Ferrer in New York.[30]

In January of 1845, there arrived three friars from Europe who to some extent relieved the shortage of priests. They were Francis Sadoc Vilarrasa from Spain, and Mannes D'Arco and James Aloysius Orengo from Italy. Vilarrasa was immediately appointed novice-master, the post he had held in the convent of strict observance at Quercia in Italy.[31] About the same time, Nicholas Raymond Young and Thomas Langdon Grace returned to the province after almost seven years of study in Italy.

Early in 1845 Bishop Miles offered St. Joseph Province a new site for ministry in the Nashville diocese: St. Peter's Parish, Memphis. He judged it to be the best parish in his diocese.[32] The provincial Wilson called for an interim chapter at which the possible accession of the Memphis parish was a chief matter of business. By accepting St. Peter's the province opened its first new mission since the death of Fenwick. Moreover, that parish had the unique distinction of being self-supporting. There were snags to overcome, however, before the Order could take possession of it.[33] For the interim, Samuel Louis Montgomery and Joseph Alemany were assigned to Tennessee to assist Bishop Miles.

In 1833 the sisters at Somerset welcomed from Kentucky two of their pioneer members, Angela Sansbury and her cousin Ann Hill. They joined the community of six at St. Mary's, including Angela's sister Benven and Ursula Grignon, Sister Mary, the first Dominican woman professed in Ohio. Mobility, which had characterized the history of the men's provinces for centuries, now became an accepted part of the women's communities as well.

Some of the young women who came to know the sisters in one of the Dominican academies asked to become Dominicans in Somerset or St. Magdalen's. By 1845 the

Stagecoach jolting across a swamp on a corduroy road

Metropolitan Catholic Almanac and Laity's Directory could preface an item about the Somerset academy of St. Mary with this fact: "There are sixteen professed sisters and five novices in this institution." The Spanish missionary Vilarrasa, in a letter to his parents, gave his impression of the Somerset sisters in these words:

In Somerset the majority are Protestants. Here we have a very edifying convent of nuns who devote themselves to the education of little girls, among them being several Protestants. These nuns observe our constitutions to the letter and wear the habit openly. They are not cloistered and by means of this wise and prudent exception are able to silence the calumnies of non-Catholics.[34]

By 1847 St. Magdalen Convent numbered twenty-one sisters and could scarcely accommodate them along with the Academy boarders.

In both communities the growth of membership and expanding ministry were overshadowed by a question that would be crucial to their continued apostolate in the United States: **How could the American sisters continue their active apostolate and at the same time follow the monastic customs which were practiced by Dominican women elsewhere in the world?** The question would last for the remainder of the century.

Monastic practices found in the nuns' constitutions included long fasts and periodic hours of the Divine Office, night and day. They allowed only minimal relationships with persons outside the cloister. But the American Dominicans understood that they had been founded for a more active ministry: to provide schooling for children and youth. To combine that ministry with monastic practice was impossible. Still, the Americans wished to live fully their vocation as members of the Order of Preachers. How could they solve this dilemma?

169

The sisters of Kentucky and Ohio decided together, with the encouragement of the friars, to present their dilemma to the Pope himself, Pius IX. They wrote a joint letter, signed by every professed member of the two communities of St. Magdalen and St. Mary. They asked, while remaining full members of the Order, to be dispensed from monastic practices which were entirely incompatible with their work of teaching. Their request was very clear, as seen in this excerpt from the letter:

> We cannot recite the Divine Office, because the number of those who are capable of teaching being very small, it would consume more time than they could possibly devote to it. Nor can we be enclosed because our Convents are not built in a suitable manner, and we have not sufficient revenues to change their present form. Again, were we enclosed, we should lose our pupils, Catholic as well as Protestants, and would then be deprived of the means of support. Wherefore, submitting these considerations to the wisdom of your Holiness, we join in one common prayer for a dispensation of being enclosed, and allowing us to recite the office of the B. V. Mary instead of the Divine Office and to grant us the favor of making the solemn profession as the Nuns of the second Order of our Holy Father St. Dominick.[35]

Cloister grilles on either side of the sanctuary at St. Magdalen chapel, Kentucky

The sisters were in fact asking to continue the practice they were following. They wished to belong to the cloistered branch of the Order (Second Order) by profession, and to the active branch [Third Order] in practice.

The letter identifies every professed sister of both convents in Kentucky and Ohio; that is, it was signed by all the existing Dominican sisters in the United States.[36] Their signatures and given locations in 1848 provide exact information that can be found nowhere else, making this a document of singular significance in the history of American women of the Order of Preachers.[37]

No reply came, probably because the letter could not have reached the Pope before he fled Rome during the 1848 uprising. The sisters' ambiguous status continued, as shown by their erection of a cloister grille in the new chapel at St. Magdalen's. The chapel was dedicated while their July 4 letter was en route to Rome.[38]

By 1847 the friars of St. Joseph Province were sharply divided between those who favored emphasis on study and observance of the 1690 Constitutions, and those who favored moderating study and observance for the sake of the mission. So sharp was their division that in October 1847 an election became impossible and the men had to ask the master general to appoint their next provincial superior. Those who emphasized study, led by Eugenio Pozzo, included Nicholas D. Young, Sadoc Vilarrasa, Charles Montgomery, and George Wilson. They favored the appointment of Joseph Alemany whose formation in the strict novitiate of Quercia, Italy, seemed to align him with their cause.[39] They flooded Rome with demands for Alemany. After their request was granted, they discovered their mistake.

Joseph Alemany was appointed provincial of St. Joseph Province on May 2, 1848. Unknown to his brethren, Alemany's missionary experience in Ohio and Tennessee had modified his views on study and strict monastic observance. He now believed that long intensive study of theology was unnecessary for the work to be done on the frontier. If mission needs conflicted with the requirements of observance, the new provincial would give priority to the good of the Church. When, for example, Vilarrasa protested the absence of James Orengo from his Ohio convent for two years on mission in Tennessee, Alemany gave Orengo permission to remain there with Bishop Miles. He stated that the province should have helped the Tennessee bishop more than it had.

In the fall of 1849 Joseph Alemany delayed calling an intermediate chapter, no doubt realizing that nothing could be accomplished in the current state of divisiveness. Then three men of the province, Fathers Nicholas D. Young, Charles Montgomery, and George Wilson, citing the authorization of seventeenth-century chapters, convoked the chapter themselves! It was to meet in October.[40] Alemany responded officially: "I now use the authority, granted me by the Master General, to cancel the Intermediate Chapter proposed by you and transfer it to the First Sunday after Epiphany, 1850." But the insurgents went ahead with their plans, and imposed six conditions on Alemany which would drastically curtail his power. For example, he was to live at Somerset rather than choose his own place of residence. He could be absent for provincial visitations only three weeks of the year. And he had no power to remove novices from their studies to be sent on mission.

In May 1850, the beleaguered Alemany sailed for Rome to attend a general chapter of the Order. He was accompanied by a friar who regularly opposed his policies, Sadoc Vilarrasa. But on arrival in Rome, they discovered that the general chapter was canceled owing to political upheaval, and the master general Ajello had left Rome. Alemany explained his position to the presiding vicar general, Thomas Cipolletti, who denied the validity of the "interim chapter" acts of the preceding October. In the midst of negotiations, Cipolletti suddenly died. His vicar sent back the acts of the irregular provincial chapter held in the previous October, but without approval.[41]

If Alemany had returned to finish his term, he probably would have governed with the moderation that was to characterize the remainder of his American apostolate. But while he was in Rome, events back in the United States led to startling changes for him and for the province. When California joined the Union in 1848, the Church was required to appoint an American bishop for the Diocese of Monterey to succeed the Mexican prelate. In 1849 Charles P. Montgomery of St. Joseph Province was named to that office. Because health and disposition made it impossible for him to accept the post, he refused the nomination. Fortunately, Rome could now turn to a perfect alternative, Joseph Alemany, the experienced Spanish-speaking missionary who had already served in Ohio and Tennessee. Because the American bishops insisted that there was no one better for the new post, Alemany was compelled to accept it. While in Rome he was consecrated Bishop of Monterey, California, on June 30, 1850. After trying to gather funds and missionaries in Europe, he went directly to California, accompanied by his former rival, Sadoc Vilarrasa, who was to establish a new Dominican province of friars. With the two men went Dominican women from Paris and Somerset to form a community of richly diverse cultures. All brought the mission of Dominic to the Pacific coast just as the search for gold was reaching its crescendo there. Their beginnings in California are told in Chapter 12.

1. See Daniel Boorstin, **The Americans: the National Experience**, Pt. Two: "The Transients" (New York: Vintage Books, 1965).

2. There were a few communities of Third Order Dominican women religious working actively in the Church in Europe, but these were not part of the mission of the friars, nor of a network of women's communities, as were those in the United States who were founded first in Kentucky in 1822.

3. Dominican friars and sisters call their houses *convents* to signify a place of common life for those who move in and out to active mission. The term *monastery* is properly used for the cloistered nuns of the Order.

4. Bishop John Baptist Purcell to the **Catholic Telegraph,** May 16, 1834.

5. See Ch. 7, "To Michigan, Wisconsin and the Mississippi Valley."

6. Taken from the **Catholic Directory** of 1834. Publishers ordinarily listed the locations of personnel as in the previous year.

7. Flaget to Louis Deluol, S.S., Bardstown, July 5, 1833, Filson Club archives, Louisville, KY (FCA).

8. Words from the Book of Deaths in the Congregation of St. Rose, Oct., 1852, SJP. His obituary was published in the **Catholic Telegraph and Advocate**, Cincinnati, OH, Oct. 30, 1852, Saint Joseph Province Archives (SJP).

9. **The Guardian**, Louisville, KY, July 7, 1860, SJP.

10. Purcell was president of the college when called to the bishopric. He was consecrated on Oct. 13, 1833, and became Archbishop of Cincinnati in 1850. The Dominicans of Somerset were within his jurisdiction until the creation of the Diocese of Columbus in 1868.

11. See the Purcell-Young correspondence of 1834-1837, SJP.

12. Nicholas Young was named vicar provincial of the American Dominicans on Dec. 3, 1832, and began his term on March 1, 1833. He became provincial on May 28, 1834.

13. Cincinnati, Feb. 6, 1834, SJP.

14. Young to Purcell, Somerset, Mar. 11, 1834, University of Notre Dame Archives (UNDA) II 4 e.

15. Stephen Montgomery, dear to Edward Fenwick as one of the first Americans in the Province of St. Joseph, caused him grief when accused of sexual misconduct. The Kentuckian was befriended by Bishop Purcell, who made him pastor of the Cincinnati cathedral parish and assumed all responsibility for him. Later, Montgomery was granted a dispensation from the Order and used his many talents in the dioceses of Louisville, Natchez, and New Orleans. See Purcell-Young correspondence, UNDA II 4 e and f; and SJP 1834-1837, SJP.

16. See the Purcell-Young correspondence of 1834-1837, SJP.

17. Anthony J. Lisska, "Rev. Nicholas Dominic Young, O.P., Early Dominican Missionary in Ohio," **Barquilla de la Santa Maria: Bulletin of the Catholic Record Society, Diocese of Columbus** (Columbus, Ohio (CRS), Dec. 1999) Vol. XIII, No. 12. p. 95.

18. Fenwick Will, Cincinnati, July 3, 1830, Cincinnati Archdiocesan Archives (CAA).

19. Details of the will and its execution are given in John H. Lamott, **History of the Archdiocese of Cincinnati** (New York: Frederick Pustet, 1921) 181.

20. Young to Olivieri, St. Joseph's, Somerset, Nov. 27, 1834, Archives General, Order of Preachers, Rome (AGOP), Mercier file. Copy SJP.

21. As his term was drawing to a close Young asked the master general, now Tommaso Cipolletti, about holding an elective chapter. Cipolletti encouraged this action. He added that, if the one chosen was Miles, as Young predicted, he confirmed the election beforehand. Cipolletti to N.D. Young, Rome, Jan. 15, 1836, SJP.

22. See Chapter 9, "Founding the Church in Tennessee."

23. Purcell to Miles, Cincinnati, March 31, 1838, SJP. The origin of the annuity question is described in Chapter 5. Purcell now claimed that he had brought up the matter frequently with N.D. Young, a claim which Young vehemently denied. (See Young to Purcell, St. Joseph's, Apr. 10, 1838, UNDA II 4 g. Copy, SJP.) Surviving evidence supports Young. There is no mention of the annuity in Purcell's earlier letters.

24. In another context Young stated that funds from Propaganda for the Diocese of Cincinnati were never shared with the Dominican parishes in the diocese. Nicholas D. Young to Raymond Van Zeeland, Somerset, Apr. 14, 1840, SJP.

25. C.P. Montgomery to Purcell, Somerset, OH, Sep. 8, 1841, UNDA II 4 g.

26. Robert White to M.A. O'Brien, Rome, Oct. 9, 1852, SJP.

27. The friars did not yet have the necessary condition for electing a provincial. See O'Daniel, **Province of St. Joseph** (New York: Holy Name Society, 1942) 89-90.

28. Pozzo to Ajello, Somerset, OH, Jan. 21, 1845, AGOP XIII, 03150, 217, SJP.

29. Because Wilson had not yet completed the twelve years of profession required to hold the provincial office, Charles P. Montgomery continued as acting provincial until Sep. of 1843. SJP records, 1843.

30. O'Daniel, **St. Joseph Province**, 175-177.

31. The novitiate at Quercia, near Viterbo, was an early sign of restoration of life in the beleaguered Order at mid-century. There monastic observance was emphasized. Men formed in that tradition included Sadoc Vilarrasa, Joseph Alemany, and Henri Lacordaire, who would soon restore the Order in France; also Vincent Jandel, who was head of the Order of Preachers after 1850. See R.P. Mortier, O.P., **Histoire des Maitres Généraux de l'Ordre des Frères Précheurs**, vol. 7 (Paris: Picard, 1914) 488-495.

32. Miles to Jarboe, Nashville, Jan. 17, 1845, SJP.

33. Dominican practice required that the parish property be deeded to the Order. This was an obstacle for many bishops. Those of the Order, including Alemany in California, proved no less resistant on this score.

34. Francis Sadoc Vilarrasa, S.T.L., in a letter of Apr. 5, 1845, to his parents, SJP.

35. Dominican Sisters to Pope Pius IX, Somerset, Ohio, July 4, 1848, AGOP XIII, 03150, 253, Copy, Archives, Columbus Dominican Sisters (CDS). Full text in Chapter 11.

36. To the west, at Sinsinawa, Wisconsin, several novices had been received into the Order by Samuel Mazzuchelli, O.P., but none made profession until 1849.

37. The personal signatures and titles of major officials in each house have allowed for correction of some accounts of terms of officials, etc.

38. See description and photo in Anna Minogue, **A Hundred Years of Dominican History** (Cincinnati: Pustet, 1921) 82-83.

39. See note 31 above.

40. Young *et al* to Alemany, Somerset, Sep. 1, 1849, SJP. Young, Montgomery and Wilson were joined by Vilarrasa and Pozzo. Cf. Montgomery *et al*, Somerset, Oct. 29, 1849, SJP.

41. The decisions Cipolletti had made were documented by Jerome Gigli, who was Vicar of the Order from July 9, 1850 until Oct. 1, when Vincent Jandel was appointed head of the Order by Pope Pius IX. See the detailed study of related documents by J.B. Walker, SJP and SDA.

CHAPTER 9

Founding the Church in Tennessee

Richard Pius Miles and Joseph Thomas Jarboe, astride their horses on a bright autumn day in October 1838, rode on, often in silence through the forested areas of Kentucky and Tennessee. They left St. Rose knowing there was no turning back. Both men, usually cheerful, showed uncharacteristic solemnity. The events of the past year weighed heavily upon them. Miles had scarcely been elected head of St. Joseph Province of friars when he was named Bishop of Nashville, Tennessee. Now Father Jarboe was accompanying him to his See almost as with one going to the guillotine.

The disturbing news of Miles' episcopal appointment had reached the Dominican friars in October of 1837. It caused ambivalent feelings for all concerned. They were glad that one of their most capable brothers had been named to the bishopric of Tennessee, but sad because they were so desperately in need of every priest in the Order. Miles himself had no mixed reaction. He was determined to accept the mitre only under formal precept. He believed his loss would be too hard on the province. ". . . I think there has been a strange blunder committed in my nomination . . . to appoint a poor Religious, who cannot command one cent, in case he accepts, to a See where there is neither a church nor a clergyman nor any means, that I know of, to procure either."[1]

Nicholas Young, never one to hide his feelings, told Bishop John Purcell of Cincinnati that he could not agree that Miles should be appointed Bishop of Nashville. "He [Miles] can expect no blessing from Heaven when he knows the present situation of the friars in this country."[2] Even Thomas Cipolletti, Master of the Order in Rome, wrote to say he was "overcome by grief at learning that Fr. Miles has been appointed to the newly created See of Nashville."[3] He urged Miles himself to write to the Pope begging to be excused from accepting the post for the good of the Order. Miles had already notified the Archbishop of Baltimore that he did not intend to accept the bishopric in Tennessee without a clear command from Rome. He was further disturbed when his friend Bishop Purcell of Cincinnati, convinced that Miles should accept the nomination, wrote, "May God plentifully reward your humility & not impute to you as a fault your distrust of His Vocation!"[4] In August of 1838, the stressful uncertainty was dispelled. Miles received word that the Holy Father insisted that he accept the Diocese of Nashville as his See. He acquiesced and began to plan the transition from being head of St. Joseph Province to first Bishop of Tennessee.

Tennessee had become the sixteenth state of the Union in 1796, with Knoxville as the state capital and John Sevier its first governor. The growth of the state was slow; in 1838 it was still considered frontier territory. Among the settlers, Catholics represented a tiny percentage, even though railroad building attracted many Irish laborers in the 1820s. Since 1808 Tennessee had constituted part of the vast diocese of Bardstown under Bishop Flaget who sent missionaries from time to time to seek out Catholics. Stephen Badin journeyed there in 1808 and again in 1809 and 1810, but the veteran missionary reported finding very few members of the Church. Other early priests from Kentucky were Robert Abell, the first pastor at Nashville, and Elisha Durbin, who retained his residence in Kentucky but traveled to Tennessee at least once a year. It was Durbin who made preparations for the coming to Nashville of its first bishop.

Bishop Richard Miles,
O.P., of Nashville

On September 16, 1838, in the absence of Flaget who was in Rome, Bishop Rosati of St. Louis performed the ceremonies in the Cathedral of Bardstown constituting Richard Pius Miles Bishop of Nashville. It had to be a day of tempered celebration for the friars, but one of joy to the few Catholics of Tennessee. Two weeks after his consecration, Miles and Jarboe traveled to Nashville. On November 10 Jarboe wrote that when they arrived in Nashville, they "took lodgings provided for us at the Washington Hotel, where the Bishop was soon visited by most of the Catholics of the place, as also by many of the citizens of other denominations who seemed pleased . . . and expressed a willingness to aid him in his many necessities."[5] Jarboe continued with words of praise for Father Durbin's preparations for the bishop. He had made repairs on the much-neglected cathedral, using $125 of his own money to cover expenses. "It is but a just tribute to this indefatigable missionary to state . . . that he has been the only priest that has visited the Catholics of Nashville for many years past . . . his praise is in all the churches."

The hardy Tennessee pioneers were, no doubt, impressed with the physical appearance of the new bishop: his six-foot, large boned and well built frame, his hair to his shoulders, as was the custom of the day. His kindly expression must have been equally attractive. "He was deeply emotional yet rarely displayed this. He was even-tempered, stable, reassuring with a resonant and mellow voice."[6] When Miles and Durbin began a visitation of the new diocese Jarboe returned to St. Rose, leaving Miles for the first time in his religious life without a Dominican confrere nearby. On this first pastoral journey through a portion of the diocese, Bishop Miles and Durbin rode horseback, stopping especially to preach among the many small pockets of scattered Catholics. On their return, they calculated they had traveled five hundred miles and that the Catholic population of the state numbered around three hundred.[7]

Over the next few years Miles welcomed several priests into his diocese. Yet he was always begging for clergy because those who came stayed only a few years. Some who served in these early years included Joseph Stokes and Michael McAleer from

Cincinnati, and William Clancy from Mobile. Other volunteers could not obtain *exeats*, even from bishops who appeared to support Richard Miles. The movement in and out of the Diocese of Nashville, as well as other frontier sees, was epitomized by one missionary, D. A. Quinn:

> Throughout this period priests come and go, appear and disappear, join an order and leave it, turn up in California and Texas, knowing that wherever they go their lot is loneliness and hardship. If they have homes, they are away from them more than in them; they rarely have churches."[8]

The first diocesan priest to offer his services in Tennessee was Joseph Stokes. He had served in the Diocese of Charleston before becoming rector of the seminary in Cincinnati. When he arrived in Nashville in September of 1839, he found Miles very ill with a respiratory infection. He stayed close to the bishop during his months of convalescence. When Miles was able to work again, he called upon Stokes to minister to the Catholics throughout the state and invite the wayward to return to the church. Stokes served in Tennessee for five years.

In the meantime, others had come to assist Miles. The second priest, William Clancy, was considered to be a maverick. His unique service was accompanying the bishop to Memphis for the first time, where he was appointed first resident pastor. There he officiated at the wedding of Eugene Magevney, a generous benefactor to the Church in Tennessee and to the Dominicans. Unfortunately, Clancy could not be induced to remain. Within a year of his coming, he left the diocese for another location in the South. William Morgan, the first man ordained for the Diocese of Nashville, joined the clergy of Tennessee at the same time as Michael McAleer in 1840. Morgan's ministry was cut short by death within a year of his arrival. McAleer served well for six years, many of them in Memphis, but was enticed to go to the more affluent diocese of New York in 1846.

Miles could always count on the support of the bishops of Cincinnati and Bardstown. He also found a concerned fellow bishop in Anthony Blanc of New Orleans who had written to offer assistance. Not only did the Bishop of Nashville ask him for "good, zealous, active Priests," but he begged for money to repair the church and to buy vestments, chalices, a cloth antependium and "a keg of pure wine for the altar."[9] To convince Blanc of his great need, he described the situation in Tennessee:

> I am consoled to find that some of my Brethren remember me in my lonely & destitute situation where I am left entirely alone to perform all the arduous duties of this hitherto cruelly neglected region & where so much aid is needed to repair the evils that have taken deep root among my poor deserted & scattered flock. I find Catholics in almost every part of the state, many of whom for many years neglected their duties & in many instances have lost their faith for want of some one to stir them up to a sense of religion: & what can a single individual do now on the verge of fifty amidst this general desolation? My great poverty deprives me of the means of offering a competent salary to a clergyman & in default of this I am doomed to struggle alone among the frightful difficulties of every species that surround me!

One solution that many United States bishops had resorted to from earliest times was a begging tour in Europe. In 1840 Miles decided to pursue that course. He spent eighteen months there, making fruitful contact with the French Society for the Propagation of the Faith and contacting seminaries to make his needs known. Upon his return he found that he still could not keep priests in his diocese beyond a few years.

Miles had not forgotten that the Dominican friars had built the Ohio Catholic Church under the leadership of Bishop Fenwick and Nicholas D. Young. He hoped that he and some of his brethren could do the same for Tennessee. While still in Europe in 1841 he wrote to Charles P. Montogomery, then Provincial at Somerset, asking that two Spanish priests who were serving in the United States at that time be sent to the Diocese of Nashville. With friars in Tennessee, he would be able to have some continuity in the various parishes in Nashville and Memphis. As a result of his request, the Spanish friar Joseph Alemany arrived in Nashville in 1842, the first Dominican priest assigned to that state.

Joseph Sadoc Alemany was born on July 13, 1814. He entered the Order of Preachers in September of 1830; in 1831 he took vows as a member of the Aragon Province of the Order. After finishing theological studies, he was ordained in 1837. A few years later, he volunteered for missionary work and was sent to the United States in 1840.[10] In 1845 Alemany moved from Nashville to Memphis where he became assistant to Father McAleer, the pastor of the fast-growing church of St. Peter's. That city numbered eight thousand inhabitants, of whom five hundred were Catholic.[11] Alemany not only worked in the city but also rode out to do missionary work in the western part of the state. When McAleer left for New York in 1846 the parish was conducted by Dominicans Joseph Alemany and Thomas Grace. Alemany remained but a short time. Early in 1847 he assumed the role of Novice Master. In 1848 he was appointed Provincial, and in 1850 was named first Bishop of Monterey, California.

An event unique in Tennessee occurred in 1842. The Sisters of Charity of Nazareth, Kentucky, accepted the invitation of Bishop Miles to establish a school for girls in Nashville. Clad in their white bonnets and dress of the day, they arrived in August and shortly after opened their school. They were the first women religious to live in Tennessee, quite a phenomenon in a state unfamiliar with Catholic practices. *The Catholic Advocate* commented that the Protestants who were present for the sisters' reception appeared to be deeply interested in these women.[12]

In 1844 when the cornerstone was laid for the new cathedral in Nashville, one more Dominican friar arrived to assist Miles. Samuel Louis Montgomery was neither young nor unknown to the bishop. They had been in the first class of Dominican friars ordained at St. Rose in 1816. Montgomery had begged the Master of the Order over a period of two years to be allowed to go to live with Miles in Nashville. His reasons included unhappiness with the state of affairs at St. Rose and personal displeasure that his younger brother, Charles P. Montgomery, now provincial of the friars, was pressing him to take the pledge to abstain from alcoholic beverages. This the older Montgomery felt was a violation of conscience. Miles appointed him Vicar of the Diocese and finance officer for the bishop's household. He remained in Nashville for the rest of his life, even outliving Miles.

After seven years of arrivals and departures of diocesan priests, Miles knew he had to invite to his diocese a group of religious men who would assure continuity in the principal parishes. His first appeal early in 1844 went to Holy Cross Father Edward Sorin, founder of the University of Notre Dame. He wrote:

> I have long wished to have some of the Brothers of St. Joseph[13] in my Diocese & am glad to indulge the hope that my wishes may be realized. Should it be possible to send me some please inform me in order that I may make preparations for them. I will cheerfully bear their traveling expenses & give the annual pension you demand.

He went on to a question raised by Sorin: would his men have to teach the girls? Miles replied:

> With regard to the several questions proposed to me: . . . I should prefer having the two sexes separated, yet where there are no means of teaching the girls separately, it would be hard to deprive them of the benefit of education for this cause and with strict vigilance on the part of teachers all the difficulties on this head might be obviated & might be taught in the same school with boys.[14]

There is no evidence that Sorin ever sent any men of his congregation to Nashville. Perhaps all his energies were concentrated by 1844 in establishing the University of Notre Dame. Or did he decline because he could not countenance his men teaching in a coeducational school?

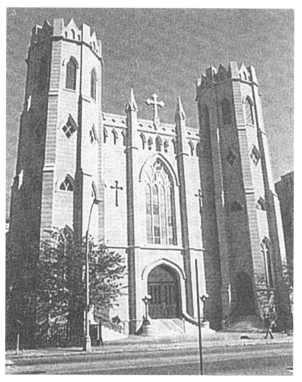

St. Peter parish church, Memphis

Miles was not to be denied. Early in 1845 he offered a parish in Memphis to his own Dominican confreres of St. Joseph Province. To Joseph Jarboe, Prior at St. Rose, he wrote:

> I have now at the command of the Order the best congregation & church in the Diocese whenever they may see proper to take possession of it, provided it be done soon. . . . It is on the Mississippi in one of the best towns of the state. . . . I think it will not require much argument to convince the superiors of the order that the offer I make will be more advantageous than others that may have been made. . . . [15]

He concluded by advising Jarboe not to lose the letter, and to answer soon. Otherwise he would be obliged to seek some other Order. The reply was affirmative and the deed to St. Peter's in Memphis was signed in 1847. The Dominican friars through the years realized Miles' dream of a large city parish with the assurance of pastoral stability. The feelings of good fortune were mutual. Miles had the continuity he sought, and the friars assumed responsibility for St. Peter's, a prosperous parish in a city with more Catholics than Nashville, the capital.

The family of
Eugene Magevney
of Memphis;
at bottom left, Sister
Agnes, foundress
of the Houston
Dominicans

A Dominican friar who served with distinction was Italian-born James Aloysius Orengo, a volunteer who arrived in Nashville in 1848. He would be the epitome of Dominican missionary activity modeled on the zeal of Edward Fenwick. His tireless journeying throughout central Tennessee for the next twenty-five years qualified him as a true builder of the Church in Tennessee. His stay might have been cut short but for the efforts of Joseph Alemany, newly-appointed provincial of the American friars. The prior at St. Rose did not feel he could allow Orengo to continue missionary work that necessitated living outside one of the friars' convents. Alemany as provincial dispensed him from this provision and allowed him to remain in the Nashville area. "It is true," he wrote, 'that you might be very useful in Ohio or other places but on the other hand I think that Bp. Miles deserves far greater help than what we give him."[16] Orengo's labors were such that "he went everywhere, knew everybody, and everybody seemed to know him."[17] He built many churches, cleared others from heavy debts and bought land for new parishes.

The 1849 epidemics of cholera and smallpox were more devastating in Memphis than in Nashville. James H. Clarkson, Dominican pastor of St. Peter's, ministered to the sick and dying. He himself became a victim of the disease in August of that year. Thomas Grace, O.P., succeeded him in pastoral duties.

Thomas Langdon Grace, born in South Carolina, attended the Athenaeum in Cincinnati and then joined the Order of Preachers, making his profession in 1831. He was sent to Rome to study, a unique privilege for American friars, and was ordained there in 1839. He held the post of professor and sub-prior at St. Rose, Kentucky, before assisting at St. Peter's in Memphis, where he became pastor in 1849. He was a friar of unusual energy and initiative. After ten years of generous service in the Memphis he loved, he accepted the office of Bishop of St. Paul, Minnesota.[18]

The decade of the forties was fraught with conflicts which sprang from nativism. Anti-Catholic prejudice abounded because the arriving Irish and many of the German immigrants were Catholics. Large numbers of Irish worked on the railroads and moved with the lengthening tracks, but many remained in the cities and competed for menial work. Despite these divisions in society, the work of the Church progressed. Bishop Miles seemed to be undisturbed by strife, never complaining of anti-Catholic bias but only of the slow pace of completing his new cathedral that was taking three years to finish.

The activities that introduced the second half of the century seemed like a full-blown drama compared to those of the forties. Despite attacks by the growing Know-Nothing Party, the Tennessee Church vibrated with life. The new spirit stemmed from the vitality of Thomas Grace and his confreres and also of Dominican women who came to share the mission of the friars. The 1853 *Catholic Almanac* reported that of the nine priests helping Bishop Miles in Tennessee, five were Dominicans: Samuel Montgomery in Nashville, James Orengo in the center of the state, and Thomas Grace, John Cleary and John Albert Bokel in the Memphis area.

The year 1850 had scarcely begun when Charles Pius Montgomery declined a commission to be bishop of Monterey, California. None of his Dominican brethren had been able to refuse in the past. Montgomery's plea of declining health apparently was believed sufficient reason for him to refuse. To Samuel Eccleston's request for other suggested candidates, Miles replied:

I regret very much to learn from your late favour that Rev. Mr. Montgomery persists in his refusal of the appointment to the see of Monterery, as I have known him to be well fitted for that office; with regard to the Rev. Mr. Grace although a very worthy & efficient clergyman I think he is too young & has not been in orders long enough. This is the only objection that could be made against him. At your request I will take the liberty to propose . . . Joseph Alemany, O.P. who stands second on the list for Santa Fe & is sufficiently known for his piety & learning to render any recommendation on my part unnecessary. . . .[19]

Alemany was in Rome to attend a Dominican General Chapter at the time the letter was written. There he was appointed as Bishop Monterery, California. When notified, he accepted.

In 1851 Thomas Grace welcomed to Memphis six Dominican sisters from Kentucky and Ohio. He had requested them from Matthew O'Brien, the new provincial, but had not expected so swift a response. The scene of their arrival is somewhat amusing in retrospect. Before preparations for their coming had been completed by

A Mississippi riverboat used by Dominicans to go to Tennessee

Grace, the six sisters, escorted by Francis Cubero, O.P.,[20] knocked on the priory door shortly after midnight, January 1, 1851. They were travel-weary, having journeyed by steamboat down the Ohio and Mississippi Rivers for four days. Eager for a good night's sleep, they awakened the pastor who was surprised and apologetic. Because there was no opportunity to find housing at that late hour, Father Grace managed to sustain conversation in his parlor throughout the night. No doubt, many heads nodded from sheer exhaustion.

This first colony of Dominican sisters came to share in the mission by teaching. They included Ann Simpson, Lucy Harper and Vincentia Fitzpatrick from St. Catharine's, Kentucky, and Magdalen Clark, Emily Thorpe and Catherine McCormick from St. Mary's in Somerset. On the morning after they arrived the pastor at St. Peter's took them to "the spacious residence of Mr. William McKeon, where they were received with all . . . warmth and hospitality."[21] Here they stayed until January 10, when they took possession of their new home, St. Agnes Academy. The writer of their annals indicated that the sisters had 300 dollars from which to deduct travel expenses. "In Louisville they purchased a few pieces of furniture and some school books which left them a balance of 50 dollars to meet all the expenses of opening and furnishing a new convent and boarding school."[22]

The sisters were pleased with their new home situated about a mile from the center of the city. The convent and academy stood in the center of a beautiful grove of native forest trees on a plot of about five acres. The annalist recorded, "The Sisters opened their school on February 4 with 20 boarders and 15 or 20 day scholars." Even before the school year ended in 1851, enrollment at St. Agnes Academy had grown so rapidly that an additional structure was needed.

Besides the regular boarders, the staff at St. Agnes housed orphans whose numbers were growing rapidly because of deaths from epidemics. By December of 1851, the number of homeless children had outgrown their original quarters. A separate institution called St. Agnes Orphanage solved the problem. Here they were provided for until a suitable home could be found for them or they could become independent. Three years later the pastor bought land outside Memphis, christened it Gracewood and transferred the orphanage there. The sisters conducted special events like picnics and fairs to support this worthy ministry. Even the special projects proved insufficient. The annalist noted that it took the closest economy on the part of the sisters to support fourteen or thirty children, male and female. "Were it not for the farm belonging to St. Peters, which the Fathers kindly allowed them to cultivate and to retain the produce, not half the number of orphans could be supported."[23]

The phenomenal growth of the St. Agnes' mission coincided with an era of extraordinary mobility of Dominican women religious. Just as sisters came from the autonomous communities of Ohio and Kentucky to staff St. Agnes, so they were ready to return or remain in any other particular house to respond to the call of the mission. The annals of St. Agnes refer frequently to sisters coming back and forth to and from Ohio and Kentucky. They had made profession, after all, in the same Order of Preachers.

Another epidemic struck Memphis in 1855. This time it was yellow fever. The low-lying swamps that surrounded the city contained ideal breeding places for the mosquitoes that carried the disease. That factor, combined with the flow of traffic upstream from New Orleans where yellow fever frequently occurred, made Memphis residents vulnerable. A contemporary Dominican of St. Agnes Academy wrote:

> The Sept. Session of '55 opened with rather a slender attendance, owing to the presence of yellow fever in the City. It made its appearance here the first time during the previous August. Although numbers were reported to have the disease, and many died; yet there was not so much as one inmate of the Acad sick for one hour all the time the fever prevailed in the city. Most, if not all the city schools suspended during the panic created by the exaggerated accounts circulated through the county. Some half dozen of our pupils took fright in consequence and went home, but returned in Nov with a large increase of new scholars.[24]

John Cleary, O.P., was not so fortunate. His missionary activities out of Memphis along the Mississippi weakened him to the point that he could not resist the fever. He died in September 1855, the first Dominican friar, but not the last, to die of yellow fever in Tennessee.

In the waning years of the fifties, prosperity was evident along with change. The dedication of the new St. Peter's Church in 1858 was indicative of the parishioners' ability to support the construction of a new building. On a more somber note, symptoms indicated that bishop Miles was suffering from declining health. In this decade of growth in Tennessee, Bishop Miles had apparently made demands for personnel from the Superior of the Charity Sisters that could not be met. As a consequence, the sisters who came to Nashville in 1842 were recalled to Kentucky. Six of them wished to remain in Tennessee and this group became independent of the Nazareth motherhouse. How well they succeeded after their separation surprised and pleased Bishop Martin Spalding of Louisville, who wrote to John B. Purcell of Cincinnati:

> By the way, the Nazareth Sisters at Nashville have prospered beyond my anticipations. In going to the South I stopped two days with our brother of Nashville, [Miles] & visited the seceding branch, [of Sisters] which is getting on famously, having already twenty one members, of whom only three are the original 'bolters.' I was agreeably disappointed, & I began to think that "Secession" after all is not so bad. It is well that each Diocese should have a motherhouse & a novitiate.[25]

On a more serious note, Spalding continued:

> I found Bishop Miles in very bad health. His cough is exceedingly troublesome & I much fear that he is not long for this world. He has sold his fine house & lot, & bought what he calls a 'rat-trap' near his cathedral. But he congratulates himself that he is at least out of debt.[26]

The health of Miles continued to decline to the point where he asked authorities in Rome to appoint a coadjutor bishop.

With the election of Joseph A. Kelly, O.P., as the new provincial of St. Joseph Province late in 1858, a series of events took place that involved the Dominicans in

Tennessee. In January a group of Dominican sisters was assigned to Memphis from St. Catharine's, Kentucky. Sisters Helen Whelan, Mary Rose Rogers, Dominica Fitzpatrick, Marie Joseph Whelan, and Lucy Mills were accompanied there by Anthony Gangloff, O.P., and the provincial Kelly, also on his way to Tennessee. In his diary Kelly wrote, "We all took the car after dinner for Louisville, staid [sic] there a night and a day, went on board the *Southerner*, and glided down to Memphis safely and pleasantly." [27] On reaching their destination, he continued:

> On awakening found myself at the Memphis bluff, it was so high that I looked in vain for the city. F. Byrne came down to the boat, with him went up to the church. . . . The new church is really a magnificent affair, it is 150 feet long, 60 wide, transept eighty; it is plastered on the outside in imitation of stone. . . . The loca-tion of St. Agnes Academy is perhaps the most beautiful in the city; the buildings are ordinary, chiefly frame. Memphis is rapidly improving. . . . The streets are unpaved which is a great drawback. Thousands of bales of cotton are to be seen in all directions.[28]

After his visit the provincial made this entry, "It seems to me that Memphis is, beyond a doubt the finest place the order possesses in this country, and presents the best opening for future success. Once I did not think so but I am convinced of it now from ocular demonstration."[29] Far less constrained was the glowing remark of the annalist of St. Agnes Academy, "St. Agnes is emphatically the Gem of Memphis, the garden of Ten.[sic], the Eden of the inmates, the abode of the Muses and the consecrated spot around which cluster all the Memphian associations of beauty and poetry."[30]

Miles received a prompt response to his request for a coadjutor. On March 15, 1859, James Whelan, O.P., was appointed to succeed to the See of Nashville upon the death of Miles. At the same time Thomas Grace received papers naming him Bishop of St. Paul.[31] The Order's loss of these two men would be a hardship, but the honor to the friars would be beneficial, as Kelly's diary entry indicated: "Our order here may now fairly begin to look up. We are not as old fogeyish or as backwards as some suppose." However, on June 10 he noted, ". . . the taking of FF. Whelan and Grace leaves us in a very crippled condition."

James Whelan was born in Ireland but came to the United States early in life. His acquaintance with the St. Joseph Province was made through Nicholas Dominic Young, who so impressed him that he entered the Order at St. Rose, Kentucky, and made his profession there in 1840. Before his ordination on August 2, 1846, he lived at St. Rose, Kentucky and St. Joseph, Somerset, Ohio, where he pursued his studies and assisted in teaching the younger members of the Order. He was described by the provincial Regent of Studies as having "good talents, an extraordinary memory; but has a cold nature. Since he does not have companions to emulate, he is very difficult to arouse to make him take a lively interest in studies. . . . he would have profited greatly by the competition of fellow students."[32]

Whelan's record of holding responsible positions in the province demonstrated his outstanding talents. The Provincial Alemany appointed him Regent of Studies and shortly afterwards president of the new St. Joseph College near Somerset. He gave evidence of a fine mind and had a reputation as an outstanding preacher. In 1854, only eight years after ordination, the friars esteemed him highly enough to elect him provincial at age thirty-one. His choice as coadjutor to Miles appeared to be the high

NASHVILLE

Second Day: December 16, 1864

Edgefield

CUMBERLAND RIVER

NASHVILLE & CHATTANOOGA R.R.

Nashville

FORT NEGLEY

FORT MORTON

FORT CASINO

MONTGOMERY HILL

NASHVILLE & DECATUR R.

BRADFORD HOUSE

GRANNY-WHITE PIKE

ILLSBORO PIKE

OVERTON HILL

FRANKLIN PIKE

Federal soldiers taking Nashville in 1862. St. Cecilia Academy (inset) was located in the area covered by the inset.

point in his exceptional career. In the cathedral of St. Louis, Archbishop Peter Kenrick consecrated Whelan on May 8, 1859. Miles remained too ill to attend the ceremony but installed his coadjutor in Nashville two weeks later.

The appointment of a coadjutor came none too soon for the ailing bishop. With the approach of winter his precarious health declined rapidly. The year 1860 opened with little hope of recovery. After receiving the rites of the Church, Miles died on February 21 at the episcopal residence. He was interred under the high altar of the Cathedral. Many were the words of praise for this first Bishop of Nashville, who with a handful of priests had built the Church in Tennessee. Newspapers carried many accounts of his life and labors, but these words epitomize the Bishop's disposition that drew many persons closer to the practice of the Catholic faith: " Never morose, and seldom low-spirited, Bishop Miles had the happy faculty, in his social relations, to be able to impart to all around him a portion of his own cheerful spirit. He was pious without affectation, charitable to the poor, and kind and affable to all."[33]

James Whelan, now Bishop of Nashville, lost no time in bringing Dominican sisters to his episcopal city. In May he purchased an estate to be used for St. Cecilia's Academy and invited women from St. Mary's in Somerset, Ohio, to staff the school. Sisters Columba Dittoe, first superior of the house, Lucy Harper, Philomena McDonough and Frances Walsh arrived in August. They were accompanied tentatively by two Dominicans from the Heilig Kreuz Monastery in Regensburg, Bavaria, Maria Benedicta Bauer and Maria Thomasina Ginker.[34]

The Dominican women from Ohio opened their school on October 4, 1861, less than two months after their arrival. St. Cecilia's Female Academy, like that of St. Agnes in Memphis, boasted of attractive surroundings. "The ground selected for the site is one of the most lovely spots in this beautiful country. It is in the midst of a garden of roses, honeysuckles, magnolias, and other flowers."[35]

Bishop Whelan's role in St. Cecilia's establishment was described in his diocesan report in 1863:

> There was great need of a Catholic institution for the education of young ladies somewhere in the vicinity of Nashville. After mature reflection and taking advice, I determined to establish such an institution for educational purposes in the vicinity of the City, a well enclosed lot of six acres known as Mount Vernon Garden about one mile north of the State house. Knowing that a first class Academy, such as only Catholic Sisters can conduct, would do an immensity of good, and be liberally supported, I spared no labor, no pains, no necessary expense to ensure the accomplishment of the undertaking. It soon became evident that my efforts would be crowned with success, and I am happy to be able to say, that St. Cecilia's Academy . . . is now a permanent institution . . . and has already secured the patronage of an extensive and wealthy portion of the country, where the Catholic system of education was not much appreciated.[36]

Whelan was delighted with the success of the academy because education had always been of major interest to him. Plans for the new facilities went forward until they had to be modified because of the war, whose approach Whelan and the sisters seemed to disregard in their correspondence. However, South Carolina's secession from the Union in late 1860 must have given a strong signal to the Nashville citizen-ry that a conflict was indeed possible and even imminent. Despite the apparent danger, the friars and sisters continued preaching and teaching even when federal troops appeared in the city.

The war years proved disastrous for James Whelan. He was compelled to resign his bishopric for reasons now unknown, but often referred to as the "case" or the "scandal." Early in 1862 Archbishop Peter Kenrick of St. Louis wrote Spalding of Louisville indicating that he was presenting "the case" of Whelan to Rome. He made no mention of any wrongdoing on the part of the Bishop of Nashville. Whelan's problems, whatever they were, must have been common knowledge to the bishops. In retrospect the closing remarks of Kenrick cast doubt upon the American bishops' nomination of the young friar:

> Whelan's name was last on the list and, having been provincial of his order appeared eligible. I do not think that I interfered in the appointment, otherwise than by withdrawing the first name . . . . We were influenced by the respect naturally felt for Bp Miles especially as he was choosing his coadjutor. No doubt the result of this unhappy nomination will be to render Propaganda still more than ever doubtful of our recommendations.[37]

About the same time, early in 1862, Nicholas D. Young wrote to Bishop Purcell, referring to an unnamed scandal concerning Whelan's behavior in a public tavern, but asked that the bishop not be suspended lest greater harm come to the Church.[38] Some conjectures concerning his resignation cited a "blunder" of more serious nature than insobriety [39] or fraternizing with Union officials in the city. [40]

Whatever his wrongdoing, Bishop Whelan felt constrained to apologize to Archbishop Peter Kenrick, Nicholas D. Young and also his confreres. [41] He notified the Archbishop of St. Louis that he had sent his resignation to the Holy See on August 15, 1862. On the same day Whelan wrote to Spalding:

> I beg leave to state that I have written to the Most Rev. Archbishop of St. Louis informing him that I have complied with the purport of the communications I received from you a few days ago . . . . Nothing on my part shall be done to embarrass still more the unfortunate state of affairs. I must confess, however, that the present condition of home affairs, business and monetary matters; owing to the Political State of the country will necessarily cause me perplexity & unhappiness. . . . will do all that I possibly can so that everything may be done as it should be and credit of the diocese not be impaired.[42]

Only in the correspondence between the archbishop and Propaganda Fide in Rome did Peter Kenrick state that the scandal was "excessive drinking in Nashville and in Cincinnati." Concerning the truth of this matter, there is no place for uncertainty, since he himself confessed to me through letters, and from face to face. . . ."[43] Whelan felt keenly his deposition, as shown in his remark to Kenrick, "I submit to the severe but I presume just and necessary chastisement. . . ." Until all decisions reached Rome and responses were received, Bishop Whelan continued to perform his episcopal duties as the war neared Nashville. When federal troops occupied the capital city, problems multiplied for all citizens. The *Freeman's Journal* reported arrests every day.

Importers of goods had to take an oath of allegiance to the Union; retailers had to take an oath not to sell to rebels.[45] By the winter of 1862, the December issue of the *Journal* reported that all who were not loyal to the government of the United States must close their stores or be arrested and have their goods confiscated. All citizens appeared to be suffering from a shortage of fuel for their homes, especially the poor. Even lighting on streets and in homes was out for days at a time.

Nevertheless, academies conducted by the sisters continued to operate and church services found Union Army personnel in attendance as well as parishioners. As a rule, the priests and sisters received no ill treatment to their persons from the occupying troops. But one Christmas Eve, several Federal soldiers demanded admittance to the St. Agnes Convent School. After some persuasion they left, but returned about 2:00 a. m. in greater numbers, insisting the door be opened. This time it was a man from the city who convinced the inebriated soldiers to leave the grounds. When Federal authorities heard of the incident, they stated that these soldiers had no authorization whatever to cause this disturbance.[46] Although no personal harm came to the sisters or their charges, their horses were confiscated when needed by the soldiers.

On July 15, 1863, Bishop Whelan sent his final report on the diocese to Archbishop Peter Kenrick. His account of St. Cecilia's Academy indicated that the property was in the hands of the sisters. They owed the Bishop of Nashville, whoever it might be, $2600. He continued,

It must be understood, that the breaking out of war in 1861, after the commencement of the new building, the blockade, the precarious state of the economy, the great price of things, etc. and the disturbed state of the society in general until this time, rendered the undertaking one of no small anxiety. We had commenced however, and were bound to persevere. Our school was never interrupted for more than about two weeks at the time of the great stampede in February, 1862. The title of this place is perfect. It is secured from taxation and when society becomes a little more settled ... there will not be the least difficulty in paying off all the liabilities. No one contributed to the amount of one dollar towards the purchase of the grounds, or the erection of the buildings. The grounds, buildings, and property of St. Cecilia's Academy is estimated by competent judges of 30 years experience in such business to be at present $70,000.[47]

Perhaps if given the choice the sisters would have preferred a more modest site and buildings. The debt must have seemed enormous, especially in war time.

Events moved rapidly for Whelan after his final report on the diocese. He left the episcopal residence in July 1863, but did not report to St. Joseph Priory until April 1866. There is evidence that he stayed with his mother in Nashville until he felt he could face his Dominican brethren. After his return to Ohio, he immersed himself in study and research. He published a pamphlet on evidence of papal infallibility.

On August 8, 1863, Joseph Kelly, having recently completed his tenure as provincial, became pastor at St. Peter's, Memphis. He announced to his congregation that Bishop Whelan had resigned and that he, Kelly, was assigned to Nashville as administrator of the diocese until a new bishop could be chosen. He thought his stay there would be brief, but he remained two years.[48]

Father Kelly, having first-hand knowledge of the successful work of the sisters in conducting an orphanage in Memphis, requested three Dominican Sisters to establish such an institution in Nashville. St. Mary's Orphanage became a reality on May 21, 1864, upon the arrival of Sisters Benven Sansbury, Josepha McGary, and Gertrude O'Meara from Somerset. With the growing number of war orphans, the boarding school did not lack occupants. Six weeks after the coming of the sisters, Gertrude O'Meara died of typhoid and was the first sister to be buried in St. Cecilia's cemetery.[49]

As the year wore on, the shelling around Nashville became ominously close. On December 1 Kelly recorded in his diary,

General Hood with the rebel army invaded Nashville. Got warning this evening that the Orphan Asylum was in danger from the batteries. Got five government wagons, an ambulance etc. some officers and citizens; . . . we were all night engaged in moving the orphans, Sisters and their effects into the city. They are now in the basement of the cathedral.

As a consequence of the shelling, the orphanage was totally destroyed. Shortly after that, all churches were confiscated for use as hospitals. The priests and sisters continued to serve in the best way possible under the circumstances but were greatly relieved that hostilities would cease when they heard of Lee's surrender in April of 1865. Joseph Kelly had to remain as administrator of the diocese until November of that year when the appointment of Patrick Augustine Feehan as Bishop of Nashville became effective.

The Dominicans had worked long to build the Church in Tennessee and they would continue to do so with Bishop Feehan as head of the diocese. Despite post-war difficulties both the friars and sisters, moved forward in their desire to spread the Word. The federal government rebuilt St. Mary's Orphanage in Nashville after its destruction in late 1864. St. Cecilia's Academy recovered slowly from the effects of the debt inherited from Bishop Whelan. In Memphis St. Agnes Academy and the Orphanage connected with St. Peter's Church enjoyed renewed vigor with additional personnel sent from Ohio and Kentucky.

1. Miles to Purcell, Somerset, Nov. 9, 1837, University of Notre Dame Archives (UNDA) II, 4 f.

2. N.D. Young to Purcell, Somerset, Dec. 31, 1837, UNDA II 4 f.

3. Cipolletti to N.D. Young, Rome, Jan. 2, 1838, St. Joseph Province Archives (SJP).

4. Purcell to Miles, Cincinnati, Mar. 1, 1838, SJP.

5. Catholic Advocate, Nov. 10, 1838, III, 316.

6. Thomas Stritch, **The Catholic Church in Tennessee** (Nashville: The Catholic Center, 1987) 47.

7. Catholic Advocate, Dec. 7, 1838.

8. D.A. Quinn as quoted in Stritch 38-39.

9. Miles to Blanc, Nashville, May 20, 1839, UNDA V 4 h.

10. In August of 1835, the Spanish government passed the Secularization Law that expelled the friars from their religious houses. John McGloin, **California's First Archbishop** (New York: Herder and Herder, 1964) 34.

11. McGloin 54.

12. Catholic Advocate, Sep. 15, 1842. This group of Sisters eventually left Tennessee and began the Congregation of the Sisters of Charity of Leavenworth, Kansas.

13. Until 1837 the Brothers of St. Joseph existed as a separate unit, but Basil Moreau united them with the Auxiliary Priests of LeMans in France under the name of the Congregation of the Holy Cross.

14. Miles to Sorin, Nashville, Apr. 9, 1844, UNDA, CSOR 2/11.

15. Miles to Jarboe, Nashville, Jan. 17, 1845, SJP.

16. Alemany to Orengo, Somerset, Dec. 26, 1848, SJP.

17. Stritch 120.

18. See O'Daniel, V.F., **The Father of the Church in Tennessee** (New York: Frederick Pustet Co., 1926) 550.

19. Miles to Samuel Eccleston, Nashville, Apr. 8, 1850, Archives, Archdiocese of Baltimore(AAB) 25 M 8.

20. Cubero accompanied Alemany to America in 1840 after their expulsion from Spain.

21. Author unknown, Annals of St. Agnes Academy commencing with the Foundation of the House, ms., Jan. 10, 1851, 1, SJP.

22. Annals, 3.

23. Annals, 8.

24. Annals, 9-10.

25. John B. Purcell became Bishop of Cincinnati in 1833 after the death of Edward Dominic Fenwick, O.P.

26. Spalding to Purcell, Louisville, Mar. 26, 1856, SJP.

27. Kelly Diary, III, Jan. 18, 1859, SJP.

28. Kelly Diary, III, Jan. 22, 1859.

29. Kelly Diary, Feb. 5, 1859.

30. Annals, 14.

31. Kelly Diary, III, Mar. 15, 1859.

32. Eugenio Pozzo, Somerset, Jan. 21, 1845, SJP.

33. The Guardian, Mar. 10, 1860. See O'Daniel 557.

34. These sisters wanted to serve immigrants from Bavaria, but could not raise sufficient funds from the small number of German-speaking residents in Nashville. They left in the spring of 1861. Rose Marie Masserano, O.P., **The Nashville Dominicans** (Roslyn Heights, New York: Roth Publishing, 1985) 2. The full story of Benedicta and Thomasina will be told in Chapter 15 and in a forthcoming history of the Racine Dominican Congregation by Suzanne Noffke, O.P.

35. "Charles" **in Freeman's Journal**, June 7, 1862.

36. Whelan to Peter Kenrick, Nashville, July 15, 1863, Diocese of Nashville Archives(DNA).

37. P.R.Kenrick to Spalding, St. Louis , Apr. 23, 1862, copy at SJP.

38. Young to Purcell, Kentucky, Feb. 10, 1862, UNDA II 5 b.

39. Stritch 144.

40. The theory of O'Daniel in **The Dominican Province of Saint Joseph** (New York: Holy Name Society, 1942) 204.

41. See Whelan to Peter Kenrick, Louisville, Feb. 5, 1862, UNDA II 5 b; N.D. Young to Purcell (quoting from Whelan's letter), Kentucky, Feb. 10, 1862, UNDA II 5 b.

42. Whelan to Spalding, Nashville, August 15, 1862, Louisville Archdiocesan Archives (LVA).

43. Kenrick to Barnabo (PF), St. Louis , May 9, 1862, Archives, Propaganda Fide (APF) v. 992, 466rv-467rv.

45. June 7, 1862.

46. Freeman's Journal, Feb. 14, 1863.

47. Bishop James Whelan Report, July 15, 1863, DNA.

48. Freeman's Journal, Aug. 8, 1863.

49. Masserano 73.

PROFILE

ANN HANLON

Sister Ann Hanlon was a woman of great desires and real accomplishments. She adjusted her dreams of doing great things for God to the gradual unfolding of His will for her in the ready-to-hand of necessity and circumstance. Her dreams were lofty ones of a life of strict observance and contemplation. Her reality was in the down-to-earth duties of someone of her direct and authoritative nature. The fast pacing of her life suggests the movement which was characteristic of the early sisters, but beneath the movement lay a concept that unified them as religious women, with differences being only those brought about by geography, the demands of the times, and, as in the life of Sister Ann Hanlon, whatever her charism called for at each juncture.

Elizabeth (Eliza) Hanlon was born July 12, 1816, the daughter of Bryan Hanlon and Brigid Connor Hanlon,[1] in what, since the foundation of the Irish state in 1922, is named County Offaly, in the province of Leinster.[2] In early Irish history, her birthplace and the neighboring county of Laois were among the most rebellious in Ireland. Later resistance to the efforts of English garrisons to bring in British settlers marked their determined character. With her father, Elizabeth Hanlon came to this country as

**Ann Hanlon,
Dominican pioneer
of Tennessee**

an émigré in 1837[3] during a time of famine and land reforms in Ireland. In America the same period was marked by mass immigration of impoverished Irish farm laborers and rural poor. The fact that Sister Ann is mentioned only a few times during her early years at St. Mary's Convent in Somerset, coupled with the fact that in subsequent references she seems to be taken for granted, perhaps indicates no claim to anything except an ordinary Irish lineage. Futhermore, Elizabeth was physically impaired; she was "crippled in body, having only the use of one leg, and unable to walk without a cane." [4] This did not seem to deter her from considerable accomplishments. We can surmise that whatever her initial motivation, she was not clearly inclined to missionary life, but was seemingly of a more contemplative disposition. Extant paintings attributed to her disclose some artistic ability. She seems however, to have planned to enter the convent in America in the late 1830's and so came to Ohio.

St. Mary's convent, Somerset, Ohio, was in its initial days of grace and struggle when Eliza, at twenty-five years of age, on September 9, 1841, received the Dominican habit and was given the religious name

Ann. Her novitiate, we are told, "commenced the tenth at three in the morning."[5] Religious profession of vows followed the next year at Somerset with Sisters Clare Osmun and Catherine Beck witnessing her vows:

I make it fully appear to my satisfaction, that I made my profession in the above mentioned convent, according to the rule and Constitutions of the order of St. Dominick [sic], Sister Helen Whelan, Prioress of said convent, being legally constituted and authorized to receive my profession, Sister Frances Whelan,	Mother of Novices and Rev. N. D. Young, Director of the Con., I so therefore, by virtue of these present and in testimony thereof , subscribed hereunto my name. This 14 day of Sept. Feast of the Holy Cross A.D. 1842. Sister Ann Hanlon.[6]

Two years later, in 1844, the young community of St. Mary's at Somerset numbered seventeen professed sisters and four novices. On November 17 of the following year, Ann Hanlon was named subprioress of this community. Then, two years after, in 1847, she assumed the position of Mistress of Novices.[7] Membership remained stable; in 1850, St. Mary's counted seventeen professed sisters, five novices, and three postulants.[8] During her time as Mistress of Novices, Sister Ann was part of a spirited movement clearly initiated by the sisters to profess solemn vows as second order religious. Her signature is affixed on a historic letter addressed to His Holiness Pius IX, and accompanied by an affidavit dated July 4, 1848.[9] The sisters petitioned for dispensation from enclosure and permission to recite the office of the Blessed Virgin Mary instead of the Divine Office. In addition they asked the favor of making the solemn profession as the Nuns of the Second Order of our Holy Father St. Dominic. Their request was accompanied by a supporting letter addressed to Master General Jandel from Robert A. White, O.P., the Vicar Provincial.[10] No reply to the sisters' petition or to the Vicar's recommendation has been recorded. At any rate, in the episode we see Ann in solidarity with her sisters in Ohio and Kentucky, capable of passion for a cause, independent, yet deeply devoted to their vocation, the Order and the Church.

In 1851 during Sister Ann's residence at St. Mary's, the first canonical visitation of the Province of St. Joseph was conducted by Visitator General Robert White who, following his sojourn at St. Mary's, noted his gratification in finding that "every attention continues to be paid by this community to the maintenance of religious discipline, and that its temporal administration has been conducted with exemplary fidelity and exactness.[11] Considering the poverty of this beginning foundation and the religious bigotry which sometimes accompanied the rise of a Catholic school, it appears that Sister Ann and the sisters at St. Mary's were nevertheless trying to follow ideals of their founder Dominic.

In 1854 James Whelan was appointed provincial of the friars, assuming jurisdiction over the Sisters. In October of the same year, Whelan appointed Ann Hanlon Prioress of St. Mary's. The provincial said that he had taken "the advice of discrete Fathers," and appointed "Sister Ann Hanlon in whose prudence and zeal we have much confidence to this office. . . .[12] In her later life among the Sisters in Nashville, Ann's prudence and zeal became legendary.

During Sister Ann's term as prioress of St. Mary's (1854-1856), James Whelan wrote two letters regarding the St. Mary's community, one to the Vicar General and one to the Master General. Although she is not mentioned in either letter, Ann was prioress at that time. To the vicar general, Whelan wrote that ". . . there are twenty-four professed sisters and two novices. . . . They have quite a good school, and are all very faithful sisters. They are poor, but notwithstanding their poverty, they have by means of their school done a great deal.[13]

But to the Master General, Whelan wrote in a somewhat different vein. While showing genuine interest in the life of the sisters, he simply said they were all very good religious but added that the community has received members "mostly from such classes as are not competent to make teachers, and . . . there are more than the income of the establishment can support. I have, Whelan said,

taken upon myself to forbid the reception of novices in either of these two houses without my special permission, and this I did for the purpose of putting a stop to the reception of useless members and to ensure the reception of those who might be useful for the welfare of their academies.[14]

How Sister Ann reacted to the Master General's evaluation, we do not know. However, when Prioress in Nashville, she adopted for the community a constitution that made provision for lay Sisters.

Furthermore Ann resigned as prioress on November 10, 1856.[15] In view of the permission she would later petition, her personal integrity could have provoked the resignation. Perhaps, too, difficulties alluded to in her letter to Master General Jandel dated December 23, 1856, were pertinent. The letter in itself is a revelation of character.

Most Rev. Father in God,

I humbly solicit your paternal indulgence while I take the liberty to address yourself in person. I am indeed grateful for the encouragement you have so kindly given me to aspire to the Second branch of our Holy Order. Your objections to my going to the continent are reasonable, and not unexpected to me. I had considered all these things myself and viewed the very darkest side of the picture. It is not gratification I seek in desiring to enter an enclosed convent. Neither do I think perfection consists in enclosure. I am well aware I might be unhappy in an enclosed Convent. Enclosure is not my only motive in seeking admission into the Second Order. I have long and earnestly desired to be in a Monastery of strict observance where the Rule and constitutions are in full force. It is about a year since I resolved to use all the lawful means in my power to obtain admission into the Second Order. I have earnestly prayed to God to place me there where I could serve Him the best.[16]

In spite of its underlying personal trauma, the letter has a certain amusing quality because it seems to argue for something one knows one does not have. But an underlying honesty is felt. Ann makes her request quite humbly—at one point even pitifully, yet without relenting. What we see in this letter is fierce determination combined with a heart-rending steadfast zeal, both qualities which mark the actions of her later years. She does not lack persuasive powers. The winning quality of the letter, however, is that in it we see the human Ann Hanlon; here we come closest to viewing her soul in its bareness and striving. At the end, after her pleading exposition, comes the line we sense she found hardest to write, "But if you do not think it proper to accede to my request this time, I will of course desist and resign myself to the decrees of Providence," even here adding a qualifier, "this time."

This last line is telling and the one which adds detail to Ann's character portrait. There is determination here which has not yet been sounded. The dream of a strict and contemplative life may have been a manifestation of a zeal not yet channeled by the real needs of her Provincial, the Master, or the Bishop. Apparently, she did "resign herself to the decrees of Providence." On May 9, 1857, Father Whelan wrote to Jandel as follows:

Again, a certain Sister asks to be permitted to go to Europe to join the Second Order. She is a very good Sister, but were her request granted, fifty others would wish to do the same. This Sister thinks, perhaps, she has been aggrieved. When the thing was proposed by her to me, I endeavored to put it out of her mind. I think Father Wilson is not doing right in giving her encouragement. She is useful here; but she has never manifested any extraordinary efforts for perfection, or displayed any remarkable degree of humility, but rather the contrary. It may be well also to state that she cannot walk without a crutch and a stick. She has the use of only one leg. This, Father Wilson [Rev. George A. J. Wilson] knew full well. When asked by some of the Sisters if she stated this fact in her application he said "She did not, as it might be an obstacle to her reception, they would find it out afterwards." Perhaps this fact has been stated, but I think not. Whatever reasons may be alleged, wounded pride is at the root. This Sister is doing very well where she is.[17]

The letter is characteristic of Father Whelan, blending as it does comments at once kindly and critical. But if Sister Ann were not "a very good Sister," and one "useful" and "doing very well where she is," he would not have made these comments. On the other hand, we wonder about the "wounded pride [which] is at the root," according to Whelan, and are curious about this comment that "she has never manifested any extraordinary efforts for perfection, or displayed any remarkable degree of humility, but rather the contrary." Some sort of pride, in fact, does appear also to be characteristic of Ann Hanlon. In her one does not see a warm and loving personality. But she had the strength of character needed for future crises, including the Civil War, yellow fever, cholera epidemics and bankruptcy, as well as founding and refounding institutions.

In 1857 a lengthy visitation report was given by Father Whelan, a report revealing the community's makeup during this period. Whelan included in his report a remodeling of the council, placing Mother Columba Dittoe, superior, Sister Benven Sansbury, subprioress and Sister Ann Hanlon, along with four other Sisters members of the council.[18] She was serving on this council when she was transferred to Memphis.

In the histories of the congregations of St. Catharine and St. Mary, the 1850s and 1860s were years characterized by mobility. Interchange of members was frequent. In 1851, sisters from St. Catharine's and sisters from St. Mary's were sent to St. Agnes Academy as the founding community. The school grew rapidly, and in 1858 Ann Hanlon, whose gifts lay more in managerial affairs, was nevertheless sent to Memphis as an art teacher.[19] She remained in Memphis for the Civil War years, an interlude which tried her spiritually and marked her indelibly. The sense of attachment to the land and natural sympathy for the underling may have enabled her to understand the struggles of the Southern people, but her realism and moral uprightness would not allow her to embrace the cause. The trials called for another kind of virtue on her part. The war years formed another chapter in her life.

Important in Dominican history of this period was Father Joseph Augustine Kelly, O.P., whose efforts and invaluable service gave hope to Dominican religious life as well as to those to whom he ministered. Father Kelly was American provincial from 1858 to 1862, and his diary for those years portrayed St. Agnes Community and the city of Memphis, both of which were on the eve of cataclysmic events.

From Kelly's diary we learn that on January 3, 1859, Father Anthony R. Gangloff, O.P., arrived at St. Catharine's to recruit sisters for the Memphis mission. Five sisters went with him. On their arrival they found the Dominican religious at St. Agnes quite well. Kelly wrote :

> The location of St. Agnes Academy is perhaps the most beautiful in the city; the buildings are ordinary, chiefly frame. Memphis is rapidly improving, the most experienced citizens are convinced that in three years it will double its present population, which is about 20 thousand." [20]

The thriving river city seemed unaware of the tensions that were brewing. Nor did the sisters have any inkling of the impending war. In August 1859, Ann Hanlon was appointed prioress. During her administration, the community planned expansion. Father Kelly recorded that

> . . . we have been thinking of having a common and select school for sisters somewhere near the church of St. Peters [sic], and I have looked for ground convenient for that purpose. I have advised our sisters to sell out their place at St. Agnes and purchase elsewhere. The proceeds of their ground would purchase double the quantity they now have, build them an academy worth 30 or 40 thousand and leave a balance on hand. We have examined several places in the suburbs of the city. [21]

In reality, this plan did not develop, since the convent minutes of 1860 indicate instead that the decision was to erect a new addition to the building because of the increase in pupils.[22]

On June 10, 1861, a notation in the minutes referred to the "unsettled and troublous times:" "It was determined to close the school without any exercises of a jubilee [sic] kind, owing to the unsettled and troublous times." This cryptic sentence is followed by another puzzling one: "Upon examining into the affairs it was found that the debt, principal and interest so long due St. Peters [sic], had been all paid except a note of $1000 not yet matured." [23] The accountability and capability of the St. Agnes community were noteworthy in matters of finance. These same qualities seem noteworthy in Mother Ann throughout her years in administration.

Mother Ann's tenure as prioress at St. Agnes (September 1, 1859, to August 4, 1862) coincided with the war years. Tennessee seceded from the Union on June 8,

1861. Overnight Memphis became one vast hospital. At the request of Bishop Whelan, newly appointed Bishop of Nashville, the sisters from Saint Agnes took charge of the city hospital which was used as a military hospital with plank pavilion wards added.[24] Mother Ann Hanlon sent Sister Magdalen Clarke, Sister Alberta Rumpff and Sister Francis Conlon to supervise at the hospital and to nurse the soldiers there.[25] All the sisters who could be spared from St. Agnes nursed both Union and Confederate soldiers.[26]

Memphis surrendered on June 6, 1862. General William T. Sherman came to control the city on July 21, and with his soldiers "pitched his tents in Saint Agnes' yard just east of the convent." [27] Meanwhile the sisters continued their visits to the hospitals, ministering to the sick and suffering.[28]

In 1862 Sister Mary Pius Fitzpatrick succeeded Mother Ann as president of the St. Agnes Society. She in turn was succeeded by Sister Veronica Ray who became president once again. Ann Hanlon again became secretary.[29] Minutes of the period showed some hope for a future after the war's end. Ann was sent to St. Louis to buy dry goods and groceries for the academy and also "to take measures to borrow money with a view to commence a new Academy, and to procure a good plan for the same."[30] Financially, the academy had survived the war with a balance of $3000 in the treasury and notes and bills of neary $10,000 due the Society.

In August 1864, the Society rented a house on Adams Street, intending to open a day school comparable to St. Agnes which served boarding students. The school, LaSalette Academy, opened in September with seventy-five pupils. Sister Ann was the first superior and director.[31] Some years later during the yellow fever epidemic of 1873, LaSalette was converted into a hospital where priests and sisters were nursed.

Sister Ann's minutes of June 20, 1865, detail the purchase of a fine, large house in Memphis. The building, located on Third Street between Poplar and Washington Streets, was bought for the purpose of opening a novitiate. Sisters Veronica and Ann were authorized to make the purchase. At this same meeting, Ann was re-elected secretary.[32] By mid-August the debt on the building had been reduced to $20,000.[33] A second lot between Poplar and Washington was purchased in September.[34] The next year the Society borrowed $5,450 for a payment due on the novitiate property.[35] The community was experiencing post-war recovery.

While still serving as secretary of the St. Agnes Society, Ann received a summons from Bishop Patrick Augustine Feehan, recently appointed Bishop of Nashville. Told to "proceed to St. Cecilia's, Nashville," on July 6, 1866, she 'tendered her resignation" as secretary and member of the St. Agnes Society.[36] With this obedience, seemingly given without reflection, Ann in many ways severed previous bonds, closing more than a chapter in her life and embarking on what would lead to unexpected challenges as well as frequent isolation as a sole, staunch woman on whom new burdens of leadership would be placed. This example of her life-long obedience is striking when viewed beside her characteristic independence.

The Nashville which Sister Ann Hanlon, along with her companion Teresa Fritch, entered in 1866 was much like the struggling post-war Memphis. Nevertheless, within a brief period of time the orphan asylum, which had been run by the sisters but destroyed during the war, was rebuilt with the help of Fr. Kelly. Bishop Whelan had resigned as administrator of the diocese in 1864, and Kelly had assumed administrative duties until late in 1865 when Bishop Feehan was appointed Bishop of Nashville. Financial accounts on the episcopal level were in major disarray.

In August 1860, the Dominican Sisters had come from Somerset to Nashville at the request of Bishop Whelan. Four sisters had made the foundation, naming it St. Cecilia's. Like their companions in Memphis, these women had witnessed the war at first hand, seen Union boats come up the Cumberland and from their windows saw the Union soldiers camped on the Academy lawn.[37] Classes at St.Cecilia Academy continued during the occupation, but financially, the war had devastated the young academy.

It was chiefly for this reason that the Nashville sisters had petitioned the Bishop for Sister Ann Hanlon.[38] To the community at St. Cecilia's, her calm and steady practicality and her direct manner of addressing situations were seen as a saving grace. On her arrival she began at once to assess finances and to stabilize the Academy. Within a year, major debts from the construction of the buildings were reduced.[39] There remained, however, a mortgage on the Academy given by Bishop Whelan to John English of Zanesville, Ohio. By the following year, 1867, debts remained burdensome, and "in pursuance of a decree of the Chancery court, the St. Cecilia Academy was sold on the 27th of July, 1867." A postscript to the story read, "Rt. Rev. P. A. Feehan purchased it for $20,300."[40]

In a like manner, the Rev. J. M. D'Arco had been given drafts on the Academy by Bishop Whelan and "to meet this claim, a second decree of the Chancery Court authorized the sale of all the personal property of the sisters, on which . . . Bishop Whelan had a lien.[41] Again Bishop Feehan purchased the items. The date of the auction was September 2, 1867, the first day of class for the fall session. Surprisingly, school began as scheduled. In November Mother Ann opened a novitiate. Meanwhile, and for the rest of the school year, she worked to pay off the debts.

By the summer of 1868, the small community of sisters in Nashville was fatigued and discouraged. The Academy's patrons, bankrupted by the war, could not pay the sisters for the education of their daughters and notes on the property could not be met. To add to their concern, Bishop Feehan informed them that he had invited Sisters of Mercy to staff his Cathedral school and he needed a place for the sisters to live. The Bishop told Mother Ann that she was released from any obligation to pay the debts—an impossible task—and that instead the sisters were free to return to Ohio.[42]

Coincidentally it seems, at this time a letter arrived from the Dominican Fathers asking for sisters to teach in Washington, D.C.[43] Assuming that St.Cecilia's would close, Sisters Philomena McDonough, Aloysia Crosson, Columba and Cecilia Dittoe accepted the invitation. In August they left Nashville, went on to Somerset, and from there on the twenty-ninth, to Washington where they opened an academy near St. Dominic's and also took charge of the parish school there.[44]

Mother Ann and two novices remained in Nashville to settle affairs.[45] She sent a wire to Sister Frances Walsh, one of the foundresses of St. Cecilia who was at St. Agnes at the time, to return immediately to Nashville.[46] Left alone with so much unfinished before her, Ann's personality exerted itself. Instead of packing and leaving, she and the two sisters began a "thirty-days prayer," arising early and reciting the fifteen mysteries of the rosary. She believed that St. Cecilia was a legitimate foundation of the Order. She could not dissolve the community and leave debts for others to pay. Before the thirty days were complete, Bishop Feehan told her that the sisters could remain if the debt could be paid. They did remain and by 1880 the debt was paid in full.[47]

On July 10, 1869, Mother Ann was reappointed Prioress; then in 1872, she was reappointed for a third term. Debts were continually reduced. During this third term, 1872-1875, Tennessee was scourged by epidemics. In Nashville cholera took a heavy toll. Mother Ann asked the sisters for volunteers to nurse the sick. Contacting the newly organized Robertson Association, the sisters joined forces and worked with community leaders "as nurses during this sickly siege.[48]

Major events punctuated Mother Ann's administration in Nashville. But clearing the community's indebtedness remained Ann's continual concern. In 1873 she registered an appeal to the War Claims Committee of the United States House of Representatives and the Court of Claims for property damages done to the Academy during the war.[49] It became a "disallowed claim," reaping no monetary assistance, but the claim demonstrated Mother Ann's watchfulness and relentless practical efforts.

By the mid 1870s Sister Ann had nearly eradicated the community's debts, built an additional building, opened a novitiate, and established the credibility of St. Cecilia convent and academy. She had completed her assignment and was ready for another person to govern. Common sense also told her to allow the new prioress freedom of movement.

But Ann was not allowed to rest. In Ocotber 1875 she and Angela Robinson were sent to Chicago to collect funds to pay off the remaining debts.[50] Now sixty years old, she was sent on mission to Chattanooga in 1876. There she became a founding sister of the Notre Dame select school and the nearby parish school.[51]

During her last term as prioress, 1878-81, Mother Ann sent Sisters Agnes Quarles and Mary Teresa Donaher to Cuba to solicit funds for the first addition to the academy building. She herself, accompanied by Philomena Williamson, undertook a trip to Mexico "for the purpose of collecting, the new building costing more than was expected, and there was no money to pay the bills."[52] They started out October 11, 1880, and returned February 27, 1881, collecting nearly $1000.

On March 12, 1881, shortly after her return, Mother Ann sent in her resignation to the Very Rev. Richard Scannell, Administrator of the Diocese. The resignation was accepted four months prior to the expiration of her term. That autumn, after two sisters resigned the office of prioress at Notre Dame Convent, Anne was appointed prioress once again. "She accepted and took charge October 8,[53] but soon, on December 30, resigned "on account of poor health."

Sister Ann Hanlon died on December 20, 1904. She has remained a legend not only at St. Cecilia, but among American Dominican Sisters. Her many accomplishments achieved in difficult circumstances could not be erased. She was a great woman, a unifier, within three Dominican congregations. In her physical features, Sister Ann Hanlon had the look of a stern and determined woman; she remained a religious whose "heart's long yearning" was for a "truly religious life." The first historian of St. Cecilia said that Mother Ann possessed a mind that was "flexible, broad, open, teachable." [54] A contemporary said that she was "rich in charity." [55]

Sister Ann Hanlon's youthful desire for a place apart from turmoil perhaps did not ever leave her. In reality, however, her life was a very active one; it was also a "truly religious life." Her qualities—the pride, the determination, the broad and teachable mind, the charity, the love of prayer—fitted her for the foundational role in American Dominican life. In the same letter to the Master General requesting enclosure, she had also written, "I have earnestly prayed to God to place me there where I can serve Him the best." As her personal calling unfolded in the events of her life, her prayer was answered.

1. Facts, Chattanooga Catholic News, Chattanooga , TN, July 30, 1892. Cf. Memorabilia, Golden Jubilee, July 25, 1892, Archives, St. Cecilia Convent, Nashville(NDS).

2. James G. Ryan, **Irish Records** (Flyleaf Press, 1988) 383.

3. Facts, July 10, 1892.

4. The Tennessee Register, Nashville, TN, Aug. 19, 1966. Cf. Sr. Miriam Walsh, **A Brief History of the Orgin and Development of St. Cecilia** (Nashville, TN: 1935) 19.

5. Council Book, 1841, Archives, Columbus Dominican Sisters (CDS).

6. Council Book, 1842, CDS.

7. Council Book, 1847, CDS.

8. "Stato delle Missioni dei Patri Domenicani nei Stati Uniti, 1850," Archives General, Order of Preachers, Rome (AGOP) XIII, 731, doc. 262.

9. Sisters of Saint Dominic to Pius IX, July 4, 1848, AGOP XIII, 731, 253. See text ch. II.

10. Sadoc Vilarrasa, O.P., to A.V. Jandel, O.P., Somerset, July 5, 1848, AGOP XIII, 731, doc. 252.

11. Council Book, Dec. 13, 1851, CDS.

12. Council Book, Oct. 19, 1854, CDS.

13. Whelan to Vicar General, Somerset, Jan. 12, 1865, AGOP XIII, 03152, 304.

14. Whelan to Jandel, Somerset, May, 30, 1855, AGOP XIII, 03152, 322.

15. Council Book, Nov. 10, 1856, CDS.

16. Hanlon to Jandel, St. Mary's,Ohio, Dec. 23, 1856, AGOP, XIII, 03152, 355.

17. Whelan to Jandel, Somerset, May 9, 1857, AGOP, XIII, 03152, 360.

18. Whelan, Report of Visitation, Aug. 8, 1857, Archives, SJP.

19. Mary Estelle Casalandra,O.P., Short History of Saint Mary of the Springs: Its History and Spirit, unpublished manuscript, 1950, 127.

20. James A. Kelly Diary ms., Jan. 22, 1859, SJP.

21. Kelly Diary, Feb. 16, 1860.

22. Council Minutes ms., St. Agnes Society, July 5, 1860.

23. Council Minutes ms., St. Agnes Society, June 10, 1861.

24. O.F. Vedder **History of the City of Memphis and Shelby County, Tennessee,** vol. 2. (Syracuse, NY: D.Mason and Co., 1888) 258.

25. E.R. Jolly, **Nuns of the Battlefield** (Providence, RI: Providence Visitor Press, 1927) 94, 97.

26. Jolly 96. Also J.P. Young, ed., **Standard History of Memphis from a Study of the Original Sources** (Knoxville, TN: H.W. Crew & Co., 1912) 341.

27. Margaret Hamilton,O.P., **History of Saint Agnes Academy Memphis, Tennessee 1851-1926** (Memphis: John Gasser Printing Co., 1926) 34. Also, **Meeting the Needs of the Times**, pamphlet, Memphis, 1951, 15.

28. Memphis Daily Argus, June 10, 1862.

29. Sister Ann served as secretary of the St. Agnes Society from September 12, 1863, until the request from Bishop Feehan that she go to St. Cecilia's in 1866. She was not secretary in 1862. Minutes record the election of Sister Veronica Ray as secretary.

30. Council Minutes, ms., St. Agnes Society, May 16, 1864.

31. Council Minutes, Aug. 20, 1864. Cf. also **Memphis City Directory 1865-6**, 16 and 18.

32. Council Minutes, June 20, 1965.

33. Council Minutes, Aug. 12, 1865.

34. Council Minutes, Sep. 2, 1865.

35. Council Minutes, June 20, 1866.

36. Council Minutes, July 7, 1866.

37. Sr. Frances Walsh, O.P., "The Annals of St. Cecilia Convent 1860-1881," 34, NDS.

38. Walsh, Annals, 38.

39. First Council Book, ms., St. Cecilia Academy, Nashville, TN.

40. "Financial Condition of the St. Cecilia Academy, 1867: Statement of Claims" [pamphlet], NDS.

41. "Financial Condition of the St. Cecilia Academy. . . ."

42. Walsh, Annals, 38.

43. V. F. O'Daniel, "Historical Souvenir of Consecration of Saint Dominic's Church" (Washington, DC, 1919) 65.

44. O'Daniel 65.

45. Sister Agnes McGarry (name spelled variously) and Sister Catherine Hoffman.

46. It is curious that Mother Ann sent for Sister Frances. The two women were opposite personality types, Sister Frances being of a congenial and sentimental nature; Mother Ann direct and unsentimental.

47. A series of entries in the first council book document significant amounts paid to Bishop Feehan from 1867 through the 1870s.

48. Nashville Republican Banner, June 21, 1873, 4. Cf. also June 23, 1873, 4, and June 24, 1873, 4.

49. Gary B. Mills, comp., **Southern Loyalists in the Civil War 1871-1880: The Southern Claims Commission, 252**. National Archives and Records Administration, claim #17205.

50. Council Minutes, St. Cecilia Academy, Oct. 28, 1875.

51. Council Minutes, St. Cecilia Academy, Jan. 3, 1876.

52. Council Minutes, St. Cecilia Academy, Oct. 7, 1880.

53. Council Minutes, St. Cecilia Academy, Mar. 12, 1881.

54. Walsh, **Brief History**, 20.

55. Walsh, **Brief History**. Cf. Sr. Dorothea Aud, O.P., "Mount Vernon Hill to Aquinas College: A Hundred Years at St. Cecilia Academy 1860-1960," unpublished manuscript, c. 1967, NDS.

CHAPTER 10

THE FRIARS AT MID-CENTURY

At the midpoint of the nineteenth century, the Dominican friars of St. Joseph Province, along with many fellow Americans, emerged from their pioneer status. Together they faced fifteen critical years in the life of the nation; a time of increasing European immigration, territorial expansion, continuing endorsement of the system of slavery and the consequent tragedy of Civil War. The years between 1850 and 1865 would also bring irreversible changes for the Church and the Order of Preachers within and outside the United States. In the midst of all changes from without, the life of the province survived, despite its own grave problems. Its mission continued.

By 1850 many elements favored the development of both urban and rural life in the region known as the Old Northwest. Immigrants and settlers claimed abundant farmland at low cost. An American genius for inventiveness provided new means of communication and transportation while civic stability, forged by the early American republic, encouraged people to live in the rising towns. [1] By 1860 the population was quickly spreading from the Appalachians to and beyond the Mississippi Valley. Between 1850 and 1865 increasing numbers of Catholic immigrants arrived. They were largely from Germany and Ireland, the former fleeing political oppression, the latter their famine-stricken Emerald Isle. Especially among the German Catholics, bishops, pastors and people now had to face a new question that would affect the Church for many decades in relation to the arrivals from Europe. Should these immigrants whose language and customs were so different from their English-speaking confreres have parishes of their own? The liturgies of all groups were in Latin; but German parishioners, struggling to learn English, found the preaching and other pastoral activities incomprehensible, or at least frustrating. Moreover, they seldom found an American parish community as close-knit as the one they left in "the old country." Like the Lutherans, they maintained that in order to keep their faith they must use the German language in worship and in the schooling of their children. Their motto was: "Language saves the Faith." They led the way for the development of ethnic parishes during the second half of the 19th century.

Following the example of Bishop Fenwick, the Dominicans understood such arguments and tried to provide priests whenever possible for the German families, as when in 1843 they opened St. Nicholas Parish in Zanesville, Ohio. In 1852 John Albert Bokel, O.P., a native of Germany, was called to Memphis, Tennessee to be "pastor of the German Catholics of this city and to care for their spiritual necessities."

He learned that forty families had already taken the initiative in the matter, and recorded:

May 23. Today I learned that the Germans were to have a meeting after Vespers at Mr. Handwerker's to find out the intention of the parish; if they wished to contribute to the support of the English church [St. Peter's, to be replaced with a larger building] or if they wished to buy a lot for themselves and to erect a church. [2]

Like many of their co-religionists, Memphis families also chose to form a separate "national parish." Despite their poverty, they supported the first German parish in Tennessee called St. Mary's. Father Bokel played his own special role, knowing where to obtain help from other German Catholics. He noted,

On June 2nd [1853] I went to St. Louis on the Steamer Bulletin to collect among the Catholics of that city money to pay as soon as possible the heavy debt on the lot. The most Reverend Archbishop [Peter] Kenrick readily gave me permission to collect. I received about $633 from my countrymen and about $370 from the others. The latter amount was for Father Grace. [3]

John Albert Bokel, Pastor and friend of German immigrants in Ohio and Tennessee

After 1850, Irish immigrants came in equally great numbers. Many unmarried women and men joined the veritable pilgrimage of exile, a custom different from that followed by most other nationalities. Most sought any kind of employment in order to relieve their relatives overseas and finance the journey of other family members from Ireland. Many of these Catholic immigrants were attracted to religious life in the United States. Among the 69 friars professed between 1850 and 1865 there were 42 born in Ireland, including 24 priests and 18 brothers. In 1856 eight of the ten Dominican friars ordained to the priesthood were natives of Ireland. This was the first and only year in which native-born Americans were outnumbered in province membership. [4] Given the ethnic pattern among American friars between 1850 and 1862, it is not surprising that three successive superiors of St. Joseph Province during that period were natives of Ireland. They were Matthew O'Brien (1850-1854), James Whelan (1854-58) and Joseph Augustine Kelly (1858-62). Under their governance the province enjoyed growth and relative stability, despite their participation in major changes in American society.

Matthew O'Brien was a strongly pastoral priest, long known for his success in welcoming converts, bringing back lapsed Catholics, and building churches and missions which he financed by begging tours. Zeal characterized his administration, although some critics considered him imprudent in admitting unsuitable candidates. In 1852, in the midst of his term, the vicar general Vincent Jandel sent an Irish Dominican, Robert White, as visitor to the American province. The

American friars, who saw him as affable and complimentary, generally liked White. But on his return to Rome his reports seemed critical, especially of St. Rose Priory. He was candid with the provincial O'Brien about the grievances of the friars there. He wrote,

I am sorry to have to allude to the subject which is somewhat disagreeable but just before I left America, I received letters which I cannot avoid noticing. At St. Rose's they were still complaining of ill treatment, & they furnished me with a catalogue of grievances which astonished me. They may be reduced to three heads: unwholesome diet in the refectory, neglect of the sick, & arbitrary conduct on the part of superiors which is almost unendurable, so much is it said to be contrary to the mild spirit of the government of our Order. I did not wish to take any step in regard to this affair, until I first made you acquainted with it. [5]

How the provincial responded to White and the friars of St. Rose is unknown, but he pleased province members in 1853 by accepting an invitation for the friars to go to Washington, D.C. There they opened St. Dominic's parish and built the church and rectory under the direction of George Wilson and Nicholas D. Young. [6] To have a mission in the nation's capital was a source of gratification to O'Brien and Young, and apparently to all the friars. Young wrote with confidence to Jandel about the *fait accompli*, "We beg your blessing & special prayers in behalf of this work, and that we may be governed in its foundation by the spirit that animated our holy Founder." [7] However, they had not consulted the vicar general, thinking it was enough to discuss the foundation with Robert White. Jandel objected strongly to the Washington establishment. While obliged to accept the action, he admonished O'Brien not to undertake new commitments with such limited numbers of friars. [8]

Matthew O'Brien, Dominican Provincial, 1850–1854

Even O'Brien's critics did not fault his decision to send men to Washington. He brought the province to the east coast and founded a parish of great promise, even financially, because it could pay for itself. The province had been virtually subsidizing the parishes it staffed in Kentucky and Ohio.

Although Matthew O'Brien was not known as an intellectual, he fulfilled as provincial the earlier desire of Nicholas Young to open the College of St. Joseph at Somerset. The building was ready in 1850 and staffing began a year later. The first president was James Whelan; other staff members combined teaching with pastoral ministry nearby. [9] At the end of 1854 there were over one hundred youths enrolled at St. Joseph's, occupying a new building. Academic degrees would be conferred on the first class three years later.

At the 1854 provincial chapter, James Whelan was elected provincial. This was the same friar who six years later was named Bishop of Nashville and whose unhappy episcopacy has been described in Chapter 9. At the age of thirty-one, he was the

**St. Joseph College,
Somerset, Ohio, 1850**

youngest to hold the office until then and already had the reputation of being a brilliant scholar. [10] After his profession in 1840, he was the only theology student, but had the advantage of studying with Eugenio Pozzo, the Italian theologian who was the first regent of studies in the province. Whelan became Pozzo's virtual assistant even before ordination, and in 1849, when Pozzo returned to Italy, replaced him as master of students. Upon the establishment of St. Joseph's College in 1851, he was named its first president, a position he held until elected to head St. Joseph Province. As provincial between 1854 and 1858, James Whelan sustained the emphasis given to study by his mentor Pozzo. He conducted regular visitation among the friars and sisters, sent written reports to the houses as well as to the Master General, urged the keeping of archives, and introduced the use of the customary Dominican form of assignment by *mandamus.* [11]

Joseph Augustine Kelly was elected provincial on October 16, 1858. Although Kelly by his office became president of St. Joseph College, he was not a profound scholar. He was both respected and liked by his confreres. [12] Like Whelan, Kelly believed that American Dominicans were best educated in their homeland rather than in Europe. Nevertheless, he sent four young men to study in Rome and France, with disappointing results: two died in Europe, and one left the Order after ordination.[13] With increasing numbers of men ready for the missions, Joseph Kelly desired to bring the Order to the eastern cities by accepting invitations to staff several new parishes. The Master Jandel grudgingly agreed to accept only one: St. Peter's in London, Ontario, which, despite a debt held a hopeful future. The friars arrived there in September 1861.[14] The development of parish ministry was one of several points on which Jandel and the American friars did not see eye to eye. The Americans knew the needs of their people as Jandel did not.

REGULA S. AUGUSTINI
E T
CONSTITUTIONES
FF. ORDINIS PRÆDICATORUM

NUNC RECENTER REIMPRESSÆ

Jussu Reverendiss. Patris ANTONINI CLOCHE,
ejusdem Ordinis Magistri Generalis .

ROMÆ, M.DC.XC.

Typis Nicolai Angeli Tinassij, *Superiorœ m permi.*

**Constitutions of the Order
of Preachers, 1690**

During the first half of the 19th century the Order of Preachers in Europe was weakened by problems, both religious and political, which were bringing all religious orders close to disaster. Following the French Revolution and the Napoleonic Wars, they were subject to political oppression and wholesale confiscation of property, the weakening of common life and the dispersal of members. To have friars living a "private life" apart from community was for the Dominicans the most serious problem, for they lost their traditional sources of strength for mission: their common prayer, purposeful study and communal decision making.

While the American province was struggling to develop its life and mission, the Dominicans in Europe were barely surviving the short, ineffective terms of leaders and the rarity of general chapters. To help revivify the Order while a general chapter was impossible to convene even for election, the Pope in 1850 appointed for six years a vicar general, Alexander Vincent Jandel. In his first letter to the friars the new head of the Order wrote candidly, "We are surrounded by ruins."[15] However, he was confident that the weakness of the Order was not unto death. Jandel was one of the men who studied at the house of strict observance in La Quercia, Italy, along with Joseph Alemany, Sadoc Vilarrasa and the preacher Henri Lacordaire who restored the Order in France.[16]

At the close of his six years as appointed vicar, Jandel was elected Master General by his brothers for successive terms until his death in 1872. The relationship of Vincent Jandel and the American friars was one of good will, but mutual understanding was hampered by cultural differences and Jandel's inclination toward the cloistral, monastic aspect of Dominican life. The French master was also mission-minded, but his giant efforts at renewal of the Order of Preachers led him to emphasize the communal character of their life as the basis for rebuilding.

The Americans of the Order from the beginning were necessarily mission-oriented. They were led by the call of the Church, the spiritual needs of the people, to be "useful" to the rapidly growing numbers who needed parishes and churches, preaching and sacraments. One problem was that although Jandel visited other countries, including England, he never came to the United States. Lacking personal knowledge of the American scene, he gave much credence to the Irish friars he sent as visitators. Their reports seemed to vacillate between flattery and sharp criticism.[17]

Jandel deplored the Americans' minimal knowledge of the Constitutions of the Order. But the few extant copies, all in Latin, had not been revised since 1690. Revision was the responsibility of general chapters, but in the turmoil of 19th-century Europe, the prescribed triennial chapters were seldom convened. Between 1806 and 1850, when eighteen general chapters should have met, only three could be held.[18] The American friars, even with their limited experience and penchant for independence, fully understood their relationship to the universal Order. They recognized in Jandel the kind of leadership that had been lacking. However, they were reasonably sure that he did not understand the Americans situation. He could not see how they were fulfilling the mission of the Order in ways different from those of their brothers in Europe. All his letters told them so.

Vincent Jandel never abandoned his hope to have all American Dominicans pursue their studies in Rome or another study center in Europe. One of his statements on the subject is found in a letter to Bishop Thomas Grace, who with other friars and bishops were petitioning for the restoration of the province founded in 1844 in Wisconsin. Jandel wrote,

> Until I shall be able to obtain a nucleus of Religious who have been trained in Europe according to our laws and who have the true spirit of the Order and are suitable for the education of youth, and for establishing an entirely new community, without any admixture of the old elements, there can be no question of opening a new Novitiate in those parts and much less of the erection of a new Province.[19]

Alexander Vincent Jandel,
Vicar General, 1850-1855;
Master General, 1855-1872

Most American friars, who discounted the value of foreign study, resisted his ideas on study. Rome in particular had proven to be an unhealthy place for some youthful members who could not survive the climate or the food.

The dream of the province founders had been to establish a college such as they had staffed at Holy Cross in Belgium and a provincial studium, or house of studies. In keeping with Dominican ideals, the need for a studium was even greater than for a college of arts and sciences. But pioneer conditions frustrated the early attempts to give a studium a firm foundation. In the United States there was no urban university to sponsor such an institution for the friars. Few men were prepared for seminary teaching, except among the French Sulpicians. Catholic youth were themselves poor and generally uneducated until colleges would be well established.

Two questions present themselves. Who were the professors assigned to teach young Dominican friars called to the priesthood? And what was the quality of education offered to them? The province founders were well educated, with the exception of Fenwick, whose studies were cut short by political conditions after the French Revolution. Thomas Wilson earned advanced degrees in theology, as did William Tuite and Robert Angier. The Americans who followed them were decidedly limited in their studies until the coming of Eugenio Pozzo, Sadoc Vilarrasa, Joseph Alemany and other Europeans fully prepared to teach theology. Under their leadership the post of Regent of Studies was established in the 1840's. Regents, however, were required to share in parish ministry, which in fact could enhance their instruction and make it more than academic. Pozzo and Vilarrasa were brilliant scholars, but Vilarrasa joined Alemany in the California foundation in 1850 and Pozzo returned to Italy in 1857.

There were now two other sources of instructors. One was the group of immigrants from Ireland, Germany and Belgium who had been well educated before joining St. Joseph Province. Included in this group were James Whelan and Joseph Kelly. There were several Americans who had studied in Europe. Thomas Grace and Nicholas Raymond Young were the most outstanding. Young would be called to parish ministry and provincial administration; Grace would be named a bishop.

The quality of education offered at St. Joseph to novices was greatly enhanced by a rich library which proved a munificent resource. It was the collection of more than two thousand volumes bequeathed to the friars by Luke Concanen, O.P., before his unexpected death in 1810. Other resources had to be built up gradually. [20] Unfortunately, the efforts of Eugenio Pozzo in the late 1840's to establish a formal studium met with little permanent success. Apparently he was incapable of adapting to the new situation. He alienated those in the province who felt that the ministry ought to determine the course of education. Had Alemany remained provincial for a full term, he may have been able, with Vilarrasa, to improve the studies of the priests while not overlooking the needs of the parishes and outlying missions. Instead, his successor, the overanxious Matthew O'Brien, tended to truncate the studies of new members in his zeal to meet the urgent needs of the American missions.

In the founding of the American province the idea of a college, even when only a dream, was inseparable from that of a house of studies. The founders had to leave Maryland for Kentucky partly because their projected college might be a threat to the one at Georgetown. But their dream did not fade from the day that the four Dominicans from Holy Cross College in Belgium launched their province and college in a Kentucky farmhouse. Although never set aside, the college idea was beset by many difficulties: the pull of men to the missions, the paucity of professors and funds and competition from two other colleges in Kentucky: St. Joseph's and St. Mary's, which were diocesan colleges at that time.

The detailed story of success and failures in Dominican higher education to 1865 is told fully by the historian James Bernard Walker, O.P., in his monograph, "The College Idea in the History of the Dominican Province of St. Joseph."[21] The chronology of higher education sponsored by St. Joseph Province to 1865, taken from that source, is here given in summary:

1806 Founding by Edward Fenwick and his first companions of St. Thomas College "on a five-hundred acre plantation in the very heart of the Catholic settlements . . . the first Catholic educational institution for boys west of the Alleghenies, and the third founded in the United States since the Declaration of Independence." (p. 314)

1807 Enrolled twenty-two, and by 1817 two hundred students; One was Jefferson Davis, later president of the Confederacy. Others were Dominican friars, including Bishops Richard Miles and Thomas Grace.

1822 Plan to move the college to Cincinnati thwarted by a restraining order that friars should not leave St. Rose for Ohio

1828 College closed, partly owing to growing competition from St. Joseph College in Bardstown & St. Mary's in Lebanon, KY

1841 Ohio novitiate opened, leading to rapid growth of a studium and hope for opening a college

1846 Opening of St. Thomas College at Sinsinawa, Wisconsin by Samuel Mazzuchelli, O.P., with incorporation by Wisconsin legislature in 1848.

1849 Transfer of administration of Sinsinawa college to Province of St. Joseph upon the resignation of Samuel Mazzuchelli as provincial of St. Charles Province

1850 St. Joseph College opened at Somerset by St. Joseph Province [22]

1853-1864 Growth of Sinsinawa college, from which foundation twenty men entered the Province of St. Joseph to become priests or lay brothers

1857 Academic degrees conferred at colleges of Sinsinawa and Somerset; both affected adversely by financial panic of 1857

1861 Tentative suspension of St. Joseph College, owing to Civil War and financial problems

1864 Tentative suspension of St. Thomas College, Sinsinawa, by Provincial Matthew O'Brien

The suspension of classes at both colleges was soon changed to their final closing by the peremptory action of the appointed provincial from Ireland, William O'Carroll. He began his term on May 1, 1865, and within two months reported to Jandel from Sinsinawa, "The two colleges, those of St. Joseph and Sinsinawa Mound are suppressed." Since he was carrying out Jandel's orders, no explanation of the action was needed. "But," he added, "Bishop Henni of Milwaukee made some pressing and even menacing entreaties to oblige us to open the college."[23]

Bishop Henni's protest had been sent to the prior at Sinsinawa, the young and inexperienced J. A. Rooney, three months before O'Carroll's coming as provincial. Henni, having heard that the provincial Matthew O'Brien was hoping to reopen the college, stated without menace or pressure,

St. Thomas Aquinas College Sinsinawa, Wisconsin, 1846–1865

I am truly glad that your provincial [O'Brien] does not give up the idea of reopening the Mound College as soon as it can be done in a satisfactory manner. For I, as the Ordinary of this Diocese, am absolutely in conscience bound to see that a property purchased and paid for Collegiate purposes be maintained for that purpose forever – the more since Father Mazzuchelli obtained all such monies, not from the order but from his friends & benefactors in Europe & likewise from the Propagation of the Faith – all of which had to be and was expended for said object . . .

I am willing to give my signature to any document, *provided it secures in full the reopening of the College* as soon as it can be creditably effected by the Fathers. [Emphasis added.][24]

Whether O'Carroll visited Bishop Henni is not known, but the college idea promoted by the province founders and supported by most of the American Dominicans was relinquished. After sixty years of struggle, their dream would now be left unrealized for sixty more years, while that of a thriving studium would await the growth and vigorous life of the province after the Civil War.

The internal problems of the American province were necessarily superseded by the attention of the friars to the problems of all Americans. In the fall of 1858, the ever-growing questions of slavery and states' rights, fanned by the Lincoln-Douglas debates, took center stage. A few days after the election of Joseph Kelly as provincial in October 1858, the presidential candidate William Seward warned the nation of the "irrepressible conflict between opposing and enduring forces" in the country. He emphasized the necessary choice of becoming "either a slave-holding nation or entirely a free-labor nation." [25]

Although Catholic slaves in Kentucky were usually called "servants," they and their owners knew they were not. Slaves belonged to the friars and sisters in Kentucky, beginning with Edward Fenwick's who arrived from Maryland with servants from the family plantation. As residents in Kentucky, the Dominicans continued to take slavery for granted. Even the friars from Europe were silent about the "peculiar institution." The Kentucky census of 1850 listed among slaveowners "St. Roses" with the following unnamed slaves:

No.	Ages	Sex	Colour
1	40	M	B
2	42	M	B
3	32	M	B
4	30	M	B
5	45	M	B
6	50	F	B
7	14	F	B
8	13	F	B[26]

The friars apparently differed little from other Catholic Kentuckians, concerning whom a recent study by C. Walker Gollar concludes:

> Lay Catholics not only accepted slave labor as a part of Southern culture, but also, essentially endorsed the institution of human bondage... More Catholics than non-Catholics owned slaves. [27]

The Council Book of St. Rose priory records the purchase and sale of slaves; also the decision of the friars, following the passage of the Thirteenth Amendment, that all blacks should be given money and provisions and should then leave the property, with one exception. "Terry may remain if she chooses so to do for her support which we willingly give her, no service being required of her." [28]

Catholic families usually encouraged the practice of religion among their slaves by providing some instruction along with participation in family worship. Since the largest parish of the region was that of St. Rose, sacramental ministries were provided for many slaves by the friars.[29] Nonetheless, as Gollar demonstrates,

Once the cross of slavery had been lifted, black people found little use for Catholicism. No record confirms this fact more clearly than does the burial register of Saint Rose. Each year from 1830 to 1865 at least twenty-five percent of the people laid to rest were slaves. But from 1866 to 1875 barely five percent of the burials were of blacks, or "negroes" and not "servants" as they formerly were called. Many other Church records prove this mass exodus from Catholicism.[30]

According to the 1860 census, the slave population at St. Catharine's included more children than at St. Rose. This was true of family units as well. Census records give no such information and the records of St. Catharine's community were destroyed by a fire in 1904.[31]

The issues of slavery and states' rights were painfully present to the American Dominicans whose territory was located both above and below the Ohio River, in regions defined as North and South. Typically, their decisions were made relative to geographical location. The Province of St. Joseph supported the Union, even though the leader at that time, Joseph Kelly, was a southerner. Among the friars, allegiances were not clear-cut, since natives of Kentucky and Maryland served in Ohio, while northerners were at work in Tennessee and Kentucky. Yet, whatever the personal allegiance of members, the friars concentrated their efforts upon ministry to the people. When war approached, friars were called to be chaplains for both armies. In December 1861, Bishop Martin Spalding of Louisville requested the prior at St. Rose to send chaplains to the Union Army encamped at Lebanon, Kentucky.[32] As a Confederate army chaplain, Joseph Jarboe from St. Rose, barely escaped death while he attended the mortally wounded in the battle of Shiloh, Tennessee.[33]

Dominican Sisters at St. Catharine's, Kentucky, converted their convent into an army hospital during the nearby Battle of Perryville in October 1862. They nursed the men of both armies.[34] In Memphis the sisters at St. Agnes Academy were asked by Bishop Whelan to take over the City Hospital for the soldiers.[35] Both sisters and friars in Kentucky and Tennessee saw soldiers pass through their grounds in thousands, or encamp close by.[36] At St. Cecilia's in Nashville, the sisters instilled courage in their resident pupils during the occupation by the Northern army. Their situation was vividly described by Sister Frances Walsh, who with three others from St. Mary's, Somerset, had founded the Nashville Dominican community in 1860 on the eve of the War. She wrote,

Without resistance Nashville yielded to the inevitable, and the Federal fleet sailed up the Cumberland. From the windows each vessel could be plainly seen down to the water's edge . . . Many of those dear girls were cut off from all communication with those they loved better than life itself. . . hostile regiments unfolded their tents in the immediate vicinity. . . . Camps and tents, officers and soldiers were familiar sights.

One day two girls were halted by an armed sentinel. They returned to the Academy grounds "in double quick . . . vowing never to leave them if by so doing they must take the detested Iron Clad Oath which meant allegiance to the Union." But officers assured the residents of their liberty of movement. Then courtesies were exchanged on both sides, and "the host that at first seemed so formidable became a protection rather than a menace." [37] Although not located on the lines of battle, both the sisters and the friars endured the privations resulting from the war, including the loss of horses and cattle to the moving troops. Nevertheless, their usual ministries continued, along with the unusual ones related to the war.

The perspective of the American Dominicans necessarily reached beyond their own concerns to the whole Church. In serving the parish, the diocese and the universal Church, friars and sisters experienced the far-reaching changes of the Church in the nineteenth century. They knew at first hand the retrogressive movements possible in both society and Church, as when the expansion of ideas aroused by the Enlightenment was confronted by the narrowing of theological perspective in the "Syllabus of Errors" of Pope Pius IX. In the United States the phenomenal growth of the Church required a rapid multiplication of dioceses. By 1852, fewer than fifty years after the single See of Baltimore had first been divided, there were thirty-two American dioceses. Dominican men and women were serving in seven of them. [38]

Beyond its ordinary ministry, one service that the American province gave the Church, albeit reluctantly, was to provide bishops for the new dioceses. Beginning with Edward Fenwick, able missionaries were called to bishoprics in every decade. They accepted with personal and provincial reluctance, and not without cost to the life and work of the Order. [39] Before the Civil War, the following Dominican men were appointed bishops:

> **1821 Edward Fenwick, Diocese of Cincinnati, Ohio**
>
> **1837 Richard Miles, Diocese of Nashville, Tennessee**
>
> **1849 C.P. Montgomery, Diocese of Monterey, California, refused.**
>
> **1850 Joseph Alemany, Diocese of Monterey, California – later San Francisco**
>
> **1859 James Whelan, Diocese of Nashville, Tennessee; resigned in 1863**
>
> **1859 Thomas Langdon Grace, Diocese of St. Paul, Minnesota**

The Church benefited from the leadership of Dominican friars as provincials, theologians or bishops. Like four of the Dominicans cited above, almost all the American bishops consecrated at this time were the first prelates in their respective dioceses. They recognized the value of meeting together for mutual assistance and decision-making, as had the prelates at the first meeting of bishops in 1810 and the seven Provincial Councils of Baltimore between 1829 and 1849. With one exception, Dominicans were present at all the meetings from 1810 through the first Plenary Council of 1852. Among those in attendance were the following:

1810 First meeting of bishops. Francis Antoninus Fleming, theologian and vicar general of Bishop John Carroll.

1828 First Provincial Council of Baltimore. Edward Fenwick, one of eight bishops of American sees.

1833 Second Provincial Council. Nicholas Dominic Young, provincial and consulting theologian.

1837 [Council convened April 16, six days before election of Miles as provincial; neither Young nor Miles could be present]

1840 Fourth Provincial Council. Richard Miles, Bishop of Nashville; Charles P. Montgomery, Dominican provincial.

1841 Fifth Provincial Council. Richard Miles, Bishop of Nashville; Samuel Mazzuchelli, theologian to Bishop Loras.

1846 Sixth Provincial Council. Richard Miles bishop, George Wilson, provincial

1849 Seventh Provincial Council. Joseph Alemany, provincial; Richard Miles bishop

In 1852 thirty-two bishops gathered in Baltimore for the first Plenary Council convened by Archbishop Francis Patrick Kenrick. Bishops Alemany and Miles participated in the major Council decisions and served on committees concerned with canon law, education, and Church property. Matthew O'Brien represented the Order of Preachers as provincial. So impressive were the united decisions of the prelates that papal approval of them was sent promptly. With the approval, however, came a warning about the danger of Americans developing a **national** Church, and also about granting too many dispensations or exceptions to Church law. [40]

For the most part, American bishops found mutual support among themselves, but international tensions supporting "ultramontanists" who were in favor of a strong papacy, occasionally affected American clergy. Most Americans, however, supported a collegial decision-making process for the American church. [41] Their views were strengthened as they observed the hostility most Protestants showed to Archbishop Gaetano Bedini who visited the United States as a papal emissary in 1852. In 1866 the bishops prepared for the opening of the First Vatican Council of 1869 during which the question of papal infallibility was raised. Some American bishops judged it to be an untimely subject, but all would finally give public support to papal authority as defined by the Church. [42] However, such issues were not of immediate concern to American Catholics. Their interests related to the need for parishes and the growing influence of pastors as well as bishops.

The orderly progress of the Dominican Province of St. Joseph at mid-century seemed to end with the provincial chapter that met in October of 1862. Unable to agree on an election, the friars once again requested the master general to appoint a provincial. Had they known the outcome of that request, the chapter might have been spurred to more decisive action. Jandel chose as provincial the nephew of Nicholas Dominic Young, Nicholas Raymond, or "Young Nick" to his brethren. He was blessed with every advantage, including his birth into a family of Maryland gentry. He had been sent with Thomas Langdon Grace to study in Rome for seven unhurried years, despite the pressing needs of St. Joseph Province. It was there that he became known to Vincent Jandel. Subsequently in detailed letters to the master general, Young cited his efforts to introduce strict observance in every house of the province. But within the first year of his tenure, he had caused scandal and had to resign. Chaos resulted. [43]

The former provincial, Matthew O'Brien, assumed authority in place of the rightful vicar, Michael Lilly. O'Brien acted so quickly that many confusing assignments complicated Dominican affairs. Discredited, O'Brien was required to cede his leadership to Lilly who completed Raymond Young's original term in 1865. Next, the provincial chapter unanimously elected the Irish prior of San Clemente in Rome, Joseph Mullooly, who promptly declined the post. Jandel then appointed still another Irish friar, William O'Carroll, who arrived at Somerset in the spring of 1865 to close an era of fifteen years of lights and shadows. [44]

The shadows made the future of the Province of St. Joseph look dismal indeed. Believing that one problem was the great distance between houses of the Province of St. Joseph, several friars asked Jandel to authorize forming at least one new province within its vast territory. In response to one petition, Jandel stated all too candidly his reason for refusing. He wrote to Bishop Grace,

> I confess to you that in my eyes, the principal motive which determines is the sad state of the province of St. Joseph; all the news that I receive of it combines to paint it under very somber colors; practical ignorance of our legislation, general lack of observance and of discipline, almost total absence of religious formation, etc. These are what stand out among all the reports and the facts of this poor province. [45]

Actually, there was already in existence another American province in California. It had been initiated in 1850. The development of that province between 1850 and 1865 is described in Chapter 12.

Despite weaknesses, St. Joseph Province had experienced growth in some areas. On the bright side were the steady increase of personnel, the opening of colleges and new missions and the faithful service given to parishes new and old. Almost all the province members and their meager resources went into this service. But they had spread themselves thin trying to meet the needs of burgeoning parishes and remote missions. Some were on the outskirts of settlements, in conditions that varied little from those of Fenwick's excursions in the forests of Ohio and Michigan. Others were ready to enter ministries in the large cities as soon as new foundations would be permitted by the Master of the Order.

Early in 1865 the roster of men in St. Joseph Province totaled forty-nine priests, at work in the following locations:

Chattanooga, Tennessee	Memphis, Tennessee	Sinsinawa, Wisconsin
Lexington, Kentucky	Nashville, Tennessee	Somerset, Ohio
London, Ontario	St. Catharine, Kentucky	Washington, D.C.
Louisville, Kentucky	St. Rose, Kentucky	Zanesville, Ohio

Between 1850 and 1865 twenty-nine lay brothers were professed in the Province. Most of them worked at Somerset, St. Rose, or Sinsinawa as farmers, tailors, carpenters and cooks. As brothers in community, they supported the other friars in their ministries.

The development of the missions of St. Joseph Province outside the heartland of Kentucky and Ohio is described in other chapters.

1. See Malcolm J. Rohrbough, **The Trans-Appalachian Frontier: People, Societies and Institutions, 1775-1850** (New York: Oxford U. Press, 1978) 347-349.

2. John Albert Bokel, O.P., "A Record Book of the German Roman Catholic Parish in Memphis Tenn. A.D. 1852," ms. Apr. 3, St. Joseph Province Archives (SJP).

3. Bokel, "Notes," June 2, 1853, SJP.

4. See J. B. Walker, "Studies of St. Joseph Province" Appendix IV, "Priests in the Province of St. Joseph," 1806-1865, ms. SJP; and Reginald Coffey, **Pictorial History of the Dominican Province of St. Joseph, USA** (New York, 1946) passim. .

5. White to O'Brien, Rome, Oct. 9, 1852, SJP.

6. The land on which the impressive Gothic church of St. Dominic was built had been part of Notley Young's 400 acres that later became Southwest Washington. See William W. Warner, **At Peace with All Their Neighbors** (Washington, D.C., Georgetown U. Press, 1994) 63.

7. Nicholas Dominic Young to Vincent Jandel, Washington, May 20, 1853, Archives General, Order of Preachers, Rome, AGOP, XIII, 03150, 284.

8. Jandel to O'Brien in margin of White to Jandel, Rome, July 25, 1853, AGOP XIII, 03150, 161.

9. As provincial Alemany had encouraged the Wisconsin province of St. Albert to merge with that of St. Joseph, and in 1850 sent men to Sinsinawa to staff the College of St. Thomas Aquinas there. See Ch.7.

10. Whelan's education began in Dublin. His family emigrated to New York and he completed his early schooling in Troy, New York.

11. See Glossary.

12. Nicholas D. Young, ever the pessimistic judge, wrote to the master general that Kelly had no understanding of strict observance and that he allowed discipline to slide as he ran around the countryside. Young to Jandel, Kentucky, Apr. 21, 1862, SJP.

13. The community at St. Rose persuaded the provincial to send their Irish students, Peter Hyacinth Doherty and

Michael James Joyce, to study in Rome. Doherty died before ordination and Joyce soon after. The third student, Leo Adams, returned briefly to Kentucky after ordination and then left the Order. Bernard Brady, the fourth Roman student, returned to Kentucky, but gave joyless service in the Order. Kelly wrote candidly to Jandel about his negative view of American friars studying in Rome. See Kelly to Jandel, Somerset, Sept. 21, 1859, AGOP XIII, 03152, 390.

14. Kelly to Jandel, Somerset, Jan. 12, 1862; and Jandel to Kelly, Rome, Mar. 18, 1862. Both in SJP.

15. R.P.Mortier, O.P., **Histoire des Maitres Generaux de L'Ordre des Freres Precheurs,** vol. 7 (Paris, Picard, 1914) 489.

16. Following the French Revolution and succeeding political upheavals, no Dominicans remained in France, where St. Dominic had founded the Order in 1215. Lacordaire brought the Order back to its birthplace in 1843. Joseph Alemany and Thomas Langdon Grace were also students there. Both found in their later mission experience a need to balance monastic observance with apostolic action.

17. White to O'Brien, Oct. 9, 1852.

18. In 1838, on Pentecost, the first general chapter since the French Revolution took place in Rome. In 1841 a chapter of fourteen delegates, all Italians, convened in Rome. The third general chapter before 1850 met in Rome in 1844. See Mortier, vol. 7, 467-480.

19. Jandel to Mazzuchelli, Fortune, Power, Mar. 22, 1864, AGOP XIII, 03152,486 bears no name of writer or addressee; it was attached to the letter of Oct. 26, 1863: Power, Mazzuchelli and Fortune to Jandel from Sinsinawa. Letters in Sinsinawa Archives (SDA).

20. See Katherine Boyd and Jordan Lenaghan, O.P., "A Theological Light on the American Frontier: Theological Texts from the Dominican Studium Library, 1805-1865." An Exhibit, 1996. Dominican House of Studies, Washington, D.C. 20017.

21. Reprinted from **The Catholic Historical Review,** 23 (1937):312-350.

22. See Jordan Lenaghan, OP,

St. Joseph College, Somerset, Ohio, 1850-1861 (New York: Dominican Province of St. Joseph, 1997).

23. William D. O'Carroll to Vincent Jandel, June 6, 1865, AGOP XIII, 03152, 513 and SJP.

24. Martin Henni to John Rooney, O.P., Milwaukee, Feb. 13, 1865, SJP and SDA XIV, 30.

25. Cited in **Almanac of American History,** Oct. 25, 1858, 274.

26. Kentucky Census of Nov. 14, 1850.

27. C.Walker Gollar, "Catholic Slaves and Slaveowners in Kentucky," **The Catholic Historical Review** 84 (1998): 42-44.

28. St. Rose Council Book ms. Dec. 27, 1865, 109, SJP.

29. The Dominican historian James Bernard Walker cites this tradition in a letter to William Hinnebusch, O.P., Sep. 25, 1975, SJP.

30. Gollar 61.

31. See Paschala Noonan, O.P,. for the history of the Kentucky Dominican Sisters, **Signadou** (Manhasset, N.Y.: Brookville Books, 1997).

32. Notes of John Albert Bokel, O.P., Dec. 2, 1861, SJP.

33. Martin J. Spalding to Archbishop John Baptist Purcell, Louisville, Apr. 16, 1862, Cincinnati Archdiocesan Archives (CAA).

34. Ellen Ryan Jolly, **Nuns of the Battlefield** (Providence, R.I.: Providence *Visitor* Press, 1927) 88-91.

35. Frances Walsh, OP, "The Annals of St. Cecilia Convent, 1860-1888," Nashville, TN, ms 29, Nashville Dominican Sisters Archives (NDS).

36. John Albert Bokel, O.P., in "Notes" wrote on Jan. 12, 1862, "Several thousand U.S. soldiers past [sic] through Springfield [close to St. Rose] for Columbus, KY. The march of soldiers continued several days." SJP.

37. Walsh, "The Annals," Nashville, Tennessee, 28-29, NDS.

38. Communities of friars and sisters were on mission in the Dioceses of Louisville, Cincinnati, Nashville and Milwaukee. Serving in the Diocese of

Boston were John McDonnell and James Henry Taaffe of the Irish province; and in New York, assisting Archbishop John Hughes, was Thomas Martin on leave from St. Joseph Province. SJP.

39. When Bishop Miles took part in the 1852 Baltimore Council, the bishops and Propaganda Fide were asked to honor the request of the Jesuit major superior that no member of the Society be named bishop. No such restraint was honored in this case.

40. Peter Guilday, **A History of the Councils of Baltimore** vol. 4 (New York: Macmillan, 1932) 181. See Propaganda Fide to F. P. Kenrick, Rome, Sep. 28, 1852. Letters and Decrees, Kenneally, **United States Documents in the Propaganda Fide Archives** vol.4 (Washington, DC:Academy of American Franciscan History, 1966) 1513 and 1514.

41. One sign of the times was the establishment in Rome in 1859, of the North American College from which some alumni, including William O'Connell, Boston's later Cardinal, brought home "Romanist" views.

42. See Gerald Fogarty, S.J., **The Vatican and the American Hierarchy** (Collegeville, Minnesota: Michael Glazier, Liturgical Press, 1990) reprint.

43. Details of the resignation and the related scandal, which included an affair with a Janesville woman, are found in the letter of N.D.Young to Jandel, Zanesville, Ohio, May 23, 1863, SJP.

44. Province records, SJP. O'Carroll's term ended in Oct. 1869 on the eve of the solemn opening of Vatican Council I.

45. Jandel to Bishop Thomas L. Grace, Rome, Mar. 20, 1864, AGOP IV, 85-86 and SJP.

CHAPTER 11

SISTERS MOBILE AND UNITED

At Somerset, Ohio, on May 9, 1851, the driver of a stagecoach waited before the beautiful Gothic chapel of St. Mary's convent for two passengers. One was the novice Aloysia O'Neill who was making her religious profession before the wondering eyes of her family, the academy students and Dominican sisters and friars. Among the silent participants was a second awaited traveler, Sister Frances Stafford. When the ceremony ended and farewells were reluctantly completed, the two women, dressed for travel, mounted the waiting coach to begin the longest and most uncertain journey of their lives. They were on the way to a new mission in California!

These travelers would not be joining a caravan of covered wagons going west. They were going east over the mountains to New York, then south by schooner along the Atlantic coast to the Isthmus of Panama. To cross that dangerous and mosquito-infested isthmus from the Caribbean to the Pacific, they would journey over its mountainous terrain by foot and muleback. If they survived, a ship would take them up the Pacific coast to San Francisco, the mecca of Americans seeking gold and adventure.

Among the passengers traveling with the two Dominican women were four Sisters of Notre Dame of Namur from Belgium. One of them, Sister Alenie, kept a chronicle of their journey, describing its incredible dangers and hardships. When their schooner finally neared San Francisco, Alenie recorded the event in these words:

> On Tuesday July 1st the fog was so dense that the Pilot steered towards Oregon, but at mid-day, perceiving his mistake, retraced the route to California. We entered the grand "Golden Gate," so appropriately named and so majestic to behold. [1]

When they sailed into the harbor the passengers could see nothing majestic in the city. However, that did not matter when the sisters found waiting at the wharf the three Dominican missionaries who had survived the perils of Panama and arrived in December 1850. They were the new Bishop of California, Joseph Alemany; his fellow missionary in the United States, Sadoc Vilarrasa; and a Belgian nun from the Paris monastery of Holy Cross, Marie Goemaere, who had answered Alemany's call to establish a community of sisters in California. [2]

**Sister Aloysia O'Neill,
at home in California**

The journey to California was only one of the dramatic and purposeful travels of American women that began to multiply at mid-century. Many wives traveled far to reach their husbands who were working in the mines, on the railroads or on the open prairies. The women and their children joined them to "settle in." Most of the mobile Americans were seeking stability for their families.

The Dominican sisters as well as the friars saw the need for increasing mobility to reach and serve the people of Church and society. They were asked to leave established communities in the nation's heartland to answer calls near and far. The friars who first founded the communities of sisters in Kentucky and Ohio were now calling them from one place to another. But what of their need for stability? Until this time that had been assured for women of all religious orders in the life of cloistered monastery. How could it be found in moving from place to place?

The American sisters, like the friars, even when "on the move," could find stability in three essential realities of their Dominican vocation: the unchanging mission of the Order to proclaim the Word of God; their lifelong commitment to that mission by vow; and the life of each local community to which they were sent.

The guide offered to each community by Dominic and his first followers was the Rule of St. Augustine, based on the **Acts of the Apostles.** Dominic believed with Augustine that the "the first purpose for which you have been formed into one community is to dwell peacefully in the convent and to be of one heart and mind in God." Augustine once described from his own experience the life and interaction of such a community in this way:

> To talk and jest together, to do kind offices by turns; to read together honied books; to play the fool or be earnest together; to dissent at times without discontent, as one might with one's own self; . . . sometimes to teach and sometimes learn; to long for the absent ones with impatience and welcome their coming with joy. These and like expressions, proceeding out of hearts of those that loved and were loved again . . . were so much fuel to melt our souls together, and out of many make but one. [3]

Until mid-century the Sisters traveled only between the two communities of Kentucky and Ohio to meet the needs in each place. Their longer mission journeys began late in 1850 with the one to California and the teaming of sisters from Ohio and Kentucky to open St. Agnes convent and academy in Memphis. In 1854 four sisters from Somerset traveled to Wisconsin to join the new Dominican community founded at Sinsinawa by Samuel Mazzuchelli. Wisconsin sisters in turn crossed the state line into Illinois to open St. Rose Academy at Galena near the Mississippi. Theirs was the first Dominican establishment in the young Diocese of Chicago. So the mobility and multiplication continued.

Like other women on the frontier, the sisters "settled in" without delay on arrival at a new place. The center of their life and mission was the local community in each

Sister Teresa Kevelahan in 1857

convent, in which they established a simple form of government. Members of each local community elected their prioress and other needed officials for brief terms. They could elect a sister of their own community to be prioress, or one from another community. An example of the latter choice was Sister Ann Hanlon of Somerset who was called to be prioress at Memphis and later at Nashville. At her death she was honored by members of all three places for her life "rich in charity." [4]

Each community took responsibility for guiding young women who applied for membership in the Order, directing them as novices and admitting them to membership at profession. For that purpose each house had its own novitiate. After profession they were ready to be called to any place where the sisters collaborated with the friars. Each local community was financially independent. When the members established a local community, they had to build and maintain the convent, school or orphanage with tuition or another source of earned services. Debts were no small source of worry.

There were no congregations of Dominican Sisters, no grouping of communities with a central government and motherhouse. All functioned within the provincial jurisdiction of the friars who founded them, and moved freely to any mission in that province. Some women who made profession in one community spent many years, and even the remainder of their lives, in another. Angela Sansbury, the first American Dominican sister, made her profession in Kentucky and died in Ohio. Teresa Kevelahan, born in a Wisconsin village named for St. Rose, entered the Sinsinawa community, went on to Kentucky, then to Nashville and then to St. Dominic's parish in Washington, D.C., where at her death sisters and parishioners testified to her sanctity.

Although the American Dominican missions of the sisters were vital and successful, the members were deeply concerned about their status in the Church and in the Order. The only religious women fully approved by the Church were cloistered and took solemn vows. Their lives were given to contemplation and liturgical prayer, helping those in any kind of need by their intercession.

When the American friars invited women to an active apostolate, they instructed them in the ways of Dominican life and gave them the Constitutions of the cloistered nuns. The friar provincial dispensed them from such impossible obligations as rising at midnight for the office of Matins. But the new communities of Dominican women had to cross and recross the line of distinction between a contemplative, cloistered life and that of active sisters in the apostolate. To their formula of profession, they added these words:

> Whereas, for want of proper inclosure, I cannot make my solemn Vows, but only simple Ones, my wish and intention as soon as proper inclosure can be procured, is to join in petitioning His Holiness to allow us to make the same Solemn vows as the Nuns of St. Dominic and the Religious Men of his Order usually make. [5]

From the beginning, then, the Dominican sisters had to deal continually with ambiguity.

So it happened that in 1848, two years before members began to venture forth to distant missions, every Dominican Sister in Kentucky and Ohio joined in sending a request to Pope Pius IX. They asked him to approve their modified way of Dominican life, explaining that as teachers they could not sustain the full liturgical prayer of the Divine Office or the strict cloister of contemplative nuns. The letter read :

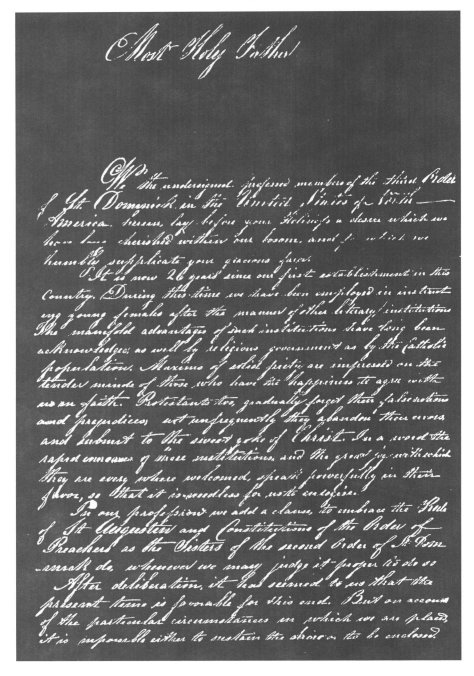

Autographed letter, U.S. Dominican sisters to Pope Pius IX, July 4, 1848

The cannot recite the Divine Office, because the number of those
who are capable of teaching being very small, it would consume
more time than they could possibly devote to it. Nor can we be enclosed
-cause our Convents are not built in a suitable manner, and we have
not sufficient revenues to change their present form. Again, if
we enclosed, we should lose our pupils Catholics as well as protestants
and would thus be deprived of the means of support. Wherefore,
-mitting these considerations to the wisdom of your Holiness, we join
one common prayer for a dispensation of being enclosed, and allow
us to recite the office of the B. V. Mary, instead of the Divine
and to grant us the favor of making the solemn profession as the
Nuns of the second Order of our Holy Father St. Dominick.
        We humbly prostrate ourselves at the feet of your Holiness

The Sisters of St. Magdalen, Ky.   The Sisters of St Mary
Sister Angela Lynch   Prioress   Sister .... Whelan Prior
Sister Magdalen Edelen Subprioress   Sister Catharine Beck Subp
Sister Villana Montgomery   Sister Ann Hanlon Mrs of Nov
        Mrs of Novices   Sister Benvin Lansbury
Sister Teresa Carlao   Sister Agnes Harbin
    Sister Rose Tennally   Sister Rose Lynch
Sister Dominica Caho   Sister Emily Thorp
Sister Columba Walsh   Sister Joanna Clarke
Sister Catharine Sneld   Sister Philomena McD
Sister Joanna Simpson   Sister Mary Joseph McK..
Sister Mary Jane Lynch   Sister Veronica Ray
Sister Mary Clements   Religious .....
Sister Margaret Queen   Sister Stanislaus McD
Sister Imelda Montgomery   Sister Velina Slevin
Sister Anne Simpson   Sister Frances Stafford
Sister Sabina McLain   Sister Margrett Ganelly
Sister Lucy Harper   S. Aloysia Magary
Sister Monica Conlon   Sister Mary Magdalen C..
Sister Frances Colon
Sister Benedicta Montgomery
Sister Vincenza Fitzpatrick
Sister Osanna Powel

The language was direct and dignified, and the request was clear. The letter was also historic, not only in content, but because it was signed by every professed Dominican sister of the United States and dated the 4th of July, 1848. There was no reply. Before the letter could reach the Vatican, Pope Pius IX had left Rome for the town of Gaeta in the south, where he remained two years while the movements for a united Italy grew stronger.

The cloud of uncertain status remained, while successive provincials sought stability for the sisters in the adaptation of their Constitutions, which were adopted or studied in this order:

1. In the early years the sisters used portions of the Constitutions of the Nuns of the Second Order of Saint Dominic, with needed adaptations and dispensations.

2. In 1857, with the encouragement of the provincial James Whelan, the sisters omitted from their formula of profession the clause concerning the intended adoption of enclosure and making solemn vows.

3. In 1858 the provincial Joseph Kelly adapted the Constitutions of the Sisters of Stone, England, for the use of the American sisters. It was often referred to as the "Kelly Rule."

The years of uncertainty about their status did not hinder the ministry of teaching which the sisters undertook as part of their Dominican call to proclaim the Word of God. Just as they joined other 19th-century women in setting out for new homes and places of service, they also moved with other women into the teaching profession. However, in the early decades of the 19th century the term "profession" was not used. Like nursing, teaching was not thought to be respectable for women. Most teachers, even of young children, were men. In 1837 a convention for teachers invited to Cincinnati "gentlemen from all parts of the Union."

The entrance of women into the teaching profession in the United States in the 1830s was stimulated by Protestant women who saw the teacher primarily as a missionary. Mary Lyon, an early leader in the movement, founded Mount Holyoke "to cultivate the missionary spirit of its pupils; the feeling that they should live for God and do something as teachers, or in such other ways as Providence may direct."[7] Women began to open schools of several kinds, ranging from classes around a kitchen table to endowed academies for young women. Early American schools owed their existence chiefly to the initiative of individuals or of churches. The idea of **common** schools financed by public funds was accepted very slowly, after being promoted by such reformers as Horace Mann. There was no broad school system, public or private, nor any strong desire for one. But there was an urgent need for the education which many families, whether immigrant or native-born, yearned to offer their children.

To that desire American Dominican women and men responded eagerly. The schools the women opened initially were academies; those of the friars were colleges. Both lacked any endowment except the gifts of those who conducted them. At that time young children were admitted to both academies and colleges along with the mature students.

Before 1865 parish schools were few. Many of them were conducted by a single schoolmaster, on the initiative of an individual parish. In fact, one of the first free schools was opened at St. Peter's Parish in New York in 1800 by the Dominican pastor William O'Brien.[8] Prompted by anti-Catholic movements in the 1850s and the growth of the Catholic population, the American bishops became increasingly concerned about Catholic education. Following the First Plenary Council in 1852, bishops exhorted Catholics to action in these words:

> Encourage the establishment and support of Catholic schools; make every sacrifice which may be necessary for this object; spare our hearts the pain of beholding the youth whom, after the example of our Master, we so much love, involved in all the evils of an uncatholic education.[9]

This impetus ultimately led the bishops in the Plenary Council of 1884 to direct that a school be opened as soon as possible in every Catholic parish.

From the start, Dominican sisters established a school wherever they formed a community. Ordinarily this was an academy for young women, but there were exceptions. At St. Magdalen's in Kentucky the sisters first opened a girls' academy, then an elementary school for boys, and later a school for black children that was short-lived. At Memphis in 1858 the sisters opened a "poor school" under the direction of Thomas Langdon Grace, O.P., to help "such Catholics as had no means of education for their families." Two sisters at St. Agnes Academy were their teachers, one teaching the girls and the other the boys. At first the Academy assumed all expenses, including those for the carriage used "to take [the sisters] to the city port... and to feed the horse."[10]

Few parish schools were conducted by Dominican Sisters before the Civil War. Among them were those opened for immigrants from Germany and Ireland, conducted by nuns from those countries. The women from Holy Cross monastery in Bavaria had hardly arrived before they opened the parish school of Holy Trinity in Williamsburg, New York, in 1853. In 1859 they sent teachers to form a new community at Second Street in Manhattan to conduct the parish school of St. Nicholas.[11] Irish nuns from a Cabra monastery came to New Orleans in 1860 to staff the parish school of St. John the Baptist for children of Irish immigrants. In 1861 Maria Benedicta Bauer opened a parish school for German children in Green Bay, Wisconsin. To her surprise it was attended by pupils ranging in age from five to twenty-five years.[12] Two sisters from Somerset in 1855 "opened a school of about 80 girls, of all sizes and shapes."[13] It was a parish school called St. Columba's Academy.

The Sinsinawa Sisters taught in district schools in the lead-mine region of southwestern Wisconsin. One of those, Borromeo Stevens, was from a Presbyterian family of Beacon Hill in Boston. As a young Dominican teacher in a rural public school of the 1860s she described her experience:

> I got my certificate, and went forth to do my patriotic and religious best in a small mining town of one short street and a wide prairie full of mineral holes. Did you ever see mineral holes? Well we didn't see the holes, but we saw the piles of yellow clay that encircles the opening to these well-like excavations, and for utter desolation and despairful dreariness nothing could compare with the scenery in the lead regions...
>
> A fervent zeal and an enthusiasm. carried me through the first three months of the school year [each term was for three months] and then I had to summon up all the courage I had inherited from my Puritan forefathers, for from the farms around... there came to me the stalwart youths who worked in summer and went to school in winter... How big and strong and invincible they seemed, but how gentle, simple and submissive they proved to be. How eager they were to learn, and how respectful they were, because I was a woman, but more, because I wore the religious garb.[13]

Many children were in need of more than schooling. Among them were the orphans who had lost their parents during the recurring epidemics of cholera and yellow fever. They were left to roam city streets unless they could be taken in by relatives or placed in institutions. For such children the Dominican Sisters from Kentucky and Ohio went to Memphis in 1852 to conduct St. Peter's Orphanage, which the

Dominican pastor Thomas Langdon Grace opened in 1853. The number of orphans grew so rapidly that the pastor bought a farm for them in 1855 called Gracewood, and asked Sister Benven Sansbury and two others to come from Somerset to direct it. In Nashville a lay group called St. Mary's Orphanage Association financed a home which Joseph Kelly opened in 1864. He asked for Sisters from Ohio and Kentucky to staff the home. The veteran Sister Benven came from Somerset once more to bring her "benevolent compassion and the wisdom of her seventy-two years."[14]

The major educational ministry of American Dominican Sisters before 1865 was to conduct academies for young women. These included the following:

1823 Springfield, Kentucky, St. Magdalen's, renamed St. Catharine's in 1851	1854 Benton, Wisconsin, St. Clara
	1855 Zanesville, Ohio, St. Columba
	1860 Nashville, Tennessee, St. Cecilia
1832 Somerset, Ohio, St. Mary's	1861 New Orleans, Louisiana, St. Mary's
1851 Monterey, California, Sta. Catalina	
1851 Memphis, Tennessee, St. Agnes	1864 Racine, Wisconsin, St. Catherine

The first academies, like the first colleges, were realistic about the range of students to be enrolled and studies offered. In many cases, along with adolescents they welcomed younger girls who would enroll in elementary classes and move on to the secondary level in the same institution. On receiving incorporation by the state, each academy could boast a legal existence important to the sisters and to their patrons. Families who enrolled their daughters helped to advertise their school. Newspapers gave them generous publicity and the United States Catholic Directory did so as well. Advertisements described the curriculum and regulations, costs and sponsorship, and even included illustrations.

Few catalogues are available from pre-Civil War academies, but a generous press provided evidence of their curriculum and scholarly achievements in coverage of commencements or "exhibitions." These were daylong reviews of the year's studies, often including public examinations. The commencement program at Sta. Catalina Academy in Benicia, California, in 1859 was similar to many of the time, as seen in this description:

Not only were artistic accomplishments exhibited at commencement, but public examinations in reading, grammar, and word analysis, geography, astronomy and maps, arithmetic, philosophy, and general science. The examinations were interspersed with musical selections, for example, arias from Bellini's Norma, Donizetti's Fille du Regine. . . . In the afternoon the exercises were, with the exception of three short dialogues and the valedictory, entirely musical. . . . There was one dialogue in French by two young ladies and a French chorus by all the pupils in the French class. [15]

Graduates of Dominican academies often chose to follow a call to religious life. Young women thus increased the sisters' membership and broadened the scope of their ministry. They brought from the academies a high level of scholarship which as teachers they would convey to other young women.

St. Cecilia's Academy, Nashville, 1860. Left: Nuns from Regensburg, Center: Founding sisters from Somerset; Right: Francisco Cubero, O.P., Chaplain. Inset: S. Frances Walsh, one of the four founding sisters

The success of the sisters' academies aroused the latent anti-Catholic antagonism which increased in the 1830s and the following decades. Bigotry reached a peak in the nation with the increase of Catholic immigration, the fiery preaching of Lyman Beecher,[16] and the rise of the Know-Nothing Party, which ran on a platform of open hostility to Catholics and immigrants. In 1852 the arrival from Rome of an emissary from the Pope, Archbishop Gaetano Bedini, fanned the flames of antagonism which had been aroused by the impassioned oratory of the anti-Catholics.

Beecher's warning to Americans about "Romish" connivings were matched by those of his zealous and gifted daughter Catharine. While she benefited countless Americans in calling young women to the teaching profession, Miss Beecher implored Americans to offset the baneful effects of education offered by Catholics. Addressing the Protestant ministers of the nation, she pleaded with them to help her establish schools, and especially academies, like those of the Catholics. Although she stated that such academies could "in no respect claim to surpass ours," she confessed her admiration for the "system" of education sponsored by the Church. She believed that Catholic education was controlled entirely by the Jesuits, men of "rigid method" who worked with the bishop in Cincinnati and other cities to plan "well-devised schemes to extend their church by the influence of education." [17] The truth was that no system of Catholic education yet existed in the country.

227

The Beechers :
Lyman, seated center; Catharine
to his right; Harriet Beecher
Stowe, far right

Catharine Beecher made a thorough study of the Catholic academies in Ohio and Kentucky. She believed that the sisters found in their Church the support which she could not obtain in the Protestant churches, either for women or for their education. She wrote of the difference between the churches,

> The grand cause of this difference is, that the clergy and leaders of the Catholic church understand the importance and efficiency of employing female talent and benevolence in promoting their aims, while the protestant churches have yet to learn this path of wisdom. The Catholic clergy exert their entire influence in creating a **public sentiment** that sustains, and even stimulates women to consecrate their time and talents to benevolent enterprises. [18]

Beecher was mistaken in thinking that there was an ecclesiastical system behind the founding of academies by religious women. There was none. All of them, including the Dominicans, acted on their own initiative, matching that of their brothers in the Order. Although bishops and priests usually encouraged the women's initiative, they did not impose their ideas on the academies. Beecher's insistence on their powerful "system" was intended to arouse the interest of the Protestant ministers and stir them to action.

Despite the warnings of Beecher and others, Protestant parents enrolled their daughters in the academies of sisters across the land. In fact, Catholic institutions welcomed Protestant pupils and pledged to respect their freedom of religion. An example of that pledge was given in one Dominican Academy prospectus:

> Pupils of every religious denomination will be admitted, and no undue influence will be used to bias the religious principles of the young ladies; nor will any of them be permitted to embrace the Catholic faith, without the verbal or written consent of the parents or guardians. Uniformity and good order, however, require the attendance of all at morning and evening prayers, and at the religious services on Sunday. [19]

Late in 1864 Vincent Jandel settled the longstanding question of ambiguous status. The American sisters, he stated, were not nuns of the Second Order but sisters of the Third Order with simple vows. And because they were engaged in the apostolate of the Church, each community was accountable to the bishop of the diocese in which they were serving. Although they were members of the Order of Preachers they were in no way under the jurisdiction of the Province of St. Joseph or any other province friars. There was consternation in every community of sisters. They, like the friars, assumed that they belonged to that province. The provincial of the friars was their provincial as well. Their reaction was recorded by the Council of St. Mary's, Somerset in these words:

> November, 1864. The General's pamphlet was received in which he hands the Third Order over to the Bishops. Mother Rose [Lynch] proposed going to Kentucky to meet the Sisters from other houses. They met, and petitioned Most Rev. A.V. Jandel to allow them their former privileges or to receive them as members of the Second Order. [20]

Every house involved in this serious question sent their superior to the meeting in Kentucky. Each one was willing to take the long, difficult journey even in wartime, from two places in Confederate Tennessee as well as from Somerset, Ohio, in order to convene at St. Catharine's in 1864. After that intercommunity meeting, as after the meeting of July 4, 1848, they sent their plea with one voice, not to the pope as they had before, but to the Master General of the Order. Their letter was signed individually by all the participating sisters:

Rose Lynch of Somerset
Imelda Montgomery of St. Catharine's, KY
Osanna Powell of St. Catharine's KY
Benven Sansbury of St. Mary's, Memphis
Philomena McDonough of St. Cecilia's, Nashville [21]

Their anguished protest arose from fear. If they were not members of the friars, under the jurisdiction of the provincial, how could they be Dominicans? To avoid the catastrophe of losing their membership in the Order of Preachers, they were willing to become cloistered nuns, even if this meant giving up their schools. But this was not to be. Four months later came Jandel's candid and courteous reply to the "united letter" of the American women. He wrote,

> I was pained at the thought of being obliged to refuse your desires so ardently expressed. But in truth I have no option in the matter of your jurisdiction but to obey the laws like yourselves. I could not assume such jurisdiction without usurping the rights of others and violating the Church's laws. You will perceive, therefore, that if I refuse your request, it is simply because I have no power to grant it. [22]

Jandel was correct about the place of the sisters in the Order. However, their active ministry was a new reality in both the Order and the Church. Many years would pass before their ecclesiastical status was clearly defined by papal decree.[23] Meanwhile, the adjustment mandated by Jandel was very difficult for the American Dominican sisters founded within the Province of St. Joseph. It took a long time for the sisters, and some of the friars, to fully implement or even accept the change of status.

The change of jurisdiction from the friars to the bishops soon ended the exchange of sisters among the various communities. They began to form congregations which established a motherhouse in a particular diocese, with branch communities in one or more other dioceses. By 1865 the increasing numbers of American Dominican sisters were augmented by newcomers from Germany and Ireland. The total number of professed sisters of the Order of Preachers in 1865 exceeded 350. At the close of the Civil War Dominican women and men were ready, with other Americans, to enter a new era in the nation and the Church.

The development of the Order in the United States was furthered immeasurably by the definition of the status of the sisters. Very soon they were called to dioceses throughout the country, where the clergy were not Dominicans. Nevertheless, their love for the Order did not decrease and they brought thousands of youth into Dominican congregations and the provinces of the friars. Seventy years after the decree of Jandel, the sisters initiated a move toward unity that has grown throughout the remainder of the twentieth century. In 1935 the major superiors of the Dominican congregations formed a conference which later became the Dominican Leadership Conference, of which both friars and sisters are members. More recently, some congregations have united with others, and many have undertaken new means of collaboration for their common mission. In the year 1999 a new kind of coming together was formed as the Federation of Dominican Sisters USA.

By the year 2000, the movement for closer union and collaboration led to an action in Kentucky of historic significance to the whole nation. The Dominican Sisters of St. Catharine, founded in 1822, joined the Sisters of Charity of Nazareth and the Sisters of Loretto, both founded in 1812, in a public act of contrition for their use of slaves. They invited African-Americans to participate in the ceremony. Sister Joan Scanlon, president of the Dominican Sisters, spoke for all in these words:

We come before you, our African-American brothers and sisters to ask for your forgiveness.

We have a shared history with you. Our fore-sisters, our people, hurt your people. Our people held your people in the bondage of slavery.

We deeply regret this. We are deeply pained by our sins of the past. We seek your forgiveness. We seek God's forgiveness.

1. Sister Mary Alenie, "Journal: Account of Journey from Antwerp to San Jose, California, 1851, entry for July 1st. Copy from Archives of Dominican Sisters of San Rafael, California.

2. See Chapter 12, "On To California!"

3. "The Confessions", **Augustine**, (Chicago: The University of Chicago, The Great Books, Chicago: Encyclopaedia Britannica, 1952) 22.

4. When the Nashville community became the Congregation of St. Cecilia, Sister Ann became the Prioress General. See her **Profile** by Sister Rose Marie Masserano.

5. Quoted in Mary Patricia Green, OP, **The Third Order Dominican Sisters of the Congregation of Saint Catharine of Siena** (St. Catharine Kentucky: 1978) 32.

6. Dominican Sisters to Pope Pius IX, July 4, 1848, Somerset, Ohio. AGOP XIII, 03150, 253, p.1.

7. Mary Lyon, quoted in Carol Ruth Berkin and Mary Beth Norton, **Women of America** (Boston: Houghton, Mifflin, 1979) 199.

8. See James Roosevelt Bayley, **A Brief Sketch of the Early History of the Catholic Church on the Island of New York** (New York: Catholic Publication Society, 2nd edition, 1870) 66. The writer was a nephew of Elizabeth Bayley Seton, who became a Catholic in St. Peter's parish. She may have been encouraged in her later establishment of schools by the success of the one at St. Peter's.

9. First Plenary Council of Bishops, "The Pastoral Letter of 1852" in Peter Guilday, **The National Pastorals of the American Hierarchy**, 1792-1919 (Washington D.C., 1923) 191.

10. "Annals of St. Agnes Academy," Oct. 1, 1858, 5, KDS.

11. Records of Dominican Sisters of Amityville, New York, AMS.

12. Records of St. Mary of the Springs, Dominican Archives.

13. Carol Milanis, **Little Essays for Friendly Readers** (Dubuque, Iowa: M.S. Hardie, 1909) 207-210.

14. Account from community records given by Monica Kiefer, OP, **In the Greenwood** (Columbus, Ohio: Springs Press, n.d.) 37.

15. **The Dominicans of San Rafael. . . A Tribute from Many Hands** (Dominican Convent of San Rafael, 1941) 37.

16. Some claimed that the burning of the Ursuline Academy in 1834 was influenced by the provocative speeches of Beecher against Catholics. For a fair report of anti-Catholic movements see Ray Allen Billington, **The Protestant Crusade, 1800-1860** (Chicago: Quadrangle Paperbacks, 1964).

17. Catharine Beecher, **An Address to the Protestant Clergy of the United States** (New York: Harper & Brothers, 1846) 33. For other Beecher sources and a splendid study of her life and work see Kathryn Kish Sklar, **Catharine Beecher** (New Haven:Yale University Press,1973).

18. Catharine Beecher, **An Address to the Protestant Clergy**.

19. Announcement of Opening of St. Catherine's Female Academy in Racine in 1864, RDA.

20. Council of St. Mary's Congregation, Council Book, 4, CDS.

21. Original in archives of CDS.

22. Vincent Jandel to Mother Rose Lynch, Rome, n.d., 1865, CDS.

23. Pope Leo XIII, with the Bull **Conditae a Christo,** issued December 8, 1900, recognized as religious all men and women who made simple vows, and clarified their role in the Church. See James R. Cain, **The Influence of the Cloister on the Apostolate of Congregations of Religious Women** (Rome: Pontifical University of the Lateran, 1965).

CHAPTER 12

ON TO
CALIFORNIA![1]

San Francisco was a genteel, "laid-back" sort of town from its early Spanish beginnings in the 1700s (then called Yerba Buena) to the drifting in of pioneering Europeans and U.S. citizens. But shortly after the cry "Gold!" was heard from Sutter's Mill in January 1848, even the most sober and settled of its citizens caught the fever and joined in the rush.

> Overnight carpenters dropped their hammers, masons their trowels, bakers their loaves, clerks their pens, to rush to the American River. Schools were closed as both teachers and pupils deserted; shopkeepers hung signs on their doors – 'Gone to the Diggings,' 'Off to the Mines' – and disappeared. By June 15 [1849] San Francisco was a ghost town, with houses and shops empty, and all who could walk, ride, run, or crawl rushing toward the Sierras.[2]

A ghost town, yes, but not for long. A year later San Francisco was alive again with those returning from the mines, rich or as poor as ever, and with latecomers from near and far stopping off to cash in. The town soon became "the City," percentage-wise as cosmopolitan as we find it today. So a wide-eyed seminarian, later ordained by the city's first archbishop, wrote to the Society of the Propagation of the faith on September 18, 1851:

> What a port! What a town! What a population! French, English, Germans, Italians, Mexicans, Americans, Indians, Canacs, and even Chinese; white, black, yellow, brown, Christians, pagans, Protestants, atheists, brigands, thieves, convicts, firebrands, assassins; little good, much bad; behold the population of San Francisco, the new Babylon teeming with crime, confusion and frightful vice.[3]

The archbishop who ordained this young enthusiast was Joseph Sadoc Alemany, a Dominican friar, appointed in 1850 expressly to serve in the wilds of the Californias, namely Alta and Baja, as well as Nevada, Utah and Arizona territory. His episcopal see was in Monterey. When Alemany arrived in the port city of San Francisco in December of 1850 he was accompanied by another Dominican friar, Francis Sadoc Vilarrasa, and a Dominican sister, Mary Goemaere, herself a Belgian immigrant. After a formal welcome on December 7, the bishop waited until December 8 to preside at the Mass of the Immaculate Conception in the small wooden church of St. Francis, the only Catholic church in San Francisco built since Mission Dolores was established. After the Mass he was presented with a gift of $1400 to cover the expenses projected for the visitation of his vast diocese.

Joseph Sadoc Alemany, O.P., Missionary named Bishop of California, 1850

Such was the modest ceremony, prayerful and practical, that began a new era in the history of the Catholic Church in California and inaugurated the ministry of the American Dominicans on the west coast. Alemany had come not just to oversee the California Church but also to establish a new province of the Dominican Order. Before his departure from Rome, Alemany had spoken to Jerome Gigli, the Vicar General of the Order, about his intentions to found a new province and had been given official permission.

Alemany's hope for a second province dated back to the days when he was provincial of the St. Joseph Province of Dominicans. At that time a young member of the Order, Peter Augustine Anderson, had come to him asking to be missioned to California. Alemany immediately granted the request, hoping Anderson would lay the ground for such a new province. The provincial was not disappointed.

Peter Anderson was born of Protestant parents in Elizabeth, New Jersey, on January 8, 1812. In 1827, when he was fifteen, his family immigrated to Ohio. Soon after this move west, his father died, leaving him the sole support of his widowed mother and younger brothers and sisters. Under the inspiration and guidance of the Dominicans serving in Ohio, Peter with his whole family entered the Catholic Church. His new-found faith ran deep. Almost immediately upon his conversion — and presumably because his younger brothers were now able to provide for the family — Peter entered the Dominican Order at St. Joseph's Priory at Somerset. In 1831 he was sent to St. Rose Priory in Kentucky where he received the habit, taking Augustine as his religious name. His year of novitiate completed, Peter made his solemn profession on August 4, 1833, at the hands of his prior, Richard Pius Miles. That year a severe plague of Asiatic cholera broke out in the Springfield, Kentucky area. The friars of St. Rose and most likely the newly-professed Anderson, and the Dominican sisters of St. Magdalen convent, risked their own lives to minister day and night to the sick and dying.

On April 4, 1840, Peter was ordained a priest at St. Rose by the same Richard Miles who had received his vows, but who was now Bishop Miles of Nashville, Tennessee. Anderson spent his first years as a priest at St. Rose, leading the contemplative life that was his as a Dominican, but he was restricted in his ministry by a stern, "hard-fisted" prior and former provincial, Nicholas Dominic Young. Beginning in 1845, Anderson took on several different responsibilities in the Order. He filled the roles of procurator, secretary of St. Joseph convent in Somerset and sacristan. Provincial George A. T. Wilson sent him in 1847 and 1848 on begging tours throughout the United States. On these expeditions he experienced mixed results, but mostly refusals. Sometimes along the way he would say Mass and preach in private homes. He traveled by steamer, train, and horseback, or by whatever means were available.

When Anderson began to dream of going on mission to California is impossible to state. By the beginning of 1849, he had talked the matter over with his new provincial, Joseph Alemany. In the light of subsequent events, we may imagine each firing the imagination of the other and together laying plans for the new foundation of the Dominican Order in the Far West. In February of 1849, Anderson was officially missioned to the Californias. His plans as they took shape centered on Alta California, by then a territory of the United States and soon to be admitted to statehood (September 9, 1850).

Preparations for his departure began at once. James Whelan, the subprior in charge of St. Joseph's, wrote to Samuel Eccleston, Archbishop of Baltimore, testifying that Peter Anderson "has obtained all necessary faculties and permission from the Provincial . . . for the purpose of going on missionary duties to California."[4] Nicholas D. Young, Anderson's vigilant and restrictive prior when at St. Rose but now enthusiastically supportive of the young priest's missionary plans, added to Whelan's letter his own recommendation. He specified to Eccleston that Peter was going to California

for the purpose of rendering assistance to those of our American Catholics who have already started . . . to that country, and if he shall find the country such as we expect, it is then our design with the approbation of the Ecclesiastical authority to establish a Community of our Order in California.[5]

The harbor of San Francisco as seen by Dominican travelers in 1850

Young asked Eccleston for a letter to the Bishop of California and to the Archbishop of Mexico. He also inquired if he knew of any other people going to California that he might arrange to accompany Anderson, but nothing materialized. On his own, Anderson traveled to New York to book any ship headed for the Isthmus of Panama, the first leg of his journey to California. It was almost a year before he could embark upon the many legs of the journey: first to the Isthmus, then by small boat and muleback to Panama City, and finally on June 17, 1850, he boarded the SS *Panama* arriving eighteen days later at the Golden Gate.

In a letter to N. D. Young, Anderson described his first days in San Francisco and the prospects for the Order:

> My reception by the Rev. Mr. Langlois, who is the presiding priest here...has been most kind and encouraging. My arrival was on Saturday morning; in the afternoon I presented my credentials. On Sunday morning I said Mass, and did the honors of the pulpit at ten o'clock service and at Vespers. Monday morning I moved my baggage to the priest's house, adjoining the church where I have a comfortable room.... Would to God, dear Father, you were here![6]

Anderson was captivated by the city, its life, its energy, its beauty, but mainly because of what his Order could offer it:

> This young giant of a city grows beyond the widest stretch of the imagination in spite of fire, wind, and dust. The tracks of the two recent conflagrations on the 18 May, the other 14th June, which totally consumed the major and best part of the city are scarcely traceable except by the newest of the buildings that have taken the place of those swept off by the two mighty elements, wind and fire combined. There is here, according to the best information I caught, a resident population of about 20 thousand.... In every part of the city can be heard the carpenter's hammer, the mason's trowel & blacksmith's anvil, whilst the Bay presents the astonishing spectacle of a forest of masts and steamboat pipes.... San Francisco, in my humble opinion, will rival New York in commercial importance.

In that same long letter to Young, Anderson expressed his conviction that the Dominicans should take advantage of California's fertile field of ministry, "It is my full conviction that the Order could be advantageously established here, no matter who becomes Bishop." [The young missionary did not yet know that Alemany had been appointed Bishop of California.] "But to accomplish this no time should be lost, prompt action on the part of the members and friends of the Order is absolutely necessary. Too much delay has already been made."[7]

Anderson spent some days in San Francisco before going to Sacramento, his assigned field of ministry. On August 6, Antoine Langlois, the Vicar General for the northern part of the state, wrote a letter to the Catholics of Sacramento introducing their new pastor and authorizing him to collect funds and procure property for the building of a church. That same day, Anderson took a steamer and arrived in Sacramento on August 7. He immediately announced his priestly intentions in the *Sacramento Transcript*. But his ministry was short-lived.

In October cholera broke out in northern California, and on the 26th of the month Anderson, who had been in San Francisco, returned to Sacramento to tend the sick and dying. The Sacramento correspondent for the *Freeman's Journal* wrote on Nov. 14, 1850: "Father Anderson has been very active in the performance of his laborious duties. He visits the hospital several times a day and also seeks out the sick and distressed in tents and other exposed situations." Sorrow was added to admiration when two weeks later on November 30, the *Journal* reported, "We are called upon to mourn the loss of one who was a father to his people, a benefactor of the poor; our esteemed and beloved pastor, Rev. P. Augustus [sic] Anderson has passed from earth, I trust to Heaven. . ."

According to the correspondent, it was on November 14 that Anderson finally realized he was seriously sick and allowed a doctor to examine him, but it was too late. He had contracted typhoid fever. Anderson died at 1:45 p.m. on Wednesday, November 27, 1850, at the age of thirty-eight, a martyr to charity. That was just eight days before Alemany and companions arrived in San Francisco.

Peter Augustine Anderson was the first to plant the seed of the Dominican mission in the western United States. The seed was his own life and death. But its nourishing and growth were in and through Joseph Alemany, Sadoc Vilarrasa and Mary Goemaere in firming up whatever beginning Anderson had made.

While still grieving the loss of Anderson, Alemany realized that work leading to a new province had to proceed. Within a few days of his arrival, he wrote to the new Vicar General, Alexander Vincent Jandel, requesting more explicit directions with regard to the province. Jandel responded graciously but also rather sharply,

> It is entirely forbidden to any Dominican religious elevated to the episcopacy to retain any jurisdiction in the Order itself: this is clear in our Constitutions and confirmed, if I mistake not, by a bull of Benedict XIIII. Since I am unable to give you the authority to establish our Order in California, I send with this answer letters patent to Father Vilarrasa to do so.[8]

Jandel's letter, however, did not reach Alemany until some weeks after its writing, thus permitting the bishop in good faith to take some initial steps in the establishment of the western Dominicans, both men and women. While Vilarrasa legally became the founder, the idea and inspiration for a province really belonged to Alemany.

In addition, when he was made bishop of the Californias, one of his first acts was to enlist Vilarrasa as companion to help in the new foundation. He further indicated his initiative and seriousness in this regard by inviting both Dominican men and women to participate in the work. This was St. Dominic's way, Edward Fenwick would say namely "to share in the mission of the Order."

The landing of the three Dominicans in the port of San Francisco was certainly significant. Still it must not be forgotten that they were not the first of their Order in California since Spanish Dominicans had ministered there in South and Central America in the 16th and 17th centuries and had gradually made their way farther and farther north finally reaching Alta California. But these friars acted with little thought of establishing a province there.

One Spanish Dominican, however, made his home in Alta, California: his name was Ignacio Ramirez de Arellano. Throughout the years of conflict between Mexico and the United States(1846-1848), Ramirez sympathized with the Americans. At the war's end he emigrated to Monterey where he eventually became pastor of the Church of San Carlos. His liking for the United States was climaxed with the entrance of Alta California into the Union in 1850. He was actively present at the state's constitutional convention that met in Colton Hall, Monterey in 1849.

As pastor of San Carlos, Ramirez had greeted Alemany when he first arrived in Monterey, January 28, 1851, with Vilarrasa. He was often by the side of Alemany at the various ceremonies and masses of welcome once his church was named a cathedral. He continued as pastor, with the assistance of Vilarrasa. Ramirez was a minister at the Solemn Mass celebrated on August 4, 1851, the feast of St. Dominic, in the chapel of the Sisters' convent of Santa Catalina, which Alemany, in his assumed role as provincial, had established on March 13. He also participated in the establishment of the men's convent of St. Dominic in Monterey on February 4, 1852. Vilarrasa's Chronicle stated: ". . . we all gathered in choir, where certain regulations made by me for the orderly administration of the convent and for regular observance were made public by Fr. Ignatius Ramirez de Arellano of the Mexican Province."[9] Ramirez remained in Monterey at least until February 2, 1853, when he entered his last baptismal date at San Carlos. When Ramirez returned to Mexico, Vilarrasa succeeded him as pastor of the cathedral church.

The surviving records and histories based upon their stories reveal that Joseph Sadoc Alemany was a holy and persistently creative churchman. He was born in Vich on July 13, 1814, in the province of Catalonia some thirty miles from Barcelona, Spain. His father was a blacksmith and his mother the daughter of a local chocolate-maker. Both parents were devout, strict Catholics. The third of twelve children, Joseph entered the Dominican Order at the age of sixteen, receiving the habit in September 1830. A year later he made his solemn profession and took the religious name of Sadoc after the Polish Dominican martyr of the 13th century. Because of the closing of all religious houses by the anti-clerical government in power, the Master General of the Order, Jacinto Cipolletti, invited him and other Spanish Dominican students to Italy for the completion of their studies. On March 11, 1837, he was ordained a priest in San Lorenzo Cathedral in Viterbo.

Shortly after ordination, at the age of only 23, Alemany was appointed assistant master of novices. Before completing his theology, he expressed his desire to go to the Philippines, but instead his superiors commissioned him to the United States. The plea of Dominican Bishop Richard Miles who told the Master General of his desperate need for priests in his extremely poor diocese had influenced the change. Accordingly, Alemany, along with two others, set sail for America on February 12, 1840.

After a long, rough voyage, Alemany and companions arrived in the United States at the beginning of April, 1840. He found that Miles in the meantime had procured some priests, so the bishop advised the young missionary to study English at St. Joseph convent in Somerset. For about two years Alemany continued his labors in Ohio, but was then called to Tennessee by Miles. From 1842 to 1845, he performed parochial duties at the cathedral in Nashville, then was sent to St. Peter's Church in Memphis. The 1847 provincial chapter at St. Rose appointed Alemany as novice master at St. Joseph in Somerset. From that time forward, changes occurred rapidly in his life. On

Francis Sadoc Vilarrasa, O.P., Founder of Holy Name Province

May 2, 1848, Rome appointed him head of St. Joseph province. In that capacity, Alemany granted permission to Anderson to go to California. It was as provincial that he was to attend the chapter in Rome. Because of political unrest in Italy this chapter was cancelled. When he returned to America in 1850, he carried the heavy responsibility of a bishop in a frontier land.

Alemany and Vilarrasa had known each other before the 1847 chapter of the province because of their association in Spain and Italy as students and young priests. Vilarrasa's background was much the same as that of Alemany. His town of birth was La Pobla de Lillet, a few miles from Alemeny's Vich, and his date of birth, August 9, 1814. He entered the Dominican Order at the Convent of St. Catherine at Barcelona, of the same province, Aragon, as was Alemany, when he was fifteen years old and chose the name Sadoc as his religious name. A year later, September 23, 1830, he pronounced his solemn vows in Spain.

Vilarrasa's theological studies were also interrupted by the religious persecution begun in Spain in 1834. In July of that year the Dominican convent in Madrid was attacked and several religious were killed while praying the Divine Office. By spring of the following year the persecution was widespread in the provinces. Faced with more violence, Vilarrasa and other members of the Aragon Province, Alemany included, accepted the invitation of the Master General to study in Italy. With courses completed, he was permitted to be ordained a priest in May of 1837. Vilarrasa spent the next two years at La Quercia near Viterbo where he served as assistant to the master of novices. In 1839 he studied further at the Minerva in Rome, and in 1841 he received the degree of lector in Sacred Theology. Fresh from his formal studies he was appointed to teach theology to the Dominican students at the la Quercia house of studies. In the fall of 1844, when George Wilson, provincial of St. Joseph's Province was in Europe, Vilarrasa volunteered for the American mission. He embarked at Le Havre on November 17, 1844, having as his traveling companions fellow Dominicans from Italy, Mannes D'Arco, Aloysius Orengo, and Americans Langdon Thomas Grace and Nicholas Raymond Young, members of St. Joseph Province who had been sent to Italy to receive their theological degrees.

In a letter to his family written in January 1845, Vilarrasa reported that, after forty-eight days of sailing and without encountering any danger, they had finally landed in New York. They disembarked on January 3, 1845, and after nine days of travel arrived at Somerset which he described as "built in the middle of the woods." In his next letter home he described a few aspects of life at St. Joseph's:

> Our convent of Saint Joseph's is as yet unfinished. The church is new, but consists only of walls and a roof with a single altar, as our funds failed us before it was completed. The altar is surmounted by a large crucifix which Father Alemany brought from the Island of Cuba... The labors of the Fathers on the missions are very great and they can never count on sleeping in the convent. It often happens, too, that when one returns worn out by his labors he has to go off again on horseback to attend to the wants of some other member of the flock, in spite of the rains and the snow.[10]

Two weeks after his arrival at St. Joseph's, Vilarrasa was again in the novitiate having been put in charge of eight novices. He did not remain long as novice master, however, for before the end of 1845, Joseph Jarboe resigned as prior of St. Joseph and Vilarrasa consented to take his place. As prior, Vilarrasa attended the provincial chapter held at St. Rose, Kentucky, in the fall of 1847. At the chapter Alemany was chosen to be master of novices at St. Rose. Accordingly, at the end of November he left Memphis, Tennessee, and came to St. Rose to take up his new position. However, unexpected things began to happen which soon ended his tenure as novice master. At this same chapter a deadlock had been reached with regard to the election of a prior provincial. George Wilson, writing to the newly elected Master of the Order, Vincent Ajello, reported from the chapter that the friars, not being able to elect a provincial, had agreed to send to the Generalate a list of those they considered eligible for the office. Three names were sent; among them was that of Joseph Alemany.

Evidently Alemany had become very popular among most of his brothers. But some were not so impressed. The most vocal of those who disapproved was Vilarrasa. In one letter to the Master of the Order he claimed to voice the mind of almost the whole province. The province was "unanimous" in the opinion, he wrote, that were either Thomas Grace (Alemany's pastor in Memphis) or Joseph Alemany named, "it will be the ruin of the province." To bolster his point of view he added, "For six years, Alemany has lived outside his convent on the missions until his recent assignment to St. Rose. . . . In these last eight months he has shown he has lost all spirit of and desire for regularity and has clearly indicated that, if he becomes Provincial, he will change everything."[11]

One wonders if Vilarrasa made his criticisms known to Alemany directly. The question remains whether Alemany knew of this particular letter or ever learned of it. Certainly there appears to have been no animosity on the part of Alemany toward Vilarrasa. Quite the contrary, the fact that Vilarrasa was Alemany's choice as companion in establishing the Western Dominican Province argues friendship and trust on the part of Alemany rather than hostility. As for Vilarrasa's feelings, all along he seems to have had some misgivings about Alemany, but he also admired him as religious, missionary and bishop, and through many years in California seemed to cooperate with him.

The California relationship between Alemany and Vilarrasa began in 1850. Both journeyed to Rome to attend a Dominican General Chapter, Alemany as provincial and Vilarrasa as definitor. It was in Europe that Alemany, now Bishop of Monterey, invited Vilarrasa to help him establish the Dominican Order in California.

Mary Goemaere, the third member of the Dominican trio to arrive in California, was to have the distinction of founding the first religious congregation of women in the new state of California and of establishing schools for the education of girls in Monterey, Benicia, and San Francisco. Catherine Adelaide Goemaere was born to artisan parents on March 20, 1809, in Warneton, a small Belgian town on the modern French-Belgian border. Almost nothing is known about Mary's early life, but later documents and accounts indicate that she had received a solid education. Her letters reveal a beautiful, legible handwriting, a skill she displayed as she administered schools, and kept account ledgers. She was also talented in the art of making lace and artificial flowers.

Sister Mary Goemaere, O.P., pioneer Dominican of San Rafael

At the age of forty, Goemaere entered a Dominican contemplative monastery in Paris, France, and on September 10, 1849, received the Dominican habit and the name of Soeur Marie de la Croix. Normally she would have professed her vows a year later and remained in the same monastery, the Monastère de la Croix, for the rest of her life. But in late August, 1850, near the end of her canonical year as a novice, her life changed. In that month, the newly appointed and consecrated California bishop, the thirty-six-year-old Joseph Alemany visited the monastery and requested help for the missions. Soeur Marie, a forty-one-year-old novice, volunteered to fulfill what she believed to be a divine call. Her acceptance of the bishop's appeal to undertake an arduous journey to a strange land began an adventure which placed her in the position of founding mother among Dominican women religious. Three weeks after answering the bishop's plea, Mary Goemaere made profession and was aboard the sailing vessel *Columbus* for the month-long sea voyage from Liverpool to New York.

Alemany, Vilarrasa and Goemaere were not the only ones to undertake the transatlantic voyage to America. Joining them in Toulouse were two novices, Rose Corbattieu and Catherine Coppe, from a French congregation headed by Mother Gerine Fabre.[12] On board the ship, Alemany wrote, "The sisters are very well and very happy; they have just finished singing several religious hymns. . . . The sisters have their English spelling books, grammars and dictionaries and we have begun our first lesson."[13] The trip was busy but uneventful. The two priests were able to offer Mass and on Sundays the bishop preached to some five hundred passengers and crew.

The group disembarked at New York on October 11. There the plans for Mary Goemaere changed. Mary would go to California instead of Ohio. Vilarrasa had accompanied the sisters from Toulouse to Somerset and there he spent some time at St. Joseph's priory preparing for the trip. The two novices remained in Somerset, and arrangements were finalized for the exchange of the two novices with two sisters from St. Mary's who were more comfortable with English and American ways, and who could go to California the following summer. They were Sisters Francis Stafford and Aloysia O'Neill. These two sisters awaited the conclusion of the younger one's canonical year. Tradition says that as Aloysia pronounced her first vows in May, 1851, the carriage waited outside to take the two sisters on the first leg of their long journey to California.

Meanwhile, Alemany, Vilarrasa and Mary Goemaere on October 28, 1850 continued on their westward trek, setting sail for the Isthmus of Panama. The journey was exhausting and inconvenient. They arrived at Chagres, Panama, during the night of November 6; the following morning they set out on the river in a small boat guided and worked by three Indians. They were three and a half days on the river, traveling by day and then debarking to spend the nights in Indian huts or small inns. From Las Cruces they went by mule to Panama City. One story about that segment of the trip reveals the practical and forceful nature of Mary Goemaere. Two mules carried the three travelers. When the mule bearing the two priests refused to proceed, Mary dealt "a vigorous blow [that] soon conquered the mule's obstinacy, and the journey was completed."[14] Taking charge came naturally to Mary Goemaere as related by sisters who knew her later. She had a "commanding appearance, and she was a strict disciplinarian, . . . adamant in her decisions."[15]

The bone-weary travelers arrived in Panama City on the twelfth of November. Four days later they sailed on the steamer *Columbus*, reaching Acapulco on November 24. The end of that long journey at San Francisco Bay on December 6, 1850, must have been an occasion of joy and delight. Their happiness, however, was diminished by the sorrowful news of Peter Anderson's death. It may be imagined how much Alemany and Vilarrasa were counting on their precursor for counsel and for future work in setting up the fledgling Western Dominican congregation of women and the province for the men. The requirements for a province (three priories) were not yet in place, hence the founding group remained the Congregation of the Holy Name of Jesus. It was not until 1912 that the congregation of men became the Province of the Holy Name of Jesus. The sisters remained the Congregation of the Most Holy Name of Jesus.

Even while, Alemany engaged himself in his duties as bishop, Vilarrasa and Goemaere made plans of their own. The three regrouped in San Francisco at the beginning of March. They left the city by steamer on March 5, 1851, and arrived in

Monument to the "Dancing Saint," Sister Dominica Arguello

Monterey the following morning. The day after their arrival, March 7, the feast of Thomas Aquinas, the bishop celebrated the Mass. It was to be one of the most significant events in the history of the western Dominicans and of the whole western U.S. Church. It was the opening of the convent under the title of Santa Catalina, the first convent ever in California. Through the arrangement of Alemany, the "school house" had been deeded by William Hartnell to the Dominican sisters for a period of twelve months. Just as at the beginning of the Order St. Dominic established a convent of nuns before organizing and housing his friars, so at the beginning of the Western Dominican Province it was the women who came first. However, the occasion must have been a modest affair for only Mary Goemaere was present.

The groundwork for this early opening of Santa Catalina was laid by Alemany in 1851. The bishop submitted a petition signed by over thirty-five men to the city Council of Monterey requesting that Colton Hall be sold or leased to him for "an academy for young ladies in this City."[16] His purpose was elaborated in a report to the committee which considered the proposed use of the city building.

The proposal clearly demonstrates what Alemany thought was important for education:

243

1. Desiring to have in California one or more institutions of learning for the literary and moral good of the community, I [Alemany] brought to the States from Europe several sisters, obtained a promise of more sisters from a female academy in the State of Ohio... in order that they all united would conduct a female Academy under certain regulations, for the order of the House.

2. The ladies shall teach reading, writing, Grammar, Geography, Arithmetic, ancient and modern history, fine needle work & music, on which various branches the pupils shall sustain a yearly examination before the public...

3. Rich families will pay a moderate sum for the education of their daughters...

4. The poor of the City shall be educated in all the branches free of all charges.

5. The orphan girls shall be fed, clothed and taught in as great a number as the circumstances of the establishment will permit. [Further on, Alemany indicated that #4 and #5 would be repayment to the city for the use of Colton Hall]

6. All shall have equal Rights, without any regard to religious distinction and no religious distinction shall be allowed, though for the sake of conformity, all shall attend religious service on the Sabath [sic] and daily morning and evening prayer. Catholic pupils shall be taught Catechism separately.[17]

Vilarrasa formally opened the convent on April 1, 1851, because Alemany had received Jandel's letter forbidding him, as bishop, to have any jurisdiction in the Order. Vilarrasa had received his appointment dated February 25 as "Commissary General" of the new congregation. On April 11, Vilarrasa received the first novice, Concepcion Arguello, the sixty-year-old daughter of a former Spanish governor of California, who received the name of Dominica. Another novice of Spanish descent, Jacinta Castro, joined the Dominican women in August 1851. In the meantime, the long-awaited sisters from Somerset, Ohio, arrived in July of that same year.

Santa Catalina school for girls opened on April 28 with eight girls. By August 1851, the school had twelve resident and sixty day students with tuition costing two dollars monthly for day pupils. Tuition charges for regular offerings and board amounted to $400. The faculty consisted of five sisters who spoke three different languages, French, English, and Spanish. Vilarrasa commented, "At first it was like the tower of Babel, not being able to understand one another."[18] Besides languages, moreover, the sisters could offer basic studies.

Within the first three years of the school's existence, nine women (three American, one Mexican, and five Spanish) joined Mary Goemaere in the Congregation of the Most Holy Name. With these additions, the school grew rapidly so that by 1852 larger quarters were needed. Alemany purchased a two-story unfinished adobe building originally meant for a hotel. Although few in number, the sisters assumed the debt of almost $3000 for finishing the building. Yet they continued to prosper. The boys' school, San Domingo, set up by Vilarrasa, struggled to survive and fared less well than that of the girls; Alemany reported in 1853 that the Dominican sisters had sixty and Vilarrasa thirty-five students.[19]

In August, 1851, Vilarrasa was appointed the sisters' spirtual director and probably lived for some time in quarters set aside for him in their convent. In addition to being chaplain, he traveled to other places in need of his ministry. In a letter to his family, he told about his work in Monterey but also in nearby Carmel where he journeyed to attend the spiritual needs of parishioners:

Monterey is one of the most delightful places that I have ever seen. A bay lies to one side and on the other beautiful oaks and pines, the leaves of which are evergreen, cover the surrounding hills. The country is very beautiful... It would be like an earthly paradise were it not for the frequent fogs. There is only one church which was erected by the Spanish... The population of Monterey consists of natives and of Mexicans. Nevertheless, there are people of nearly every nation here, particularly North Americans.[20]

His account of Carmel was distinctly different from that of Monterey.

Carmel is four miles from Monterey. A few ruins of the Mission buildings of the same name are left. Not many years ago more than five hundred Indians lived at the Mission. The church is very well preserved. There are many bears in that part. I have seen their tracks many times on the highway... The mission of Carmel was founded by Father Junipero Serra, a Franciscan in 1790.

Establishing a house of Dominican friars in Monterey at last became possible with the arrival of six young men from Catalonia on December 26, 1851. The first of the postulants clothed on February 4, 1852, was Francisco Macario Juan Vinas, or Vinyes, who some years later would succeed Vilarrasa as head of the province. Others in the order of their acceptance were Pedro Juan Francisco Fosas, Ramon Antonio Domingo Costa, Ramon Caietano Cerver, Andres Enrique Jose Berenguer, and Alberto Ramon Pedro Romeu. Now that there were more members in the community a Dominican priory could be established and so Alemany provided property and buildings for the first Dominican house of friars in the western United States. The convent served both as novitiate and house of studies.

Strict observance began as soon as the candidates were formally clothed in the habit of the order. Vilarrasa pictured for his family the nature of their life in Monterey:

In our convent, through observance, we do not know the taste of meat, but we have good fish and eggs. Everyday at three in the morning we say Matins; at six we have meditation, Prime, Conventual Mass, and at seven we take coffee and then have recreation for half hour. At eleven thirty we say the rosary, then Terce and Sext... Dinner follows. At two in the afternoon we have Vespers, and at six fifteen Compline, Salve, meditation, spiritual reading, supper and recreation.

This monastic regimen was approved by Jandel, the Master of the Order, with only a few minor changes. But the satisfaction felt from having a regular regimen could not override other needs that pressed upon the pioneers in the nascent congregation. Vilarrasa lamented the lack of funds and insufficiency of alms and other offerings needed for building a real convent. The shortage of priests was a nagging concern. Both Vilarrasa and Alemany persisted in petitioning Rome for clergy and religious. Vilarrasa wrote the Master of the Order that he was alone with no one to take his place; that when the bishop was away from Monterey the sisters did not have Mass. Clearly he was pleading for more missionaries, but nothing came of his request.

During the novitiate year 1852-1853, two brothers left: Thomas Fosas and Hyacinth Soler. The others made their solemn profession on March 7, 1853. The novitiate was not left barren for long. On August 28, 1853, Antoine Langlois, age forty-five, received the habit. It was Langlois who, as vicar General for Northern California, had welcomed the three pioneer Dominicans to San Francisco in December of 1850. Born in the province of Quebec on March 9, 1812, he was ordained a priest in 1838. He volunteered in 1841 for missionary work in the Oregon Territory. A fellow missionary there persuaded him to work with the Forty-niners, the term used to describe gold miners who were flocking into San Francisco. Perhaps it was Anderson at whose side Langlois sat when the pioneer Dominican died who inspired him to join the Dominicans. Whole-heartedly he entered into the new life of a friar.

Life was austere. The ranchos surrounding Monterey were mainly for cattle, and most food stuffs had to be imported. The Annals of the sisters indicate that sugar came from Chile and butter from Ireland. In 1852, imported flour cost $80 a sack. There was constant danger of famine if the ships were prevented by storms from arriving on time.

By 1853, Vilarrasa began contemplating a change of venue for the little community. Monterey was beautiful and serene, but unreliable for support. Besides, the population and prospects for future development lay in the north, in and around San Francisco. During the First Plenary Council of the American Hierarchy held in 1852, prospects regarding the future of California came under discussion. Some thought that the California diocese was to be divided into Monterey stretching southward to the Mexican border and San Francisco embracing all north to the Oregon border. Alemany was sure to become Archbishop and Ordinary of the northern diocese.

In anticipation of that move by the Sacred Congregation, Vilarrasa requested and received all necessary permissions from the Master of the Order. The rumor proved true. The anticipated division of the diocese was decreed in July of 1853. Alemany became archbishop of the metropolitan see of San Francisco and Thaddeus Amat, a Vincentian, took his place as bishop of the diocese of Monterey.

Until early January, 1854, Vilarrasa puzzled over where to move the novitiate. Finally his choice fell on Benicia where he moved his small community in March of 1854. Alemany gave the Dominicans the parishes of Benicia and Martinez with their churches. The sisters, now comprising seven professed sisters, three novices, along with some fifty students moved to Benicia. The prioress, Mary Goemaere, had chartered a schooner to take the sisters, the furniture and the students there; the cost was a total of $500. Soon after their arrival in August 1854, their convent school for young women was set up and functioning. There were four other schools in Benicia at the time, all of good reputation, but the sisters' school, now named St. Catherine's, quickly became a worthy rival.

From the time of their arrival in California, the Dominican men and women had forged a close working relationship. Now this was confirmed at Benicia. Both the men and women were part of the Holy Name Congregation and Vilarrasa, as Commissary, was the Dominican superior in California; it was he who wrote the first constitution for the sisters. Both opened schools in Monterey and in Benicia, but only the girls' school remained successful. In fact a building program was launched by Mary Goemaere for St. Catherine's school. Goemaere continued to guide her young group and instill in them a sense of Dominican life and apostolate.

In retrospect, one can question Vilarrasa's choice of Benicia. It was just a small lazy town founded in 1847. But it blossomed during the 1850s. With the presence of the military and their families and the continual influx of Forty-niners, the city continued to expand. It even became for a few months the state capital. By 1860, the gold fields were depleted and the city became a sleepy town again with a dwindling population. Vilarrasa wrote that the church at Benicia, intended as a parish remained unfinished with a debt of two thousand dollars. Because there was also no dwelling nearby the church site for the friars, Vilarrasa built "a very humble house without cells, such as we had in Monterey, and for this purpose the Archbishop assisted us with a sum of five hundred dollars."[22] Still by 1859, thanks to donations of the faithful, the debt on the church was completely liquidated. The initial convent for the friars built in 1855, however, had to be enlarged the following year at a cost of seventeen thousand dollars. That debt took fourteen years to pay off. Hammer and nails, together with full conventual religious life, daily ministry required by the parish and its mission in Martinez, and teaching and priestly duties at the sisters' convent and their school must have weighed heavily upon the shoulders of the only two priests, Vilarrasa and Langlois.

The burden shared by those two priests was lightened in a few years. Vilarrasa recorded in his chronicle, "On December 19, 1857, Brothers Vincent Vinyes and Dominic Costa received the Order of Priesthood at the hands of the Most Reverend Archbishop Alemany in the church of Benicia.

Early convent of the Friars in Benicia

They were the first priests of the Order to be ordained in California."[23] Of the original six Catalan novices, two had left before profession, and of the four who made solemn profession, one had died and one had returned to his native Spain. Vinyes and Costa, while helping in the priestly ministry, continued their studies in Benicia under Vilarrasa, and on May 21, 1860, Vinyes received the degree of Lector of Theology and Philosophy. Vinyes was appointed vicar of the convent of Benicia and began to share with Vilarrasa in the intellectual formation of the novices and students. But Costa left California in 1863 to join the Province of St. Lawrence in Chile. In the same year, Dominica Arguello, the first candidate the sisters had

247

received, died. Although advanced in age upon entrance, Dominica had spent twelve years in the young congregation.

Life for the friars in Benicia was much the same as it had been in Monterey. The daily horarium was in force which meant some three hours in choir in common prayer, one of these hours at two or three o'clock in the morning. There was daily parish liturgy, and, when possible, Mass for the sisters at nearby St. Catherine's. There were baptisms and marriages, instructions for converts, some teaching at St. Catherine's and religious instruction for children. Because of the heavy load of duties, Vilarrasa persisted in begging the master of the Order for reinforcements from Europe, but to no avail.

Mother Mary also had her periods of loneliness and frustration as she wrote to the head of the Order, Jandel:

My very Reverend Father, in order to explain everything to you without tiring you, I want only to tell you that I have been poor, alone and abandoned during the eight years we have been in California. I came from Paris in 1850 with Monsignor Alemany and our good little Father Vilarrasa. The Monsignor's intention, when I left Paris with him, was that I should go to Somerset to our Dominican Sisters' Convent in order to teach French there, and upon arriving in New York he changed his mind and told me to follow him to California. This I did willingly thinking that by doing all that he told me I could not fail to do the will of God... I came there and began a community out of obedience, knowing neither English or Spanish and not being able to speak to anyone because I met no French people during these eight years that we have been here. The good God blessed our work and He alone knows what I have to suffer and what I still suffer now; ...We are in all twelve professed sisters, two novices and two postulants... Our boarders are 70 in number and we have in addition a dozen day students. There is here... much good to be done but there are no workers; what can we do without a priest? Monsignor is occupied with his diocese and the good little Father Vilarrasa with his community; and the poor sisters with their boarding school are abandoned. We could do so much if you would be so good as to send us a few more priests, if only for a few years. Oh! If you would come to California and see for yourself our situation, I am sure that you would consider doing more than you do....[24]

Apparently Mother Mary's letter failed to convince the Master General to send more friars.

Despite the lack of clergy, the convent and school continued to flourish. One source reported, "The school in Benicia soon acquired such widespread popularity that there were not accommodations for all the pupils who applied."[25] That same account indicated that a new building constructed at a better location became a reality when the cornerstone was laid in 1859. Alemany assisted at the ceremony directed by the friars of St. Dominic's Priory. The new structure was completed in 1860 when additional members entered the novitiate and the school's enrollment increased.

Besides the new building, the sisters experienced other changes at the close of the decade of the 1850s. The constitutions of the English Dominicans of Stone replaced the original Rule written by Vilarrasa. This was done by order of the Master of the Order. Beginning in February of 1859, the sisters in California followed a rule meant for Third Order religious women. The sisters continued to recite the Office of the Blessed Virgin, and consider the daily Mass as not obligatory. Jandel ordered that those constitutions be printed and each sister receive a copy.[26]

However few friars there were, regular observance was not neglected in Benicia, thanks to the vigilance and example of the commissary general. In addition, Vilarrasa also shared in missionary work, offering parish missions in and around San Francisco and at one point, giving an archdiocesan retreat for priests. But most of the traveling was left to the other priests stationed at St. Dominic's. For the most part, Vilarrasa tended to the parish, and most especially, to the important work of formation and the maintenance of regular observance. Throughout his lifetime there is not the slightest hint that he ever let up on his love for and insistence upon the monastic, communal aspect of the Dominican vocation, no matter how unreal or impractical it might often seem. As major superior, moreover, he planned for an expanding ministry for the congregation. In the fifties and sixties, there were, besides Benicia, Martinez, and Vallejo, three parishes begun in San Francisco: St. Bridget's, St. Francis, and Notre Dame des Victoires. He was the one responsible for enabling these parishes to be begun and for sending friars to preach the Word.

Thus the life of the Dominican priests in California revolved around their own community life and parish duties. This included serving mission churches assigned to the parish. In one instance it resulted in initiating the erection of a new mission.

In 1864 Vincent Vinyes was called to the Empire Mine in Martinez to tend to a seriously injured miner. He took the opportunity to call together the Catholics of the area and celebrated Mass with them in the home of John Mulhare, whose home was a short distance from Antioch. This led to the building of Holy Rosary Church, another Dominican parish. Today the friars continue to serve there.

St. Vincent Ferrer's in Vallejo also evolved from a mission to a thriving parish. It was in 1855, the year following the transfer of their novitiate and studium to Benicia, that the Dominicans began to minister on a regular basis in Vallejo. Like other small northern California settlements in the forties, Vallejo, named after its founder, General Mariano Vallejo, grew in population and size with the gold rush and the establishment in 1852 of the naval base on Mare Island. By the time the Dominicans arrived in Benicia, it had become a fair-sized town requiring the Church's attention. Accordingly, each weekend one of the friars would either walk or ride a horse from St. Dominic's to Vallejo some eight miles distant. An old time resident of Benicia, James Bolton, recalled seeing Vilarrasa making the trek from Benicia to Vallejo and back again on foot. Finally some generous neighbors presented him with a donkey. It was not until ten years later that St. Dominic's in Benicia was able to supply St. Vincent's with its first resident pastor.

There was ambiguity with regard to parish ministry. By ministering in parishes the friars could satisfy an urgent need in the diocese at large; they could expand the Order by using the parishes as a source of vocations. But by so doing, they found themselves unable to live the monastic life to its fullest. The Dominican women, on the other hand, suffered no such ambiguity as the friars. The life of the sisters revolved around education, both for themselves and for their pupils. They were able to live conventual life and teach.

It was obvious in those early years of the Congregation that in order to subsist, the friars needed the income that parishes could provide. Vilarrasa's solution was the building of a priory with a conventual church attached. That arrangement became a reality in October of 1863 when Alemany granted permission to the province to build a house of the Order with a public church in a western area of San Francisco near the squares called Lafayette, Hamilton and Alta. These squares bound the area that later occupied St. Dominic's church which was to be conventual, not parochial, in status and function. That church continued to exemplify the work of the Dominican friars.

The sisters and friars maintained their close relationship in carrying on the mission of the Order even after Mary Goemaere no longer was in charge. Sister Mary ended her term as prioress after eleven years, resigning in 1862. Under her leadership, the convent and school had been moved from Monterey to Benicia, the school's name was anglicized to St. Catherine's Academy, and the language of instruction became English. Many supplies for the school and convent were sent by her Parisian monastery. Mother Mary's last official act as superior general of the California Dominican women was to open St. Rose Academy in San Francisco in 1862. Shortly after its foundation St. Rose was moved onto the property of St. Dominic's Church and rectory in San Francisco. The sisters and friars were once again ministering together.

Mother Mary continued to live and work at St. Catherine's in Benicia, teaching, keeping the books and making lace and artificial flowers for the chapel. She was succeeded by Sister Louisa O'Neill, once a member of the Somerset, Ohio, community. Louisa carried on the good work begun by her predecessor, helping the sisters to bring the spirit of the Dominican Order to all their endeavors.

1. This chapter was adapted by Loretta Petit, O.P., from **Mission West** by Fabian Stan Parmissano, O.P., with the author's permission. It was supplemented by Patricia Dougherty, O.P., of San Rafael.

2. Ray Allen Billington, **The Far Western Frontier,** 1830-1860 (New York: Harper & Brothers, 1956) 219-220.

3. Joseph Venisse, **Annales** XXIV (November 1852) 412. Adapted from John Tracy Ellis in McGloin's life of Alemany.

4. Whelan to Eccleston, Somerset, Mar. 7, 1849 , Archives, Archdiocese of Baltimore (AAB) 26 R 3.

5. Young to Eccleston, Somerset, Mar. 7, 1849, AAB 26 R 3.

6. Anderson to Young, San Francisco, July 12, 1850, St. Joseph Province Archives (SJP).

7. Anderson to Young, July 12, 1850.

8. Alemany File, Western Dominican Archives (WDA) XIII: 3.

9. Vilarrasa File, WDA XIII, 4.

10. Vilarrasa to his parents, Somerset, Apr. 5, 1845, SJP.

11. Vilarrasa to Alberti, Somerset, July 5, 1848, Archives General, Order of Preachers (AGOP) XIII, 03150, 252.

12. Maria Pia Quoci, O.P., to Mary Nona McGreal, Rome, May 31, 1992, Project OPUS files. Rose and Catherine completed their novitiate and made profession in 1851 in St. Mary's Congregation in Somerset. Catherine served in Ohio and Kentucky where she died in Louisville at the age of 51. "French Rose," as she was called, taught French in Ohio and ministered in various capacities in Tennessee. She nursed the sick in the yellow fever epidemic of 1876 in Memphis and died a victim of the disease.

13. Alemany to Rev. Mother Superior (Toulouse), Aboard the *Columbus*,

Sept. 11, 1850, Archives of Dominican Sisters of Albi, France.

14. M. Aloysius Boschen, "Dominicans in California," Part I, **Dominicana**, 1 (Dec., 1900): 340.

15. Mary Hyacinth Kilgannon, O.P., "The History of Saint Catherine's Academy: 1851-1854 in Monterey, California; 1854-1862 in Benicia, California," Unpublished master's thesis, Dominican College, San Rafael, 1967, 12.

16. Alemany Folder 2, Archives of San Rafael Sisters(SRA).

17. "Communication to the Committee by Hon. Council of the City of Monterey in reference to a female academy in Colton Hall," signed by Alemany, Feb. 7, 1851, SRA.

18 . Vilarrasa to Parents, Brothers and Sisters, Oct. 2, 1851, **Revista Catolica** XX (Jan., 1852) 93-96, SRA.

19. "Report submitted to the State

Superintendent of Public Instruction, 1853" cited in Francis J. Weber, **Joseph Sadoc Alemany: Harbinger of a New Era** (Los Angeles: Dawson's Book Shop, 1973) chart opposite p. 34.

20. Villarrasa to his family, Monterey, Oct. 2, 1851, WDA XIII, 4.

22. Vilarrasa Journal, WDA XIIII, 4 (1854).

23. Vilarrasa Chronicle, WDA, XIII, 4, 1857.

24. Goemaere to Jandel, Benicia, Oct. 19, 1858, AGOP, XIII, 41.

25. Ligouri Ash and Agnes Cahill, "Memoirs of Mother Mary," ms., (1925) 13, SRA.

26. Cf. "Memoirs" 14.

THE KELLY DIARY
VOLUME II
JANUARY 24 – MAY 21, 1858

J oseph Augustine Kelly, O.P. opens the four volumes of his diary with a description of his setting out on his first return to Ireland:

> 1853. May 1st. Departed from St. Rose's Kentucky, in company with Thomas Duffy for Europe. We drove to Louisville in a fine buggy, and made a grand appearance on the way, except that the seat was minus of cushions, thanks to the courtesy of our good Prior; but the defect was supplied with a grand quilt. We bid an affectionate farewell to the brothers, and the venerable spire of our convent was lost in the distance. Our spirits were high and joyous. . . . We wiffed away our segars and rolled to Bardstown.

Like many who were entering American religious communities in the mid-nineteenth century, Kelly was born in Ireland, in Dublin to be exact; and was baptized at Sts. Michael and John Church on July 12, 1827. He had one sister, Mary Ann. After the death of his mother the small family left for the United States, landing in Philadelphia in December 1837, but moving to Louisville, Kentucky, a few months later.

Daniel Kelly, the father, built up a thriving construction business and although apparently uneducated himself (he signed his will with an X), he sent his son to St. Joseph's College in Bardstown for a year, and then to the Jesuit college of St. Mary's. Shortly after completing studies there in February 1844, Kelly entered the Dominican Order. On June 13 he received the habit at St. Rose, Kentucky. While recording this fact Kelly left no clue about his reasons for becoming a Dominican. According to the diary, he continued his studies at St. Rose and at St. Joseph's in Ohio. On July 26, 1850, he was ordained to the priesthood together with his classmates James Edelen, Peter Walker and John Raymond Cleary. A few months later at the age of twenty-three, Kelly was appointed prior of St. Joseph Convent by the provincial Matthew O'Brien. From that time he was almost always in positions of responsibility in the province.

In 1856 the provincial James Whelan appointed Kelly president of St. Joseph College in Somerset, Ohio. The college was opened on September 2, 1851, at the site of the original Ohio convent of the friars in Perry County. The first president was James Whelan, who after his election as provincial, was replaced in 1854 by Philip

Dominic Noon. When Noon's health broke down, Kelly was named as his successor. The Civil War, among other causes, was a factor in the closing of the college in 1861.

In October, 1858, at the age of 31, Joseph Kelly was elected by the friars to be their provincial. After completing his term of office in 1863, he became pastor at St. Peter's Parish, Memphis. Thereafter he remained in Tennessee, where he was honored by his grateful contemporaries as "father of the orphans" and selfless caregiver among victims of the yellow fever epidemics.

The first of four volumes of Kelly's diary is devoted almost entirely to his trip home to Ireland; the second records part of his term as college president; the third, his years as head of St. Joseph Province. The fourth volume briefly covers many of his remaining years. The diaries, meant for his own remembering, are frank but discreet. Through them a human picture of the man emerges. Although most entries are brief and to the point, they reveal his enthusiasm and universal curiosity.

The diaries show that Kelly loved to be with people. Fairly abundant are such entries as "To bed tonight near twelve. FF [James Vincent] Daley, [Joseph F] Dunn, [Michael Dominic] Lilly, [John Antoninus] Rochford, and myself drawing out the time till then in social chat and amusement," (April 14, 1858). The diaries express his concern over occasional long evenings of "amusement and chat" with his confreres when he was college president. He worried whether socializing was a frivolous waste of time, but finally decided in the negative because the friars had to bear heavy parochial duties, teach college classes, and exist in what was virtually a boarding school of male adolescents.

Kelly also kept in close touch with his neighbors, especially parents of students or relatives of the friars. The second volume of the Diary contains many phrases like "visited Wade's family, dined with them and sleighed home through the mud" (February 29, 1858); "Called on some of my Zanesville friends" (March 18); "With Father Dunn drove to John Noon's this evening, had a pleasant time." (April 21). On April 28 he took the altar servers on an overnight picnic at Noon's.

The Irish-born friar delighted in meeting new people wherever he went, invariably making life-long friends. When provincial business caused him to go to Arkansas he introduced himself to Bishop Edward Fitzgerald of Little Rock; soon they became good friends, over the years exchanging correspondence and visiting. Kelly even introduced the friars to Little Rock and the healing waters of Hot Springs. He felt welcome in the homes of Bishops Peter Kenrick of St. Louis and Martin J. Spalding of Louisville. In the latter city he frequently visited his father.

Generally accepting people as they were, he was not blind to the faults of real trouble makers. Few ever spoke more honestly to the Master General Jandel than Kelly, who told him that those Jandel had favored were perceived quite differently by the friars.

Kelly loved to travel; while in office he took full advantage of the opportunities to be on the move. When Giuseppe Larocca, O.P., Master General, visited the country in 1881, Kelly was amazed that he could complete a convent visitation in less than two days. For Kelly such a visit took at least two weeks, and often more. He was not content simply to meet with the brethren and examine the account books. In

**Joseph
Augustine
Kelly, O.P.**

Washington his visitation included seeing the historic sites, museums and public buildings with side trips into Maryland and Virginia to meet old friends and the relatives of his fellow friars. Visitation at Sinsinawa involved stops at many river towns and trips as far as St. Paul. His participation in a general chapter in Rome in 1862 led to a tour of several countries of western Europe. These are recorded in great detail in the related Diary.

Clearly Joseph Kelly preferred the active life. Although he was a college president and seminary professor, he was less a scholar than an administrator. Although he read widely he confessed to the weakness for newspapers shared by his fellow Americans. "I find that giving so much attention to papers is rather a loss of time, and yet I have so strong a passion for devouring them that I cannot overcome it" (February 28). The Irish preacher Thomas Burke was convinced that American friars read nothing else.

What appears most characteristic about Joseph Kelly was a devotion to duty that led him to do what had to be done, although he was repeatedly given difficult assignments. When conditions in wartime Nashville led to the withdrawal of Bishop James Whelan, Kelly became administrator of the Diocese of Nashville. He collected funds, built an orphanage and rescued sisters and orphans when the city was besieged. When federal armies destroyed the orphanage he had just erected, he persuaded the federal government to build an even larger one for the orphans. His "sick calls" in the river city of Memphis often brought him to barroom floors and back alleys to victims of violence. These were cared for with the same diligence and promptness as that given to prominent citizens.

Even when his position was of a stop-gap nature, as when appointed administrator of the Nashville diocese, he did not use the situation as an excuse for inaction. When he saw problems, he sought and found solutions This was especially true regarding the orphans in Nashville and later in Memphis. Fittingly, the last item in his Diary for June 14, 1885, reads: "Baptized thirteen orphans today." He died in the following August.

Archivist's note:

This is the second of the four extant volumes of Father J.A. Kelly's Diary. It does not bear his name, but the handwriting is unquestionably his. Besides, other facts also prove that it is his. The presidency of St. Joseph's College is one of them. The Diary covers January 24, 1858, to May 21, 1858. There is every reason to believe that other volumes of his Diary recording events of other periods in his life were written. They have yet to be found. This volume was discovered at St. Patrick's, Columbus, Ohio, after the death of Father Kelly in Memphis on August 7, 1885.

Pages from the Diary of Joseph Augustine Kelly, O.P.

January 24, 1858, Sunday morning

My term of Presidency has so far run over a year and a half, and still continues. It is an office of some honor, but of trouble and difficulties more than enough to outbalance it. All is not gold that glitters, is an old proverb and a true one. My present position verifies it. It is said that it is great to be president of a College, but the greatness, according as we look at it may be in different lights. To the looker on it may seem a post of dignity; to the incumbent it is a post of endless annoyance. It seems to me that a president is a target, at which everyone, may hurl a lance with safety to himself, but not without danger to the said target. Prefects are not always disposed to follow a straight line, and sometimes wander into crooked ways, but on this head, I cannot complain much. A half a hundred boys are to be made to do their duty, and yet not to be offended; each one has his whims to be gratified. Some don't like so much study, others think there is too much recreation; some think their teacher is incompetent, partial, unjust &c; others look on the same individual as a paragon of perfection. Then there are the parents, more childish often than the children. One will have his child punished, another is opposed to it; one believes with Solomon that the rod must not be spared, another wiser stipulates that the jacket is not to be dusted in this free country. Expel a boy and he is an enemy of the college for life. Pa and ma discover on a sudden that the college is badly conducted, that other institutions are far superior; they invariably find that their boy has been ill fed, ill clothed, ill instructed, and totally neglected. Such are the beauties of expulsion. . . . Passing events of the day I will jot down from time to time, as an experiment in writing, and also to look over them hereafter with pleasure if not with profit. Distance lends enchantment to the view.

Jan. 28 Thursday

The Philopoedian Society today got up a new bookcase. It is 20 feet long, will hold a large number of books, looks well. It is the third case purchased since the formation of the society, each one being larger and more costly than the other. The other society now speaks of making an addition to their library. There is quite a rivalry between the two societies, each striving to outstrip the other. It is a laudable ambition and makes both prosper and flourish the more. The two libraries contain at present about fifteen hundred volumes of choice reading in history &c. The societies we may say have just attained the age of reason, being but seven years old and in this short time, the members have purchased all the books themselves with some assistance from the Faculty. Judging the future by the past, their prospects are really brilliant.

Jan. 31 Sunday

Finished reading the Book of Genesis today. I intend to read the Bible through this year, taking it up on Sundays and occasionally at other times.

Feb. 1

Last evening rode over with J. Crosson to his mother's and there passed a pleasant night. The old lady presented me with a pair of socks, the wool of which she spun and knitted herself, though eighty years of age. Rode to James Fink's, dined and enjoyed a few hours of social chat. Then returned home through a storm which now covers the ground.

Feb. 10

We received a newspaper edited and owned by P. Noon, Ebbensburg Pa. A former student. V[?] Bennet, also an old student is now a member of the Iowa legislature. Thus St. Joseph's is beginning to be glorified in her children.

Feb. 11

Went from Somerset to Zanesville in a buggy with F. Edelen. Though cold we had rather a pleasant drive. Went to the depot with F. Bokel in a carriage to meet Dr. Brownson and conduct him to the hotel. In the evening he lectured in Nerritt's hall to a large audience, for one hour, and three quarters. He is not an orator, but speaks like a philosopher, with calm and solid reasoning. His subject was: "Popular objections to the church." These objections he said were not at the present day scriptural, but social and worldly. Catholicity was objected to because hostile to civilization, because it restrains reason, investigation &c. He showed that reason is allowed full play; enquiry is allowed outside the church. . . . All were pleased with the lecture, and could have listened for longer time. It made an impression on the Protestants present.

Feb. 12

In Zanesville. Passed most of the morning with Dr. Brownson. He is quite large. Weighs probably 200 pounds, has a fine appearance; small piercing eyes, grey hair, grey whiskers and an imperial. He looks indeed as if he did not forget the feasts though he keeps the fasts. He is very conversable, very pleasant. He chews much tobacco, and has a singular way of working his upper lip when he has said a good thing or is about to laugh. The upper lip is thin while the lower is very thick and hanging. He speaks out plumply what he thinks of any person or thing. His father was an officer in the Spanish army; his mother from Scotland. He says Archbishop Hughes[1] is no theologian.

Feb. 13

The circulation of Brownson's Review is about 1800. And I suspect pays pretty well. He complains of his lectures not being very well attended generally. Lately in Cincinnati he received but ten dollars for a lecture. I rather like *Harper's*; it has a great deal of trash, is very bigoted, but yet contains some good articles. The editorial article at the end of each number is generally worth the price of the magazine. I find that Catholic editors who strongly condemn it, are generally the first to purchase and read it. Our Fathers in Zanesville[2] have discovered that Carroltons Irish tales are immoral and have proscribed them.

Feb. 16

Listened with much pleasure to our boys practicing negro melodies; they do them in splendid style and will I am sure create a sensation by their performance. They have a banjo, bones, triangle, violin, &c. The songs are interspersed with conundrums, wit, &c &c. Having been thinking how well our boys agree together. Since I have been here, they have never had a fight, or a serious disagreement; minor differences sometimes arise, but are of short duration. This speaks much in their favor, and considering the number and diversity of characters and dispositions, is I think something very remarkable. Last week a large boy cut off a portion of the legs of his pants, hemmed and gave them to small boy (T.M. McCormick) who was new; another gave him a jacket, another a vest, and in the end he had a good suit of clothes. Their kindness and charity in this might even put their professors to blush. . . . But we are weighed down with heavy debts. Our debt this time last year was computed to be fifteen thousand dollars, and of course is still large though somewhat diminished. Often during one day we have half a dozen calls for money. People think we are a bank stashed with money.

Feb. 19

Quite cold; snow, and sleet falling all day; sleighing good. F. Daly has just arrived from Memphis, he walked in upon us quite unexpectedly this evening. . . . He left St. Louis yesterday and reached Lexington at twelve o'clock today; this is fast traveling even in this fast age.

Feb. 23

Still very cold; sleighing is excellent, and horse flesh suffers in consequence. The boys; have been sliding down hill all day on home made sleighs, having fine sport. Witnessed their fun for some time, and trying it myself, had a glorious upset, and tumble on the snow.

Feb. 25

For the first time visited Wade's family, dined with them and sleighed home through the mud for half the way, the snow having pretty much vanished under a warm sun. Our conversation was all about Ireland and the Irish, Wade always addressing me as the gentleman from Dublin; he declared he would know me if he met me in Sockville Street &c. . . . It is strange and sad to think how fond our young men are of liquor; it is their ruin and their curse. Some are expelled every year for this cause, others know they will incur the same penalty, and yet their passion is so strong that they will blindly give way to it. In the excitement of the moment, they forget the sin, the shame and the disgrace it draws upon them. How the heart of parents must bleed over such children.

Feb. 26

Did not read a great deal today. I have a great many interruptions during the day, my room being a kind of public resort, where our folks come to chat and give in their experience. This robs me of much time which I think I could employ more profitably. It happens on some days, though not often. I cannot find time to say my office between the "calls" and have to defer it till night.

Feb. 28

Raining this morning, snowing all the evening. Preached today to a rather small Congregation; -- William came over this morning and gave me an apple saying it was for my sermon. There being seven [Friars] that preach, that duty devolves on each one but once in seven weeks.

March 1

Having written to Mrs. Beeson last week to send money to take her son home, as I designed to expell him, she reached here this evening. She came from St. Louis to intercede for him, and to beg that he may be forgiven. She pleads like a lawyer, and entreats as only a mother can for an erring son. Have been reading for the last three months from time to time Victor Cousin's history of Modern Philosophy. It is a very able and learned work, the language beautiful and eloquent, but it is in places so abstruse and profound, that I cannot fathom it . . . . He prefers modern to scholastic philosophy. Scholastic philosophy was fettered and tied down to religion; the modern is free and independent in all things.

March 2

I have yielded to the entreaties of Mrs. Beeson and consented to keep her son; tomorrow she starts home rejoicing.

April 1

All fools day. Enjoyed some hearty laughs at the pranks of the boys; some of them were rapping at my door before I got up, being sent on a wild goose chase, by their more wide-awake companions. . . .

April 2

There is much talk among ourselves right now about a college in Memphis; it is affirmed to be just the place, fine location, wealthy people, great facilities. The college could be built on some year's credit and would pay for itself at the appointed time. Must be built soon, or others will embrace the opening before us. . . . If St. Joseph's were out of debt, I should be in favor of closing the college, and the building could be used for our own brothers, establishing here one novitiate for the province.

April 4

The greatest and most general revival ever got up in this country is now being carried on. Preachers are daily holding forth in almost every town and hamlet from N. York to N. Orleans. Many so called conversions are reported, but no cases of restitution are recorded.

April 5

Some people are predicting the end of the world, on account of the religious revivals going on, the greatest it is said in the last hundred years, but their imagination runs away with their judgement. In N. York and other cities merchants close their stores for days to attend meetings, but the thing is rather overdone, many are making fools of themselves & sensible one's [sic] are disgusted.

April 6

This evening F. Lilly, Dunn, & Rochford and myself have just finished a two-hour game. Resumed classes and studies today; boys nearly all back. . . . Read two articles in *Brownson's Review*, for this quarter. One of Bishop Spaulding [Spalding] on mormonism and the poor, in which he reviews Mayhew's book on the poor of england. Shows that in London alone there are 30,000 who live in cellars in a state of sin and starvation. Proves english poor to be far more debased than the poor of france, spain, germany, &c.

April 7

Mr. Robinson of Cincinnati was here today; a fine portly looking man. Had a call from M. Scott and J. Crosson. . . . Finished reading *Brownson's Review*. It contains a long article on colleges, from a contributor, who is entirely opposed to our present school system. Some of his ideas I can endorse, the majority I wholey reprobate. He is in favor of having one high toned university, which would suffice for the whole country. Our colleges are he thinks, but boarding schools, not superior to common schools; would have them called grammar schools. He says they have too much of an ecclesiastical complexion, teachers being students of divinity, or priests who have charge of congregations. Thinks it's a mistake to suppose that teachers from this fact, have moral influence over the boys.

April 8

The gem it is said cannot be polished without friction, and man cannot be perfect without trials. In this view, the President of a college must be the most perfect of men. Job was never President of a college, had such been the case, he would perhaps have lost his patience occassionally [sic]. Bishop Spalding once remarked to me that being President, was next to being naked on a cross; don't know that it is so bad as all that, but it is something like it, at any rate. If my daybed be hard, I have a feather bed at night, which is some little consolation, as it gives me repose and pleasant dreams. Looked through "Nick Nap," a comic monthly of N.York. The pictures display taste and ability and the whole affair is pretty well gotten up.

April 13

F. Shoulipnikoff, at twelve last night, left the convent, throwing off his habit, and returning to the world. All our brethren were glad of it, and he had the sympathies of none. Manus ejus contra omnes, et manus omnium contra eum; he thought everything Dominican wrong.

April 16

Received an invitation from Revd. N.R. Young to preach the panegyric on St. Dominic next August in Washington city. Hope to do so, as I am desirous of seeing the wonders of the capital city.

April 17

After supper E. Brooke arrived from Washington as a student; his father studied seven years at St. Rose's, in the days of the college there. Learned from him that a boy at Georgetown College can advance in the English branches only in proportion as he advances in the classics; all are obliged to study Latin and Greek: boys jugged must always learn their lines in Latin.

April 18

A couple of hours with Chad Magruder in correcting his graduating speech on the influence of Patriotism; it is beautifully written. . . . Siesta after dinner; chat and amusement with FF. Lilly, Dunn, and Br. Clement till supper.

April 22

Social chat and amusement with F. Daly, Dunn, Fr. Rochford, which was continued until eleven tonight. I have come to the conclusion that this is a waste of time, is paying too dear for the whistle, and I shall discountenance it hereafter.

April 24

With T. Sligar, drove to Zanesville in the buggy this morning; though somewhat cool, we had a pleasant time. . . . Heard confessions, which though once a familiar, is now almost a new occupation. Encountered some strange cases, illustrating the feelings of the Revd guides of souls here, who are more strict than the law itself. A woman told me she had never been a drunkard, but still was forced to take the total abstinence pledge before she was allowed to go to communion. Said she was forced to it, and did not intend to keep it at the time, and wants to know, if she sinned, in breaking such a pledge. Thus great rigor often begets sin, instead of destroying it. Some of the people are kept on the stool of repentance for months at a time. Though the intention may be good, we cannot applaud the act. Our law is one of mercy, of gentleness, and of love.

April 25

F. Cubero stood at the church door to see if any lady entered with obvious hoops; he found one, and told her she had better go home, or some where else as it was no use for her to come to church. The preceding Sunday he preached on women's hoops and men's chewing tobacco, declared they were an abomination to the Lord, and would be turned out of church by physical force, if they came there. Comment is unnecessary.

April 26

I see that 100 short sermons, the creed, commandments &c translated from the revel of H. J. Thomas, a canon of Liege, by a professor of a western college (i.e. Sinsinawa) is just published. The sermons are brief, lucid, have great directness, and compression of argument, are very good for country congregations. It is rather creditable to our folks of the big mound and no doubt gives them a large opinion of themselves.

April 28

I have long promised our boys who serve mass a picnic; tomorrow is the day and they are all on tiptoe, as lively as a piece of old cheese able to walk. This evening we set out in the express, old Whitey heading towards J.Noon's and inclining his head every other step, approving of our trip. A malicious person might say Whitey did this on account of a certain lameness of limbs, but those who can appreciate his worth know better. W. Rouelt, T. Murray, M. English, J. Hill, E. Flouston, T. Kehoe, T. Tiner made up the company, and a right merry set they were. Half the boys in college say they want to learn to serve mass in order to enjoy a future picnic. A dozen have offered themselves as drivers of our one horse carriage and all rejected. . . is well pleased with himself, thinks he is better looking than his fellows, our coach drives up and off we go at two miles an hour.

April 29

Thursday; a beautiful day, very warm. Last night at John Noon's, the boys had a glorious time. F. Roch played the violin, they sung [sic] and danced, and talked, and laughed and were as merry as grigs. Had beds on the floor and slept twice two double. Went to McCluney church after breakfast, sauntered about awhile, then to Smith's, and saw the additions and improvements they're making, F. D'Arco being the architect. Back to Noon's, smoked til thirsty, remedied the evil by generous draught of port, and sat down to noble old gobler [sic], which soon was dissected and done for. Mustered our force and set out homeward, passing through Rehoboth and Lexington. Everybody talked while no body listened; fun, wit worthy of older heads, and songs shortened the road. The only regret expressed, was that the sport could not be prolonged for a week or two.

May 2

This evening with F. Rochford, went to J. Crossons. John was glorious and jubilant having another heir, which I baptized Thos. Joseph.

May 13

We begin to think of long office again, nine psalms and nine lessons; we have not devotion enough to make us rejoice at the prospect and the proximity of the time. Mr. Slevin called in the evening. Passed some time at Sr. Fanny's[3] conversing with Mrs. Tiner and Lizzie and Georgie. Read Chateaubriand on the hierarchy.

May 21

Read Chateaubriand. The knights sometimes formed friendships among themselves, the blood of each was mingled in one cup, and as a pledge of the mutual fidelity, they wore either a golden heart, a chain, or a ring. Love of fair lady had in such cases but a secondary claim on their hearts. . . . The days of chivalry are long since over; mammon and money are the gods of our time.

1. Archbishop John Hughes (1797-1864) was the first archbishop of New York.

2. Charles Pius Montgomery, O.P., (1806-1960) and Francis Cubero, O.P. (1807-1893) were good men but their narrow interpretation of morality was an affliction for the parish. The Diary will give several other instances

3. Sister Fanny and Sister Teresa Naughton were Dominican tertiaries who spent their lives giving domestic service at St. Joseph's.

IMMIGRANTS CALLED BY IMMIGRANTS, 1853-1865

CHAPTER 13

A CALL HEARD IN BAVARIA

Quite clearly, the participants had got their signals mixed. Mother Benedicta Bauer of Heilig Kreuz monastery assured the bishop of Regensburg,[1] Germany, that her volunteers for an American mission would be perfectly safe because the Benedictine monk Dom Boniface Wimmer promised to provide for their spiritual welfare and assist them in their temporal affairs. On April 4, 1853, he had written that the sisters might start for America as soon as the arrangements could be made. He would receive them at St. Vincent's College in western Pennsylvania where they could study the English language. He, himself, "would attend to everything else."[2]

With the missionaries already three days into their transatlantic journey, Dom Wimmer sounded an entirely different tune in a letter to his friend Abbot Gregory Scherr of Metten, Germany. "In the near future I shall have to go to New York again to meet Dominican Sisters that the Convent of the Holy Cross is sending me as a cross (as if I did not as yet have enough crosses)." He would have to displace his own people in order to house the nuns "until such a time that I can find a suitable place for them." Williamsburg, Brooklyn, was a possibility since it had a German pastor, Father Raffeiner, who was "disposed to take them." The monk wished he had never gotten mixed up in the project to begin with. He blamed Mother Benedicta, who "did not cease to beg me and so I agreed, or rather promised, to help as much as I could to find a place for them outside of our diocese."[3]

Two letters, two well intentioned people, two very different versions of a German mission project that would eventually lead to twelve active congregations of Dominican women in the United States—"the Regensburg Tree." First, there would have to be a collision of the two plans on a dock in lower Manhattan, and once again, adjustment of a dream to the reality of where the real need existed.

Sometime in 1851, during a recruitment and fund raising trip to his homeland, Dom Boniface Wimmer, OSB, paid several visits to his Dominican cousin, Sister Elizabeth Kissel, at Holy Cross Monastery, Regensburg.[4] The monk had left his abbey of Metten in 1846, accompanied by a group of students and candidates for the dual purpose of founding a Benedictine community and serving German immigrant Catholics in the United States.[5] Much more than the Irish, who spoke the prevailing language of the new nation, did German Catholics worry about American immigrants losing the faith if they could not worship and be taught in their native tongue. As one German-speaking priest explained it, "In English you must count your dollars, but in German you speak with your children, your confessor and your God."[6]

Under the slogan "Language saves faith," German missionary priests in the United States went about setting up German-speaking parishes and schools. During his visits to Holy Cross in 1851, Dom Wimmer painted a desperate picture of little German children losing their religion because there was no one to teach them catechism in the mother tongue. One of the nuns who must have listened to those talks, Sister Seraphine Staimer, wrote how the priest's descriptions fired the prioress, Mother Benedicta Bauer, with "the urgent desire to found a convent of our Order in America."[7]

The house which gave birth to that enthusiasm was a contemplative monastery of the Dominican Second Order, in existence since 1233. During the Napoleonic wars, when most Dominican houses in Germany were dissolved, Holy Cross had survived by opening a school for girls on its premises. It was not by choice that the nuns had taken up teaching. Instead Prince Karl von Dahlberg had ordered it. He was the governing authority because the religious houses of Regensburg had been awarded him as an indemnity in 1803. The Prince decided that two of the convents—Dominicans and Poor Clares—might remain open if the sisters provided educational services to the children of the city. Much against their will, the religious of Holy Cross allowed three of their better educated nuns to become teachers.

Holy Cross School was an immediate success. Eventually ten members, or approximately one fourth of the community, entered the active ministry. Each day they traveled from the convent to a separate school building erected across the street via an enclosed passageway which shielded them from public view. Lay or "extern" sisters escorted pupils to and from the street, supervised meals and met with parents, so that the choir nun teachers could continue to fulfill their cloister requirements. Meanwhile, the chanting of the Divine Office and other aspects of their penitential life went on as they had for the previous six hundred years.[8]

Surely this was the lifestyle Mother Benedicta intended to reproduce, under Dom Wimmer's direction in the hills of western Pennsylvania. But the future of the plan remained precarious; Valentine Riedel, Bishop of Regensburg wanted no part of it. For two years he refused permission for the sisters to go to America.[9] There is no record of how Mother Benedicta succeeded in changing his mind, but change it she did. By April of 1853, the project was moving ahead with Reidel's blessing.

That two-year hiatus may at least partially explain why Dom Wimmer was no longer anxious to sponsor a Dominican foundation of teaching nuns in Western Pennsylvania. During the interim, he recruited a group of German Benedictine women from the Convent of St. Walburg, Eichstat, Bavaria. They had found their way from New York to Latrobe in July of 1852 and began to work among the German immigrants.[10] Nevertheless, Wimmer's letters to Mother Benedicta early in 1853 seemed to encourage her to go ahead with the venture. In them, the Benedictine mentioned that he had consulted with the Dominican friars at the First Plenary Council of Baltimore. Nothing in Dominican records substantiates that contact. In fact, it would be almost forty years before the Brooklyn sisters made contact with any Dominican men.[11]

Happily oblivious to Dom Wimmer's change of heart, Mother Benedicta went about assembling the first American mission band. Only one of those four pioneers left a personal record of the discernment process she went through before volunteering. During her last illness, Mother Augustine Neuhierl gave this account:

> Six years ago the holy Angels visited me, asking me do I wish to go to a new Convent. I always answered "No." Thereupon they stayed away. The Infant Jesus came also, asking me did I want to go to America, saying it would be well with me and He would help me. I said, if it is His holy will, then I will go.[12]

The volunteers for the American mission came forward; They included Augustine Neuhierl and Josepha Witzlhofer. At this point, Mother Benedicta had two teachers for the mission. Both prospective missionaries had come from middle class families in the Regensburg area. Teresa Witzlhofer and Marie Josephine Neuhierl entered Holy Cross a year apart, Teresa in 1838 and Marie Josephine in 1839. Both girls had already completed with distinction educational programs which prepared them to teach. Teresa brought with her a certificate signed by the Royal District Inspector attesting that she had "finished the course of instruction required of the teachers of girls and has acquired such perfection in all the arts that she may preside in any school for girls."[13]

Marie Josephine's pastor at Walderbach signed a school certificate attesting that she was "gifted from God with extraordinary talents" and "especially called and adapted for the intellectual and pious education of youth."[14] Once she began to consider going on mission to America, her superiors "encouraged her desire, and sent her to the Institute of Englische Fraulein at Altotting [from the Autumn of 1852 until Spring of 1853] for the purpose of mastering the English language.[15]

Holy Cross School could not have functioned without the help of the lay sisters. For this reason Sisters Francesca Retter and Jacobina Riederer, both of whom had expressed their willingness to emigrate, were chosen.[16] By 1853, the American venture moved ahead at full speed. Quoting Dom Wimmer's instructions to her ordinary, Mother Benedicta asked him to issue a "Dismissory, that is, a Latin testimonial to the effect that these Sisters are sent to the missions in America to found a convent of their Order." She also transmitted the monk's assurance that "they are directed for the time being to me as their counselor and protector."[17]

On May 10, the four volunteers presented themselves to the bishop at the chancery offices in Regensburg where he examined them orally and then had them sign the petition to emigrate. His Dismissory, given on May 29, noted that "The Reverend Boniface desires that we send to America some Sisters from the Holy Cross Monastery . . . well qualified for educating young girls."[18] Riedel's permission also noted that Sister Josepha Witzlhofer had been appointed superior of the quartet and outlined the relationship that the American foundation was to have with Holy Cross:

> They remain in the congregation to which they are bound by their sacred vows and under the jurisdiction of the prioress of Holy Cross until such time as their numbers increase sufficiently to erect a new monastery in America, or in case of exigency that they be allowed to return to the Holy Cross Monastery

That specification about the building of an American monastery was going to prove vitally important when, seven years later, a different bishop and prioress in Regensburg began to harass Sister Josepha for making unauthorized foundations in the United States.

With official permission secured, the nuns were ready to consider practical matters: travel arrangements and luggage—how to go and what to take. Dom Wimmer had put Mother Benedicta in touch with Father Joseph Mueller, court chaplain to King Ludwig of Bavaria and director of the Ludwig-Missionsverein.[19] Founded in Munich in 1838, the Verein was intended to assist German Catholic mission projects in Asia and America. Between 1844 and 1916, the society donated nearly $900,000 to the American missions. Part of that sum helped the Holy Cross sisters to finance their first American monasteries.[20] Father Mueller saw to the purchase of tickets aboard the steamship *Germania* from Bremerhaven to New York and offered to accompany the little band as far as Leipzig.

For their part, the community at Holy Cross put together a purse of 4,000 guldens ($1,500) and filled twenty chests with articles to furnish the new chapel and convent.[21] Otherwise the pioneers traveled light. In the custom of the day for cloistered religious, each woman folded her habit and veil into a carpet bag along with personal articles, office book and constitutions, then put on dark secular clothes for the duration of the trip.

With Father Mueller accompanying them, the band of missionaries left Regensburg by stage the evening of July 25, 1853. After thirty-three hours of travel, the group reached Leipzig on July 27. Describing the journey for the community at Holy Cross, Father Mueller recorded:

> [We] had ourselves carried to the hotel Stadt Breslau and rested for a few hours. At 6 a.m. I set out to find the Catholic Church . . . drove back to the hotel to get the Sisters and then read Mass for a safe voyage. Then we took breakfast and prepared for the journey. I hurriedly wrote several letters of recommendation . . . and at 11 a.m. accompanied them to the railway station, for there was a good deal of baggage.[22]

At the time, supervising the "good deal of baggage" must have seemed the most needed piece of assistance on the part of the priest. However, it was one of the "hurried letters of recommendation" that turned out to be most vital to the success of the mission once the women reached New York.

On his return from the station, the Verein director wrote Mother Benedicta that her "good children" would arrive in Bremen at ten the next morning and wait for the departure hour. From that point until they landed in Manhattan almost a month later, the only record is an entry in the Annals of the Propagation of the Faith in Munich. "On August 1, four Dominican sisters from Regensburg sailed from Bremerhaven on the streamer *Germania* for North America, to establish a convent in Carrolltown, Diocese of Pittsburgh."[23]

After almost a month at sea, the *Germania* made port in lower Manhattan on the morning of August 26. The four German sisters waited until noon for Dom Wimmer

Holy Cross Monastery, Regensburg, Bavaria

to arrive and finally conceded that he would never appear. It was at that point that one of Father Mueller's letters saved the day. Sister Josepha was carrying a note addressed to another Father Mueller, Redemptorist pastor of the Most Holy Redeemer parish on East Third Street.[24] Sister Augustine's six-month course in English was immediately put to use.

After arranging to store the chests temporarily on the pier, the sisters hired a carriage to take them the two miles to Holy Redeemer rectory. There they were welcomed by Father Kleineidam and Brother Nicholas. Refreshment was provided and the Redemptorists set about finding temporary lodging for the travelers until contact could be made with Dom Wimmer. By late afternoon, part of the mystery had been solved. Then a partial explanation was made concerning the harrowing experience of the morning. Father Nicholas Balleis,[25] the Benedictine pastor of St. Mary's, Newark arrived at the parish. He apologized for misreading the steamship schedule and explained that Dom Wimmer had delegated him to meet the sisters.

Together, Redemptorists and Benedictines arranged for the two choir nuns to stay in Manhattan with a family named Zeigler while the lay sisters would return to Newark with Father Balleis and be quartered with his parishioners, the Blaggis. Pointedly absent was any mention of travel to Pennsylvania. But at least the German quartet had been welcomed, lodged and fed by the end of that first day. But what had gone wrong with the plans for a convent in Carrolltown?[26]

In the week that followed, Father John Stephen Raffeiner, stationed at the German parish of Holy Trinity in Williamsburg, Brooklyn, visited them. Was this a coincidence? Apparently Dom Wimmer had been in contact with Raffeiner and thought that the priest "would take them if the archbishop permits it."[27] The Brooklyn pastor came each week to the Redemptorists for confession; on his visit during the last week of August, he met the two choir nuns from Holy Cross and ascertained that they would be available to teach. Writing to Mother Benedicta in mid-September, Dom Wimmer confirmed the arrangement:

> It was only on the fifth day after their arrival that I found it possible to see and care for them. Since I knew of no place in the land at this time where they might locate, I came to an agreement with the reverend Raffeiner, Vicar General of New York, that he would receive them at his parish church in Williamsburg, a suburb of New York.[28]

Dominican Convent Williamsburg, 1854

As far as the nuns were concerned the Redemptorists played a bigger role in their establishment than Dom Wimmer was willing to admit. They had their own way of acknowledging the fact. That first Brooklyn school they dedicated not to Saint Boniface or Saint Benedict, but to Saint Alphonsus, patron of the Redemptorist order.[29]

Sisters Josepha and Augustine began teaching in September. One hundred forty girls filled the basement of Holy Trinity Church. From the beginning, the enterprise was an unmitigated success. The convent situation was not so fortunate. Dom Wimmer gave the Holy Cross prioress an account of the living conditions. They were clearly inadequate even by Wimmer's analysis:

> Since there is no convent there, they had to be domiciled for the time being in the rectory which is attached to the old church. Don't be alarmed at that. The pastor, the above-mentioned Rev. Vicar, is an old gentleman, a good priest, and has only one assistant. The rectory is roomy. I remained there four days in order to arrange everything so that by the end of the week the four Sisters had complete enclosure not only on the outside from the people, but also on the inside from the priests. They are rather confined, but it will do. They have a kitchen, a study, and a dormitory sufficiently large for all four. . . . I gained an uninterrupted connection with the church and a large room under the church which the Sisters may use for their wash, a storeroom, or they could even sleep there if they wished.[30]

What is missing from this description is the fact that the part of the rectory assigned to the sisters was a dirt-floored basement. Before the winter was over, they did indeed sleep in "the large room under the church," but it was unheated and constantly damp. All four contracted heavy colds. Sister Francesca's illness progressed into tuberculosis. She would die of it the following year.

Both lay sisters had an additional burden which consisted in having to cook for the two priests. Their mentor admitted it was "disturbing and annoying." Nevertheless, he "was not able to make any other arrangements." Apparently Father Raffeiner had received the sisters "especially that he might be provided with a cook and also economize."[31] To save the sisters, a widow was finally engaged to do the other housekeeping chores for the two men, but the nuns were told to pay her wages. Dom Wimmer reported the financial situation as "2,500 gulden in their possession, which will soon be spent, because they have to buy cupboards, etc. The school money will provide for the necessaries of life."[32]

Tuition amounted to twenty-five cents a week per student, enough only for the "necessaries" for the sisters. As Dom Wimmer put it, "At present there can be no thought of building a convent." For this reason he encouraged Sister Josepha to accept "any good candidates that present themselves." Besides, it was necessary to train teachers who were "well versed in English." He promised to be responsible for such decisions, reminding the German prioress that "I am in a better position to know American needs than you in far off Holy Cross."

The only hint as to the missionaries' state of mind appeared in the last paragraph of the monk's account. "At first they were rather disheartened and diffident, but before I left, they were full of courage and confidence." This observation was the only evidence that the chaotic arrival had dampened the high spirits with which they set out. As for Dom Wimmer himself, there is some question as to how he felt about the whole episode when he wrote: "If I managed this affair well or not, I do not know. My intention was good; of that I am sure." Whatever doubts he may have had disappeared at the end. "Everything has turned out so well that one must believe it to be the will of God that matters culminated in this manner."[33]

The Benedictine founder told the Dominican prioress that he could not go to Williamsburg very often as it was a 400-mile journey. He did keep up with the progress of the new foundation. Early in December, Wimmer returned to New york to help the nuns acquire a lot on the corner of Graham and Montrose Avenues, a purchase that consumed the last of their funds. On Christmas Eve, he sent his friend Abbot Gregory Scherr of Metten an account of the school. "Before the arrival of the Sisters, two men teachers never had more than 150-170 boys and girls together and now the Sisters alone have 225 girls in their classes and are expecting more."[34] In February, he boasted, "The good ladies have now 243 in their school, the half of which number came from Protestant schools or did not attend any."[35]

That December visit seems to have been the last time the "protector" acted directly on their behalf. However, during the course of the winter, the German sisters found a new clerical champion. Shortly after their arrival, Catholics on Long Island were detached from the diocese of New York and became the diocese of Brooklyn. A young Irishman, John Loughlin, was appointed bishop and Father Raffeiner served as his vicar general. The new bishop could converse in German and must have met the Regensburg nuns when he visited Holy Trinity. By early spring he offered them a loan of $4,000 to purchase a small house. It stood between the church and the lot on

M. Emilia Barth, second prioress of the Dominican Sisters of Williamsburg

which they planned to build.[36] On May 16, 1854, the sisters moved into their first real convent. At this point they had what they would call a weather-tight home.

Now the nuns were to encounter the first complications related to their canonical status as enclosed nuns. Their basement quarters at Holy Trinity had been linked with both church and school in such a way that cloister was not violated when they moved from one to the other. Teachers could move from convent to school through a closed passageway making the classroom wing technically a part of the monastery. But once Sister Josepha and Sister Augustine began to walk from the little house down the block to St. Alphonsus school, cloister was broken. If they had a dispensation, it seems to have been one from Father Raffeiner or Bishop Loughlin that went unrecorded.

According to The Catholic Almanac for 1855, St. Alphonsus' enrollment skyrocketed to 300. This meant that each nun taught a class of 150! Although there is no extant correspondence between Sister Josepha and Mother Benedicta that year, the American superior must have asked for help. Once more Father Mueller guided a group of Holy Cross women across Germany, giving them a sizeable donation from the Ludwig Missionsverein towards the construction of a convent on the Brooklyn lot.[37]

Three choir nuns, Sisters Seraphine Staimer, Aemilia Barth and Michaela Braun, left Regensburg April 13, 1855, and landed in America May 9, 1855. Their physical presence as teachers for the understaffed school was cause enough for rejoicing, but the financial help they brought made the expedition a double blessing. Besides the initial gift, the Missionsverein promised the Brooklyn community an annual donation of 1500 gulden ($600) for the next five or six years to help them become self supporting. According to Mother Seraphine, the sisters first paid their debt to the bishop and then began to make plans for "a real convent" on the corner of Graham and Montrose.

In addition to the windfall from Europe, the sisters themselves managed to save five to six hundred dollars from their annual income. In addition, the nuns began a cottage industry that utilized the artistic training they had developed in Germany. Just one drawing for articles painted and embroidered by the sisters realized $800. It was to set the stage for the many raffles and bazaars in years to come. "In this way," wrote Mother Seraphine, "about $2000 was saved in two years."[38]

Just two weeks after the arrival of the newcomers, Sister Francesca Retter died from the tuberculosis she had contracted during that first winter in the basement. It must have been a terrifying initiation for the newcomers, perhaps an experience which Sister Michaela was unable to get over. Mother Seraphine recorded that Michaela was "unable to accustom herself to conditions in Williamsburg and returned to Ratisbon after two years."[39]

The school continued to flourish. From the very beginning, Dom Wimmer had reported that parents and children were "delighted. . . when they heard that the Sisters were to come and when they saw them."[40] One tangible evidence that the nuns lived up to expectations was the rising enrollment. Another appeared in the form of a letter sent to the Katholische kirchen-Zeitung in May of 1856 by a parishioner who signed himself "Philos." Describing a First Communion ceremony at Holy Trinity, he said:

> The children sang a very beautiful Communion hymn especially adapted for such occasions. It was composed by Rev. Sister Augustine OSD, the well qualified teacher in the second class of the Girls School here. I must at once observe on this occasion that the Sisters of St. Dominic in the three years of their stay here, have already acquired great merits in the education and training of youth.[41]

Still no American candidates had presented themselves for entrance. Shortly before ground was broken for the new convent in June 1857, Sister Josepha sent a plea for aid to the motherhouse: "We have four hundred children taught in only three divisions; send us, therefore, more Sisters."[42] This brief petition went out just after the coming of Margaret Bosslet, the first American postulant, who entered as a lay sister.

Before any further help arrived, the American contingent celebrated a major triumph. Bishop Loughlin dedicated their new convent at the corner of Graham and Montrose on November 9, 1857.[43] Since the original dismissory from Bishop Riedel had specified that the mission group was subject to the motherhouse "until such time as their numbers increase sufficiently to erect a new monastery in America,"[44] later authorities decided that this was the point at which the five German sisters and their precious American postulant[45] became an independent entity.

Rather than celebrating a new status which they may not have known they possessed, the community which moved into Holy Cross Convent on Graham Avenue that November was focused on finding new members. Early in the next year, Father Ambrose Buchmeier of St. Nicholas parish in Manhattan, asked for sisters to teach in the girls' division of his school. Dom Wimmer had once told Mother Benedicta Bauer that "Father Ambrose scolded me sternly because I did not tell him about the Dominican Nuns because he would have taken them."[46] Five years later, the Manhattan pastor was making another try. At the time, Sister Josepha had to say "no" for they could barely cope with the numbers in St. Alphonsus.

However, unknown to the American foundation, Mother Benedicta was in the process of leaving her office as prioress at Holy Cross and planning to go on mission to America. The former superior, accompanied by choir nuns Thomasina Ginker and Cunigunda Schell and a prospective postulant, Crescentia Traubinger, arrived at Williamsburg on October 22, 1858. Margaret Bosslet, who had been received as Sister Rosa the previous April, now had a companion in the novitiate. Crescentia became a postulant on her first day in America, spending almost two years as a candidate until she in her turn received the habit and the name "Dominica." The two young choir nuns settled happily into the school. Mother Benedicta began to work in her specialty area giving music instruction.

Some years later, Sister Seraphine would write, "Mother Benedicta did not like it in Williamsburg."[47] She did not elaborate, but whatever her objections, she made them known to their mentor in Germany, Father Joseph Mueller, who discouraged the idea of leaving to make a new foundation and counseled patience: "You know that in America you would not find the Convent of the Holy Cross. America is a mission country which demands much self-abnegation."[48]

As it turned out, one of Mother's traveling companions left the Williamsburg house before she did, and that too was a source of tension. Mother Josepha had decided that the Brooklyn community was now large enough to spare teachers for Father Buchmeier's school in lower Manhattan. To St. Nicholas parish on East Second Street she sent Sisters Augustine Neuhierl, Cunigunda Schell and Rosa Bosslet.[49] Their friend Father Ambrose had furnished a narrow Manhattan brownstone house next to the church as a convent for his long awaited German Dominicans. They still had to break cloister in order to reach the school, but there was no harrowing winter in a drafty basement for the new foundation, which was eventually dedicated to the Holy Rosary.

From Mother Benedicta's point of view, the problem lay in the fact that Sister Cunigunda had been destined to accompany her in founding a convent that would properly duplicate their Regensburg home elsewhere in America. Instead, the various chroniclers of the Williamsburg community agreed that both Cunigunda and Dominica found the New York foundation so much to their liking that they did not want to leave.[50] Regensburg's version of the touchy situation described that choice as "a new and bitter trial" for "poor Mother Benedicta" and blamed "The Sisters at Williamsburg [who] had advised these Sisters to stay at the convent where they had the assurance of a permanent place, whereas there would be much uncertainty in a new foundation."[51]

As a member of the founding trio for Second Street, Manhattan, Sister Cunigunda, like her two companions, met with no uncertainties. Father Ambrose saw to it that they were comfortably provided for. During the earliest days when there was no chapel in the narrow brownstone, he allowed them to say the Divine Office in the sacristy of St. Nicholas Church.[52] When the fledgling community expanded, they were able to acquire the adjacent brownstones and interconnect them so that the Dominican community of the Most Holy Rosary had a ready-made headquarters consisting of several adjoining houses on East Second Street.

Historians may question as to the time when the Manhattan house began to move toward independent status, but as members of the Dominican Second Order, there was never any doubt that they would one day become a separate community. In the European monastic tradition, as soon as a new foundation possessed sufficient income and the requisite numbers to live a regular religious life, it could become an independent community. In the early 1860s, it was not a matter of whether Holy Rosary would separate from its parent in Williamsburg; the question was when.

By the time she had been ten years in Brooklyn, Mother Josepha Witzlhofer was overtaken by the tuberculosis scourge that would kill so many religious in the late nineteenth century. At some point, Sister Augustine asked for more personnel to be assigned to the Manhattan house and was told to "admit [her] own candidates."[53] Opening a separate novitiate in Manhattan would be a definitive step towards independence, one that the Holy Rosary superior was at first reluctant to take. She continued to rely on the Williamsburg house during Mother Josepha's lifetime.

After Josepha died on April 9, 1864, Bishop Loughlin appointed Sister Seraphine in her place. At the end of the next school year, matters came to a head. Father Augustine Dantner from the German parish of St. John on Manhattan's 30th Street came looking for teachers. The contact was apparently made through Sister Augustine who then asked Mother Seraphine, and received a promise of sisters for the new school. However, as September approached, Williamsburg had no one to send. To avoid the embarrassment of going back on a promise, Sister Augustine halved her faculty at St. Nicholas. To St. John's went Sisters Cunegunda, Ambrosia, Theresia and Magdalena, leaving the Second Street school understaffed.

The following spring, Sister Augustine took the step she had been avoiding for the previous several years and admitted the first postulants to Holy Rosary, Sisters Alberta Krein and Catherine Muth. Candidates continued to come, and Second Street was on its way to independent status, an event which took place legally in 1869. Within the next two decades, the Brooklyn and Manhattan communities made decisions which placed them farther apart geographically.

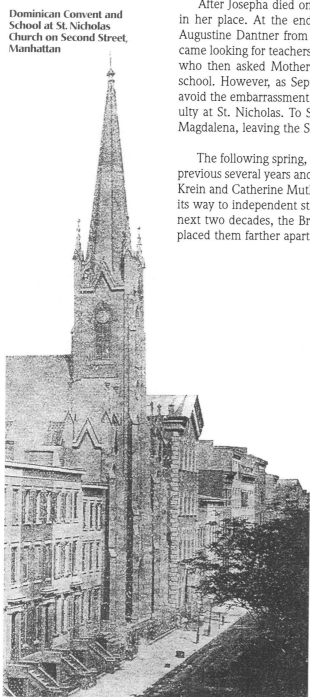

Dominican Convent and School at St. Nicholas Church on Second Street, Manhattan

Before relations between the Brooklyn and Manhattan convents became strained, a decision by Mother Benedicta Bauer led to a third Regensburg foundation in America. During the spring of 1860, two unhappy religious decided to leave Booklyn; one opting to return to Holy Cross, the other to move still further away to the interior of the new country. After seven years of trial, Sister Jacobina Riederer received permission to return to Regensburg.

The "quit claim" which marked Jacobina's leaving the convent on Graham Avenue was signed by five professed religious of the community: Sisters Josepha, Augustine, Serephine, Aemilia and Cunigunda.[54] Absent were the signatures of Benedicta Bauer and Thomasina Ginker, indicating that they were considered guests rather than permanent members. While Sister Jacobina was recrossing the Atlantic in the month of April, Mother Benedicta was corresponding with her Regensburg successor, Mother Agnes Loehner.

If there was some strain between Benedicta and the Williamsburg community, Mother Agnes' reply to her request for permission to go elsewhere could not have helped the situation. There was a new bishop in Regensburg, and the Holy Cross prioress had consulted with him. First, she relayed his instructions. "Those in America must become independent. But before taking that step they must declare if it be their intention to stay in America or return to the Motherhouse."[55] Mother Agnes went on to say that she had already sent several letters to Williamsburg suggesting that the American house separate from the motherhouse. She had received a panic-stricken refusal to her first communication and no answer to subsequent letters.

Mother Agnes did not say when the refusal had been sent. It may have dated from the era before the last consignment of missionaries from the Motherhouse arrived, when the new Holy Cross was still in need of both personnel and financial assistance from Europe. Technically, they were independent as of November 1857, when the "new convent in America"[56] was dedicated. Bishop Synestry's Dismissory for Mother Benedicta and her companions specified that they were "under the jurisdiction of the prioress of Holy Cross convent . . . till the time when a new convent erected in America will be approved by legitimate authority."[57] Surely John Loughlin, Bishop of Brooklyn, had approved the erection of the convent on Graham Avenue before he dedicated it. The problem lay in the fact that as a busy missionary the bishop seldom put things in writing.[58] If he had, the prioress of the new Holy Cross might have been spared much grief.

That Sister Josepha was indeed a prioress in 1858 was attested to by Bishop Synestry himself when he wrote that "the prioress of the sisters who have already gone to the missions" had consented to accept the quartet coming from Regensburg.[59] However, the European prelate was unwilling to cede her the full power of that position. This became all too apparent when the American superior received an official decree from Regensburg dated October 26, 1860, charging her with having made invalid foundations.

If she took this decree seriously, Mother Josepha would have had to recall the sisters from Manhattan and the Midwest. She did no such thing, thereby suggesting that either Bishop Loughlin or Father Raffeiner advised her to ignore the instructions from Europe. Nothing came of von Synestry's complaint to Rome; rather, the silence of the years which followed seemed to indicate tacit permission for the American foundations to go their own way.[60]

Apart from the Bishop of Regensburg's threatening decree, both Williamsburg and its daughter community in lower Manhattan reached the midpoint of the 1860s peacefully with good prospects for steady growth. Mother Benedicta and Sister Thomasina had left for the Midwest in June of 1860. After an odyssey that took them from Ohio to Tennessee to Wisconsin, they found a permanent home in the city of Racine on the western shore of Lake Michigan.

By the end of the Civil War in 1865, Holy Cross had established three branches in the United States: Brooklyn, Manhattan and Racine. Over the next seventy years there were destined to be nine more branches ranging from California, Washington and Kansas to New Jersey, Ohio and Michigan. They would usually begin as responses to the call of a German pastor seeking teachers for his parochial school and broaden out into multiethnic communities answering a variety of needs. In all of them flourished the spirit of those four women standing on a Manhattan dock with plans gone awry, who then picked up the pieces and started off in a new direction.

1. Nineteenth and early twentieth century accounts refer to the city and the diocese as "Ratisbon" which was its Celtic name meaning "settlement on the waters." Contemporary usage has gone over to the German title of "Regensburg," derived from the fact that the city is located just below the point where the river Regen flows into the Danube.

2. Holy Cross Chronicle, ms., Regensburg, Excerpt III, 3-6. Copy in Racine Dominican Archives (RDA). Cited by S. Mary Hortense Kohler, O.P., in **Life and Work of Mother Benedicta Bauer** (Milwaukee: Bruce Publishing, 1937) 43-44.

3. Dom Wimmer to Abbot Gregory, July 29, 1853. This letter was found in the Archives of St. Vincent's Archabbey, Latrobe, PA, by Felix Fellner, OSB, who sent it, along with two others, to Rev. Eugene Crawford when the latter was writing the history of the Amityville Dominicans. Cited in **Daughters of Dominic on Long Island,** (New York: Benziger, 1938) 1: 42. Primary sources assembled by Father Crawford are contained in the Crawford File, Amityville Dominican archives (AMF).

4. When writing to the Bishop of Regensburg in April of 1853, Mother Benedicta Bauer states that Dom Wimmer had "called at the convent several times" two years earlier. M. Benedicta Bauer to V. Von Riedel, April 4, 1853.

5. From an account of the founding of the Dominican Congregation of the Holy Cross, Brooklyn, NY, written by Sister Maud Bonten, O.P., using information supplied by Mother Ignatia of Holy Cross, Regensburg in 1928. Copy in the AMF.

6. Quoted in **The Church of St. Joseph of Yorkville** (New York: 1932) n. pag. Cited by Jay P. Dolan in **The American Catholic Experience** (New York: Doubleday, 1985) 169.

7. Mother Seraphine Staimer, Diary, 1. Begun in 1865 and kept until shortly before her death in 1889. Mother Seraphine began her account by describing the visits of Dom Wimmer to Holy Cross and the journeys of the missionaries to America.

8. 750 Jahre Dominikanerinnen-kloster Heilig Kreuz, trans. Sister Teresa Margaret Hoessbacher, O.P., (Munchen: Verlag Schnell & Steiner, 1983) 20-22, AMF.

9. Staimer, Diary, 1.

10. Sister Mary Regina Baska, OSB, **The Benedictine Congregation of Saint Scholastica,** 10-12. Cited by Eugene Crawford in **Daughters of Dominic on Long Island,** 1: 61. Oral comparisons of tradition between Regensburg Dominicans and Eichstat Benedictines usually produce exclamations of "You too?" in the matter of Dom Wimmer's recruitment techniques and failure to carry through on promises of travel assistance to western Pennsylvania. Crawford characterizes the monk as a man with "too many irons in the fire."

11. Mother Benedicta to Bishop von Reidel, May 1853, Copy in Racine Dominican Archives(RDA). Cited by Kohler 94-95 and Crawford 43-44. Amityville's oral tradition tells of two sisters in Manhattan on business during the 1880s ringing the doorbell of St. Vincent Ferrer's rectory and asking to talk to a Dominican priest as they had never met one.

12. Sister Eugenia Glaab, O.P., Notebooks and History Chronicle, ms., Early Foundation History files, Hope Dominican Archives(HPEA). Sister Eugenia recorded this account several times. In the margin of the Chronicle, she appended "I Sister M. Eugenia was present and heard these words from the lips of Mother M. Augustine."

13. Crawford, **Daughters,** 1: 215. School certificates for the sisters who came from Germany were brought across the ocean with them and are on file in the various motherhouse archives.

14. *Chronik,* Foundation History, Book 7, HPEA.

15. Sister Maria Monica, prioress of Holy Cross convent, Regensburg to Mother Prioress [Hyacinth Scheininger], June 17, 1889. Trans. By Sister Eugenia Glaab. Mother Augustine Neuhierl File 4, Box 35, HPEA. The dates for Mother Augustine's stay at Altotting were supplied by Mother Amanda Kluge of Holy Cross in her letter to the Newburgh Vicaress General Sister Mary Ruth Tole, Aug. 5, 1954.

16. Holy Cross Chronicle, Excerpt 3, 1, RDA.

17. Mother Benedicta to Bishop Riedel, May 1853.

18. Bauer to Riedel, May 1853.

19. Mother Benedicta to Bishop Riedel, May 1853.

20. Theodore Roemer, **The Ludwig-**

Missionsverein and the Church in the United States (1859-1918) (New York: Joseph Wagner, 1933) 1, 138. Cited by Sister Hortense Kohler in **Life and Work of Mother Benedicta Bauer,** 90. In addition to the Brooklyn foundation, Mother Benedicta's community at Racine also received Verein funds.

21. Schrems, **Kurze Geschichte des Dominikanerinnen-Klosters vom Heiligen Kreuz in Regensburg und Seiner Filialen,** Manuscript V, 35; *Account Book and Notebook,* 1: 13. RDA. Cited by Kohler in Mother Benedicta Bauer, 105-06.

22. Joseph Mueller to Mother Prioress [Benedicta Bauer], Leipzig, July 27, 1853, Newburg Dominican Archives(NDA) Box 1, Folder 4.

23. Annalen der Verbreitung des Glaubens, Munich, 1853. 21: 382, Copy in AMF, Crawford File.

24. New York City's German community began petitioning for a German language parish in 1808 and received the first of several with the establishment of St. Nicholas on East Second Street in 1833. The Redemptorists were given charge of the new Most Holy Redeemer Church in 1844. See Jay P. Dolan, **The Immigrant Church** (Baltimore: John Hopkins University Press, 1975).

25. Nicholas Balleis, OSB, came to America from a monastery in Austria in 1836, the first of his Order to arrive in the United States. He worked as a missionary in the New York area and was pastor of St. Mary's, Newark (presently a Benedictine parish), in 1853. Alexius Hoffman, OSB to Sister Jane Marie Murray, O.P., of Grand Rapids, n.d., John Byrne, CSSR, to Rev. Eugene Crawford at Amityville, Dec. 14, 1936.

26. Chronik, Foundation History, Book 7, 5-6, HPEA. See also Holy Cross Chronicle, copy in RDA.

27. Wimmer to Scherr, July 29, 1853.

28. Dom Wimmer to Mother Benedicta Bauer, Latrobe, PA, Sept. 18, 1853, Copy in RDA.

29. The Catholic Almanac, 1855 (Baltimore: Lucas Brothers) 190. Cited by Crawford in *Daughters of Dominic,* 1: 69.

30. Wimmer to Bauer, Sept. 18, 1853.

31. Wimmer to Bauer, Sept. 18, 1853.

32. Wimmer to Bauer, Sept. 18, 1853.

33. Wimmer to Bauer, Sept. 18, 1853.

34. Dom Wimmer to Abbot Gregory Scherr, St. Mary's, Elk Co., Christmas Eve, 1853.

35. Wimmer to Scheer, February 24, 1853. Copy in the Amityville Archives, Crawford file.

36. Staimer, Diary, 4, AAD.

37. Staimer, Diary, 5, AMF. Mother Seraphine writes that Sister Josepha had petitioned the motherhouse for more sisters. She puts the donation at 6000 gulden ($2400) "to build a Dominican Convent" and attributes it directly to King Ludwig, calling him "one of our greatest benefactors."

38. Staimer, Diary, 6.

39. Staimer, Diary, 5.

40. Wimmer to Bauer, Sept. 18, 1853.

41. Philos, *Katholische Kirchen Zeitung,* New York, Thursday, May 22, 1856, 359. Copy in the Crawford file, AMF.

42. Sister Josepha Witzlhofer to Mother Benedicta Bauer, Williamsburg, Apr. 3, 1857. Copy in the AMF.

43. Staimer, Diary, 6.

44. Riedel, *Dismissory,* May 29, 1853.

45. At this point, the community consisted of Sisters Josepha Witzlhofer, Augustine Neuhierl, Jacobina Riederer, Seraphine Staimer, Emilia Barth and postulant Margaret Bosslet.

46. Wimmer to Bauer, Latrobe, Sept. 18, 1853. Copy in RDA.

47. Staimer, Diary, 6.

48. Joseph Mueller to Mother Benedicta Bauer, Munich, July 12, 1859, RDA.

49. *Chronik,* 10, HPEA.

50. See Kohler, 161; Crawford, 84.

51. Holy Cross Chronicle, Excerpt V, 3. Cited by Kohler, 161.

52. Glaab, Notebooks, HPEA.

53. Sister Augustine Neuhierl to Mother Hyacintha Oberbrunner, Dec. 1, 1866, RDA. Mother Hyacintha was successor to Mother Benedicta Bauer, and Mother Thomasina Ginker of the Wisconsin community, who had died within a year of each other. In the course of a request to borrow teachers from Racine, Sister Augustine reviewed her personnel difficulties with the Williamsburg house.

54. Property deeds, AMF.

55. Mother Agnes Loehner to Mother

Benedicta Bauer, Ratisbon, May 12, 1860, RDA. Cited by Crawford, 1: 85-87.

56. This was the condition for independence laid down by Bishop Riedel in his Dismissory of 1853. Once a new convent in America could be built, then the missionaries would no longer be subject to the Motherhouse.

57. *Dismissory* issued by Bishop Ignatius von Synestry of Ratisbon on Aug. 15, 1858.

58. The Brooklyn diocesan archives file on Bishop Loughlin for this period contains only a few letters and a rather sketchy diary.

59. Synestry, *Dismissory*, Aug. 15, 1858, RDA.

60. By the time the Regensburg decree arrived in Brooklyn, Mother Benedicta and Sister Thomasina were already in Nashville helping the Somerset sisters to establish the Academy of St. Cecilia. Contrary to von Synestry's charge, Mother Benedicta had received permission from Mother Agnes at Holy Cross to begin her western venture.

CHAPTER 14

FROM IRELAND TO THE SOUTHLAND

Braving the storms of the transatlantic crossing in the fall of 1860 created but small concern for the seven Dominican nuns from the monastery in Cabra, Ireland. To leave their long-established life in the cloister posed an equally great challenge. They anticipated privations and hardships in accepting the assignment to New Orleans in the United States. But they never dreamed that a war was about to break out between the North and the South. Clearly, news of a war would not have changed their minds. Through the centuries their congregation had endured many displacements and persecutions in Ireland. Exile, poverty, lack of personnel, persecution because of religious habit and religious name had been constant problems; these hardships had not kept their predecessors from maintaining their objective to live the life of Second Order followers of Dominic.

The story of the Cabra Dominican Monastery "is a faithful reflection of the trials and struggles of Ireland."[1] Every Irish man and woman experienced political turmoil, war, plague and famine. Even in this environment, some pious women in Galway in 1644 opened a house known as the Convent of Jesus and Mary under the direction of Gregory French, O.P. They were recognized and approved by the Order and by the Holy See as the first monastery of Dominican nuns in Ireland since the Reformation. Because they considered education as a particularly Dominican apostolate, they supported themselves by opening a school for girls. In a mere eight years after their establishment, their cloistered life in Galway came to an end in 1652 because of Oliver Cromwell's repressive regime. They were given the option to "renounce their religious life and return to their families to live as lay people, or to choose exile. . ."[2] They chose the latter.

The young community of Irish nuns, fourteen in all, emigrated to Spain. There they were received in Bilbao and various other monasteries. Only two of these sisters, Mary Lynch and Julian Nolan, returned after a thirty-four year exile. Those two had come back to Galway in 1686 at the request of the Dominican Irish Provincial who wanted them to reestablish their monastery of the Incarnation. Sister Mary Lynch, now sixty, and Julian at seventy-five, had to call upon their last reserves of mind and body to start again. Julian was the prioress and Mary became subprioress and mistress of novices. Together they refounded the Convent of Jesus and Mary and invited others to join. As their numbers increased they were able to resume all their monastic practices.

But there was still no rest for vowed religious. A new penal code made effective in 1698, banished "forever" all clergy and women religious. This time the sisters decided to remain, opting to stay in Ireland where they lived with friends or relatives in the Irish countryside.[3] At other times they remained in the monastery. For safety reasons they altered their way of life by removing all signs of the cloister, wearing the garb of the day and engaging in domestic work for their support. This changed way of life proved extremely traumatic.

These adverse conditions affected the two foundresses the most. Julian died in these surroundings in 1701 and Mary took on the burden of prioress. The difficulties the nuns endured in Galway also disturbed the Irish Provincial. He contacted the Archbishop of Dublin, Edward Byrne, to ask if eight of the nuns in Galway might live in his diocese where they could more easily live their monastic life in the anonymity of a large city. Permissions from both the archbishop and the Master of the Order were forthcoming.

In the spring of 1717, the eight led by Sister Mary Bellew, who was appointed by the Dominican provincial, found refuge in Channel Row, near Dublin. When the penal laws were rigorously enforced, the nuns wore secular garb, used their baptismal names and engaged in dress-making for a living. They were known as "Mrs. Bellew's family."[4] Within the house the "seamstresses" lived their monastic life. This new monastery of Jesus, Mary and Joseph in Channel Row was recognized by Church and Order authorities as a bona fide cloistered community, completely independent of the former convent in Galway.

St. Mary's Convent, Cabra, Dublin

Young women continued to join them despite their clandestine existence. When a sufficient number entered, they opened a school and took in boarders. Many of these boarders were children of the gentry who had not fared well under penal laws. By the middle of the eighteenth century the small community could boast of twenty-eight members. They gladly paid the fines levied by the government for continuing to have the liturgy celebrated in their monastery. As the years passed, with increased pressure of the penal laws and impoverishment of their benefactors, their numbers declined until only three nuns remained. Those three moved again, this time in 1805 to Clontarf where they again opened a school.

The nineteenth century brought better times. Women religious were again able to wear their religious garb. When Mother Ann Columba Maher was elected prioress, she was predicted to be "one whose mission it will be to restore her community to all its full vigour and splendor."[5] However growth was slow and the years at Clontarf were characterized by material and spiritual poverty. They could not keep their school open because of the dearth of nuns and there were so few priests that they could celebrate Mass only once a week.

Cabra became their next home in 1819. The five members from Clontarf moved to Cabra where they opened a school for the poor. The second quarter of the nineteenth century brought problems of a different nature. Because of the difficulty of obtaining Dominican friars as chaplains, with the nuns reduced in numbers and desperately poor, Mother Columba's successor, M. Magdalen Butler, agreed to transfer the group from the jurisdiction of the Dominican Master General to that of the Archbishop of Dublin. Their very survival was at stake. They also adopted the Little Office instead of the Divine Office in order to give more time to the instruction of the poor. Vincentian priests instructed the group and assisted them to draw up a constitution.[6] In twenty years, fifty-three new members made profession. Finally came a period of comparative prosperity. Even the prosperous years brought an unexpected change. In 1836, a group from Cabra decided to set up a new monastery on Mount Street, independent from Cabra. Both operated schools for girls greatly in demand in Irish society. The Mount Street monastery and school eventually moved to Sion Hill.

Even this diminution in numbers did not deter Mother Anne Columba Maher from trying new ventures. In 1844, the Cabra nuns opened a residential school for those "totally or partially impaired in hearing and in speech," the first of its kind in Ireland.[7] This type of school proved to be a blessing for the people of Ireland and became a model imitated by branch monasteries from Cabra. The decade of the 1860s for the Cabra nuns has been designated by some as their "apostolic decade." Despite their small numbers and their cloistered status, this small monastery looked outward to assist where needs were great and requests were mounting for religious women in the schools. In that ten-year period, members from Cabra sent forty-two nuns on mission to four continents. They went to Lisbon, Portugal; Capetown, South Africa; Adelaide, South Australia; New Orleans, United States.

The call to New Orleans came from the parish priest at St. John the Baptist Church in that city. Father Jeremiah Moynihan welcomed the seven Cabra Dominicans who arrived in 1860. They were Sisters Mary John Flanagan, founding prioress, Mary Magdalen O'Farrell, subprioress, Mary Hyacinth McQuillan, Mary Xavier Gaynor, Mary Ursula O'Reilly. These "choir" or teaching sisters were joined by two lay sisters, Osanna Cahill and Bridget Smith, who did the cooking, washing and manual labor.

These pioneers served in a parish school, an unusual practice in the United States because most communities of women religious began with an academy of their own. Only later did teaching in parish schools become common for congregations of sisterhoods.

Jeremiah Moynihan had long been working to bring sisters to New Orleans from Ireland. His archbishop, Antoine Blanc, also favored the plan; the parish priest was willing to buy a house for the sisters. First the Sisters of Mercy had received the call to serve, but did not wish to send anyone from Ireland. Early in 1860, Sister M. DeRicci Maher, Prioress at Cabra, received a request from Moynihan. She wrote to her congregation, "The sisters appointed to go [to New Orleans] will have a good deal to endure . . . and will be solicited from the names given in for the purpose. We will pray the Rosary of the Blessed Virgin for the purpose for the next ten days."[8]

Moynihan expressed his joy to his archbishop at the answer from the prioress:

I look upon myself as the most fortunate man that ever came to America, and, of course, under God. The sisters of Mercy it is impossible to get. To be candid, I am not sorry, because they are not so educated as the nuns I am getting, their primary object is the visitation of the poor and sick and education is only secondary with them, so that I was almost praying that I may not get them. The nuns who are to accompany me are of the Order of St. Dominic, tip top educators, can teach French, music, etc. . . . I do not expect to be in New Orleans before the 1st of November. I would not think of taking those ladies there before then. It will be a rich scene to witness me sweeping the Catholic girls out of the corporation schools.[9]

Mother Mary John Flanagan

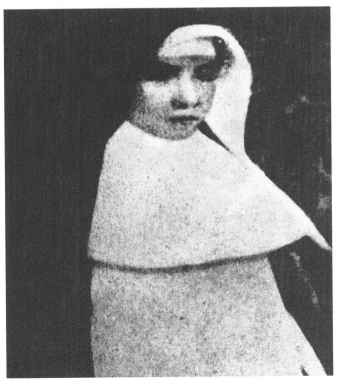

The jubilant priest further said he apprised the sisters of the comparative privations which they would likely undergo, but that New Orleans was a field ripe for harvest. He planned to have his cottage next to the church prepared for the sisters. It was obvious that he could not prepare them for the events that would unfold in the United States at this crucial time.

The sisters, accompanied by their pastor, left Ireland in October 1860 and docked on November 5. Within a month of their arrival they were teaching 200 girls at St. John the Baptist School. The Christian Brothers taught the boys. Their housing on Dryades Street, however, was not yet ready for occupancy. The ever-gracious and hospitable Ursulines extended hospitality to the Dominicans until their house could be furnished.

Within two weeks, the sisters began living in their still scantily furnished four-room cottage; it became their first American monastery. The oratory and community room were combined; the other rooms served as refectory and kitchen with sleeping quarters in a poorly ventilated attic that could be reached by ladder. The beds were of wood with corn shock mattresses. Wooden boxes once used for soap and starch constituted their only furnishings.[10]

At the time the sisters arrived, troubling events developed rapidly. First they learned that Archbishop Antoine Blanc, who had so enthusiastically authorized their coming, had died a few months earlier and a new archbishop had not yet been named. In December, South Carolina seceded from the Union and in the following month Louisiana followed suit. By February 1861, the Confederate States of America, which Louisiana joined, was formed. "The whole nation was in turmoil and the South seethed with discontent and with a determination to protect, even with the force of arms, what they claimed were states' rights."[11]

Despite the uncertain conditions of the time, the sisters decided to open a select academy in 1861. St. Mary's Dominican Academy, legally known as the New Orleans Female Dominican Academy, prospered from its inception. Needless to say, the sisters enjoyed having a fine academy where they could continue their tradition of excellence in education, but they were also able to move into a new brick dwelling recently completed by the pastor and connected to the new academy. The school was placed under the direction of Sister Mary Magdalen O'Farrell.

Mother Mary John and her subprioress frequently consulted Father Moynihan about school affairs. These meetings at the convent resulted in some unpleasantness among the sisters. Sister Ursula O'Reilly seemed to head the malcontents. For example, it was she who wrote to the new archbishop, Jean Marie Odin, complaining of the frequent visits that Father Moynihan made to the convent. Mary John's letter to the archbishop sheds light on the situation:

I hope I have not left you under a wrong impression with regard to the matters about which you spoke last evening. I consider it would be very unjust on my part not to inform Your Grace that as far as mention was made of frequent visits. Father Moynihan is in no way to blame as it was by my invitations that he came. From the very commencement he was most exact not in the least to interfere with our duties or rule and constantly insisted on us never being absent or late at any duty on his account. As we were all strangers here Father Moynihan through every kindness came to look after different matters and continually having to heart our comfort and happiness he left no part of the cottage or ground adjoining which we considered to require alteration or improvement undone. Consequently this more or less caused these visits. Again when forming the plan for the New Convent and all the time that it was building a visit from him once a week or month would not have been sufficient . . . . To speak candidly, My Lord were I to judge from Sister Mary Ursula's discontented manner and haughty demeanor I could scarcely suppose that in making these complaints she was activated by any other motive than a mere opener or plan to leave this. From what I can conclude by her remarks she considers she was in a manner deceived in joining the Community at Cabra.[12]

In concluding that letter, Mother Mary John submitted to Odin her resignation from the position of prioress as well as that of her subprioress. "I am convinced that the Sisters would be better pleased and would be more unified if others were placed in our Offices. We have considered this over and over again and come to the same conclusion . . . the Sisters have no confidence whatever in me."

Federal ships in New Orleans harbor, 1862

Mary John was correct in one aspect of that letter and much mistaken in another. Ursula did return to Ireland and soon after left the convent for secular life. The archbishop did not accept the resignations indicated and Mary John continued to be elected prioress by "the same Sisters who she thought had no confidence whatever in her." In the next thirty-two years she served as prioress intermittently for a total of twenty-five years.

But more serious troubles occupied the thoughts of the sisters and indeed all the people of New Orleans. The blockade by Union forces tightened in 1862 so that New Orleans faced dire hardship. The sisters chose not to leave, though invited by the Cabra monastery to return to Ireland. Instead they determined not to close their schools and deprive the students of their education. In fact, in 1863 these hardy pioneers decided to accept boarders in their academy and expand their facilities. When they could no longer accommodate the number of applicants, they looked for another site. One was available in nearby Greenville. The property of the Mace Academy was sold at auction and the sisters acquired it in 1864 for the sum of $10,425. The following year all the boarding students were transferred to the suburban site and the school was named St. Mary's. Mary Joseph Kavanagh, the first native of New Orleans to enter the community, was appointed Mistress of Schools.

New Orleans never suffered shelling by the Union armies, but soldiers were a familiar sight as they camped under the trees at the site of the boarding school and occasionally ventured into the chapel to pray. The young southern women probably found it difficult to accept "the enemy" even in a place of worship.

The year 1865 brought an end to hostilities, but not to hardships. But with determination and renewed hope in the future, these nuns worked together to expand their Dominican mission of teaching.

1. Cabra Annals, ms., 3, Cabra Dominican Archives, Copy in New Orleans Dominican Sisters Archives (NOSA).

2. *Weavings, Celebrating Dominican Women,* n.p., 1988, St. Mary's New Orleans Archives (SMNO).

3. Manuscript by Therese Leckert, O.P., SMNO.

4. *Weavings,* p. 7.

5. Annals, Cabra Dominicans, 1814, 76, Copy in SMNO.

6. This change of jurisdiction and recitation of the office caused confusion later. Generally, cloistered nuns (Second Order) recited the Divine Office and had Dominican priests as their ecclesiastical superiors. Third Order (apostolic, active women religious) prayed the Little Office and were under the jurisdiction of the bishop of the diocese. See the scholarly work of Margaret Smith, O.P., from the Dominican Sisters of Eastern Australia, "The Great Schism of the West," unpublished ms., a research paper concerning the Irish Dominican Sisters and their affiliated congregations, 1988, Sydney, Australia.

7. *Weavings,* p. 15.

8. M. DeRicci Maher to My dear Sisters, Cabra, Apr., 1860, SMNO.

9. Moynihan to Blanc, Ireland, June 28, 1860, SMNO.

10. Mary DeRicci Albrecht, O.P., "Brief History of Dominican Sisters, Congregation of St. Mary New Orleans, LA.," ms., 1985, SMNO.

11. Roger Baudier, **The Catholic Church in Louisiana** (New Orleans, n.p., 1939) 411.

12. Mary John Flanagan to Jean Marie Odin, Dryades Street, New Orleans, Jan. 10, 1862, SMNO.

CHAPTER 15

FROM REGENSBURG TO RACINE: AN ODYSSEY

Maria Benedicta Bauer, a nun of Heilig Kreuz (Holy Cross) Monastery in Regensburg, Bavaria, had long followed with interest a mid-nineteenth century movement among Bavarian nuns to undertake a mission of education for the masses of German Catholics who were emigrating at that time to the United States. Galvanized primarily by the directors of the Ludwig Missionsverein and its collaborators in America, these nuns were prepared to leave their cloisters to teach the children of the emigrants.[1]

Maria Benedicta herself had been prepared to join the effort as early as 1827. That particular mission, for reasons unknown, was cancelled. But later, as prioress of her convent, she sent Holy Cross women to America in response to a plea from the Benedictine Abbot of Latrobe, Pennsylvania, Boniface Wimmer. The first of these women established a school in Williamsburg (now Brooklyn), New York, in 1853. They were joined by a second contingent in 1855. From the Williamsburg foundation (now headquartered in Amityville on Long Island) was to be born a long line of new congregations, fondly known as "The Regensburg Tree." The Racine Dominicans would spring up as a shrub beside that tree when Maria Benedicta Bauer would follow her sisters to the United States. She was intent, however, on establishing her own motherhouse.

Maria Benedicta was born Maria Anna Bauer on July 17, 1803, fourth of the six children of the blacksmith Johann Michael Bauer and his wife Anna Margaret Klotzl of Pielenhofen, Bavaria.[2] Only months before Maria Anna Bauer's birth, the Great Secularization was inaugurated in Bavaria, when nearly all religious communities were dispersed by order of the Napoleonic government, and their properties confiscated for state use. The proud Cistercian monastery that had dominated and largely ruled tiny Pielenhofen since 1237 was sold off in bits and pieces. In 1806 when Maria Anna was three years old, one small section of the central building was given over to twenty-nine Carmelite nuns from Munich and Neuburg who had refused to renounce their vows. There they would be allowed to live out their days on a meager government pension, but they were forbidden to receive any new members. It is probably these women who are referred to when the adult Maria Anna, by then the prioress Maria Benedicta, mentions in her journal the "pious sentiments which were imparted to me by pious nuns even from my childhood."[3]

M. Benedicta Bauer,
1853

Though no records of the Pielenhofen state school of that period have survived, it was almost certainly there that Maria Anna received her early education. In any case, it has been established that she did not attend either of the only two Bavarian nuns' schools to have survived the secularization, Holy Cross and Santa Klara in Regensburg.`

At the age of seventeen, three years after the end of the Napoleonic domination of Bavaria, the blacksmith's daughter entered the Dominican monastery of Holy Cross to become part of a story that was already six hundred years old.[4] There, after a year of candidature and another of novitiate, she made her first profession of vows in 1822. Her solemn profession would, by Bavarian civil law, have to wait until she was thirty-three years old. She spent most of her early convent years teaching in the state school for girls for which the nuns had been forced to assume responsibility in 1803 as the price of their continued existence as sisters. Already a fairly accomplished pianist and organist, she was soon given charge also of musical education within the community.

On January 16, 1845, Maria Benedicta Bauer was elected prioress of Holy Cross, then a community of sixteen choir nuns and eight lay sisters.[5] By the time she would be elected to her fifth three-year term, the community would have grown to thirty-one choir nuns, twenty-one lay sisters, five novices, and four candidates.[6]

Her terms as prioress were marked by a vigorous, if not always popular, campaign of reform in a community whose discipline had suffered much from the adaptations at first made necessary by the Secularization of 1803 to 1817, but later simply tolerated. Her efforts at outreach included a proposal in 1855 to receive and educate a number of ransomed African slave girls who would eventually be returned to Africa as teachers.[7] She was also bent on the material improvement and expansion of the monastery. To that end she engaged in several remodeling projects and founded the first branch houses of Holy Cross, each with its own school for girls of the farming and laboring classes.[8] Through this last enterprise, an occupation that had barely survived forty years became an aggressively pursued ministry for the Regensburg Dominican nuns. For the prioress, the establishment of branch houses seems to have been first of all a ministerial effort within the broader post-Secularization "re-Catholicizing" of Bavaria. But she apparently saw it also as an opportunity to transfer nuns who were having problems within the Regensburg monastery to communities where they might fare better or be less trouble to her.

Maria Benedicta Bauer's days as prioress in Regensburg ended abruptly during her fifth term in June 1858, when she was deposed from office and disenfranchised for life within the community by the new bishop of Regensburg, Ignatius von Senestrey. His charge against her was that she had abused her authority and "grossly mismanaged" the finances of the community.[9]

It is true that the prioress could be harsh when crossed. How often she lamented in her journals, "Ach, meine Heftigkeit!" ("Ach, my heavy-handedness!"). Her correspondence provides a number of examples of her often caustic and impulsive manner. Yet it is equally clear that she dearly loved her sisters and was generally very warmly maternal in her dealings with them. She wrote in her journal:

> I never (in my innate simplicity) had any doubt that any but one only of those currently in this convent had any persistent resentment toward me personally. Nor did I feel the least resentment toward one or the other. And if at times I have been Hot-tempered and cross with one or the other, they all know that I always mean well, and then, I always try to make up for my fault. - So I believe there is scarcely anyone I have to suspect of harboring an ongoing resentment against me. - In the future I shall try mightily to rid myself even of this bruskness, rudeness, hot-temper[10]

As for her alleged financial mismangement, the accusation seems to stem from her efforts at expansion and renovation, and especially from her having used patrimony funds for those purposes. But the expansion and renovation projects initiated by her seemed in general to have been justified. And her use of the patrimony of some of the nuns (carefully documented by her) was probably based on counsel she had received from the Master of the Order, who refused to allow the Bavarian nuns to make solemn profession if the community would ever be in need of funds. In that case nuns under simple vows could donate their patrimony to the monastery.[11]

On examination, the bishop's basic case against the prioress is far from convincing. She in fact emerges as fundamentally vindicated in her administration, an administration made especially difficult by internal divisions, wrought primarily by an unscrupulous chaplain on whose dismissal she had finally insisted in April 1856. At the vortex of the dissension within the community were two young nuns, Cäcilia Solleder and Reginalda Brenner, both resentful of the chaplain's dismissal and of the prioress' policies in general. In the wake of discipline imposed on Cäcilia and the prioress' subsequent efforts to persuade the pair to join the missionaries in Williamsburg, they had secretly left the monastery in April 1858. It was they who had leveled the accusations upon which the episcopal investigation focused following their departure.

Maria Benedicta's removal from office left her with a bleak future if she remained within the walls of Holy Cross. But there is no evidence that she contested it. She returned instead to her longstanding desire to emigrate to the United States. Now fifty-five years old and already showing signs of the stomach cancer that would eventually cause her death, the ex-prioress sailed for Williamsburg via Bremen in September 1858. She was accompanied by three others. Maria Thomasina Ginker was twenty-four years old, three years professed, and novitiate companion of the two nuns who had been at the heart of the prioress' grief. Cunigunda Schell, twenty, was still a novice when the possibility of a new American mission materialized. Her profession was accelerated so that she could make her vows before departure. Finally there was the watchman's daughter from Regensburg, Crescenzia Traubinger, who was fifteen years old. She had been encouraged to enter the monastery by Maria Benedicta Bauer. Now she became a candidate expressly to join her in looking for a new convent home.[12]

Archival documents make it clear that Maria Benedicta Bauer intended from the beginning to establish her own motherhouse in the United States. Nevertheless, she lived and taught with the sisters in Williamsburg until she had managed to devise a plan for action. This she did in consultation with Joseph A. Kelly, the provincial of the Dominican friars in Somerset, Ohio.[13] In June 1860, she and Maria Thomasina Ginker traveled by train and stagecoach to Somerset, where they were to spend some time with the "English sisters," learning the language there instead of at Williamsburg where there had been little opportunity or incentive to learn it in the totally German school and community. Their two original companions elected to remain in Williamsburg.[14]

The "English sisters" were, of course, the small band of Dominicans who had been sent out in 1830 from St. Catharine's in Kentucky to the little hilltop town of Somerset on the National Road. By now they had a thriving convent and boarding school not far from the friars' church and priory at Holy Trinity. Both of the new Bavarian arrivals found Somerset a refreshing interlude. But by August it seemed the dream of a new motherhouse of their own was about to be fulfilled. The Dominican bishop of Nashville, James Whelan, had requested sisters from Somerset to establish an academy in his city. According to Maria Benedicta, the sisters "asked the two of us to settle in Nashville with the four sisters who had been called, to help them out with music and other necessary preparations for the coming recital. We accepted this on condition that we might, after the recital, share in the field of labor in the German parish in Nashville. This the bishop promised, and with this intention he took us with him."[15] Bishop Whelan's version suggests a slightly different dynamic: "S. Benedicta expressed a desire to come with them and I consented."[16] The four Somerset sisters, the two Regensburgers and the bishop left Somerset on August 15, 1860. They made their way by stagecoach, rail, river steamer and again rail, arriving in Nashville early on Sunday morning, August 19.[17]

The Regensburg sisters' sojourn in Nashville lasted only a few months. Maria Benedicta was increasingly vexed by the non-cloistered lifestyle of the American sisters. "These good sisters have as yet no rule as religious-no more than layfolk in the Third Order. So apparently they have no special obligations! But we have to conform as one house to all of the customs and practices here, since we are just foreign sisters from Germany."[18] Besides, both of the Bavarians found the southern climate and food a hardship. "The climate here has been so detrimental to my health," wrote Maria Benedicta, "that on my arrival here I was very ill for six weeks. And what is even worse is the English cooking, which I can tolerate less and less. Often I can't eat for a week at a time, since my digestive system is failing and I have to struggle constantly with vomiting. As a result my constitution, so healthy otherwise, will not stand up much longer. I often feel completely drained of strength."[19]

Although the missionaries wrote home to the Ludwig Missionsverein as late as December 12 to beg for funding for the motherhouse they hoped to build in Nashville the following spring,[20] they were fast coming to realize that the German parish there was too poor and disorganized to support a school. Perhaps, too, the fact that the St. Cecilia sisters owned slaves (as did most southern religious groups) disturbed the Bavarians; for Bavarians were notorious in the South for their anti-slavery activities.

By the end of December Maria Benedicta began corresponding with Michael Deisenrieder, a Bavarian priest of the Milwaukee Diocese whom she had apparently

**John Martin Henni,
first Bishop
of Milwaukee,
1844–1881**

either met in Europe or to whom she had been referred by the chaplain of the Missionsverein, about the possibility of a move north. But Maria Benedicta had certainly heard of Bishop John Martin Henni's open and welcoming policies and of his particular eagerness to recruit German-speaking clergy and religious for his diocese. Thus with the first signs of spring, the two sisters were traveling once again, barely a month before the outbreak of the Civil War.

A brief stay in Milwaukee brought them two new companions–candidates from Mother Caroline Friess' large supply! Mother Caroline was a Bavarian and the girlhood friend of the nun that Maria Benedicta had chosen as first superior of her branch house in Niederviehbach.[21] The two young women were not the first that the superior of the School Sisters of Notre Dame had given away to foster the new foundations of others. Within six years, one of them, Maria Oberbrunner, would be the prioress of the group she was volunteering to join, sight unseen![22]

At this time they also met with their new bishop, John Martin Henni, who suggested that they make Green Bay their temporary home. The German parish of St. Mary of the Assumption there had recently built a new school and would welcome trained and experienced teachers.

After yet one more journey by train and stagecoach, the two nuns and their two new candidates arrived in Green Bay on Good Friday, March 29, 1861. They quickly divided the new schoolhouse into classrooms and living quarters, and by Easter Tuesday began to register pupils. Maria Benedicta had determined from the start that the school was to be open to boys as well as girls and to children of any religious persuasion. It is uncertain whether this decision was purely her own, since earlier reports in the Green Bay newspapers had stated that the parishioners had promised the same. But by this time the sisters had already experienced Williamsburg, a school with both boys and girls. The welcoming of Protestants, however, would surely have been a bit strange to Bavarians, in whose native land Protestants were not even welcome to live! Bishop Henni may have influenced the nuns to assume a more open attitude.

What astonished Maria Benedicta most of all as registration proceeded was the ages of those who came. "The girls range in age from five to twenty-five. At first we were under the impression that these really grown-up 'ladies' had come to register their children, but they were registering themselves as pupils!"[23] On April 9 classes began.

In spite of the bishop's repeated insistence that Green Bay was no place for a permanent foundation, by early May the always impulsive Maria Benedicta had purchased lots adjoining St. Mary's Church for her motherhouse. And though she resisted telling the local newspapers until she had written to inform Bishop Henni of the step she had taken, The Green Bay *Advocate* carried the story just a week after her letter to the bishop! The bishop apparently felt it better not to respond directly for a while. But he did send the rector of his seminary, Father Michael Heiss, who wrote to his friend: "In August I must go to Green Bay to give a retreat to the Dominican sisters who are building a convent there."[24] Heiss was well enough impressed to endorse the sisters' plea to the Ludwig Missionsverein for funding for the project.[25]

The earliest surviving word from Bishop Henni on the matter came only after Maria Benedicta had written in early December to ask permission to begin building the following spring.[26] Then later in the same month she wrote to tell him that she was beginning to realize that

> Green Bay is so small, and the German parish so poor that they send scarcely thirty-six children to the school, and hardly half of these are able to pay two shillings a month. We receive as a rule no more than four or five dollars a month, but our expenses are usually half again as much. Besides, our holy rule says we are never to build a convent if there is no prospect for continued existence.[27]

Henni reminded her quite gently in his response: "You, dear Sister, probably already know that I've always objected to the founding of a motherhouse in Green Bay. I gladly consent to your establishing a school there, but the motherhouse must always have an independent location and more spacious grounds. . . . I am sure that there are more suitable places."[28] A month later he wrote with suggestions of several possible Wisconsin locations, urging that she take a trip to visit each of them in spring.[29]

There is no evidence at all that Maria Benedicta ever followed his suggestion. On May 1 she signed the deed to a house and lot in Racine, and on May 12 she and her small community, along with a few boarding students and orphans, arrived to take possession.[30] The nuns opened their first Racine school in the basement of St. Patrick's Church on June 1, raising money to supplement tuition by giving concerts at which their superior performed on the organ.[31]

By 1863 the sisters were teaching in several schools in Racine and one in Port Washington. The next year saw the establishment of an academy for girls within the new motherhouse that had been built at Pearl and Chippeway Streets (later renamed Park Avenue and Twelfth Street).

Racine, Wisconsin, in 1858, looking south across the Root River from St. Patrick's Parish

When tuition, concerts and grants from the Ludwig Missionsverein did not bring in sufficient funds to support the schools, the nuns received Bishop Henni's permission to beg from door to door. Maria Thomasina found this task not entirely pleasant, as she wrote to Rev. Paul Kagerer of the Ludwig Missionsverein:

Last autumn, so that we would be able to pay the pressing debts we had assumed for the needed addition to the building [for the academy], I actually had to go out, with our bishop's permission, to take up a collection among the people. That was a difficult duty for me, but the example of our holy father Dominic gave me courage to go from house to house and beg for a kind donation from the people. I devoted six weeks to this duty, and here and there had to put up with great unpleasantness. But in this case the unpleasantness could only lead to trust, since our begging got us out of our pressing need.[32]

All this while, the sisters were continuing to live the monastic regimen of the Second Order and to maintain cloister to whatever extent they could. The stomach cancer that had surely been present already for a few years before Maria Benedicta left Regensburg became more serious in early 1865. By June of that year she was confined to bed, and Maria Thomasina found herself taking on more and more responsibility for the young community. The prioress died on October 13, 1865, leaving eight professed sisters, seven novices, and eleven candidates.

Because there were not enough perpetually professed sisters to hold a canonical election, Bishop Henni appointed the thirty-one-year-old Maria Thomasina Ginker to be prioress. She was in office less than a year when she contracted typhoid fever from a novice she was nursing. Unaware of the gravity of her illness, she decided to preach the community's annual retreat in late August 1866, when the scheduled preacher cancelled at the last minute. The retreat, for which her carefully written conferences still survive, ended with the reception of three novices on August 28. The second prioress of the Racine Dominicans died on September 6.

Maria Benedicta Bauer's work in this country had been marked from the beginning by her determination to Americanize. She had emphasized in all of her advertising for her schools that both English and German would be used. As she had done in her schools in Bavaria, she recruited as students especially the children of the working class. The latter emphasis continued to be strong in the community after Mother Benedicta's death in 1865. Efforts at adapting to the American culture, however, became much weaker during the long administration of Maria Hyacintha Oberbrunner, especially with the advent of Jodocus A. Birkhaeuser, who served as chaplain from 1868 until his death in 1908. Their influence served to keep the Racine Dominican community heavily German in its internal life as well as in is ministerial choices even into the 1920s.

1. The *Ludwig Missionsverein* of Munich was established in 1838. Supported by donations from interested Catholics and particularly from its royal patron, King Ludwig I, the society made grants to fund the travel costs and foundations of Bavarian missionaries.

2. The children born to Johann Michael Bauer and his wife were Johann Baptist (1798-1806), Anna Maria (1800-1808), a stillborn infant (1802), Maria Anna (1803-1865), Michael (1806-1879), and Maria Katharina (1809-1811). Anna Margaret Klotzl, however, had a daughter by a previous marriage, Maria Margaretha Schmid, born in 1793. She has to be the unnamed sister mentioned several times in M. Benedicta's journals, since the other girls had all died earlier. (M. Benedicta's journals, all from 1854 and 1855, are in the Racine Dominican Archives(RDA).

3. *Tagebuch II,* "Retreat Notes, 1854."

4. The monastery of Heilig Kreuz had been established in 1233.

5. Chapter Acts, Heilig Kreuz, January 16, 1845 (Bischofliches Zentralarchiv Regensburg (hereinafter BZAR) K1 114/19: *Priorinwahlen: 1832-1900,* and *Schematismus der Geistlichkeit des Bistums Regensburg fur das Jahr 1844* (Regensburg: Georg Joseph Manz, 1845).

6. Schematismus der Geistlichkeit des Bistums Regensburg fur das Jahr 1857 (Regensburg: Georg Joseph Manz, 1857).

7. While Maria Benedicta's own proposal seems not to have materialized, a group of such girls was actually received by the School Sisters of Notre Dame in Munich about the same time. Every one of these girls, however, died of lung diseases and emotional trauma before their planned transfer to the United States. (M.B. Bauer correspondence: BZAR, K1 114/6, *Klausurdispense: 1832-1944;* Notre Dame documentation from SSND Archives.)

8. Documentation for the various renovation projects as well as for financial aspects of the branch foundations is found in Maria Benedicta Bauer's notebooks, Racine Dominican Archives. Correspondence concerning the branch houses of Niederviehbach (1847), Mintraching (1853), and Williamsburg (1855) is found in BZAR, KL 112/1: *Filialkloster Niederviehbach,* K1 114/29, *Filialkloster Mintraching:* 1852-1860; and K1 114/31, *Filialkloster in Williamsburg* (USA): 1853-1895. Other documentation in the archives of the *Ludwig Missionsverein,* Munich, and Kloster St. Maria, Niederviehbach.

9. Letter of Bishop von Senestrey, announcing the deposition of the nuns of Heilig Kreuz and its branch houses (BZAR K1 114/2: *Oberhirtliche Visitation,* 1837-1921). No such letter, it seems, was sent to the nuns in Williamsburg, although they were still subject to the prioress of Holy Cross.

10. *Tagebuch II,* June 15, 1854. The one whom she suspects resents her is probably Reginalda Brener, friend of Cäcilia Solleder. The reasons for Reginalda's resentment will be dealt with shortly.

11. Letter of Dominicus Lentz, O.P., socius to the Master, to Maria Benedicta Bauer, Jan. 27, 1857. BZAR K1 114/2: *Oberhirtliche Visitation,* 1837-1921.

12. BZAR, K1 114/31, *Filialkloster in Williamsburg (USA): 1853-1895.*

13. This correspondence has not survived, or at least it has not yet been found.

14. Crescenzia Traubinger had in the meantime been received into the Williamsburg community as Sister Maria Dominica. Both she and Cunigunda Schell, already professed, lived out their lives as members of the Williamsburg group.

15. Letter of Maria Benedicta Bauer to Bishop John M. Henni, Jan. 14, 1861, Archives, Archdiocese of Milwaukee (MAA).

16. Letter of Bishop James Whelan to Bishop John M. Henni, Nashville, March 7, 1861, MAA.

17. Sister Mary Frances Walsh, who chronicled the journey and the early years at St. Cecilia's in Nashville (The Annals of St. Cecilia Convent: 1860-1888), never mentions the presence or participation of the two Bavarian nuns. This could be explained by the fact that she was concentrating only on her own congregation. Certain discrepancies, however, between her account and Maria Benedicta's lead one to suspect that the omission reflects the tension which seems to have grown between Maria Benedicta (and possibly Maria Thomasina) and the former Somerset sisters by the time they parted company

18. Maria Benedicta Bauer to Bishop John M. Henni, Jan. 14, 1861, MAA.

19. Maria Benedicta Bauer to John Henni.

20. Archives, *Ludwig Missionsverein,* Munich (#395).

21. Maria Amanda von Schenk, first of the superior Niederviebach convent.

22. As Mother Maria Hyacintha, she would be appointed by Bishop Henni to succeed Mother Benedicta and Mother Thomasina after the untimely deaths of the two foundresses within a year of each other (October 1865 and September 1866). The other candidate from the Notre Dame community was Cunigunda Loesch. She became Sister Rosa, but was later obliged to leave the Racine community when Bishop Henni refused her a temporary leave of absence to recover her health.

23. Maria Benedicta Bauer to Bishop Henni, June 6, 1860, MAA.

24. Michael Heiss to Kilian Kleiner, July 5, 1861, MAA.

25. Heiss to Kleiner, Aug. 30, 1861, MAA. "They certainly are fully deserving of favorable consideration by the esteemed Board of Directors."

26. Bauer to Henni, Dec. 10, 1861, MAA. There is, of course, the possibility that he did write immediately, but that Maria Benedicta found the response too embarrassing to keep! (All of Henni's extant letters to her are in the Racine Dominican Archives, with no copies in Milwaukee.)

27. Bauer to Henni, Dec. 28, 1861, MAA.

28. Henni to Bauer, Jan. 3, 1862, RDA.

29. Henni to Bauer, Jan. 12, 1862, RDA.

30. The German Catholic newspaper, *Wahrheits Freund,* under the date of May 28, reports that "On the twelfth of this month the venerable Mother Benedicta Bauer of the Order of St. Dominic with eleven companions arrived here with the intention of founding a motherhouse of her Order in Racine." The pastor, Matthew W. Gibson, tells of the coming of M. Benedicta and "Sister Thomas" and their eight novices, two of whom "were received last week in my Parish." (Letter to *Propaganda Fide,* Sept. 8, 1861, Archives, *Propagands Fide,* Rome) Documents in the Racine Dominican Archives account for three novices (Sisters Hyacintha Oberbrunner, Rose Loesch, Raymunda Muller) and two candidates (Barbara Fox, Mary Endres), and at least one boarder, Mary Rositer. Since there is no record of Sister Dominica (Barbara) Huber, who had been received in Green Bay, it is assumed she had left the community.

31. *Racine Weekly Journal,* May 28, 1862, 3, and June 11, 3. Parents often could not pay the tuition because the Civil War had so tightened their finances.

32. Maria Thomasina Ginker to Paul Kagerer, Racine, June 10, 1865, Draft Copy in RDA.

GLOSSARY

Bishop A member of the hierarchy of the Church, given jurisdiction over a diocese; or an archbishop over an archdiocese

Bull (From *bulla*, a seal) A solemn pronouncement by the Pope, such as the 1537 Bull of Pope Paul III, Sublimis Deus,proclaiming the human rights of the Indians (See Ch. 1, n.16)

Chapter An assembly of members or delegates of a community, province, congregation, or the entire Order of Preachers. A chapter is called for decision-making or election, at intervals determined by the Constitutions.

Coadjutor Bishop One appointed to assist a bishop in his diocese, with the right to succeed him as its head.

Congregation A title given by the Church to an approved body of religious women or men.

Convent The local house of a community of Dominican friars or sisters.

Council The central governing unit of a Dominican priory, province, congregation, monastery, laity and the entire Order.

Diocese A division of the Church embracing the members entrusted to a bishop; in the case of an archdiocese, an archbishop.

Divine Office The Liturgy of the Hours. The official prayer of the Church composed of psalms, hymns and readings from Scripture or related sources.

Episcopal Related to a bishop and his jurisdiction in the Church; as in "Episcopal See."

Exeat Authorization given to a priest by his bishop to serve in another diocese.

Faculties Authorization given a priest by the bishop for priestly ministry in his diocese.

Friar A priest or cooperator brother of the Order of Preachers.

Lay Brother A term used in the past for "cooperator brother."

Lay Dominican A professed member of the Dominican Laity, once called "Third Order."

Mandamus The official assignment of a friar or a sister to a Communit and ministry related to the mission of the Order.

Master General (or simply Master) The major superior of the friars and the nuns of the Order of Preachers; the successor to the founder of the Order of Preachers, who was called Master Dominic.

Monastery A community of contemplative, cloistered nuns in the Order of Preachers.

Novice A man or woman admitted to a novitiate for the studies and formation required before making religious profession.

Nun A Dominican woman belonging to a cloistered, contemplative monastic community.

Prior The elected superior of a priory or province of friars; or of a chapter of lay Dominicans.

Prioress The elected superior of a congregation, province, priory of sisters or chapter of lay Dominicans.

Propaganda Fide The original title of the ecclesiastical Congregation for the Propagation of the Faith, now called the Congregation for The Evangelization of Peoples.

BIBLIOGRAPHY

Agonito, Joseph. *The Building of an American Catholic Church: The Episcopacy of John Carroll.*
New York: Garland, 1988.

Ahlstrom, Sydney. *A Religious History of the American People.* 2 vols. Garden City, NY: Doubleday, 1975.

Ashley, Benedict M., O.P. *The Dominicans.* Collegeville, MN: Liturgical Press, 1990.

Barry, Colman J., O.S.B. *The Catholic Church and German Americans.* Milwaukee: Bruce, 1953.

Baudier, Roger. *The Catholic Church in Louisiana.* 2 vols. New Orleans, Chancery Office, 1939.

Bayley, James Roosevelt. *A Brief Sketch of the Catholic Church on the Island of New York.*
New York: Catholic Publications Society, 2nd edition. 1870.

Bennett, William Harper. *Catholic Footsteps in Old New York.* New York: Schwartz, 1909.

Berlin, Ira and Leslie S. Rowland, eds. *Families & Freedom: A Documentary History of African
American Kinship in the Civil War Era.* New York: The New Press, 1997.

Billington, Ray Allen. *The Protestant Crusade, 1800-1860.* Chicago: Quadrangle, 1964.
Far Western Frontier, 1830-1860. New York: Harper, 1956.

Blessing, Patrick. *Religion, Culture and the Vigilance Movement, San Francisco 1856.* Cushwa Working
Paper Series 8, Number 3. Notre Dame: UP, 1980.

Bohr, David. *Evangelization in America.* New York: Paulist, 1977.

Boles, John B. *Religion in Antebellum Kentucky.* Lexington: U of Kentucky, 1976.

Boorstin, Daniel. *The Americans.* New York: Vintage Books, Random House, Vol. 2: The National
Experience, 1965; Vol. 3: The Democratic Experience, 1973.

Brock, William Ranulf, *The United States, 1789-1890.* Ithaca, N.Y.: Cornell UP, 1975.

Bryce, Mary Charles, O.S.B. *Pride of Place: The Role of the Bishops in the Development of Catechesis
in the United States.* Washington, D.C.: Catholic University, 1984.

Butler, Loretta M. and Jacqueline E. Wilson. *I Write My Name: African-American Catholics in the
Archdiocese of Washington, 1634-1990.* Archdiocese of Washington, Office of Black Catholics,
Hyattsville, MD. 2000.

Carey, Patrick, ed. *American Catholic Religious Thought: Shaping of a Theological and Social Tradition.*
New York: Paulist, 1987.
People, Priests, and prelates: Ecclesiastical Democracy and the Tensions Of Trusteeism.
Notre Dame: UP, 1987.

Carthy, Mary Peter, O.S.U. *Old St. Patrick's: New York's First Cathedral.* New York: USCHS, 1947.

Chinnici, Joseph P., O.F.M. *Living Stones: The History and Structure of Catholic Spiritual Life in the
United States.* New York: Macmillan, 1989.

Code, Joseph Bernard. *Dictionary of the American Hierarchy, 1789-1964.* New York: Wagner, 1964.

Coffey, Reginald, O.P. *The American Dominicans: A History of St. Joseph's Province.* Washington D.C.:
Vernon Publishing, 1970.

Cogley, John. *Catholic America.* New York: Dial, 1973.

Cohalan, Florence D. *A Popular History of the Archdiocese of New York.* New York: USCHS,1983.

Coleman, Terry. *Passage to America: A History of Emigrants from Great Britain And Ireland
to America in the Mid-Nineteenth Century.* London: Hutchinson, 1972.

Commager, Henry Steele, and Allan Nevins, eds. *The Heritage of America: Readings in American
History.* New York: Little, 1974.

Crawford, Eugene J. *Daughters of Dominic on Long Island: the Brooklyn Sisters of St.
Dominic.* New York: Benziger, 1938.

Crews, Clyde. *An American Holy Land: History of the Archdiocese of Louisville. 1775-1985.*
Wilmington, DE: Michael Glazier, 1987.

Curti, Merle. *The Growth of American Thought.* New York: Harper, 1943.

Davis, Cyprian, O.S.B. *Christ's Image in Black: The Black Catholic Community Before the Civil War.*
Cushwa Working Paper Series 21, Number 1. Notre Dame: UP, 1989.
History of Black Catholics in the United States. New York: Crossroad, 1990.

DeTocqueville, Alexis. *Democracy in America.* 2 vols. New York: Vintage, 1945.

Dirvin, Joseph I., C.M. *Mrs. Seton, Foundress of the American Sisters of Charity.* New York: Farrar, 1962.

Dolan, Jay P. *The American Catholic Experience: A History from Colonial Times to Present.*
Garden City, NY: Doubleday, 1985.
Ed. *The American Catholic Parish: A History from 1850 to the Present.* 2 vols. New York: Paulist,
1987. Vol.I, The Northeast, Southeast and South Central States. Vol.II, The Pacific, Intermountain
West, and Midwest States.
The Immigrant Church: New York's Irish and German Catholics, 1815-1865. Notre Dame: UP,
1983.

Dominicans of San Rafael. *A Tribute from Many Hands.* San Rafael, CA: Dominican Convent
of San Rafael, 1941.

Ellis, John Tracy. *American Catholicism*. 2nd ed. Chicago: UP, 1969.
    ed. *Documents of American Catholic History*. Vol. I. 1493-1865. Wilmington, DE: Michael
        Glazier, 1987.
Ellis, John Tracy, and Robert Trisco. *A Guide to American Catholic History*. 2nd ed. Santa Barbara:
    ABC-Clio, 1982.
The Encyclopedia of the American Religious Experience. 3 vols. New York: Scribner's, 1988.
Ewens, Mary, O.P. *The Role of the Nun in Nineteenth-Century America*. New York: Arno, 1978.

Fenning, Hugh, O.P. *The Irish Dominican Province, 1698-1797*. Dublin: Dominican Publications, 1990.
Franklin, John Hope. *From Slavery to Freedom: A History of Negro Americans*. New York: Knopf, 1974.
Franks, Karen Marie, O.P., ed. *Strength of Our Roots, Faith in Our Vision: Brief History and Biographies:
    1850-2000*. San Rafael: Dominican Sisters of San Rafael, 2000.

Gannon, Michael V. *The Cross in the Sand*. Gainesville: UP, 1965.
Gaustad, Edwin Scott. *Historical Atlas of American Religion*. New York: Harper, 1976.
Glazier, Michael and Thomas Shelley, eds. *The Encyclopedia of American Catholic History*.
    Collegeville, MN: The Liturgical Press, 1997.
Gleason, Philip. *Keeping the Faith: American Catholicism, Past and Present*. Notre Dame: UP, 1987.
Green, Mary Patricia, O.P. *The Third Order Dominican Sisters of the Congregation of St. Catharine
    of Siena: Their Life and their Constitutions, 1822-1869*. St. Catharine, KY: 1978, reprint.
Guilday, Peter. *A History of the Councils of Baltimore (1791-1844)*. New York: Arno, 1969.
    John Gilmary Shea, Father of American Catholic History, 1824-1892. New York: USCHS, 1926.
    Ed. *The National Pastorals of the American Hierarchy, 1792-1919*. Westminister, MD:
        Newman, 1954.
Gutierrez, Gustavo. *Las Casas in Search of the Poor of Jesus Christ*. Maryknoll, New York: Orbis, 1992.

Handlin, Oscar. *The Uprooted*. New York: Grosset & Dunlap, 1951.
Hanley, Thomas O'Brien, ed. *The John Carroll Papers*. 3 vols. Notre Dame: UP, 1976.
    Vols 1, 1755-1791; 2, 1792-1806; 3, 1807-1815.
Hedrick, Joan. *Harriet Beecher Stowe*. New York: Oxford, University Press, Inc., 1994.
Hennesey, James, S.J. *American Catholics: A History of the Roman Catholic Community in the United
    States*. New York: Oxford, 1981.
Hoy, Suellen and Margaret MacCurtin. *From Dublin to New Orleans: The Journey of Nora and Alice*.
    Dublin: Attic, 1994.
Hudson, Winthrop. *Religion in America: An Historical Account of the Development of American
    Religious Life*. 3rd ed. New York: Scribner's, 1981.

Jarrett, Bede, O.P. *The English Dominicans*. New York: Benziger, 1921.
Jolly, Ellen Ryan. *Nuns of the Battlefield*. Providence, RI., Providence Visitor, 1927.
Jurgens, William. *A History of the Cleveland Diocese*. Cleveland: Diocese of Cleveland, 1980.

Kaufman, Polly W. *Women Teachers on the Frontier*. New Haven: Yale UP, 1984.
Kelly, Mary Gilbert, O.P. *Catholic Immigrant Colonization Projects in the United States, 1815-1860*.
    Monograph Series, Vol.XVII. New York: USCHS, 1939.
Kenneally, Karen, C.S.J. *American Catholic Women: A Historical Exploration*. New York: Macmillan,
    1989.
Kiefer, Monica, O.P. *A History of the Dominican Sisters of St. Mary of the Springs*.
    Columbus, OH: Dominican Sisters, 1972.
Kohler, Mary Hortense, O.P. *The Life and Work of Mother Benedicta Bauer*. Milwaukee: Bruce, 1937.
    Rooted in Hope. Milwaukee: Bruce, 1962.

Lamott, John H. *History of the Archdiocese of Cincinnati, 1821-1921*. Cincinnati: Pustet, 1921.
Larkin, Emmet. *The Historical Dimensions of Irish Catholicism*. New York:Arno, 1976.
Liptak, Dolores, R.S.M., ed. *A Church of Many Cultures: Selected Historical Essays on Ethnic American
    Catholicism*. New York: Garland, 1988.

McCaffrey, Lawrence J. *The Irish Diaspora in America*. Bloomington: Indiana UP, 1976.
McCarthy, Joseph M., ed. Benedict Joseph Fenwick, S.J., *Memoirs to Serve for Future Ecclesiastical
    History of the Diocese of Boston*. New York: USCHS, 1976.
McGreal, Mary Nona, O.P. "Dominicans," *Encyclopedia of American Catholic History*. Ed. Michael
    Glazier, Collegeville, MN: Liturgical Press, 1998.
Marks, Paula Mitchell. *Precious Dust: The American Gold Rush Era: 1848-1900*. New York: William
    Morrow, 1994.
Marty, Martin. *An Invitation to American Catholic History Basics of Christian Thought*. Vol. 4. Chicago:
    Thomas More, 1986.
    Righteous Empire: The Protestant Experience in America. New York: Harper, 1977.
Masserano, Rose Marie, O.P. *The Nashville Dominicans: A History of the Congregation of Saint
    Cecilia*. Nashville, TN: Dominican Sisters, 1985.
Mattingly, Ramona. *The Catholic Church on the Kentucky Frontier, 1785-1812*. Washington, D.C.:
    Catholic UP, 1977.
Mazzuchelli, Samuel. *The Memoirs of Father Samuel Mazzuchelli*. Chicago: Priory Press, 1967.

Meagher, Timothy J. Urban *American Catholicism: The Culture and Identity of The American Catholic People.* New York: Garland, 1988.

Melville, Annabelle M. *John Carroll of Baltimore.* New York: Scribner's, 1955.

Miller, Perry. *Life of the Mind in America: From the Revolution to the Civil War.* New York: Harbrace, 1970.

Misner, Barbara, S.C.S.C. *Highly Respectable and Accomplished Ladies: Catholic Women Religious in America, 1790-1850.* New York: Garland, 1988.

Morison, Samuel Eliot, and Henry S. Commager. *Concise History of the American Republic.* New York: Oxford, 1977.

Murray, Mary Cecilia, O.P. *Other Waters: A History of the Dominican Sisters of Newburgh, N.Y.* New York: Old Brooksville, 1993.

New Catholic Encyclopedia. 19 vols. New York: McGraw Hill, 1967-1996.

Nichols, Roy Franklin. *The Stakes of Power, 1845-1877.* New York: Hill, 1961.

Nichols, Thomas L. *Forty Years of American Life. 1821-1861.* New York: Stackpole, 1937.

Nolan, Charles E. *A History of the Archdiocese of New Orleans.* Strasbourg, France: Editions du Signe, 2000.

Noonan, Paschala, O.P. *Signadou: A History of the Kentucky Dominican Sisters.* St. Catharine, KY: 1998.

O'Connor, Paschala, O.P. *Five Decades: History of the Congregation of the Most Holy Rosary, Sinsinawa, Wisconsin 1849-1899.* Sinsinawa, WI: 1954.

O'Daniel, Victor, O.P. *The Dominican Province of St. Joseph.* New York: Holy Name Society, 1942.

Paré, George. *The Catholic Church in Detroit, 1701-1888.* Detroit: Gabriel Richard, 1951.

Perko, Michael J., S.J., ed. *Enlightening the Next Generation: Catholics and Their Schools, 1830-1980.* New York: Garland, 1988.

Petit, Loretta, O.P. *Friar in the Wilderness: Edward Dominic Fenwick O.P.* Chicago: Project OPUS, 1994.

Prucha, Francis, S.J. *American Indian Policy in the Formative Years, 1780-1834.* Cambridge: Harvard UP, 1962.
　　Bibliographical Guide to History of Indian-White Relations in the United States. Chicago: U of Chicago, 1977.
　　The Great Father: The United States Government and the American Indian. Lincoln: Nebraska UP, 1986.

Rice, Madeleine Hooke. *American Catholic Opinion in the Slavery Controversy.* New York: Peter Smith, 1964.

Rohrbough, Malcolm J. *The Trans-Appalachian Frontier: People, Societies, and Institutions, 1775-1850.* New York: Oxford UP, 1978.

Ryan, Thomas Richard. *Orestes A. Brownson: A Definitive Biography.* Huntington, IN: Our Sunday Visitor, 1976.

Schauinger, Joseph Herman. *Cathedrals in the Wilderness.* Milwaukee: Bruce, 1952.
　　Stephen T. Badin, Priest in the Wilderness. Milwaukee: Bruce, 1956.

Schlesinger, Arthur M. Jr. ed. *Almanac of American History.* New York: Putnam, 1983.

Schwind, Mona, O.P. *Period Pieces: An Account of the Grand Rapids Dominicans, 1853-1966.* Grand Rapids: Grand Rapids Dominicans, 1991.

Shanabruch, Charles. *Chicago's Catholics: The Evolution of an American Identity.* Notre Dame: UP, 1981.

Shaughnessy, Gerald. *Has the Immigrant Kept the Faith?* New York: Arno, 1969.

Shea, John Gilmary. *A History of the Catholic Church Within the Limits of the United States.* 4 vols. New York: Privately printed, 1886-1892.

Sklar, Kathryn Kish. *Catharine Beecher.* New Haven: Yale UP, 1973.

Spalding, Thomas W. *Martin John Spalding: American Churchman.* Washington, D.C.: Catholic University, 1973.

Stritch, Thomas. *The Catholic Church in Tennessee: the Sesquicentennial Story.* Nashville, TN: Catholic Center, 1987.

Trisco, Robert Frederick. *Bishops and Their Priests in the United States.* New York: Garland, 1988.

Tyler, Alice Felt. *Freedom's Ferment: Phases of American Social History to 1860.* Minneapolis: UP, 1944.

Warner, William W. *At Peace with All Their Neighbors.* Washington D.C.: Georgetown U., 1994.

Weber, Francis J. *Joseph Sadoc Alemany: Harbinger of a New Era.* Los Angeles: Dawson, 1973.

White, Joseph M., ed. *The American Catholic Religious Life: Selected Historical Essays.* New York: Garland, 1988.

Wright, Louis B. *Culture on the Moving Frontier.* Bloomington, IN: UP, 1955.